S0-AYC-414

HISTORIES OF THE HOLOCAUST

HISTORIES OF THE HOLOCAUST

DAN STONE

CABRINI COLLEGE LIBRARY
610 KING OF PRUSSIA ROAD
RADNOR, PA 19087

OXFORD
UNIVERSITY PRESS

D
804.348
.5763
2010

#5030 74/33

*This book has been printed digitally and produced in a standard specification
in order to ensure its continuing availability*

OXFORD
UNIVERSITY PRESS

Great Clarendon Street, Oxford OX2 6DP
Oxford University Press is a department of the University of Oxford.
It furthers the University's objective of excellence in research, scholarship,
and education by publishing worldwide in
Oxford New York
Auckland Cape Town Dar es Salaam Hong Kong Karachi
Kuala Lumpur Madrid Melbourne Mexico City Nairobi
New Delhi Shanghai Taipei Toronto
With offices in
Argentina Austria Brazil Chile Czech Republic France Greece
Guatemala Hungary Italy Japan South Korea Poland Portugal
Singapore Switzerland Thailand Turkey Ukraine Vietnam

Oxford is a registered trade mark of Oxford University Press
in the UK and in certain other countries

Published in the United States
by Oxford University Press Inc., New York

© Dan Stone 2010

The moral rights of the author have been asserted

Database right Oxford University Press (maker)

Reprinted 2011

All rights reserved. No part of this publication may be reproduced,
stored in a retrieval system, or transmitted, in any form or by any means,
without the prior permission in writing of Oxford University Press,
or as expressly permitted by law, or under terms agreed with the appropriate
reprographics rights organization. Enquiries concerning reproduction
outside the scope of the above should be sent to the Rights Department,
Oxford University Press, at the address above

You must not circulate this book in any other binding or cover
And you must impose this same condition on any acquirer

ISBN 978-0-19-956680-8

For my wonderful *Mischlinge*, Libby and Greta,
for when they need to know

Acknowledgements

First of all thanks to Christopher Wheeler at Oxford University Press for encouraging me to write this book and for being such a wonderfully engaged editor. Thanks too to Matthew Cotton and Natasha Knight at OUP for their assistance.

Thanks to Ulrike Smalley and Suzanne Bardgett at the Imperial War Museum for helping me obtain permission to use Alicia Melamed Adams's striking painting for the cover of the book. I am very grateful to Alicia for granting me permission to reproduce her artwork.

For taking the time to read chapters of the book, I am extremely grateful to: Donald Bloxham, Amos Goldberg, Dirk Moses, and Barbara Rosenbaum. A special thank you to Rudolf Muhs, for checking (and greatly improving) my translations from German, and to my PhD student Becky Jinks, who patiently read through the whole manuscript and offered many helpful suggestions. Obviously, all remaining errors are my responsibility.

I would like to thank Donald Bloxham for allowing me to read *The Final Solution: A Genocide* (OUP, 2009) in advance of publication, and Alison Bashford, Alon Confino, Amos Goldberg, Antero Holmila, Wulf Kansteiner, Dirk Moses, Chris Probst, Wolfgang Seibel, Zoë Waxman, and Jürgen Zimmerer for providing me with copies of forthcoming publications.

The research for this book would have been immeasurably harder without the resources of the German Historical Institute, London, and, especially, the Wiener Library, London. I am grateful to the staff of both institutes for their assistance.

My thanks to the many friends and colleagues who discussed aspects of this book with me or whose scholarship has set a fine example: Scott Ashley, Tony Barta, Daniel Beer, Doris Bergen, Paul Betts, Cathie Carmichael, David Cesarani, Tim Cole, Alon Confino, Ann Curthoys, Ned Curthoys, John Docker, Robert Eaglestone, Saul Friedländer, Peter Fritzsche, Christian Gerlach, Julie Gottlieb, Helen Graham, Raphael Gross, Sara Guyer, Antero Holmila, Joel Isaac, Olaf Jensen, Adam Jones, Pete Kakel, Wulf Kansteiner, Richard King, Tony Kushner, Barry Langford,

Tom Lawson, Florin Lobonţ, Peter Longerich, Wendy Lower, Dirk Moses, Rudolf Muhs, Richard Overy, Andy Pearce, Christopher Probst, Mark Roseman, Michael Rothberg, Dirk Rupnow, Dominik Schaller, Wolfgang Seibel, Tim Snyder, Scott Straus, Susan Rubin Suleiman, Chris Szejnmann, Philippe Vervaecke, Arne Johan Vetlesen, Zoë Waxman, Anton Weiss-Wendt, Eric Weitz, Hayden White, Christian Wiese, Michael Wildt, and Jürgen Zimmerer.

Finally, thanks as always to my family: my parents Avril and Graham (see if you can get past p. 7), Hilary (see if you can remember the title—clue: it's a bit like the last one), and my pride and joy, Libby and Greta.

Contents

Abbreviations

CEH	*Central European History*
GH	*German History*
HG	*The Historiography of Genocide* (Dan Stone, ed., Basingstoke: Palgrave Macmillan, 2008)
HGS	*Holocaust and Genocide Studies*
HH	*The Historiography of the Holocaust* (Dan Stone, ed., Basingstoke: Palgrave Macmillan, 2004)
JCH	*Journal of Contemporary History*
JGR	*Journal of Genocide Research*
JMH	*Journal of Modern History*
VfZ	*Vierteljahrshefte für Zeitgeschichte*
YVS	*Yad Vashem Studies*

Introduction

Towards an Integrated Historiography
of the Holocaust

Auschwitz was no instructional institution . . . You learned nothing there,
and least of all humanity and tolerance.

Ruth Klüger[1]

I n 1987, Michael Marrus published *The Holocaust in History*.[2] That book,
a model of scholarship, has provided a generation of students and
scholars with the clearest guide to the already massive historical research
on the subject of the genocide of the Jews in Nazi-occupied Europe. Over
twenty years later, Marrus's book remains very serviceable, and this book
is conceived as something of a supplement to it. But since the end of the
Cold War, the historiography of the Holocaust has grown exponentially,
as archives in the former communist countries have become accessible,
and lines of inquiry have developed that have opened up new ways of
understanding the unfolding and nature of the genocide of the Jews. This
book is meant first and foremost as a guide to the historiography of the
last twenty years, although I hope readers will find that it engages critically
with the literature and does more than merely point out schools of thought
or areas of debate.

For the purpose of this book, the Holocaust is understood as the genocide
of the Jews, as they were defined by the Nazi regime, during World War II

1. Ruth Klüger, *Landscapes of Memory: A Holocaust Girlhood Remembered* (London: Bloomsbury, 2003), p. 70.
2. Michael R. Marrus, *The Holocaust in History* (London: Penguin, 1989 [1987]).

and, importantly, as a key part of Germany's war effort. Europe's Romany (Gypsy) population was also the victim of genocide under the Nazis. Many other population groups, notably Poles, Ukrainians, and Soviet prisoners of war were killed in huge numbers, and smaller groups such as Jehovah's Witnesses, Black Germans, and homosexuals suffered terribly under Nazi rule. The evidence suggests that the Slav nations of Europe were also destined, had Germany won the war, to become victims of systematic mass murder; and even the terrible brutality of the occupation in eastern Europe, especially in Poland, can be understood as genocidal according to the definition put forward by Raphael Lemkin is his major study, *Axis Rule in Occupied Europe* (1944), the book that introduced the term 'genocide' to our vocabulary. Part of the reason for the emphasis on the Jews in today's understanding, though, is a correct assessment of the fact that for the Nazis the Jews were regarded in a kind of 'metaphysical' way; they were not just considered as racially inferior (like Romanies), deviants (like homosexuals), or enemy nationals standing in the way of German colonial expansion (like Slavs). In the Nazi *Weltanschauung* (world view), history was understood as the struggle between good and evil, represented by the 'Aryan' and 'non-Aryan' races, in particular Germans and Jews. Nazi Germany was a racial state, that is to say, the whole of the Third Reich was based on a racialized view of the world; as Rudolf Hess, Hitler's deputy, put it, Nazism was nothing more than 'applied biology'. But the Jews were to some extent outside of the racial scheme as defined by racial philosophers and anthropologists. They were not mere *Untermenschen* (sub-humans) to be contrasted with the Nazi dream of the *Übermensch* ('overman' or superman), but were regarded as a *Gegenrasse*, a 'counter-race', that is to say, not really human at all. Nazism encouraged research into and was to some extent based on race science, a science that was by no means unique to Germany in the first half of the twentieth century. Yet the persecution of the Jews actually made little sense from the point of view of race science, for the Jews were regarded as racially powerful, a unique people who despite the absence of their own territory had supposedly maintained their racial purity through two millennia. The persecution of the Jews then, as I will show in this book, owed more to mystical antisemitism and political conspiracy theories than it did to eugenics and the triumph of modern science and technology. 'Holocaust', then, refers to the genocide of the Jews, which by no means excludes an understanding that other groups—notably Romanies and Slavs—were victims of genocide. Indeed, as we will see later, the murder of the Jews, although a project in its own right, cannot be properly historically situated without understanding the 'Nazi empire' with its grandiose demographic plans.

Considerable changes have taken place recently in our understanding of the development of Holocaust historiography. Earlier historians (such as Abel Herzberg, Jacques Presser, Philip Friedman, Josef Wulf, and Leon Poliakov) worked very hard to raise awareness of the murder of the Jews. It is no longer possible to claim that there was silence in the postwar period—just as there had not been in the pre-war and wartime years—but only varieties of selective speech.[3] Nevertheless, since the end of the Cold War the historical literature on the Holocaust has mushroomed, in line with the development of 'Holocaust Studies' as a discipline and, more recently, of 'genocide studies', a field that often takes the Holocaust as a paradigm or at least as a case study with which other cases of genocide can be compared. This book does not diminish the achievements of earlier scholars but rather takes them for granted (it remains for someone to write a monograph on early Holocaust historiography to complement recent research). The focus here is on the post-1989 period since the volume of work is so massive that a guide to it is sorely needed.

Like the books which it analyses, this volume is also a product of its time. The focus on race—whether 'scientific' or 'mystical'—reflects the major historiographical trend of the last twenty years: the turning away from social history and the focus on 'ideology' in the broad sense, and the emphasis on 'race' above all. There are signs that this trend is already beginning to reach its natural conclusion. One historian notes that we may, paradoxically, have 'Nazified the Nazis'; that is, historians run the risk of taking the Nazis at their word too literally in seeing race at the heart of everything to do with the Third Reich, making the regime appear far more coherent than

3. David Bankier and Dan Michman, eds., *Holocaust Historiography in Context: Emergence, Challenges, Polemics and Achievements* (Jerusalem: Yad Vashem, 2008); Dalia Ofer, 'The Strength of Remembrance: Commemorating the Holocaust During the First Decade of Israel', *Jewish Social Studies*, 6, 2 (2000), pp. 24–55; Robert G. Moeller, *War Stories: The Search for a Usable Past in the Federal Republic of Germany* (Berkeley: University of California Press, 2001); Alexander Victor Prusin, ' "Fascist Criminals to the Gallows!" The Holocaust and Soviet War Crimes Trials, December 1945–February 1946', *HGS*, 17, 1 (2003), pp. 1–30; Hasia Diner, 'Post-World War II American Jewry and the Confrontation with Catastrophe', *American Jewish History*, 91, 3–4 (2003), pp. 439–67; Lawrence Baron, 'The Holocaust and American Public Memory, 1945–1960', *HGS*, 17, 1 (2003), pp. 62–88; Gabriel N. Finder, 'Yizkor! Commemoration of the Dead by Jewish Displaced Persons in Postwar Germany' in *Between Mass Death and Individual Loss: The Place of the Dead in Twentieth-Century Germany*, eds. Alon Confino, Paul Betts, and Dirk Schumann (New York: Berghahn, 2008), pp. 232–57.

was actually the case.[4] One can already see that a renewed focus on the intricacies of Nazi rule and experience of everyday life, especially during the war, is calling into question some of the conclusions of the 'racialized' understanding of the Third Reich. Richard Bessel, for example, notes that, by the end of the war, violence was all that the regime had left to offer, and it was being applied fairly indiscriminately to *Volksgenossen* ('racial comrades') just as to *Volksfremden* (the 'racially alien'), and Nikolaus Wachsmann, among others, has shown how the 'concentrationary universe' developed to some extent from the treatment of 'ordinary' prisoners in the German penal system.[5] But the significance of the insights gained by focusing on race should not be underestimated. Moishe Postone argues that 'focusing on antisemitism as an ideology is essential for any attempt to historically grasp the Nazi program of total extermination'.[6] And Peter Fritzsche's recent book, *Life and Death in the Third Reich*, constitutes an exemplary statement of the so-called 'voluntaristic turn', that is, the claim that the Nazi regime was ruled less by terror than by consensus.[7] And when it comes specifically to the Holocaust as opposed to the Third Reich in general—there are now two quite separate bodies of literature—the racial paradigm looks set to endure for some time yet, though it is naturally complemented by other approaches.

The other notable feature of this book is its focus on the perpetrators. Where Marrus devoted more or less equal space to the classic tripartite division between perpetrators, victims, and bystanders, I devote most attention to the former, and the latter figure relatively little. This focus is first of all a reflection of the state of the literature: the development of *Täterforschung* (perpetrator research), understood broadly not only to mean the biographies of key figures but analyses of organizations and networks of persecution, is one of the most noteworthy developments of the last two decades. But it also reflects my opinion that, if one truly wants to

4. Alon Confino, 'A World Without Jews: Interpreting the Holocaust', *GH*, 27, 4 (2009), pp. 540–1.
5. Richard Bessel, 'The War to End All Wars: The Shock of Violence in 1945 and Its Aftermath in Germany' in *No Man's Land of Violence: Extreme Wars in the Twentieth Century*, eds. Alf Lüdtke and Bernd Weisbrod (Göttingen: Wallstein, 2006), pp. 69–99; Nikolaus Wachsmann, *Hitler's Prisons: Legal Terror in Nazi Germany* (New Haven: Yale University Press, 2004).
6. Moishe Postone, 'The Holocaust and the Trajectory of the Twentieth Century' in *Catastrophe and Meaning: The Holocaust and the Twentieth Century*, eds. Postone and Eric Santner (Chicago: University of Chicago Press, 2003), p. 87.
7. Peter Fritzsche, *Life and Death in the Third Reich* (Cambridge, MA: The Belknap Press of Harvard University Press, 2008).

understand the unfolding of the Holocaust and the Nazis' beliefs that lay behind their decisions, one must examine the perpetrators.

Having said that, I hope readers will not feel that I have neglected the victims. The argument that Holocaust historiography often overlooks the victims and ends by speaking of Jews as mere objects to whom things happened—thus dangerously replicating Nazi ways of thinking—is one that has made a powerful impact on historians, who have begun to turn to Jewish life and culture before, during, and after the Holocaust in order better to understand how the Jews responded to their persecution. These studies, many of which draw innovatively on cultural theory and anthropology, provide an important corrective to the years of previous neglect. When one considers the richness of the Jewish source material, this is indeed a welcome development. 'Studying the resources and opportunities possessed by Jews', writes David Engel, 'is one of the most important tasks of the Jewish historian.'[8] But, even so, one cannot escape the fact that the vast majority of Jews caught in the Nazi empire had little room for manoeuvre, and that ultimately their destinies largely remained outside of their control. They did not all suffer the same fate, as I discuss throughout the book, for competition amongst the Nazis—about the use of forced and slave labour, for example—and their allies—about the limits of national sovereignty, for example—influenced the outcome significantly. And in the context of the ghettos, camps, and DP camps, there is much to say about Jewish responses to persecution, as some of the most innovative recent work on 'cultural resistance', orthodox Jewry, or rescue initiatives proves. But there is no chapter specifically on 'victims' as in Marrus's book. Rather, I wanted my historiographical account to accord with Saul Friedländer's ambition of creating an 'integrated' history of the Holocaust, in which the perpetrators and victims are discussed side by side. Nevertheless, the book begins and ends with the perpetrators, not just because they are the subject of the bulk of the literature but because in understanding any case of genocide our most urgent task as historians is to try to understand those who carried it out.

A book such as this cannot offer a comprehensive history of the Holocaust, nor can it provide a full guide to either the unfathomably large scholarly literature (by historians, theologians, sociologists, philosophers,

---

8. David Engel, 'Holocaust Research and Jewish Historiography: Mutual Influences' in *Holocaust Historiography*, eds. Bankier and Michman, p. 79.

literary theorists, political scientists, social psychologists, educationalists, and others) or the vast array of representations of the Holocaust produced by film-makers, artists, photographers, novelists, poets, musicians, or the many and varied attempts to memorialize the Holocaust in museums and monuments. The literature on National Socialism is large enough—in 2000, the standard bibliography listed 37,000 titles[9]—and that of the Holocaust is now just as big, if not bigger. The library at Yad Vashem in Jerusalem receives some 4,000 books per year in every European language as well as others. I cannot hope to examine all of this literature. What I aim to do is to offer a way into the various ways of approaching the Holocaust through the medium of history. This approach obviously requires history to be painted with a broad brush, but I hope to show in my overview of the historiography that the Holocaust developed differently in different places; the extraordinary geographical spread of the persecution cannot be understood if one thinks in terms of a simple blueprint for genocide. I show too that although there was no clear plan for genocide until as late as 1941–42, nevertheless the logic of the Nazi *Weltanschauung* from the founding of the party and through the Nazi regime's actions from 1933 were inherently genocidal. Theoretically speaking, I follow Franco Moretti's concept of 'distant reading', eschewing close reading of texts in order to try and gain a sense of the bigger picture, and to discern major trends and challenges to understanding.[10]

In Chapter 1, I demonstrate that although it was a Nazi-directed programme, 'Holocaust' is an umbrella term encompassing many examples of indigenous persecution that burst out under Nazi protection, especially in Romania, Slovakia, Croatia, the Baltic States, and France. Nazism burst the bounds of German ultra-nationalism and sought, especially under the SS's vision, to create a pan-European racial community, with the Germans and their racially valuable allies at the top and Slavs at the bottom, reduced to slaves. In this vision of a Nazi empire, Jews had no place at all. The Holocaust, then, was a European project, and the belated recognition of this fact helps explain why at the turn of the twenty-first century European states finally began to acknowledge that it has something to do with them.

9. Michael Ruck, *Bibliographie zum Nationalsozialismus* (Darmstadt: Wissenschaftliche Buchge-sellschaft, 2000).
10. Franco Moretti, 'Conjectures on World Literature', *New Left Review*, 1 (2000), pp. 56–8. My thanks to Joel Isaac for this reference.

Next, in Chapter 2, I introduce readers to some of the key interpretive debates in the historiography, in particular those between 'intentionalists' and 'structuralists', and between those who stress 'modernity' and those who put more emphasis on 'ideology'. Although the structuralist argument that there was no blueprint for genocide, and that the road to Auschwitz was 'twisted' is correct, one must also note the genocidal fantasy that lay at the heart of Nazism from its inception. Thus, whilst a simplistic intentionalist position that sees the Holocaust as the realization of a plan held by Hitler since 1919, 1925, or 1933 is not tenable, the more we discover about the penetration of Nazi antisemitic indoctrination into every sphere of life in the Third Reich, the more it becomes clear that whilst policy-making and individual decisions may have been made on an ad hoc basis, they were made within a framework of vicious, paranoid Jew-hatred. As I show in Chapter 3, the Holocaust was 'modern' insofar as it took place in a 'modern' society, was organized bureaucratically, and relied in part on technological killing methods. But this is hardly surprising, as its setting was a modern European state; but not all modern European states commit genocide. Thus, the 'deep essence' of the Holocaust was an outburst of transgressive violence that owed more to fantasy-thinking than to the logic of reason, 'biopower', or the 'dialectic of Enlightenment'. But as I show, thinking about the Holocaust in these terms does not exculpate modern society altogether; rather, the rationalized structures of modernity not only channelled but created the fantasies of Nazism.

Following on logically from these debates, I then move on, in Chapter 4, to an analysis of race science and its contribution to the Holocaust. This is an especially complex topic because it is widely believed that Nazism was a theory of the lionization of the 'Aryan' race and that Jews were persecuted as 'non-Aryan'. However, although academic race science was important and the complicity of many medics, geneticists, and anthropologists with Nazi crimes must not be overlooked, I argue that the genocide of the Romanies (the *Porrajmos*) owed more to race science than did the Holocaust. Likewise, the sterilization laws and the Euthanasia project, for all their significant links of personnel and technology with the Operation Reinhard death camps, make sense in terms of negative eugenics in a way that eliminating the Jews does not. Race science lent respectability to mystical theories about Jews that existed without the input of scientists. In fact, the regime increasingly distanced itself from academic race science, which, with its hair-splitting distinctions between 'race', '*Volk*', and 'nation', and its rejection of hardline

Nordicism, had the potential to undermine Nazi racial propaganda. Hitler and Himmler called upon science when they wanted to—Hitler described 'the discovery of the Jewish virus' as akin to the eradication of disease thanks to Pasteur and Koch and talked of Nazism as 'the final step in the overcoming of historicism and the recognition of purely biological values'—but in the final analysis Nazism was a philosophy of 'thinking with the blood' that owed little to, was even fundamentally dismissive of, reason, logic, and science. Its attack on the Jews was based on a fantasy; Hitler was, as Norbert Elias put it, the 'rainmaker' or 'shaman' who performed the magic necessary to realize the fantasy. In the same breath as praising Pasteur and Koch, Hitler exclaimed: 'How many diseases have their origin in the Jewish virus!'—a statement that owed nothing to science.

One of the most recent attempts to understand the Holocaust is through comparative genocide studies, and, in Chapter 5, I turn next to the idea of Nazi colonialism and examine the Holocaust in comparison with earlier colonial genocides, such as took place in the European settlements of North America and Australia. The claim that the Holocaust is 'unique' is one that for some time has been indefensible in academic circles, and here I show why. Yet studying the Holocaust in relation to other cases of genocide does not mean diminishing either the Holocaust or other genocides (which are sometimes seen as important only insofar as they 'measure up' to the Holocaust). Actually, the Holocaust is not a good yardstick for thinking about genocide in general, for most cases of genocide do not resemble it in certain key respects. Yet the Holocaust was genocide, and it shares many features with genocides that have occurred elsewhere, as Lemkin wanted us to see. In this chapter, I show why thinking comparatively and in terms of a theory of genocide is helpful in understanding the Holocaust. But I also point to the limits of the comparison: whilst the occupation of eastern Europe is helpfully thought of as a kind of colonization, the idea of 'colonial genocide' is less relevant for understanding the Holocaust as a pan-European project. When one considers the hunting-down, deportation, and murder of the Jews of western or southern Europe, the concept of colonial genocide becomes less relevant than other ways of approaching the Holocaust. What remains clear, however, is that the murder of the Jews was not a total break with what had gone before but was a radical version of experiences that have taken place throughout modern history, especially in the European overseas colonies.

Finally, in Chapter 6, I turn to cultural history as a way of understanding the victims and, most significantly, the perpetrators. Through a discussion of the creation of the Nazi *Volksgemeinschaft* (people's community)—currently a very productive area of research—as well as key institutions such as the Churches, I show that the recent emphasis on the Third Reich as a 'consensus dictatorship' has much to recommend it, a finding that allows historians to place the Holocaust in relation to debates about the earlier phase of persecution of Jews (1933–38), by, for example, showing the ways in which Kristallnacht and other forms of Nazi violence fuelled the ever-more dangerous Nazi fantasies about the existential threat that Jews supposedly posed to the security of the 'Aryan race'. Thinking about 'fantasies' is now common to cultural historians, but it remains somewhat rare amongst Holocaust historians, for whom such approaches seem dangerously close to letting slip the rationality of the historical method and giving way to or replicating Nazi 'irrationality'. But by turning the focus away from 'modernity', 'rationality', and 'race science', one can see that the fundamental driving force of the Holocaust was the leading Nazis' insistence on 'thinking with the blood'. Race mattered to the Nazis not because it was scientifically verifiable (it was not) but because they wanted their theories of race to be true. Thus, it behoves historians to try and understand the narratives and ways of thinking and acting that the Nazis promoted in order to make sense of the world that they had conquered.

Not only can a book such as this not cover in detail every historical work on the Holocaust; there are also huge areas of Holocaust-related scholarship which I do not touch on at all. Apart from the vile phenomenon of Holocaust denial, which is not discussed here—since its basic statements about the past are false, it cannot be considered as a historical narrative; rather, it is a tool of neo-Nazism—the Holocaust has given rise to some of the most thoughtful works of philosophy and literature of the late twentieth century, as well as some of the most moving artworks, broadly conceived. The Holocaust is often regarded as the harbinger of postmodernism, with its distrust of 'grand narratives' of human progress or reason; along with the decolonization struggle, it was central to the civil rights movement and the rise of liberalism after 1968; and it has contributed in a surprising way to the contemporary dominance of minimalism as the leading aesthetic in the architecture of museums and memorials. The writings of Tadeusz Borowski, Jean Améry, Primo Levi, and other survivors are among the most remarkable texts of the twentieth century, as indeed are texts written in the ghettos and camps by those who did not survive, most notably the massive *Oneg Shabbat* archive of the Warsaw Ghetto and the so-called *Scrolls of Auschwitz* written by men forced to work in the gas chamber and crematoria complex. The philosophies of Jacques Derrida, Emil Fackenheim, Theodor W. Adorno, and Emmanuel Levinas are incomprehensible without the Holocaust. Likewise the novels and short stories of Imre Kertész, Piotr Rawicz, Raymond Federman, Jorge Semprun, Sara Nomberg-Przytyk, Ida Fink, and Henryk Grynberg, the poetry of Paul Celan, Edmond Jabès, or Jerzy Ficowski. The very genre of testimony owes its existence and popularity today to a very great extent to the Holocaust. Finally, our western obsession with 'memory culture', heritage, and the redemptive power of remembering and commemorating the past is also linked to the rise to centrality of Holocaust consciousness. Although I cannot discuss these trends here, I hope that readers will find that what I have written is informed by them and a certain sensibility that is attuned to the achievements of post-Holocaust thought is in evidence. Although this is a study of historiography, my belief is that the best historians draw on material from many disciplines and ways of thinking in order to make sense of the world, for everything that human beings create in the world is itself part of history and can (and should) be historicized. My own work has been influenced (and hopefully, informed) by philosophy, literary theory, and anthropology, and my belief is that history as a discipline operates best when it is open-minded about method, sources, and style.[11] That is why the book is titled *Histories of the Holocaust*: not only are there many competing (and complementary) narratives of the Holocaust, whose main arguments I try to illuminate here, but there never will be a satisfactory single, total narrative; nor should there be. The vast multiplicity of studies that currently proliferate more than ever are themselves the best resistance that historians can offer to the tendency in modern (and 'postmodern') culture to simplistic 'final solutions'. The 'unfinishing' with the past, the

---

11. See, for example, my *History, Memory and Mass Atrocity: Essays on the Holocaust and Genocide* (London: Vallentine Mitchell, 2006); *The Holocaust and Historical Methodology* (ed., New York: Berghahn, forthcoming); 'Beyond the Mnemosyne Institute: The Future of Memory after the Age of Commemoration' in *The Future of Memory*, eds. Rick Crownshaw, Jane Kilby, and Antony Rowland (New York: Berghahn, 2010) pp. 17–36; and, for an example of the relevance of literature for understanding the past and historical method, 'Surviving in the Corridors of History, or History as Double or Nothing' in *Federman's Fictions*, ed. Jeffrey R. Di Leo (Albany: State University of New York Press, 2011) pp. 203–13.

fact of permanent change, is the historian's contribution to the variety of ways of being human and thus of promoting freedom.

Finally, as my epigraph from Ruth Klüger's memoir indicates, studying the Holocaust does not leave one optimistic about the human condition. Has the Holocaust brought about a 'break with history'? Does it signal the end of our belief in progress? Or has it become just another addition to the slaughter-bench of history? Why has the Holocaust assumed the central position it has in western society today? I do not doubt the good intentions of the politicians and educationalists who want us to learn about the Holocaust. But we need to consider what we are learning. Far from becoming, as some argue, the basis of a 'cosmopolitan memory' that is at the forefront of promoting human rights, the more one discovers about the Holocaust the less comfortable one feels about the future of the human species. The propensity for ideological demagoguery and organized violent frenzy has not gone away in the twenty-first-century world. As we human beings set about destroying our planet, the likelihood is that a combination of environmental degradation and violent ideologies will lead to genocide on an unprecedented scale. Reading about Anne Frank or flying schoolchildren on day trips to Auschwitz, however well meaning, are insufficient to counter this terrible scenario.

*

As I sat down to write the first chapter of this book, I became increasingly overwhelmed by the enormity of the task. The scholarly literature on every conceivable subject of the Holocaust, from the murder of the Jews of Riga to Jews in hiding in the south of France, is so vast and conducted in so many languages that no person can possibly master it all. The pan-European dimension of the Holocaust, discussed in Chapter 1, is more obvious and comprehensible than it has ever been. The sources that I have consulted for this book are mostly in English and German, and sometimes French, with occasional references to books appearing in other languages (which I can struggle to read). Fortunately, it seems to be the case that the majority of significant works appear in those languages, whether in translation or not, with perhaps the major exceptions being Hebrew and Polish. Thus, I hope it is not to do too much of a disservice to colleagues writing in, say, Hungarian or Russian to say that many works written in the eastern European languages tend to be detailed local studies or, where they have wider significance, generally get translated into English or German. Still,

I am aware that, even with rather substantial footnotes, my references barely scratch the surface of the scholarly literature, and my text necessarily remains in most instances quite superficial. I apologize to colleagues whose work is not mentioned; this is through oversight or lack of language skills. Even so, I hope that this book does offer a helpful guide to the main trends in the recent historiography, and I trust that those interested in pursuing any particular theme in greater depth will soon discover that there is far more out there than I have been able to document.

I

The 'Final Solution'

A German or European Project?

> There is little sense in trying to offer a historiographical summary of the Holocaust in Europe.
>
> Marc Olivier Baruch[1]

Introduction

Between 8 and 19 August 1941, a *Sonderkommando* unit working together with Ukrainian militiamen murdered the Jewish men and women of Byelaya Tserkov, a town 70 kilometres from Kiev. Their children were locked in a building on the edge of town. Most were killed on 19 August, but some 90 were left behind, locked inside. Following the requests of military chaplains Ernst Tewes and Gerhard Wilczek to Lieutenant-Colonel Helmuth Groscurth to deal with the awful condition of the children, they were executed on 22 August. Since the Germans could not agree on which of their units would shoot them, they ordered the Ukrainians to carry out the task. Groscurth commented in his report to von Reichenau that 'Both infants and children should have been eliminated immediately in order to have avoided this inhuman agony'.[2]

---

1. Marc Olivier Baruch, 'Perpetrator Networks and the Holocaust: The Spoliation of Jewish Property in France, 1940–1944' in *Networks of Nazi Persecution: Bureaucracy, Business and the Organization of the Holocaust*, eds. Gerald D. Feldman and Wolfgang Seibel (New York: Berghahn, 2005), p. 190.
2. Ernst Klee, Willi Dressen, and Volker Riess, eds., *'Those Were the Days': The Holocaust as Seen by the Perpetrators and Bystanders* (London: Hamish Hamilton, 1991), pp. 138–54 (Groscurth p. 151).

On 11 June 1942, Adolf Eichmann informed the SS officials responsible for Jewish Affairs in Brussels, Paris, and The Hague that deportations of Jews would begin. Jews already assembled at the transit camps of Westerbork (Holland), Drancy (France), and Malines (Belgium) were to be deported as of 15 July, 17 July, and 4 August respectively. The result was the deportation and murder of about 75% of the Dutch Jews in Auschwitz and Sobibor, 25% of the French Jews, and approximately 50% of the Belgian Jews.[3]

In the district of Moghilev, the Jews were under brutal but disorganized Romanian occupation and, like the other Jews in Transnistria (the area of Romanian-occupied Ukraine between the Bug and Dniester rivers), they suffered terribly. The following comes from a report written by M. Katz, the former President of the Jewish Committee of Moghilev:

> In the ghetto of Halcineţ people ate the carcass of a horse that had been buried. . . . The authorities poured carbonic acid on it, yet they continued eating it. I gave them some money, food, and clothing and took their promise not to touch the carcass. I placed them in a nearby village and paid the rent for three months in advance.
>
> The Jews in Grabvitz lived in a cave. I had to remove them to the village against their will. They couldn't part from the 700 graves of their loved ones. . . . I found similar scenes at Vinoi, Nemerci, Pasinca, Lucineţ, Lucincic, Ozarineţ, Vindiceni: everywhere men exhausted, worn out; some of them worked on farms, others in the tobacco factory, but the majority lived on begging.[4]

These were the lucky ones, the Jews who had as yet not been deported across the Bug to be shot by the Germans.

At 4am on 26 November 1942, Norwegian plain-clothes policemen rounded up 532 Jews from their homes and drove them, in black taxis, to Oslo harbour. There they waited in line until they were ordered to board the German ship *Donau*, which took them to Germany and then, by freight train, to Auschwitz. Only nine survived and returned to Norway at the

3. Maxime Steinberg, 'The *Judenpolitik* in Belgium Within the West European Context: Comparative Observations' in *Belgium and the Holocaust: Jews, Belgians, Germans*, ed. Dan Michman, 2nd edn (Jerusalem: Yad Vashem, 2000), pp. 202–3. On Belgium see also Jean-Philippe Schreiber, 'Belgium and the Jews Under Nazi Rule: Beyond the Myths' in *Nazi Europe and the Final Solution*, eds. David Bankier and Israel Gutman (Jerusalem: Yad Vashem, 2003), pp. 469–88.
4. Radu Ioanid, *The Holocaust in Romania: The Destruction of Jews and Gypsies Under the Antonescu Regime, 1940–1944* (Chicago: Ivan R. Dee, 2000), p. 204.

end of the war. Most of the rest were gassed on arrival at the extermination camp in early December 1942.[5]

What connects these events? They occurred at different times in very different parts of Europe. The phenomenon we call the Holocaust was in reality a mass of separate events, united by virtue of the fact that they occurred because of the Nazi mania to kill all the Jews of Europe. As Saul Friedländer notes, 'the events we call the Holocaust represent a totality defined by this very convergence of distinct elements'.[6] But this fact begs many questions: how was a continent-wide operation logistically possible? Who helped? And why? These questions are dealt with in this chapter, which examines the extent to which collaboration across Europe allowed the Holocaust to occur on a scale that would have been impossible were only Germans involved.

It is immediately striking in the above descriptions that in each case local collaborators played a significant role. With respect to Belgium, for example, Maxime Steinberg writes: 'The German variable is not enough on which to build the parameter that accounted for that aspect of the occupation [i.e., Jewish policy]: the Jews themselves and the Belgian society in which the "Final Solution" was applied must also be included among the many variables of that event.'[7] In this chapter, I will show how the Holocaust was in reality a series of 'Holocausts', sometimes carried out with very little German prompting or supervision; and I will examine the reasons why so many people across Europe supported the aims of Nazism and, in many cases, took part in the Holocaust. Whilst it is true to say, as the adage goes, 'no Hitler, no Holocaust', and thus 'no Germans, no Holocaust', it is also not the case that the Germans were a uniquely 'exterminationist' antisemitic nation.[8] Many outbreaks of violence against Jews took place under Nazi protection, but once one sees 'Holocaust' as

5. Arne Johan Vetlesen, *Evil and Human Agency: Understanding Collective Evildoing* (Cambridge: Cambridge University Press, 2005), p. xii.
6. Saul Friedländer, *The Years of Extermination: Nazi Germany and the Jews 1939–1945* (London: HarperCollins, 2007), p. xv.
7. Steinberg, 'The *Judenpolitik* in Belgium', p. 200.
8. As Daniel Jonah Goldhagen argued, in *Hitler's Willing Executioners: Ordinary Germans and the Holocaust* (London: Little, Brown and Company, 1996). For analyses, see Ruth Bettina Birn, 'Revising the Holocaust', *The Historical Journal*, 40, 1 (1997), pp. 195–215; Christopher R. Browning, 'Daniel Goldhagen's Willing Executioners', *History & Memory*, 8, 1 (1996), pp. 88–109; A. Dirk Moses, 'Structure and Agency in the Holocaust: Daniel J. Goldhagen and His Critics', *History and Theory*, 37, 2 (1998), pp. 194–219.

an umbrella term instead of a monolithic, micro-managed project, one sees the shocking extent of collaboration and antisemitic initiative in occupied Europe.

In the mid-1990s, the *Wehrmachtsausstellung* ('Crimes of the Wehrmacht' exhibition) travelled across Germany and Austria, revealing the full participation of ordinary soldiers in the crimes committed by the Nazi regime. Although historians had known for decades that massacres of civilians had not only been carried out by the SS, the legend of the 'clean Wehrmacht' remained pervasive in Germany, and not just in right-wing circles. The curators went to great lengths to find photographs, which in many cases had been sitting in the pockets of uniforms that had been hanging in lofts and cellars for decades.[9] Now that the real extent of German participation in mass murder is clear,[10] it is time also to reveal the true nature of European collaboration. That we can do so is testament to the achievement of the many regional studies of the Holocaust that have been published since the end of the Cold War, with the opening up of archives across former communist east Europe.

The opening of these archives has meant that historians have focused primarily on local collaboration and administration in eastern Europe. Many Holocaust survivors from that region famously claimed that their neighbours (whether Ukrainians, Poles, Lithuanians, or whoever) were 'worse

9. Hannes Heer, Walter Manoschek, Alexander Pollak, and Ruth Wodak, eds., *The Discursive Construction of History: Remembering the Wehrmacht's War of Annihilation* (Basingstoke: Palgrave Macmillan, 2008); Klaus-Michael Mallmann, Volker Rieß, and Wolfram Pyta, eds., *Deutscher Osten 1939–1945: Der Weltanschauungskrieg in Photos und Texten* (Darmstadt: Wissenschaftliche Buchgesellschaft, 2003); Daniel Uziel, 'Wehrmacht Propaganda Troops and the Jews', *YVS*, 29 (2001), pp. 27–63; Hannes Heer and Klaus Naumann, eds., *War of Extermination: The German Military in World War II, 1941–1944* (New York: Berghahn, 2000); Hannes Heer, *Tote Zonen: Die deutsche Wehrmacht an der Ostfront* (Hamburg: Hamburger Edition, 1999); Hamburg Institute for Social Research, eds., *The German Army and Genocide: Crimes Against Prisoners, Jews, and Other Civilians, 1939–1944* (New York: New Press, 1999); Walter Manoschek, ed., *Die Wehrmacht im Rassenkrieg: Der Vernichtungskrieg hinter der Front* (Vienna: Picus, 1996).
10. Mark Mazower, *Hitler's Empire: Nazi Rule in Occupied Europe* (London: Allen Lane, 2008), p. 10; Peter Fritzsche, *Life and Death in the Third Reich* (Cambridge, MA: The Belknap Press of Harvard University Press, 2008), pp. 159, 184, and 199–200; Edward B. Westermann, *Hitler's Police Battalions: Enforcing Racial War in the East* (Lawrence: University Press of Kansas, 2005); Jürgen Matthäus, 'What about the "Ordinary Men"? The German Order Police and the Holocaust in the Occupied Soviet Union', *HGS*, 10, 2 (1996), pp. 134–50; Hannes Heer, 'Killing Fields: The Wehrmacht and the Holocaust in Belorussia, 1941–1942', *HGS*, 11, 1 (1997), pp. 79–101; Norman Naimark, 'War and Genocide on the Eastern Front', *Contemporary European History*, 16, 4 (2007), pp. 259–74; Dieter Pohl, *Die Herrschaft der Wehrmacht: Deutsche Militärbesatzung und einheimische Bevölkerung in der Sowjetunion, 1941–1944* (Munich: R. Oldenbourg, 2008).

than the Germans'.[11] This assertion, whilst understandable emotionally—it must be more shocking to find people you know attacking you, than experiencing brutality at the hands of an invading force, which can more readily be grasped as 'what happens in war'—is not borne out by the facts. Nevertheless, it has become clear that the murder of the Jews in eastern Europe would have been much harder for the Germans to carry out were it not for the assistance of the local inhabitants. But the same is true of western Europe, and it is important not to maintain stereotypes about eastern European 'primitiveness' or 'superstition' when more systematic, state-level collaboration occurred in France, Norway, or the Netherlands.

In the 1930s, the rise of Nazism was not an aberrant phenomenon. Almost every European state abandoned democracy—in any case a post-Great War imposition in many countries—in favour of authoritarianism of one variety or another. The exceptions, such as Britain, the Scandinavian countries, France, Switzerland, and Czechoslovakia, all had indigenous fascist movements, some more threatening to the established order than others.[12] All were vilified by the fascist powers for being inefficient and soon to be superannuated. And during the war, Nazism presented itself as more than an occupying force driven by nationalist dreams of territorial expansion; rather, Nazism, so its ideologists claimed, would go beyond the nation-state and defend European civilization from the Bolshevik threat, uniting Europe behind a vision of racial unity and economic integration. Nazism, in other words, was a transnational phenomenon, for in every European country, both the occupied and unoccupied, there were sections of the population (often quite small, but influential) who sympathized with Nazi aims. When it came to overturning the 'decadence' of nineteenth-and early twentieth-century liberalism, the effete political culture with its *Herrenklub* elitism, and the emasculated cultural sphere, with its celebration of sexual and artistic licence, certain groups across Europe were ready to throw their lot in with the Nazis. This has been shown even for

11. See, for a recent example, Daniel Mendelsohn, *The Lost: A Search for Six of Six Million* (London: Harper Perennial, 2008).
12. For lesser known examples, see: P. F. Sugar, ed., *Native Fascism in the Successor States, 1918–1945* (Santa Barbara: ABC Clio, 1971); Herman Kopecek, '*Zusammenarbeit* and *spoluprace*: Sudeten-German-Czech Cooperation in Interwar Czechoslovakia', *Nationalities Papers*, 24, 1 (1996), pp. 63–78; David Kelly, 'The Would-Be Führer: General Radola Gajda of Czechoslovakia', *Journal of Slavic Military Studies*, 12, 3 (1999), pp. 163–77; Beat Glaus, *Die Nationale Front: Eine Schweizer faschistische Bewegung, 1930–1940* (Zurich: Benziger, 1969).

areas that had long been regarded as exceptions, such as Slovenia.[13] From
the conservative nationalist to the radical fascist, Nazism appeared to
offer participation in European 'recovery' and a bulwark against 'godless
communism'. As Tim Kirk notes, 'The possibility of a fascist or *"fascisant"*
new order in Europe had been a future that had appealed to a much wider
constituency than the Nazi Party and its supporters.'[14] As the past tense of
Kirk's sentence implies, most of these collaborators would learn the hard
way that Nazi claims of creating European unity were a charade, behind
which stood only exploitation and appropriation in favour not of 'Europe'
but the German continental empire. As Martin Dean notes, 'harsh German
measures ultimately only worsened the very problem they were trying to
solve.'[15]

    The same was true of the Holocaust. There was no greater symbol
of the degenerate modernity that Nazism rejected than 'the Jew', especially
'the international Jew', the supposed string-puller behind the British and
American democracies as well as the communist USSR.[16] In an age of
ultra-nationalism following the break-up of the old European empires, and
with the rise of exclusivist ideologies that demanded ethnic preference
and national homogeneity, the Jews—'rootless cosmopolitans', in the
communist parlance—were quick to be targeted; in the eastern half of
Europe for their supposed communist affiliations, and in the west for their
cosmopolitan 'modernism' and their lack of rootedness. These stereotypes
about Jews worked themselves out differently in different locales, albeit
with remarkable consistency in terms of their power to mobilize people.
The Holocaust, then, was a transnational phenomenon, not just because
Jews lived everywhere in Europe but because many European states, under
the extreme circumstances of World War II, took upon themselves the
task of solving the 'Jewish question' in their own way. One could talk

13. Gregor Joseph Kranjc, 'Obligatory Hatred? Antisemitic Propaganda and the Slovene Anti-
    Communist Camp', *East European Jewish Affairs*, 37, 2 (2007), pp. 189–216. On the Nazis'
    popular appeal, see Peter Fritzsche, *Germans into Nazis* (Cambridge, MA: Harvard University
    Press, 1998).
14. Tim Kirk, 'Working Towards the Reich: The Reception of German Cultural Politics in
    South-Eastern Europe' in *Working Towards the Führer: Essays in Honour of Sir Ian Kershaw*,
    eds. Anthony McElligott and Tim Kirk (Manchester: Manchester University Press, 2003),
    p. 220.
15. Martin Dean, *Collaboration in the Holocaust: Crimes of the Local Police in Belorussia and Ukraine,
    1941–44* (Basingstoke: Macmillan, 2000), p. 26.
16. See David Bankier, 'Signaling the Final Solution to the German People' in *Nazi Europe*,
    eds. Bankier and Gutman, pp. 15–39; Jeffrey Herf, *The Jewish Enemy: Nazi Propaganda during
    World War II* (Cambridge, MA: The Belknap Press of Harvard University Press, 2006).

of a 'transnational Holocaust', but a more appropriate term would be 'Holocausts', for the degree of independent action engaged in by the Third Reich's allies is impressive. As Marrus noted of western Europe, 'the Nazis relied on local agencies to prepare the Jews for their own destruction. Remarkably few Germans were available for such work.'[17] In eastern Europe too, the Nazis' task would have been considerably harder were it not for local assistance. In what follows, I do not present a comprehensive survey of the Holocaust in each country of occupied Europe, but look to the historiography to see how far this idea of 'Holocausts' can be taken, and how far the idea of the genocide as a 'European project' has any meaning other than geographical.

'Holocausts': Eastern Europe

A well-known example of the phenomenon of non-German involvement at the early stage of the Holocaust, indeed, before the 'Final Solution' as a coherent, Europe-wide project had been set in motion, can be seen in the Baltic States, where 80% of the Jewish population was killed by the end of 1941. In Estonia, the *Einsatzgruppen* very quickly destroyed the small Jewish population of about 4,400 (although it should be noted that more than three quarters of this number escaped into the Soviet Union, leaving fewer than 1,000 Jews in Estonia at the start of the German occupation).[18] Indeed, the SS officers in charge, such as Martin Sandberger, head of *Sonderkommando* 1a, and his boss, Walter Stahlecker, commander of *Einsatzgruppe* A, took great pleasure in rendering Estonia *judenrein* before any other area occupied by the Germans; Rudolf Lange, the head of *Einsatzkommando* 2 and commander of the security police in Riga, notoriously boasted about his

---

17. Michael R. Marrus, *The Holocaust in History* (London: Penguin, 1989), p. 70. See also Marrus, 'The History of the Holocaust: A Survey of Recent Literature', *JMH*, 59, 1 (1987), pp. 114–60.
18. Meelis Maripuu, 'Kollaboration und Widerstand in Estland 1940–1944' in *Collaboration and Resistance During the Holocaust: Belarus, Estonia, Latvia, Lithuania*, eds. David Gaunt, Paul A. Levine, and Laura Palosuo (Bern: Peter Lang, 2004), pp. 403–19. See also Ruth Bettina Birn, *Die Sicherheitspolizei in Estland 1941–1944: Eine Studie zur Kollaboration im Osten* (Paderborn: Schöningh, 2006); Wolfgang Benz, 'Die Ermordung der baltischen Juden und die einheimische Bevölkerung' in *Deutsche, Juden, Völkermord: Der Holocaust als Geschichte und Gegenwart*, eds. Jürgen Matthäus and Klaus-Michael Mallmann (Darmstadt: Wissenschaftliche Buchgesellschaft, 2006), p. 141; Anton Weiss-Wendt, 'The Soviet Occupation of Estonia in 1940–41 and the Jews', *HGS*, 12, 2 (1998), pp. 308–25; Weiss-Wendt, *Murder Without Hatred: Estonians and the Holocaust* (Syracuse: Syracuse University Press, 2009).

achievements at the Wannsee conference in early 1942.[19] But the SS and Wehrmacht did not do this alone.

In his instructions to the *Einsatzgruppen* leaders just after the start of Operation Barbarossa, Heydrich ordered that 'No steps will be taken to interfere with any purges that may be initiated by anti-communist or anti-Jewish elements in the newly occupied territories. On the contrary, these are to be secretly encouraged.'[20] In Lithuania, sections of the local population set about attacking the Jews with only the slightest provocation from the Germans. Along with other locals, the infamous 'death dealer of Kaunas' was photographed clubbing Jews to death with an iron bar as German soldiers looked on, laughing.[21] The group of 300 men led by the journalist Klimatis carried out at least one murder operation independently of the Germans, killing almost 4,000 Jews.[22] Lithuanians carried out some 500 separate pogroms before the Germans took over and made the murder process more systematic.[23] Even so, in general, the numbers involved in such displays of brutality were relatively small, and the Germans did not always find it easy to persuade local people to take part. Vygantas Vareikis argues that explaining the destruction of Lithuanian Jewish communities as a result of traditional anti-Judaic stereotypes and interwar propaganda is 'grossly over-simplified'. Only the brutal conditions of the interwar and war years mobilized these stereotypes to such an extent and gave them

19. Andrej Angrick and Peter Klein, *Die 'Endlösung' in Riga: Ausbeutung und Vernichtung 1941–1944* (Darmstadt: Wissenschaftliche Buchgesellschaft, 2006), pp. 271–5.
20. Reinhard Heydrich, instructions to *Einsatzgruppen* leaders, 2 July 1941, in J. Noakes and G. Pridham, eds., *Nazism 1919–1945: A Documentary Reader. Vol. 3: Foreign Policy, War and Racial Extermination* (Exeter: Exeter University Press, 1988), p. 1092.
21. Klee et al., *'Those Were the Days'*, pp. 23–37.
22. Peter Lawrence, 'Why Lithuania? A Study of Active and Passive Collaboration in Mass Murder in a Lithuanian Village, 1941' in *Why Germany? National Socialist Anti-Semitism and the European Context*, ed. John Milfull (Oxford: Berg, 1993), p. 214. See also Arūnas Bubnys, 'The Holocaust in the Lithuanian Province in 1941: The Kaunas District' in *Collaboration and Resistance*, eds. Gaunt et al., pp. 283–312 for a wider perspective.
23. Joshua Rubenstein, 'The War and the Final Solution on the Russian Front' in *The Unknown Black Book: The Holocaust in the German-Occupied Soviet Territories*, eds. Joshua Rubenstein and Ilya Altman (Bloomington: Indiana University Press, 2008), p. 12. See also Karen Ehrlich Friedman, *German/Lithuanian Collaboration in the Final Solution, 1941–1944* (PhD thesis, University of Illinois at Chicago, 1994); Knut Stang, 'Kollaboration und Völkermord: Das Rollkommando Hamann und die Vernichtung der litauischen Juden' in *Die Gestapo im Zweiten Weltkrieg: 'Heimatfront' und besetztes Europa*, eds. Gerhard Paul and Klaus-Michael Mallmann (Darmstadt: Primus, 2000), pp. 464–80; Stang, *Kollaboration und Massenmord: Die litauische Hilfspolizei, das Rollkommando Hamann und die Ermordung der litauischen Juden* (Frankfurt/M: Peter Lang, 1996) for details of the names and activities of the men involved in the auxiliary battalions.

credence.[24] Still, the role of local collaborators was not insignificant and, as Jürgen Matthäus writes, the Holocaust 'could not have evolved on Lithuanian soil if imported German violence had not harmonized with residual anti-Jewish sentiment among the local population'.[25]

In Latvia too, the locals could—as a few did—enlist for German civil and military institutions, but only on the Germans' terms.[26] But although it proved hard to incite the local population into 'spontaneous' pogroms, and although Latvian 'collaboration' was generally confined to day-to-day administration, the formation of the Arājs and Vagulāns commandos brought a substantial collaborationist force into existence. The Arājs force of 300 men in 1941, which grew to 1,200 in 1943, was responsible for the murder of at least 26,000 civilians and was involved in the murder of maybe as many as 60,000 (out of a total of 85,000 killed in Latvia), mostly Jews. In particular, the Arājs commando played a role in the infamous Rumbula massacre of 30 November and 8 December 1941, in which most of Riga's Jews were killed, as well as in the killing of the Reich Jews who were deported to Latvia in early 1942. Latvian auxiliary police units were also involved in atrocities, although not on the same scale as the commandos.[27] The murder of the Jews of Latvia, then, was unmistakably a German project; but it was carried out also by Latvians: 'It is fair to state that in the implementation of the Holocaust in Latvia, there was no sphere in which Latvians were not involved.'[28]

The images from Kaunas or Rumbula remind us that the initial stages of what we now call the Holocaust occurred in the areas of eastern Europe that had been annexed by the Soviet Union under the terms of the

24. Vygantas Vareikis, 'In the Shadow of the Holocaust: Lithuanian Jewish Relations in the Crucial Years 1940–1944' in *Nazi Europe*, eds. Bankier and Gutman, pp. 251, 262.
25. Jürgen Matthäus, 'Controlled Escalation: Himmler's Men in the Summer of 1941 and the Holocaust in the Occupied Soviet Territories', *HGS*, 21, 2 (2007), p. 230.
26. Andrew Ezergailis, ' "Neighbors" Did Not Kill Jews!' in *Collaboration and Resistance*, eds. Gaunt et al., p. 212, and, in the same volume, Antonijs Zunda, 'Collaboration in German-Occupied Latvia: Assessments of the Historical Literature', pp. 111–26.
27. Andrew Ezergailis, *The Holocaust in Latvia: The Missing Center* (Riga: Historical Institute of Latvia/Washington: United States Holocaust Memorial Museum, 1996), ch. 6 (commandos) and ch. 10 (auxiliary police). See also Martin Evans, 'Memories, Monuments, Histories: The Re-Thinking of the Second World War since 1989', *National Identities*, 8, 4 (2006), pp. 317–48; Bella Zisere, 'The Memory of the Shoah in Post-Soviet Latvia', *East European Jewish Affairs*, 35, 2 (2005), pp. 155–65.
28. Katrin Reichelt, 'Kollaboration und Holocaust in Lettland 1941–1945' in *Täter im Vernichtungskrieg: Der Überfall auf die Sowjetunion und der Völkermord an den Juden*, ed. Wolf Kaiser (Berlin: Propyläen, 2002), pp. 115–6. Reichelt (p. 116) considers the number killed by the Arājs commando to have been considerably lower than Ezergailis' estimate.

Molotov–Ribbentrop pact. In this area, which (along with part of eastern Poland) the Nazis designated *Reichskommissariat Ostland*, the most recent studies, based on detailed archival and oral research, indicate 'the shockingly vast web of complicity on the part of many thousands of Europeans who willingly participated in the humiliation, plunder and murder of their Jewish neighbours'.[29] Yet the Holocaust on Soviet territory outside of the annexed territories remains one of the least-well-known parts of this history.[30] The notion of 'factory-line genocide', if it is appropriate at all, only holds good for the later stages of the Holocaust, after the 'Final Solution' had been decided on. Before 1942, nearly one million Jews were murdered in the USSR, primarily by shooting in pits on the edges of towns and villages. Recovering this history is vital not only in order that we might know what happened—the Holocaust in the Soviet Union was messy and at times inconsistent, as in Pinsk, where 18,000 Jews were still alive after the first *Aktion*, which killed 7,000–8,000[31]—but so that our understanding of the Holocaust is not restricted to clichéd images of 'industrial mass murder'. This history is now to some extent becoming clearer, with the first major monograph on the subject recently appearing.[32] Although less well known, the collaboration that occurred after the 'first sweep' of the *Einsatzgruppen* was actually of greater value to the Germans, both in locating Jews and maintaining the occupation.

An important recent publication in English is the *Unknown Black Book*, which collects accounts from the first wave of killings. The book, first published in Russian in 1993, confirms the fact that, as Yitzhak Arad writes,

29. David Gaunt and Paul A. Levine, 'Introduction' in *Collaboration and Resistance*, eds. Gaunt et al., p. 32.
30. Wendy Morgan Lower, 'From Berlin to Babi Yar: The Nazi War Against the Jews, 1941–1944', *Journal of Religion and Society*, 9 (2007), pp. 1–14.
31. Tikva Fatal-Knaani, 'The Jews of Pinsk Through the Prism of New Documentation', *YVS*, 29 (2001), pp. 149–82, esp. p. 164.
32. Yitzhak Arad, *The Holocaust in the Soviet Union* (Lincoln: University of Nebraska Press, 2009). Earlier works include: Yitzhak Arad, 'The Holocaust of Soviet Jewry in the Occupied Territories of the Soviet Union', *YVS*, 21 (1991), pp. 1–47; Lucjan Dobroszycki and Jeffrey S. Gurock, eds., *The Holocaust in the Soviet Union: Studies and Sources on the Destruction of the Jews in the Nazi-Occupied Territories of the USSR, 1941–1945* (Armonk, NY: M. E. Sharpe, 1993); Zvi Gitelman, ed., *Bitter Legacy: Confronting the Holocaust in the USSR* (Bloomington: Indiana University Press, 1997). For recent surveys, see Dieter Pohl, 'Die Wehrmacht und der Mord an den Juden in den besetzten sowjetischen Gebieten' in *Täter im Vernichtungskrieg*, ed. Kaiser, pp. 39–53; Harvey Asher, 'The Holocaust and the USSR' in *Lessons and Legacies, Vol. 7*, ed. Herzog, pp. 253–68; Vadim Altskan, 'Soviet Archival Sources for Studying the Jewish Experience During the Holocaust' in *Ghettos 1939–1945: New Research and Perspectives on Definition, Daily Life, and Survival* (Washington, DC: Center for Advanced Holocaust Studies, USHMM, 2005), pp. 147–57.

'Without the active support of the local inhabitants, tens of thousands of whom served in police units, the Germans would not have been able to identify and exterminate as many Jews in the occupied territories of the Soviet Union.'[33] For most locals, participation did not include taking part in murder; but the accounts describe neighbours waiting to help themselves to the Jews' possessions, from clothes to apartments: 'Having caught the scent of booty, all sorts of dirty scoundrels came running from every direction.' As Rubenstein notes, particularly in the Baltic states and western Ukraine, 'it was as if the population understood, without much prodding by the Germans, that there were no limits on what they could do to their Jewish neighbours.'[34]

Many of the 'regional studies' that have been written since the end of the Cold War suggest that Nazi policy towards the Jews developed in tandem with plans for 'resettling' ethnic Germans and argue that the decision-making process was usually ad hoc, owing more to local initiative than to directives from Berlin. I will assess these claims in the next chapter. An earlier example is Shmuel Spector's *The Holocaust of Volhynian Jews* (1990), an unusual regional study not only because its author is Israeli (most are German) but because he focuses on the victims rather than on the perpetrators and covers the prehistory of the Jews under Polish and Soviet rule. Spector writes that in the early days of Nazi occupation, 'a wave of pogroms swept over the Jews' that was 'carried out by the Ukrainian population in places where an interim period of sorts ensued between the phasing out of Soviet rule and the arrival of German officials'. Most of these pogroms were, he argues, driven by the desire for Jewish property. For example, in Horyngrad-Krypa on 7 July 1941, the first day of the occupation, Ukrainians equipped with 'axes, knives and boards spiked with nails set upon the local Jews, murdering thirty'. The *Einsatzgruppen* report of 16 July spoke of 'welcome activity against the Jews' that was performed 'by the Ukrainian population in the first hours after

33. Yitzhak Arad, 'The Destruction of the Jews in German-Occupied Territories of the Soviet Union' in *The Unknown Black Book*, p. xvi. See also Arad, 'The Local Population in the German-Occupied Territories of the Soviet Union and its Attitude toward the Murder of the Jews' in *Nazi Europe*, eds. Bankier and Gutman, pp. 233–48; Ilya Ehrenburg and Vasily Grossman, eds., *The Complete Black Book of Russian Jewry* (New Brunswick: Transaction, 2001); Martin Dean, 'Local Collaboration in the Holocaust in Eastern Europe' in *HH*, p. 128.
34. Lev Rozhetsky, 'My Life in a Fascist Prison'; Rubenstein, 'The War and the Final Solution', both in *Unknown Black Book*, pp. 128 and 13.

the Bolshevik withdrawal'.[35] All of these studies refer to such actions by indigenous populations.

Much recent research has focused on the Holocaust in the lands that today constitute Ukraine, which, as Ray Brandon and Wendy Lower remind us, was for a short period in 1941 home to some 2.45 million Jews, the largest Jewish population in Europe.[36] Lower notes that for Ukrainians, in the early days of the occupation, 'there was reason to believe that German rule might bring more freedom and prosperity'. The Germans gave the impression that Ukrainian nationalist movements would be tolerated and, accordingly, the Germans found it relatively easy to recruit for a Ukrainian 'Order Service', or militia, especially in formerly Polish Eastern Galicia.[37] Lower explains that 'The Germans needed indigenous helpers to administer and exploit the newly conquered territory' and that these helpers—albeit a minority—actively participated in the murder of Jews.[38] She approvingly cites John Paul Himka, who writes that 'during the Nazi occupation of Ukraine, criminality moved from the margins of society to its centre, and individuals with an inclination to rob, extort, and kill were not lost in the larger crowd of humanity, but rather stepped to the fore.'[39] Indeed, referring to pogroms in the Zhytomyr region in 1941, she writes: 'In general, German officials instigated the pogroms, but they preferred not to bloody their own hands since local militiamen (Ukrainians and ethnic Germans), anti-Semites, and plunderers were so obliging.'[40]

35. Shmuel Spector, *The Holocaust of Volhynian Jews 1941–1944* (Jerusalem: Yad Vashem, 1990), pp. 64, 65, 67, 69.
36. Ray Brandon and Wendy Lower, eds., *The Shoah in Ukraine: History, Testimony, Memorialization* (Bloomington: Indiana University Press, 2008).
37. Wendy Lower, *Nazi Empire-Building and the Holocaust in Ukraine* (Chapel Hill: University of North Carolina Press, 2005), pp. 37, 38, 49. See also Lower, 'A New Ordering of Space and Race: Nazi Colonial Dreams in Zhytomyr, Ukraine, 1941–1944', *German Studies Review*, 26, 2 (2002), pp. 228–54; 'Hitler's "Garden of Eden" in Ukraine: Nazi Colonialism, *Volksdeutsche*, and the Holocaust, 1941–1944' in *Gray Zones: Ambiguity and Compromise in the Holocaust and its Aftermath*, eds. Jonathan Petropoulos and John K. Roth (New York: Berghahn, 2005), pp. 185–204; 'The "*reibungslose*" Holocaust? The German Military and Civilian Implementation of the "Final Solution" in Ukraine, 1941–1944' in *Networks*, eds. Feldman and Seibel, pp. 236–56; 'Facilitating Genocide: Nazi Ghettoization Policies in Ukraine, 1941–1944' in *Life in the Ghettos During the Holocaust*, ed. Eric J. Sterling (Syracuse: Syracuse University Press, 2005), pp. 120–44.
38. Lower, *Nazi Empire-Building*, p. 51.
39. Lower, *Nazi Empire-Building*, p. 90, citing John Paul Himka, 'Ukrainian Collaboration in the Extermination of the Jews During the Second World War: Sorting Out the Long-Term and Conjunctural Factors' in *The Fate of the European Jews, 1939–1945: Continuity or Contingency?*, ed. Jonathan Frankel (New York: Oxford University Press, 1997), p. 172.
40. Lower, *Nazi Empire-Building*, p. 91.

As in the Baltic states, in Ukraine these collaborators were in a minority. These thuggish elements were not trusted by other locals, and they could indulge in what from the German point of view were unwanted and unwarranted acts of violence. Nevertheless, the Germans relied on these helpers for the identification of Jews and, in general, 'with nearly every step of the "Final Solution" leading up to the point of execution',[41] collaborators were involved. OUN (Organization of Ukrainian Nationalists) groups, Aharon Weiss shows, 'unquestionably supported the Nazi policy of extermination of the Jews, and actively participated in its implementation'.[42]

Where the archives have been most helpful is in proving 'official' collaboration, that is, the establishment of local auxiliary police forces and the like. In his *Collaboration in the Holocaust* (2000) and in numerous articles, Martin Dean has brought this sordid history to light. Focusing especially on Belorussia and Ukraine, Dean investigates the reasons behind the formation of and willingness to join the *Schutzmannschaften*, or auxiliary police forces that the Germans established in occupied eastern Europe. Noting that the position of the population can only be understood in the light of pre-1941 Soviet occupation, Dean explains the 'uncomfortable compromise between distant plans for colonization and the practical necessity of exploiting the native population for the German war effort'. The result of this ambivalence was that 'the Germans only made firm allies of those loyal collaborators who joined their service'.[43] The Germans used these locals first, because of a shortage of manpower and, second, because of the commitment of the men to their task. For most able-bodied men, the only other options were deportation to Germany or joining the partisans in the forest, and many joined the *Schutzmannschaften* 'from a combination of anti-communism and personal ambition'. Some 25,000 men in areas under German civil administration volunteered in the first months of the occupation and, whilst 'Local participation in no way diminishes Nazi responsibility for these

41. Lower, *Nazi Empire-Building*, p. 92. For an approach more focused on the Ukrainian population than Lower's, see Karel C. Berkhoff, *Harvest of Despair: Life and Death in Ukraine under Nazi Rule* (Cambridge, MA: Harvard University Press, 2004), ch. 3. See also Timothy Snyder, *The Reconstruction of Nations: Poland, Ukraine, Lithuania, Belarus, 1569–1999* (New Haven: Yale University Press, 2003), ch. 8.
42. Aharon Weiss, 'The Attitude of the Ukrainian Nationalist Groups Towards Jews During the Second World War' in *Nazi Europe*, eds. Bankier and Gutman, p. 269. See also Dieter Pohl, 'Ukrainische Hilfskräfter beim Mord an den Juden' in *Die Täter der Shoah: Fanatische Nationalsozialisten oder ganz normale Deutschen?* ed. Gerhard Paul (Göttingen: Wallstein, 2002), pp. 205–34.
43. Dean, *Collaboration*, p. 57.

terrible crimes . . . it became a significant feature in the implementation of the Holocaust in these areas.'[44]

Some historians have, however, sought to go beyond this approach, arguing that official collaboration is 'merely the tip of the iceberg'. Vladimir Melamed argues on the basis of oral testimonies and a wide range of sources that 'territorial, national, and political aspects did play a role when it comes to the typology of perpetration and collaboration . . . it is improbable to regard all these atrocities as pre-planned and masterminded by the Germans'.[45] Gabriel Finder and Alexander Prusin have shown 'the significant role of Ukrainian police forces in the implementation of the Final Solution' in eastern Galicia.[46] Leonid Rein too seeks to reveal the attitude of the general population. Naturally, this is something that is hard to get at, but Rein attempts to do so for German-occupied Belorussia.[47] In Belorussia, some 80% of the prewar Jewish population was killed. The evidence is hard to read, though, where collaboration is concerned, for Belorussian collaboration was extremely heterogeneous.[48] Although nationalist groups appeared and were encouraged by the Germans, the general population, as Dean also argues, seems to have been reluctant to engage in antisemitic violence. 'Everywhere in Belorussia where mass murders of the Jewish population took place', Rein writes, 'we find evidence of the active participation of local police forces.' But those who benefited from the elimination of the Jews encompassed a much wider section of society than the police. This participation was driven by greed as much as by antisemitism, although the two are hard to separate: the

44. Dean, *Collaboration*, pp. 60, 71, 162, 167. See also Dean, 'The German Gendarmerie, the Ukrainian *Schutzmannschaft* and the "Second Wave" of Jewish Killings in Occupied Ukraine: German Policing at the Local Level in the Zhitomir Region, 1941–1944', *GH*, 14, 2 (1996), pp. 168–92; 'Microcosm: Collaboration and Resistance During the Holocaust in the Mir Rayon of Belarus, 1941–1944' in *Collaboration and Resistance*, eds. Gaunt et al., pp. 223–59; 'Where Did All the Collaborators Go?', *Slavic Review*, 64, 4 (2005), pp. 791–8; '*Schutzmannschaften* in Ukraine and Belarus: Profiles of Local Police Collaborators' in *Lessons and Legacies*, Vol. 7, ed. Herzog, pp. 219–32; 'Soviet Ethnic Germans and the Holocaust in the Reich Commissariat Ukraine, 1941–1944' in *The Shoah in Ukraine*, eds. Brandon and Lower, pp. 248–71, for similar conclusions.
45. Vladimir Melamed, 'Organized and Unsolicited Collaboration in the Holocaust', *East European Jewish Affairs*, 37, 2 (2007), p. 219.
46. Gabriel N. Finder and Alexander V. Prusin, 'Collaboration in Eastern Galicia: The Ukrainian Police and the Holocaust', *East European Jewish Affairs*, 34, 2 (2004), p. 96.
47. Leonid Rein, 'Local Collaboration in the Execution of the "Final Solution" in Nazi-Occupied Belorussia', *HGS*, 20, 3 (2006), p. 383.
48. Olga Baranova, 'Nationalism, Anti-Bolshevism or the Will to Survive? Collaboration in Belarus under the Nazi Occupation of 1941–1944', *European Review of History*, 15, 2 (2008), pp. 113–28; also Pohl, 'Ukrainische Hilfskräfte'.

idea that the Jews (even rural Jews) were wealthy was a long-standing stereotype, which the Germans sought to encourage. Rein's evidence does not allow him to go much further than Dean, but his conclusion—which perhaps goes beyond what his evidence suggests—is that all sections of the population were involved in one way or another, whether this was driven primarily by nationalism, as in western Belorussia, or sheer opportunism, as in the cases of Communist Party and Komsomol members in eastern Belorussia.[49]

Rein's reference to Communist Party members collaborating with Nazism might at first glance seem paradoxical. Yet the work of Jan Gross on Poland makes it more explicable. Gross caused a heated debate in Poland with his book, Neighbors (2001), which detailed the murder of the Jewish half of the population of Jedwabne in 1941. Emotions flared because in this case the murderers were not Germans but Catholic Poles. Jedwabne is in the Białystok region of eastern Poland, and had been occupied by the Soviets between September 1939 and June 1941. Gross's work was so inflammatory in certain quarters because it directly challenged the Polish narrative of victimhood. Or rather, if it did not deny Polish suffering during World War II, it pointed out that Poles could also be victimizers. Gross asserted that the local population greeted the Wehrmacht enthusiastically in 1941, and then accused the Jews of doing the same to the Red Army in 1939; in other words, 'it appears that the local non-Jewish population projected its own attitude toward the Germans in 1941 (this story remains a complete taboo and has never been studied in Polish historiography) onto an entrenched narrative about how the Jews allegedly behaved vis-à-vis the Soviets in 1939.'[50] Furthermore, he went on to argue that the very people—the 'rabble'—who had collaborated with the Germans would go on to become 'the backbone of the Stalinist apparatus of power five years later'; they were people who lacked moral fibre and a sense of social solidarity that would have helped in resisting Nazism and communism.[51] Gross's work gave rise to a great deal of commentary, not all of it complimentary. Apart from outright denials, some historians sought to dispute the fundamentals of Gross's findings by massive attention to minute details, burying the wider picture under a pile of supposed inaccuracies. Dariusz Stola calls this

49. Rein, 'Local Collaboration', pp. 393, 396, 399.
50. Jan T. Gross, Neighbors: The Destruction of the Jewish Community in Jedwabne, Poland (Princeton: Princeton University Press, 2001), p. 155.
51. Gross, Neighbors, p.165.

procedure 'quasi-negationism', by which he means 'a most detailed critique of sources, to conclude that nothing can be said precisely and unquestionably about an event'.[52] But the Polish Institute for National Remembrance, which was established as a result of the debate, has largely confirmed Gross's findings.[53] Gross has defended his ideas—indeed, extended their scope—in his more recent book, *Fear* (2006), which examines antisemitism in postwar Poland, again arguing that there were important lines of continuity between Nazi and communist treatment of Jews, and that the communists' attitude towards Jews was driven largely by the need to ingratiate themselves with the local population, thus acquiring a source of legitimacy that they otherwise lacked. As Gross puts it, 'we must recognize the fact that in the brief span of five years following the end of the war—while Communist rule in Poland was being consolidated and, if my argument stands, *as a constitutive part of the process*—Poland was rendered *Judenrein*'. This process culminated in the antisemitic purges of 1968, when the 'national road to socialism' ended in 'national socialism plain and simple'.[54] What Gross shows is that there were more local collaborators than historians had previously imagined, even in a country like Poland which suffered immensely under German occupation, losing proportionately more of its population than any other country in Europe. His work is being taken up by other scholars, who are now researching in greater detail Polish participation in the Holocaust.[55]

---

52. Cited in Michael Shafir, *Between Denial and 'Comparative Trivialization': Holocaust Negationism in Post-Communist East Central Europe* (Jerusalem: Vidal Sassoon International Center for the Study of Antisemitism, 2002), p. 26.

53. On *Neighbors*, see *Transodra*, 23 (2001): *Die 'Jedwabne-Debatte' in Polen: Dokumentation*, ed. Ruth Henning; Antony Polonsky and Joanna B. Michlic, eds., *The Neighbors Respond: The Controversy over the Jedwabne Massacre in Poland* (Princeton: Princeton University Press, 2004), and the discussions in *Slavic Review*, 61, 3 (2002), *East European Politics and Societies*, 16, 1 (2002), *YVS*, 30 (2002), and *HGS*, 17, 1 (2003). See also Jerzy Jedlicki, 'Historical Memory as a Source of Conflicts in Eastern Europe', *Communist and Post-Communist Studies*, 32 (1999), pp. 225–32; Ewa Wolentarska-Ochman, 'Collective Remembrance in Jedwabne: Unsettled Memory of World War II in Postcommunist Poland', *History & Memory*, 18, 1 (2006), pp. 152–78, and the reply by Sławomir Kapralski in the same issue.

54. Jan T. Gross, *Fear: Anti-Semitism in Poland After Auschwitz. An Essay in Historical Interpretation* (New York: Random House, 2007), p. 243; Gross, 'After Auschwitz: The Reality and Meaning of Postwar Anti-Semitism in Poland' in *Lessons and Legacies, Vol. 7*, ed. Herzog, p. 95. But note the criticisms of David Engel, 'On Continuity and Discontinuity in Polish-Jewish Relations: Observations on *Fear*', *East European Politics and Societies*, 21, 3 (2007), pp. 534–48, and the comments of Omer Bartov, 'Much Forgotten, Little Learned', *YVS*, 35, 2 (2008), pp. 267–87.

55. Mikołaj Kunicki, 'Unwanted Collaborators: Leon Kosłowski, Władisław Studnicki, and the Problem of Collaboration among Polish Conservative Politicians in World War II', *European Review of History*, 8, 2 (2001), pp. 203–20; Klaus-Peter Friedrich, 'Collaboration in a

In Poland generally, there has been an explosion of interest in the Holocaust, and a wave of publications in Polish that is gradually being incorporated into English.[56] The journal *Zagłada Żydów: Studia i Materiały* (*Holocaust: Studies and Materials*) marks a new scholarly seriousness in Polish historiography, with important contributions from Dariusz Libionka, Sławomir Buryła, Sara Bender, and others.[57] Apart from editions of primary sources, Polish historians have focused on the ghettos and the camps in Poland, Jews in hiding,[58] the Polish underground, studies of Jewish provincial communities, and testimonies of and interviews with survivors, including the large number of neglected diaries and early postwar testimonies in Warsaw's Jewish Historical Institute. Historians have also become more aware of the significance of the war in Poland between 1939 and 1941 for paving the way for a radicalization of policy vis-à-vis the Jews in the context of the invasion of the Soviet Union. As with other regional studies, examinations of Poland reveal the importance of understanding developments on the ground, far from Berlin. And scholars have provided a more differentiated account of the ghettos as well as a more mature assessment of the fraught topic of Polish–Jewish relations.[59] This

"Land without a Quisling": Patterns of Collaboration with the Nazi German Occupation Regime in Poland During World War II', *Slavic Review*, 64, 4 (2005), pp. 712–46 (but note John Connelly's response in the same issue); Akina Skibińska and Jakub Petelewicz, 'The Participation of Poles in Crimes Against Jews in the Świętokrzyskie Region', *YVS*, 35, 1 (2007), pp. 5–48; Carla Tonini, 'The Polish Underground Press and the Issue of Collaboration with the Nazi Occupiers, 1939–1944', *European Review of History*, 15, 2 (2008), pp. 193–205. See also the interesting observations by Padraic Kenney, 'Martyrs and Neighbors: Sources of Reconciliation in Central Europe', *Common Knowledge*, 13, 1 (2007), pp. 149–69. Collaboration by Poles and Jews is the theme of volume two of *Zagłada Żydów*.

56. Important studies such as Andrzej Żbikowski's edited volume on Poles and Jews during World War II (2006) and Barbara Engelking's book on Polish denouncers of Jews deserve to be made accessible to an English-speaking audience.

57. See the review of the journal in Natalia Aleksiun, 'Winds of Change in Poland', *YVS*, 37, 1 (2009), pp. 193–9. A selection of articles from the first three volumes (2005–07) is available in English as *Holocaust: Studies and Materials: Journal of the Polish Center for Holocaust Research* (2008).

58. Gunnar S. Paulsson, *Secret City: The Hidden Jews of Warsaw 1940–1945* (New Haven: Yale University Press, 2002).

59. For example: Peter F. Dembowski, *Christians in the Warsaw Ghetto: An Epitaph for the Unremembered* (Notre Dame: University of Notre Dame Press, 2005); Joshua D. Zimmerman, ed., *Contested Memories: Poles and Jews During the Holocaust and its Aftermath* (New Brunswick: Rutgers University Press, 2003). For overviews of the Polish literature, see Dieter Pohl, 'War, Occupation and the Holocaust in Poland' in *HH*, pp. 88–119; Dariusz Stola, 'New Research on the Holocaust in Poland' in *Lessons and Legacies, Vol. 6*, ed. Diefendorf, pp. 259–84; Natalia Aleksiun, 'Polish Historiography of the Holocaust—Between Silence and Public Debate', *GH*, 22, 3 (2004), pp. 406–32.

is quite an achievement in the sometimes trying political circumstances of post-communist Poland.

The historians who have contributed to this maturation of the historiography have done so partly by investigating the participation of locals but also showing the limits of this participation and explaining the pressures on people that in many instances proved more compelling than ideological affinity with Nazism. Furthermore, as Gross's work shows, the experiences of the victims in eastern Europe is now being investigated in some detail, and various microhistories are under way that seek to provide a 'thick description' of the world that was destroyed.[60] Nevertheless, a synthetic work on the Holocaust in Poland—along the lines of Arad's on the Soviet Union—is still to be written.

In some ways following a similar historiographical trajectory, but in other ways very different, is the case of Hungary. Historians have long identified the special characteristics of the Holocaust in Hungary: the murder in 1944 of the largest surviving community in Europe, telescoping what took years to happen elsewhere into weeks. Historians have also known from the start that the German *Sonderkommando* under Eichmann could not have deported 440,000 Hungarian Jews to Auschwitz (of whom about 60,000 survived) without the support of the Hungarian gendarmerie or the authorization of Admiral Horthy.[61] Recent research is fleshing out

60. Omer Bartov, *Erased: Vanishing Traces of Jewish Galicia in Present-Day Ukraine* (Princeton: Princeton University Press, 2007). See also Bartov, 'Eastern Europe as the Site of Genocide', *JMH*, 80, 3 (2008), pp. 557–93; Yehuda Bauer, 'Jewish Baranowicze in the Holocaust', *YVS*, 31 (2003), pp. 95–151; Bauer, 'Nowogródek: The Story of a *Shtetl*', *YVS*, 35, 2 (2008), pp. 35–70; Bauer, *The Death of the Shtetl* (New Haven: Yale University Press, 2010); Christopher R. Browning, 'The Holocaust in Marcinkance in the Light of Two Unusual Documents' in *The Holocaust: The Unique and the Universal: Essays Presented in Honor of Yehuda Bauer*, eds. Shmuel Almog et al. (Jerusalem: Yad Vashem, 2001), pp. 66–83; Browning, *Collected Memories: Holocaust History and Postwar Testimony* (Madison: University of Wisconsin Press, 2003), chs 2 and 3.

61. Randolph L. Braham, *The Politics of Genocide: The Holocaust in Hungary* (Boulder: Social Science Monographs, 1994); David Cesarani, ed., *Genocide and Rescue: The Holocaust in Hungary 1944* (Oxford: Berg, 1997); Randolph L. Braham and Scott Miller, *The Nazis' Last Victims: The Holocaust in Hungary* (Detroit: Wayne State University Press, 1998); Randolph L. Braham and Attila Pók, eds., *The Holocaust in Hungary: Fifty Years Later* (New York: Columbia University Press, 1997); Randolph L. Braham, 'Hungary' in *The World Reacts to the Holocaust*, ed. David S. Wyman (Baltimore: Johns Hopkins University Press, 1996), pp. 200–24; Randolph L. Braham, 'Hungarian Jews' in *Anatomy of the Auschwitz Death Camp*, eds. Yisrael Gutman and Michael Berenbaum (Bloomington: Indiana University Press, 1994), pp. 456–68; Yehuda Bauer, *Jews for Sale? Nazi–Jewish Negotiations 1933–1945* (New Haven: Yale University Press, 1994), chs 8–12; Shlomo Aronson, 'Israel Kasztner: Rescuer in Nazi-Occupied Europe; Prosecutor at Nuremberg, and Accused at Home' in *The Holocaust: The Unique and the Universal*, eds. Almog et al., pp. 1–47.

these insights. This means less a discovery of local collaboration than a detailed inquiry into its motivation, nature, and extent, as well as detailed studies of rescue operations and local case studies (such as Judit Molnár on Pécs and Szeged).[62] There is now a very large literature on the Holocaust in Hungary. The considerable extent of Hungarian involvement in the murder of the Jews is beyond doubt. As Ernst Kaltenbrunner, head of the RSHA (*Reichssicherheitshauptamt*/Reich Security Main Office), put it, he could 'hardly do without the contribution of the Hungarian police and gendarmerie'.[63] But equally indubitable is the fact that without the impetus provided by the German occupation in March 1944, the Hungarian Jews would not have been deported to Auschwitz. Debate continues regarding the extent to which Hungarian involvement was a result of local initiative or German orders, with the weight of evidence seeming to suggest the latter, though certainly not to the exclusion of the former.[64] What continues to demand an explanation, then, is the eagerness with which the Hungarians followed the Germans' demands, a history that requires careful local analysis—district by gendarmerie district—that can also take into account the massive plunder of Jewish property that occurred as part of the process.

In the Hungarian case too, the contribution of victim-centred historiography is just as significant as for Ukraine or the Soviet Union. Anna Szalai has examined the responses of Hungarian Jews to anti-Jewish legislation between 1938 and 1942, and Guy Miron has looked at the historical memory among the Jewish community in 1938–39, both showing that the Hungarian Jews' understandable patriotism was misplaced.[65] Methodological innovation is also more apparent with respect to Hungary, with its long-established historiography, than in the context of other countries. Tim Cole brings methods derived from cultural geography to bear on his analysis of the ghettoization of Budapest, and apart from providing a

---

62. See, for example, Randolph L. Braham, 'Rescue Operations in Hungary: Myths and Realities', Judit Molnár, 'Two Cities, Two Policies, One Outcome: The De-Judaization of Pécs and Szeged in 1944', both in *YVS*, 32 (2004), pp. 21–57 and 97–129.
63. Cited in Molnár, 'Two Cities', p. 100.
64. Cf. Christian Gerlach and Götz Aly, *Das letzte Kapitel: Der Mord an den ungarischen Juden* (Stuttgart: Deutsche Verlags-Anstalt, 2002)—which stresses Hungarian initiative—with the criticisms of their work by László Karsai, 'The Last Chapter of the Holocaust', *YVS*, 34 (2006), pp. 293–329.
65. Guy Miron, 'History, Remembrance, and a "Useful Past" in the Public Thought of Hungarian Jewry, 1938–1939'; Anna Szalai, 'Will the Past Protect Hungarian Jewry? The Response of Jewish Intellectuals to Anti-Jewish Legislation', both in *YVS*, 32 (2004), pp. 131–70 and 171–208.

detailed historical survey of the Jews and the Holocaust in Hungary, Laura Palosuo employs gender analysis and oral history, placing the experiences of the victims at the centre of her original study.[66] She argues that age, gender, social class, and other factors all made a difference to how Hungarian Jews experienced the Holocaust, whether in hiding, in the deportation process, in the Budapest ghetto or during the late, chaotic stages of the war before the Soviet occupation. 'Trouser inspection', the method by which Jewish men were identified, is especially prominent among the recollections of Palosuo's informants, thus revealing that whilst the Germans targeted all Jews as Jews, persecution was experienced differently by men and women. And with respect to class, although the wealthy, with their connections, were better able to survive, they also in general found it harder to adapt to changing circumstances. As one woman says, 'I think for those rich people it was more difficult even than for us. Because there was nothing to take from us.'[67]

All of this recent research suggests that the Germans were the instigators of the Final Solution, but that without local help, their 'success' would have been hampered and their 'progress' considerably slower. At the same time, it conforms to the established model of a German-inspired project on a continent-wide scale. There are, however, a few countries where this model is not wholly applicable. In these instances, local participation went beyond engaging in a German-led project, to use the opportunity offered by the war and Germany's attack on the Jews to initiate 'indigenous Holocausts'. The difference is between occupied countries in which local thugs, opportunists, and antisemites were actively engaged, and collaborationist regimes where the attack on the Jews emanated partly from the state itself. We see this state of affairs in Slovakia, Croatia and, most clearly, in Romania.

By comparison with other European countries, the murder of the Jews in Slovakia remains surprisingly under-researched, and more monographs on the Holocaust in Slovakia are among the most pressing desiderata in Holocaust historiography, especially given the predominance of apologetic historiography.[68] Although much is known about the Holocaust in Slovakia, the literature tends to be confined for the most part to the general outline

66. Tim Cole, *Holocaust City: The Making of a Jewish Ghetto* (New York: Routledge, 2003); Laura Palosuo, *Yellow Stars and Trouser Inspections: Jewish Testimonies from Hungary, 1920–1945* (Uppsala: Uppsala Programme for Holocaust and Genocide Studies, 2008).
67. Palosuo, *Yellow Stars*, pp. 181 (trouser inspections) and 150.
68. A starting point is Ivan Kamenec, *On the Trail of Tragedy: The Holocaust in Slovakia* (Bratislava: H&H, 2007). See also Tatjana Tönsmeyer, *Das Deutsche Reich und die Slowakei 1939–1945: Politischer Alltag zwischen Kooperation und Eigensinn* (Paderborn: Schöningh, 2003).

of the murder process and to the Nazi–Jewish negotiations that occurred in the late stages of the war, although a number of well-known memoirs, especially from escapees, enrich the picture. Apart from Ivan Kamenec's *On the Trail of Tragedy*, Livia Rothkirchen's articles on the subject and her book on the Jews of Bohemia and Moravia, which touches on Slovakia, remain the standard works.[69]

Wartime Slovakia, one of the most loyal of the collaborating regimes, was led by Andrej Hlinka and Jozef Tiso, both priests. It was a product of an ultra-nationalist, antisemitic, anti-Hungarian, Catholic milieu, and is aptly described as 'clero-fascist'.[70] Its armed party units, the Hlinka Guard, were modelled on the SA. Tiso's world view echoed Hitler's: 'Jewry will be expelled from our national life for good, for in Slovakia it was always an element of subversion and operated as the principal carrier of Marxist and liberal ideas. These people are a great moral threat because of their usury, their swindling, and their lasciviousness.'[71] From 1940, the Slovakian government introduced a raft of antisemitic legislation, and forcibly 'Aryanized' Jewish property. As of 1942, the Jews of Slovakia were deported to the ghettos and death camps of occupied Poland; 58,000 were deported in the first wave. Many Jews were also murdered in Slovakia itself, mainly by German units.

However, it should also be noted that already in 1938, that is, before the war and the establishment of the Slovak puppet state, the 'autonomous' (i.e. within post-Munich Czechoslovakia) Slovakian regime deported—without being ordered to by Eichmann—some 7,500 Jews to a no-man's-land between Slovakia and Hungary, in protest at the forcible surrender of territory to Hungary after the Vienna Award (2 November 1938). The fact that some Jews in Slovakia were Hungarian-speaking helps explain this action, which Eduard Nižňanský sees as an important precursor

69. Livia Rothkirchen, 'The Situation of Jews in Slovakia Between 1939 and 1945', *Jahrbuch für Antisemitismusforschung*, 7 (1998), pp. 46–70; Rothkirchen, 'Czechoslovakia' in *The World Reacts to the Holocaust*, ed. Wyman, pp. 156–99; Rothkirchen, 'The Protectorate Question and the "Jewish Question", 1939–1941', *YVS*, 27 (1999), pp. 331–62; Rothkirchen, *The Jews of Bohemia and Moravia: Facing the Holocaust* (Lincoln: University of Nebraska Press, 2006). See also the Slovakian government-sponsored publication that followed a March 1992 conference: Dezider Tóth, ed., *The Tragedy of Slovak Jews, 1938–1945* (Branská Bytrica: Ministry of Culture of the Slovak Republic and the Museum of Slovak National Uprising, 1992).
70. Rothkirchen, *The Jews of Bohemia and Moravia*, p. 139.
71. Cited in Eduard Nižňanský, 'Die Deportation der Juden in der Zeit der autonomen Slowakei im November 1938', *Jahrbuch für Antisemitismusforschung*, 7 (1998), p. 38.

to the Final Solution in Slovakia, and indicative of the regime's willingness to act on its own initiative where the Jews were concerned. On 9 February 1939, Tiso declared: 'In Slovakia the Jewish question will be solved justly, charitably and humanely.'[72]

On 23–24 October 1941, Tiso and his deputy, Vojtech Tuka, visited Hitler's headquarters and requested Himmler's assistance in deporting the Jews from Slovakia.[73] This initiative from below meant that, by the autumn of 1942, about 60,000 Jews had been deported. There followed two relatively quiet years, thanks partly to Vatican intervention and partly to negotiations with the underground 'Working Group' (led by Gisi Fleischmann and Rabbi Michael Dov Weissmandel),[74] but the Slovak Uprising of summer–autumn 1942, in which many Jews participated, resulted in the murder of 2,257 Jews and the deportation of 2,396 more. And, with the appointment of Alois Brunner, Eichmann's deputy, as commandant of Sered concentration camp in September 1944, a further 13,500 were deported from Sered between October 1944 and March 1945.[75] With Tiso justifying his regime's actions to the Holy See until the very end of the war—'Holy Father, we shall remain faithful to our programme'[76]—it is clear that the Holocaust in Slovakia was far more than a German project, even if it was carried out in the context of a 'puppet' state.

A similar conclusion can be reached about Croatia. Indeed, the Ustashe regime of the clerical fascist *poglavnik* (leader), Ante Pavelić, was very similar to Tiso's Slovakia, although the violence it unleashed, primarily against Croatia's two million Serbs, was, if anything, even more extreme. Historians such as Jonathan Steinberg have emphasized the independent line and the brutality of Croat action against Serbs, Jews, and Romanies. But the historical literature remains quite sparse, and recent work on the numbers of dead in Yugoslavia during World War II has been inspired by and in response to the propaganda that fuelled the wars in former Yugoslavia in the 1990s. Hence the focus especially on Bosnia-Herzegovina. The work

---

72. Nižňanský, 'Die Deportation der Juden', p. 38. See also Kamenec, *On the Trail of Tragedy*, pp. 122–3 for similar quotations.
73. Rothkirchen, 'The Situation', p. 52.
74. Bauer, *Jews for Sale?*, pp. 74–75, 79–101, esp. pp. 91–101, which demonstrates that the Working Group's belief that they were responsible for halting the deportations was wrong.
75. Rothkirchen, 'The Situation', p. 62; Ivan Kamenec, 'Die erfolglosen Versuche zur Wiederaufnahme der Deportationen slowakischer Juden', *Theresienstädter Studien und Dokumente*, 9 (2002), pp. 318–37.
76. Rothkirchen, 'The Situation', p. 63.

of the Sarajevo-based Research and Documentation Centre in accounting for those murdered in Bosnia in the 1990s needs to be correlated with accurate figures for the 1940s, if some of the fuel is to be removed from contemporary ethnic strife in Bosnia.[77]

When Pavelić returned from Italian exile to establish his new regime, the Ustashe went 'raging mad', according to Edmund von Glaise Horstenau, the German envoy to Zagreb. The descriptions of the tortures suffered by the victims are rather different from what is conjured up by the notion of 'industrial genocide'. Steinberg gives accounts of bodily mutilation and peasants having to be paid to drag corpses out of rivers to prevent them floating downstream into the Italian zone. The Jasenovac camp, set up and run by the Croat regime, was the centrepiece of this indigenous genocide, which took the lives of between 300,000 and 400,000 Serbs and 45,000 Jews. Only with the Italian occupation of Croat territory did this mayhem cease, much to the annoyance of Italy's allies, the Germans.[78] Then, of course, it was left to the Germans to implement the Final Solution in Serbia according to their own methods, and Serbia became the second country under German occupation after Estonia to be declared '*judenfrei*'.[79]

Saul Friedländer notes: 'In their mixture of Christian beliefs, fascist policies, and savage murderousness, the Croat Ustasha and the Romanian

77. Research and Documentation Center Sarajevo (CD-Rom, 2007); Ewa Tabeau and Jakub Bijak, 'War-Related Deaths in the 1992–1995 Armed Conflicts in Bosnia and Herzegovina: A Critique of Previous Estimates and Recent Results', *European Journal of Population*, 21, 2–3 (2005), pp. 187–215; Tomislav Dulić, *Utopias of Nation: Local Mass Killings in Bosnia and Herzegovina, 1941–42* (Uppsala: Uppsala University Press, 2005); Robert M. Hayden, 'Recounting the Dead: The Rediscovery and Redefinition of Wartime Massacres in Late- and Post-Communist Yugoslavia' in *Memory, Opposition, and History under State Socialism*, ed. Ruby S. Watson (Santa Fe: School of American Research Press, 1994), pp. 167–84; Hayden, 'Mass Killings and Images of Genocide in Bosnia, 1941–5 and 1992–5' in *HG*, pp. 487–516.
78. Jonathan Steinberg, *All or Nothing: The Axis and the Holocaust 1941–43* (London: Routledge, 1990), p. 30; Friedländer, *The Years of Extermination*, pp. 228–30. See also Stevan K. Pavlow-itch, *Hitler's New Disorder: The Second World War in Yugoslavia* (New York: Columbia University Press, 2008); Jonathan E. Gumz, 'Wehrmacht Perceptions of Mass Violence in Croatia, 1941–1942', *The Historical Journal*, 44, 4 (2001), pp. 1015–38; Michael Phayer, *The Catholic Church and the Holocaust, 1930–1965* (Bloomington: Indiana University Press, 2000), ch. 3; Mark Biondich, 'Radical Catholicism and Fascism in Croatia, 1918–1945', *Totalitarian Movements and Political Religions*, 7, 2 (2007), pp. 383–99.
79. Walter Manoschek, 'The Extermination of the Jews of Serbia' in *National Socialist Extermination Policies*, ed. Herbert, pp. 163–85; Christopher R. Browning, *Fateful Months: Essays on the Emergence of the Final Solution*, rev. ed. (New York: Holmes & Meier, 1991); Browning, 'The Wehrmacht in Serbia Revisited' in *Crimes of War: Guilt and Denial in the Twentieth Century*, eds. Omer Bartov, Atina Grossmann and Mary Nolan (New York: New Press, 2002), pp. 31–40; Barry M. Lituchy, ed., *Jasenovac and the Holocaust in Yugoslavia: Analyses and Survivor Testimonies* (New York: Jasenovac Research Institute, 2006).

Iron Guard, or even Antonescu's regime, had much in common; the same extremist ingredients characterized the Ukrainian nationalists, mainly Bandera's faction in the OUN, and the sundry groups of Lithuanian and Latvian "partisans." For all these radical killer groups, local Jews were a prime target.'[80] Ideologically speaking, this is correct, but in many other respects Romania is a *sui generis* case. Although the level of collaboration in the countries discussed above was significant, even in Croatia and Slovakia one sees regimes that were basically acting under the aegis of a German project in order to unleash local hatreds with the help of indigenous nationalists, Nazi sympathizers, and antisemites. In Romania, the scenario was rather different. After the Wehrmacht, the Romanian army was the largest force to invade the Soviet Union, and in Transnistria the Romanians occupied a large slice of Ukraine that included the city of Odessa. Until fairly recently, the Holocaust in Romania had been unfortunately overlooked in the historiography. It is clear that here the 'Jewish problem' would be solved 'in the Romanian way', as Jean Ancel notes.[81] That is to say, although the murder of the Jews took place under the umbrella of the German-led programme, the murder of the Jews of Romania (excluding northern Transylvania, ceded to Hungary in 1940) and Transnistria was essentially an independent undertaking. As with the Croats, the 'unsystematic' and brutal nature of the treatment of the Jews in Romania elicited complaint from the Wehrmacht and the SS, and delighted Hitler.

The murder of the Jews of Romania and Romanian–occupied Ukraine has to be seen in the light of interwar Romanian history. Probably more than any other country in Europe, even Hungary, interwar Romanian politics was dominated by antisemitism. Ultra-nationalism was the norm, fuelled by the huge expansion of the country at the end of World War I, when the Treaty of Trianon granted Transylvania, Bukovina, and Bessarabia to Romania, and a massive programme of nation-building began that combined the typical accoutrements of a modern technocracy with ethnic selection that sought to eliminate Jews, Phanariots (Greeks), Hungarians, and Germans from positions of power and set ethnic Romanians on a course of 'ethnic uplift'.[82] When King Carol abdicated in 1940 after a series

---

80. Friedländer, *The Years of Extermination*, p. 230.
81. Jean Ancel, 'The Romanian Way of Solving the "Jewish Problem" in Bessarabia and Bukovina, June–July 1941', *YVS*, 19 (1988), pp. 187–232.
82. Irina Livezeanu, *Cultural Politics in Greater Romania: Regionalism, Nation Building and Ethnic Struggle, 1918–1930* (Ithaca: Cornell University Press, 1995).

of chaotic administrations, the way was clear for Marshal Antonescu to take over, at first in league with the ultra-radical Iron Guard, and then alone, after he purged and expelled the Iron Guard. Although not a 'Nazi' in the sense of the Guardists, Antonescu was a more stable ally for the Germans—'we will go 100% to the death alongside the Axis'—and his hatred of Jews ran deep.[83] With the onset of war, Antonescu made it clear that Romania would be unleashing its own solution to the Jewish question. He explained the meaning of the war as a zero-sum game that pitted Romanian survival against Jewish, in the same manner as Hitler: 'Should we miss this historical opportunity now, we'll no longer exist. We shall be entirely doomed to destruction. It is my duty to protect this nation with my last energy.'[84]

In Transnistria, extreme brutality was the norm. Historians have now provided a quite full account of the ghettos there and the awful experiences of the Jews forced into them. Ioanid estimates that of the 217,000 Romanian and indigenous Jews who died in Transnistria, no more than 50,000 were killed by the Germans.[85] Dennis Deletant describes the 30 months of the ghettos' and camps' existence in Transnistria as 'calamitous', and Dalia Ofer talks of a 'catastrophe'.[86] Deletant gives a figure of 220,000–260,000 Jews and some 20,000 Romanies killed there.[87] Likewise, the Romanian army's treatment of the Ukrainians was horrific, and many fled to join the OUN or German auxiliary forces in eastern Galicia.[88]

Romania is thus the prime example of an independently executed Holocaust, albeit one undertaken only once Hitler had revealed to Antonescu his plans for the Jews, thus providing him with a 'green light'. If the Conducător's regime proved itself to be shockingly brutal in 1941, Romania's

---

83. Dennis Deletant, *Hitler's Forgotten Ally: Ion Antonescu and His Regime, Romania 1940–1944* (Basingstoke: Palgrave Macmillan, 2006), p. 54.
84. Antonescu, 5 September 1941, cited in Lya Benjamin, 'The Jew's Image in Antonescu's Political Texts' in *The Holocaust and Romania*, eds. Ionescu and Rotman, p. 124. On the Iron Guard, see Leon Volovici, *Nationalist Ideology and Antisemitism: The Case of Romanian Intellectuals in the 1930s* (Oxford: Pergamon Press, 1991); Z. Ornea, *The Romanian Extreme Right: The Nineteen Thirties* (Boulder: East European Monographs, 1999); Rebecca Haynes, 'Work Camps, Commerce, and the Education of the "New Man" in the Romanian Legionary Movement', *The Historical Journal*, 51, 4 (2008), pp. 943–67.
85. Ioanid, *The Holocaust in Romania*, p. 193.
86. Deletant, *Hitler's Forgotten Ally*, p. 186; Dalia Ofer, 'The Holocaust in Transnistria: A Special Case of Genocide' in *The Holocaust in the Soviet Union*, eds. Dobroszycki and Gurock, p. 135.
87. Deletant, *Hitler's Forgotten Ally*, p. 171.
88. Andrej Angrick, 'The Escalation of German–Rumanian Anti-Jewish Policy after the Attack on the Soviet Union', *YVS*, 26 (1998), p. 213. See also Angrick, 'Die Einsatzgruppe D und die Kollaboration' in *Täter im Vernichtungskrieg*, ed. Kaiser, pp. 71–84.

independent line is also in evidence in the abrupt halt of the murders in late 1942. After the vicious outburst of violence in 1941–42, the Romanians, after preparing in mid-1942 for the deportation of the Jews of the *Regat* (the 'old kingdom' of Moldavia and Wallachia) and southern Transylvania to the Nazi death camps in Poland, gradually at first and then rapidly changed their position. Not only did Antonescu's regime resist deporting the Jews after October 1942 (with the exception of 'communist Jews' to Transnistria in 1943–44), but it actively sought to protect them, trying to exempt Romanians in German-held territory from deportation to death camps and assisting Jews in leaving for Palestine. Jews in Romania, as Vladimir Solonari notes, 'were still heavily discriminated against, exposed to various vexations and harsh confiscatory taxation, but the majority of them survived the war'.[89] As a result, apologists have sought to defend Antonescu, overlooking his record prior to mid-1942. The actual scenario is summed up well by Solonari:

> The Jews [of Bessarabia and Bukovina] became the first targets of Antonescu's plan because he knew of the Nazis' plans to subject Jews in the east to 'special treatment', was absolutely convinced—in the summer and fall of 1941—of an easy and quick German victory in the world war, and was aware that the Romanian army was ready and eager to participate in the mass killing of Jews. That other parts of the original plans were never fulfilled was mostly due to the changing fortunes of war and Ion Antonescu's growing skepticism of Germany's chances of coming out on top in the world struggle.[90]

In other words, the abandonment of the plan to deport the Jews of the *Regat* was pure opportunism, based on an accurate assessment of the outcome of the war. The plan was not, as Ancel notes, 'abandoned for humanitarian reasons or any sudden awakening of conscience'. Indeed, the perception of Romania's leaders that the Jews would prove useful bargaining chips in their negotiations with the Allies was itself evidence of 'the antisemitic perception that Jews ruled the world'.[91]

89. Vladimir Solonari, ' "Model Province": Explaining the Holocaust of Bessarabian and Bukovinian Jewry', *Nationalities Papers*, 34, 4 (2006), p. 471. The best way to understand the position of the Jews in Bucharest is through Mihail Sebastian's diary, one of the most extraordinary documents to have emerged from the Holocaust: Sebastian, *Journal 1935–1944: The Fascist Years* (Chicago: Ivan R. Dee, 2000).

90. Solonari, ' "Model Province" ', p. 492. See also Solonari, *Purifying the Nation: Population Exchange and Ethnic Cleansing in Nazi-Allied Romania* (Baltimore: Johns Hopkins University Press, 2009).

91. Jean Ancel, 'The German–Romanian Relationship and the Final Solution', *HGS*, 19, 2 (2005), p. 264.

The Romanian army's real record in Bessarabia, Bukovina, and Transnistria is now clear. Ancel notes: 'Virtually anyone who was armed took part in the slaughter of tens of thousands of Jews in Bessarabia and Bukovina: the Romanian army, the German army, Einsatzgruppe D, the Romanian gendarmerie and police, and even local Romanian and Ukrainian civilians.'[92] The International Commission on the Holocaust in Romania confirmed the findings of historians such as Jean Ancel, Lya Benjamin, Radu Ioanid, and Vladimir Solonari, that Romania under Antonescu was responsible for the murder of over 400,000 Jews.[93] By contrast, in Moldova, the post-Soviet country that comprises most of former Bessarabia, apologetic, nationalist historiography has yet to be subjected to the same sustained critique as in Romania, no doubt a result of that small country's beleaguered situation (the threat of separatism from the tiny self-declared republic of Transdniestria, with its Russian-speaking minority) and the Romanian-speaking elite's nation-building aspirations.[94] In Romania, where there was almost nothing known about the Holocaust before the end of the Ceauşescu regime—or rather, from a point at which 'fascism' was a term directed at the Hungarians—there now exist research centres conducting detailed studies into all aspects of the Holocaust in Romania, from the observations of French diplomats to Jewish emigration from Constanţa.[95] Important documentary collections have been published, and the USHMM (United States

92. Ancel, 'The German–Romanian Relationship', p. 257.
93. Available online at the USHMM website. See also the essays in Randolph L. Braham, ed., *The Destruction of Romanian and Ukrainian Jews During the Antonescu Era* (New York: Columbia University Press, 1997); Ruxandra Cesereanu, 'The Final Report on the Holocaust and the Final Report on the Communist Dictatorship in Romania', *East European Politics and Societies*, 22, 2 (2008), pp. 270–81; Vladimir Tismaneanu, 'Democracy and Memory: Romania Confronts its Communist Past', *Annals of the American Academy of Political and Social Science*, 617 (2008), pp. 166–80.
94. Florin Lobonţ, 'Antisemitism and Holocaust Denial in Post-Communist Eastern Europe' in *HH*, pp. 440–68; Vladimir Solonari, 'From Silence to Justification? Moldovan Historians on the Holocaust of Bessarabian and Transnistrian Jews', *Nationalities Papers*, 30, 3 (2002), pp. 435–57; Diana Dumitru, 'The Use and Abuse of the Holocaust: Historiography and Politics in Moldova', *HGS*, 22, 1 (2008), pp. 49–73; Dmitry Tartakovsky, 'Conflicting Holocaust Narratives in Moldovan Nationalist Historical Discourse', *East European Jewish Affairs*, 38, 2 (2008), pp. 211–29; Dumitru, 'The Attitude of the Non-Jewish Population of Bessarabia and Transnistria to the Jews During the Holocaust: A Survivor's Perspective', *YVS*, 37, 1 (2009), pp. 53–83.
95. See, for example, the essays in Mihail E. Ionescu and Liviu Rotman, eds., *The Holocaust and Romania: History and Contemporary Significance* (Bucharest: Institute for Studies of Defense and Military History, 2003); Randolph L. Braham, ed., *The Tragedy of Romanian Jewry* (New York: Columbia University Press, 1994).

Holocaust Memorial Museum) has a thriving research section on Romania, having obtained over one million relevant documents. Debate continues on whether the Romanian treatment of the Jews indicates the existence of a systematic plan for the Final Solution in mid-1942[96] as well as on many other issues, but most noteworthy of all is the fact that the historiography of the Holocaust in Romania has developed with such rapidity.

By contrast with eastern Europe, in some respects, the Holocaust in western Europe remains surprisingly unintegrated into the general synthetic works. Images of the deportations from western Europe are seared into our contemporary consciousnesses, but the opening of the archives since 1989 has driven the historiography of the 'Final Solution' primarily by analysing the 'wild east'.[97] Recent historical research, apart from adding greater detail to the picture of what transpired, helps us understand how the Holocaust in western Europe belonged to the bigger picture. Where the murder of Jews in the Soviet Union was carried out in face-to-face shootings reminiscent of colonial massacres (see Chapter 5), most Jews in the west were targeted only once the plan to murder all of the Jews of Europe had been conceived. That is not to say that a prior process of radicalization was not important; the reverse in fact is true. First, the conquest of France made continent-wide solutions to the 'Jewish question' more likely. And second, once one considers the question of collaboration, especially in France, it is obvious that the deportations 'to the east' were made easier by virtue of the fact that antisemitic legislation and propaganda was already in full force. The murders in the USSR paved the way for the Holocaust as a continent-wide programme; in the west one sees that programme under way once it had been formulated, which occurred not least because of the conquest of western Europe.

'Holocausts': Western Europe

Although it took North American historians to start the discussion, by the 1990s most people in France were familiar with the fact that the Vichy regime had pre-empted German orders and acted on its own initiative

---

96. Cf. Angrick, 'The Escalation' with Ancel, 'The German–Romanian Relationship'.
97. Ben Shepherd, *War in the Wild East: The German Army and Soviet Partisans* (Cambridge, MA: Harvard University Press, 2004).

in introducing antisemitic legislation in 1940.[98] By the time that the Jews were to be deported from France, two years after this legislation, the measure did not seem so extreme to the French authorities, following as it did the gradual exclusion of the Jews from French life. Henry Rousso may be overstating the case when he argues that an ongoing obsession with the past is incommensurate with its historical significance,[99] but really heated debates in French memory culture are now more likely to concern the Algerian War (1954–62) and the continuities between Vichy and Algeria than 'only' the Holocaust in France.[100] Where once historians shied away from the subject, there is now widespread acceptance that the deportation of Jews—particularly of those refugees who had fled to France in the 1930s, and who did not have French citizenship—was an initiative of the French authorities as much as it was at the behest of the Nazi occupiers.[101] The work of historians and the trials—albeit delayed and obstructed—of Vichy officials such as René Bousquet, Paul Touvier and, especially, of Maurice Papon, have revealed the role played by the French police in rounding up Jews and taking them to internment camps such as Drancy pending their deportation 'to the east'.[102] The bureaucracy of murder, from checking local census files and other documents in

98. Michael R. Marrus and Robert O. Paxton, *Vichy France and the Jews* (New York: Basic Books, 1982). See Bertram M. Gordon, 'The "Vichy Syndrome" Problem in History', *French Historical Studies*, 19, 2 (1995), pp. 495–518; Gordon, 'World War II France Half a Century After' in *Fascism's Return: Scandal, Revision, and Ideology since 1980*, ed. Richard J. Golsan (Lincoln: University of Nebraska Press, 1998), pp. 152–81; Michael R. Marrus, 'Coming to Terms with Vichy', *HGS*, 9, 1 (1995), pp. 23–41; Jacques Adler, 'The Jews and Vichy: Reflections on French Historiography', *The Historical Journal*, 44, 4 (2001), pp. 1065–82; Henry Rousso, *The Haunting Past: History, Memory, and Justice in Contemporary France* (Philadelphia: University of Pennsylvania Press, 2002); and Georges Bensoussan, *Auschwitz en héritage? D'un bon usage de la mémoire* (Paris: Éditions Mille et Une Nuits, 1998) for discussion of the supposed Vichy 'obsession'.

99. Éric Conan and Henry Rousso, *Vichy: An Ever-Present Past* (Hanover: University Press of New England, 1998).

100. For example: Benjamin Stora, *La gangrène et l'oubli: la mémoire de la guerre d'Algérie* (Paris: La Découverte, 1992); Jim House and Neil Macmaster, *Paris 1961: Algerians, State Terror, and Memory* (Oxford: Oxford University Press, 2006). For a useful survey, see William B. Cohen, 'The Algerian War and French Memory', *Contemporary European History*, 9, 3 (2000), pp. 489–500.

101. See Vicki Caron, *Uneasy Asylum: France and the Jewish Refugee Crisis, 1933–1942* (Stanford: Stanford University Press, 1999). See also Adam Rayski, *The Choice of the Jews under Vichy: Between Submission and Resistance* (Bloomington: Indiana University Press, 2005).

102. Donald Bloxham, 'From Streicher to Sawoniuk: the Holocaust in the Courtroom' in *HH*, pp. 407–11; Richard Golsan, ed., *Memory, the Holocaust, and French Justice: The Bousquet and Touvier Affairs* (Hanover: University Press of New England, 1996); Golsan, ed., *The Papon Affair: Memory and Justice on Trial* (New York: Routledge, 2000).

order to locate Jews to the transportation process itself, involved little German input.

Throughout western Europe, the model of a regime that was antisemitic but not actively murderous was more or less followed elsewhere, though only in Norway and France does one see collaborationist regimes that eagerly set about dealing with the Jews. Whilst the various types of regimes in Nazi-occupied western Europe identified and rounded up Jews, they were not killing them themselves. Nor would they have been without the occupation. Nevertheless, when French or Dutch fascists argued for the cleansing of their countries of Jews, it is clear that collaboration in genocide was widespread. In the Netherlands, despite considerable antipathy towards the German occupiers, the Dutch police were important to the deportation of the Jews, 75% of whom (from a total of 140,000) were murdered. This may have been because of a 'conformist authoritarian social stance' among the police rather than any real ideological support for Nazism, but the outcome was the same.[103]

Although the figures are different, both in absolute numbers and in percentage terms, in Belgium and Norway one sees a similar pattern: despite the hatred for the occupiers among much of the population (especially in Norway, where, paradoxically for the Nazis, the population was the epitome of the 'Aryan'), the bureaucrats who identified, rounded up, and sent Jews away to their deaths were largely locals, with a thin layer of German supervision.[104] Besides, the numbers only represent the extent to which the Nazis had achieved their aims given the prevailing circumstances in each country by the end of the war, not the limits to their abilities.[105] Thus, in France, the country with the highest survival rate (some 20% of France's Jews were killed, about 76,000) the likelihood of survival was increased given the size and natural attributes of the country and, crucially,

103. Gerhard Hirschfeld, *Nazi Rule and Dutch Collaboration: The Netherlands under German Occupation, 1940–1945* (Oxford: Berg, 1988), p. 318. See also J. C. H. Blom, 'The Persecution of the Jews in the Netherlands: A Comparative Western European Perspective', *European History Quarterly*, 19, 3 (1989), pp. 333–51; Bob Moore, *Victims and Survivors: The Nazi Persecution of the Jews in the Netherlands, 1940–1945* (London: Arnold, 1997); Ido de Haan, 'Routines and Traditions: The Reactions of Non-Jews and Jews in the Netherlands to War and Persecution' in *Nazi Europe*, eds. Bankier and Gutman, pp. 437–54.

104. David Fraser, *The Fragility of Law: Constitutional Patriotism and the Jews of Belgium, 1940–1945* (London: Routledge, 2009), analyses the role played by the Belgian government and judiciary in the expropriation of Jewish property and the deportation of the Jews.

105. See Michael R. Marrus and Robert O. Paxton, 'The Nazis and the Jews in Occupied Western Europe, 1940–1944', *JMH*, 54, 4 (1982), p. 712.

the thinness of German occupation outside of Paris. Even given the keen assistance of the Vichy regime, at least at certain points, survival rates were far higher than in the Netherlands, where the landscape and density of population offered few hiding places, where the Jews were concentrated in Amsterdam and, significantly, where there was an occupation rather than collaborationist regime in power. Likewise in Norway, the vast majority of the country's 1,800 or so Jews were in Oslo and they were easily identified and rounded up. The exceptions are Italy and Denmark, where large numbers of Jews were saved and where those Jews who were deported had to be caught by the Germans themselves or, in the case of Italy, were victims of the extreme circumstances of northern Italy after 1943. Thus, whilst Marrus and Paxton are no doubt right to say that 'German power, and also the ability of the Nazis to apply their power, were decisive in determining how far the destruction process went by the time of liberation',[106] it is equally clear that the deportations that did take place throughout western Europe required the assistance—with varying degrees of willingness—of the local authorities: 'Without the extensive cooperation of indigenous police forces and other officials, the Germans were therefore incapable of realizing their plans for the murder of west European Jews.'[107]

Much of this history of the Holocaust in western Europe has been well known for several decades. Recent research brings nuance to the picture, by carrying out innovative comparative studies (as opposed to simply listing death rates country by country), and by explaining the relationship between the Holocaust in western and eastern Europe. Wolfgang Seibel has investigated 'polycracy' in western Europe, showing that apparently fragmented administrations could still deport large numbers of Jews if the 'core group of perpetrators', the SS and police, were centralized. But he also remarks that the existence of 'intermediary actors' between the core group and their victims introduces a degree of variability and complexity to the picture. The apparent paradox of polycratic administrations and relatively effective rates of Jewish deportation rests, according to Seibel, on the relative strength of the SS in the power struggles within each jurisdiction.[108] This insight might help to answer Ahlrich Meyer's question about why deportations began in France earlier than elsewhere in western

106. Marrus and Paxton, 'The Nazis and the Jews', p. 714.
107. Marrus and Paxton, 'The Nazis and the Jews', p. 706.
108. Wolfgang Seibel, 'The Strength of Perpetrators—The Holocaust in Western Europe, 1940–1944', *Governance: An International Journal of Policy, Administration, and Institutions*, 15,

Europe (in March 1942) as well as explaining how what began as military 'Sühnemaßnahmen' (retributive measures) became incorporated into the Final Solution following Himmler's visit to Paris in early May 1942.[109] Pim Griffioen and Ron Zeller further nuance this analysis, by showing that, in the cases of France and the Netherlands at least, the 'relative freedom of action of the *Judenreferat* [Jewish desk] of the German Security Police proved more important' than other factors, such as the availability of transport or the size of the transit camps. Whereas in France the SS acquiesced, quite remarkably, in the Vichy regime's decision to interrupt deportations in October 1942 and between March and June 1943, in the Netherlands the deportation of the Jews became more exclusively a German affair over time, until the point at which the attitudes of local administrators could be more or less ignored.[110] In Belgium, as Maxime Steinberg's path-breaking research shows, the role of the SS was indeed crucial in the first wave of deportations, the so-called '100 days' between August and October 1942; but, as Insa Meinen has proven, 'more than half of the Jews deported from Belgium were arrested either as individuals or in small groups, not

---

2 (2002), pp. 211–40. See also Seibel, 'Managing Polycracy: Nazi Bureaucrats as Institutional Entrepreneurs and the German Occupation of Belgium 1940–1944' (forthcoming).

109. Ahlrich Meyer, 'Der Beginn der "Endlösung" in Frankreich: offene Fragen', *Sozial.Geschichte*, 18, 3 (2003), pp. 35–82. See also Meyer, *Täter im Verhör: Die "Endlösung der Judenfrage" in Frankreich 1940–1944* (Darmstadt: Wissenschaftliche Buchgesellschaft, 2005); Wolfgang Seibel, 'A Market for Mass Crime? Inter-Institutional Competition and the Initiation of the Holocaust in France, 1940–1942', *International Journal of Organization Theory and Behavior*, 5, 3&4 (2002), pp. 219–57; Barbara Lambauer, 'Opportunistischer Antisemitismus: Der deutsche Botschafter Otto Abetz und die Judenvernichtung in Frankreich (1940–1942)', *VfZ*, 53, 2 (2005), pp. 241–73; Laurent Joly, *Vichy dans la 'solution finale': Histoire du commissariat général aux Questions juives (1941–1944)* (Paris: Bernard Grasset, 2006), pp. 329–34; Martin Jungius and Wolfgang Seibel, 'The Citizen as Perpetrator: Kurt Blanke and Aryanization in France, 1940–1944', *HGS*, 22, 3 (2008), pp. 441–74; Florent Brayard, 'To What Extent Was the "Final Solution" Planned?', *YVS*, 36, 1 (2008), pp. 73–109, esp. 99, 103.

110. Pim Griffioen and Ron Zeller, 'Anti-Jewish Policy and Organization of the Deportations in France and the Netherlands, 1940–1944: A Comparative Study', *HGS*, 20, 3 (2006), p. 460. See also Pim Griffioen and Ron Zeller, 'A Comparative Analysis of the Persecution of the Jews in the Netherlands and Belgium During the Second World War', *Netherlands' Journal of Social Sciences*, 34, 2 (1998), pp. 126–64; Simon Kitson, 'From Enthusiasm to Disenchantment: The French Police and the Vichy Regime, 1940–1944', *Contemporary European History*, 11, 3 (2002), pp. 371–90; Guus Meershoek, 'The Amsterdam Police and the Persecution of the Jews' in *The Holocaust and History: The Known, the Unknown and the Reexamined*, eds. Michael Berenbaum and Abraham J. Peck (Bloomington: Indiana University Press, 1998), pp. 284–300; Henry L. Mason, 'Accommodations and Other Flawed Reactions: Issues for Verwerking in the Netherlands' in *Lessons and Legacies, Vol. 3: Memory, Memorialization, and Denial*, ed. Peter Hayes (Evanston: Northwestern University Press, 1999), pp. 93–108.

in large-scale operations'. The German authorities, not the Belgian, were primarily responsible for the later arrests and deportations.[111]

Marnix Croes has investigated this question in even greater detail for the Netherlands, showing that survival rates in the different areas of the country display considerable variation, depending on the assiduity with which Jews were hunted down rather than, as one might suppose, the consistent application of the Dutch civil service to its dubious task or the high rate of NSB (*Nationaal-socialistische Beweging*/National Socialist Movement) membership. Indeed, the detail of their survival figures for the various Dutch provinces—in the region of 20% in Groningen, Drenthe, and Noord-Holland as opposed to about 50% in Limburg, Zeeland, and Utrecht—means that he can write: 'Local variations in survival rates suggest that we change the question from "Why did so few Jews survive in the Netherlands?" to "What factors influenced the chances of survival at the individual, municipal, regional, and higher levels?" ' Persecution in Amsterdam, where the Jews were overwhelmingly concentrated, was especially fierce. The same, he suggests, is true of Belgium, where there is a marked difference between the 65% survival rate in Luik, 63% in Brussels, and the 35% in Antwerp.[112] All of this complicates the picture, making it very difficult to look to urban–rural distinctions, class or religious affiliation in accounting for destruction rates. Whilst this invalidates black-and-white assessments, such complexity is of course the stuff of real life, and this recent historical research confirms the fact that motivations are rarely predictable, that behaviour is inconsistent, and that social life does not conform to neat patterns.

This complexity is revealed too in research on France. As we have seen, whilst the fact of collaboration remains a point of consensus among historians, different agencies, including the police, lent varying degrees of support to the deportations. After 1943, Pierre Laval's government increasingly dragged its feet where deportations were concerned. Ulrich Herbert has argued that the radicalization of anti-Jewish policy in France was already under way in 1940 and that decision-making for the 'Final Solution' was driven by local initiatives from the upper echelons of the

111. Maxime Steinberg, *La Persécution des Juifs en Belgique (1940–1945)* (Brussels: Éditions complexe, 2004); Insa Meinen, 'Facing Deportation: How Jews Were Arrested in Belgium', *YVS*, 36, 1 (2008), pp. 39–72.
112. Marnix Croes, 'The Holocaust in the Netherlands and the Rate of Jewish Survival', *HGS*, 20, 3 (2006), p. 486.

Wehrmacht and the SD (*Sicherheitsdienst*/Security Service) as much as by central directives in Berlin.[113] Fritzsche and Longerich both argue that 'the defeat of France opened new possibilities, raising expectations for a comprehensive "final solution" '.[114] The failure to realize the Madagascar Plan also radicalized policy. Whilst it was not a plan for mass murder as such, what Friedländer refers to as 'the Madagascar fiction' was genocidal, in the sense that the Nazis deliberately chose an inhospitable island and, in terms of Nazi ideology, a place where the Jews could not survive as parasites on a superior culture.[115] With Britain still controlling the high seas, the plan was dropped within months, but it contributed considerably to the dynamic that encouraged radical proposals for handling the 'Jewish question', by henceforth requiring comprehensive continent-wide solutions. I will return to this issue in the next chapter.

The experience of the victims too has been investigated in greater detail. Jean-Marc Dreyfus has researched what he calls 'almost-camps' in Paris. These were facilities that cannot be labelled either as concentration camps (they were not controlled by the SS) or as transit camps, but nevertheless were places where French Jews were held and forced to work. The 'almost-camps' of Austerlitz, Lévitan, and Bassano, formerly a warehouse, a furniture store, and fin-de-siècle townhouse respectively, were created to assist with the *Möbelaktion*, the operation that coordinated the looting of all Jewish-owned residences in France, Belgium, and the Netherlands. The shortage of labour in France meant that Jews who were administratively tied to Drancy were brought in as forced labourers. These Jewish labourers were kept in conditions that were superior to those in Drancy, and although some 21% were deported to Auschwitz or Bergen-Belsen in June and July 1944, those who were still in them when they were liberated in August walked home after the liberation. With the revelations in the press of what transpired in the death camps, those who survived in Paris stayed silent, and

---

113. Ulrich Herbert, 'The German Military Command in Paris and the Deportation of the French Jews' in *National Socialist Extermination Policies*, ed. Herbert, pp. 128–62.
114. Fritzsche, *Life and Death*, p. 188; Peter Longerich, *Politik der Vernichtung: Eine Gesamtdarstellung der nationalsozialistischen Judenverfolgung* (Munich: Piper, 1998), p. 274.
115. Friedländer, *The Years of Extermination*, p. 82. On Madagascar, see Magnus Brechtken, *Madagaskar für die Juden: Antisemitische Idee und politische Praxis 1885–1945* (Munich: R. Oldenbourg, 1997); Longerich, *Politik*, pp. 274–92; Longerich, *The Unwritten Order: Hitler's Role in the Final Solution* (Stroud: Tempus, 2001), pp. 55–6; Eric T. Jennings, 'Writing Madagascar Back into the Madagascar Plan', *HGS*, 21, 2 (2007), pp. 187–217.

only recently has the existence and history of these 'almost-camps' been described.[116]

In general, the experience of the Jews has been investigated in extraordinary detail, using a vast range of sources in many languages. Yiddish and eastern European sources have made their entrance on to the English-language historiography in an unprecedented way in the last decade. Whether discussing music in the ghettos and concentration camps, the role of the *Judenräte* (Jewish Councils) in the ghettos, or death marches, the emphasis on recovering the voices and experiences of the victims—at the very least so that historians do not replicate the Nazi description of the Jews as mere *Stücke* (pieces)—has made great headway. Saul Friedländer's achievement in his two-volume synthesis is to provide a multi-vocal narrative in which perpetrators' orders and actions are mingled with Jewish responses, from submission to resistance, and the actions or inactivity of the bystanders, whether countries or institutions, such as the Vatican or the Red Cross. Understanding the nature of the killing process requires focusing on perpetrators and their accomplices. But it is no longer acceptable for general histories of the Holocaust to overlook the fact the victims were real people with emotions and varying responses to persecution.

One of the paradoxes of the Holocaust is that Jews in Axis countries were relatively safer than in Nazi-occupied ones. The Jews of Finland were not deported; Finland's relationship with Nazi Germany has been subjected to detailed scrutiny, however, in recent years and, as with the 'neutral' countries, the picture is by no means black and white.[117] Had Hungary not sought to switch sides in early 1944 it is likely that the occupation of March 1944 would not have occurred and thus that the Jews—and not just those in inner Budapest, where they for the most part survived in a very precarious situation—would have been spared. As we have seen, in Romania, although Antonescu was responsible for the murder of perhaps 400,000 Jews, once the tide of the war turned against the Axis, the Jews

116. Jean-Marc Dreyfus, ' "Almost-Camps" in Paris: The Difficult Description of Three Annexes of Drancy—Austerlitz, Lévitan, and Bassano, July 1943 to August 1944' in *Gray Zones: Ambiguity and Compromise in the Holocaust and its Aftermath*, eds. Jonathan Petropoulos and John K. Roth (New York: Berghahn, 2005), pp. 222–39. For a fuller description see Jean-Marc Dreyfus and Sarah Gensburger, *Des camps dans Paris: Austerlitz, Lévitan, Bassano, juillet 1943–août 1944* (Paris: Fayard, 2003).

117. Antero Holmila, 'Finland and the Holocaust: A Reassessment', *HGS*, 23, 3 (2009), pp. 413–40.

of 'Old Romania' were also saved, albeit in desperate circumstances. The
Bulgarian regime deported the Jews in the territories it occupied, that
is, Macedonia and Thrace, but the Jews of Bulgaria proper, those with
Bulgarian citizenship, were not deported, even if the national mythology
of Bulgaria's 'goodness' has been challenged recently.[118]

But the case that has attracted the most research and speculation is that
of Italy. Jews under Italian protection fared much better than those under
French or Croatian rule, and some of the Jews of Rome and northern Italy
were deported only after the Italians had deposed Mussolini and left the
Axis in 1943, the country was under German occupation, and the north
had descended into the frenzy of the violent Italian Social Republic (RSI),
with its capital in Saló on Lake Garda. It has long been known that more
than 6,000 died in the Holocaust, but that 85% of Italy's Jews survived.[119]
Recent research continues to attempt to account for the Italian resistance
to Jewish persecution, but also offers more detail of what did transpire in
Italy, from the racial laws of 1938 to the deportations of 1943–45. The
number of Jews killed has been adjusted upwards and the percentage of
survivors downwards. Richard Breitman's analysis of British decodes of
SS and SD radio messages between Rome and Berlin confirms the fact
that, without local assistance, it was far harder for the Germans to hunt
down and deport Jews. It also demonstrates the involvement of the very
top in the decision-making process, especially when things got difficult
for the Germans.[120] Maura Hametz shows that celebrating Italy's 'brava
gente' should not prevent us from understanding that Italian fascism could
devastate Jewish lives. Her study of Trieste, the site of the major transit
camp and torture centre, the Risiera di San Sabba, reveals that less than
10% of the Jewish community of about 5,000 there survived the war.
She also shows that, in contrast to the Germans investigated by Breitman,
the centre, that is, Rome, was less important in this instance than the
development of local fascist policies. Again, however, these developments
must be seen in the context of 1943, when Trieste, just outside the RSI,
became the capital of the Third Reich's Adriatic Coastland (*Adriatisches
Küstenland*). Political opponents may have been exterminated at San Sabba,

---

118. Ethan J. Hollander, 'The Final Solution in Bulgaria and Romania: A Comparative Perspec-
     tive', *East European Politics and Societies*, 22, 2 (2008), pp. 203–48.
119. Susan Zuccotti, *The Italians and the Holocaust: Destruction, Rescue and Survival* (Lincoln:
     University of Nebraska Press, 1996).
120. Richard Breitman, 'New Sources on the Holocaust in Italy', *HGS*, 16, 3 (2002), pp. 402–14.

but Jews were deported out of Italy. Unlike in Jasenovac or Transnistria, local fascists in Trieste were not directly involved in the genocide of the Jews.[121]

Liliana Picciotto's important research, which formed the basis of the Italian book of remembrance for the Italian Jews,[122] underscores the point that the Holocaust 'was foreign to the Italian mentality and became possible only when the international situation transformed the Italian–German alliance into a German occupation of Italy, on September 8, 1943'.[123] Her detailed study explains the 30 November 1943 decision on the part of the RSI to instigate its own anti-Jewish policy as an attempt to assert some kind of independence vis-à-vis the Germans. Under this regime, the Italians hunted down the Jews and the Germans then took over the responsibility for deporting them, initially from the jails of Milan, Florence, and Bologna, and later (from 30 January 1944) from the camp at Fossoli di Carpi to Auschwitz, or, in Trieste, from the jail until late March 1944, when the San Sabba rice mill was ready to be used instead. Smaller numbers were deported from other centres.[124] According to Picciotto, whose statistical calculations are the most detailed and careful available, nearly 7,000 Italians Jews were deported, and about 25% of the Italian Jewish population was killed in the years 1943–45, about the same as in France. The murder of the Italian Jews only occurred once the country was occupied by the Germans, but, contrary to the *brava gente* myth, the Italians' involvement was as important to the Germans' efficient perpetration of the genocide as was that of the French or Hungarians. Besides, as MacGregor Knox

121. Maura E. Hametz, 'The Ambivalence of Italian Antisemitism: Fascism, Nationalism, and Racism in Trieste', *HGS*, 16, 3 (2002), pp. 376–401. See also Michael Wedekind, *National- sozialistische Besatzungs- und Annexionspolitik in Norditalien 1943 bis 1945: Die Operationszonen 'Alpenvorland' und 'Adriatisches Küstenland'* (Munich: R. Oldenbourg, 2003).
122. Liliana Picciotto, *Il libro della memoria. Gli ebrei deportati dall'Italia 1943–1945* (Milan: Mursia, 1992 and 2002).
123. Liliana Picciotto, 'Statistical Tables on the Holocaust in Italy with an Insight on the Mechanism of the Deportations', *YVS*, 33 (2005), p. 314. See also Picciotto, 'The Shoah in Italy: Its History and Characteristics' in *Jews in Italy under Fascist and Nazi Rule 1922–1945*, ed. Joshua D. Zimmermann (Cambridge: Cambridge University Press, 2005), pp. 209–23, and Michele Sarfatti, *The Jews in Mussolini's Italy: From Equality to Persecution* (Madison: University of Wisconsin Press, 2006).
124. Picciotto, 'Statistical Tables', pp. 320, 324. See also Picciotto, 'The Italians and the Jews During the Fascist and German Persecutions' in *Nazi Europe*, eds. Bankier and Gutman, pp. 491–518; Davide Rodogno, '*Italiani brava gente?* Fascist Italy's Policy Toward the Jews in the Balkans, April 1941–July 1943', *European History Quarterly*, 35, 2 (2005), pp. 213–40; Guri Schwarz, 'On Myth Making and Nation Building: The Genesis of the "Myth of the Good Italian", 1943–1947', *YVS*, 36, 1 (2008), pp. 111–43.

points out, Italian actions (or non-actions) before the German occupation owed more to the Italian desire to establish their sovereignty rights than to feelings of tenderness towards Jews.[125]

Naturally, one suspects that a victorious Third Reich would sooner or later have successfully pressed for the deportation of Jews in all of these places, as it did the Jews of Rhodes or Salonica, and as it tried (but failed) to do in Albania.[126] But the limits of Nazi rule are apparent here: the Jews could be used as pawns in great power rivalries, bargaining chips in postwar negotiations. The 'Final Solution' was not so pressing a 'project' for Germany's allies as for the Germans. Hence the legend that Antonescu was a 'rescuer' of Jews: a claim that is partly true but that totally ignores his earlier role, which fully justified his being hanged as a war criminal.[127]

Why Collaboration?

Nazism was more than extreme nationalism. It advocated empire based on racial affinity and 'European union' based on economic exploitation for the benefit of the dominant race. Hence apart from the large armed forces provided by Germany's allies, especially Hungary, Romania, and Italy, whose role has been greatly underrated (combined they provided more than 1.5 million men to the German war effort), there were SS units from across Europe, albeit of limited size, numerous auxiliary police forces across the Nazi empire, and many Europeans who saw the best guarantee of their own nation's future prosperity lying in cooperation with Nazi Germany.[128] This cooperation was assisted by the local variations of

125. MacGregor Knox, 'Die faschistische Italien und die "Endlösung" ', *VfZ*, 55, 1 (2007), pp. 53–92.
126. On Greece, see Mark Mazower, *Inside Hitler's Greece: The Experience of Occupation, 1941–44* (New Haven: Yale University Press, 1993), ch. 19; on Albania, Bernd J. Fischer, *Albania at War, 1939–1945* (London: C. Hurst, 1999); Miranda Vickers, *The Albanians: A Modern History* (London: I. B. Tauris, 1995), ch. 7.
127. Mark Temple, 'The Politicization of History: Marshal Antonescu and Romania', *East European Politics and Societies*, 10, 3 (1996), pp. 457–503; Michael Shafir, 'Marshal Antonescu's Postcommunist Rehabilitation: *Cui bono?*' in *The Destruction of Romanian and Ukrainian Jews During the Antonescu Era*, ed. Randolph L. Braham (Boulder: Social Science Monographs, 1997), pp. 349–410; Henry F. Carey, 'Genocide Denial and Antonescu as Democratic Role Model: 1984 in the Twenty-First Century', *Romanian Journal of Society and Politics*, 1, 1 (2001), pp. 33–69; Mihai Chioveanu, 'A Deadlock of Memory: The Myth and Cult of Ion Antonescu in Post-communist Romania', *Studia Hebraica*, 3 (2003), pp. 102–23.
128. Naturally, such collaboration was at the Germans' bidding; see Jan Gross, 'Themes for a Social History of War Experience and Collaboration' in *The Politics of Retribution in*

the anti-Bolshevik message, which in France went hand in hand with the overturning of the secular tradition of the Third Republic—the Vichy regime was essentially the victory of the anti-Dreyfusards—and in Ukraine, the Baltic States or the Caucasus the promise of independence from the USSR. Some 800,000 Russians served the Germans, either militarily or in administrative capacities, including significant military units under the command of General Andrei Vlassov.[129]

However, there were more mundane reasons too. Research into the actions of those who joined *Schutzmannschaften* reveals that 'personal greed, careerism, anti-communism, peer pressure and even alcoholism' were contributing factors.[130] Under 'the corrupting environment engendered by the German occupation' in Ukraine, 'nationalist aspirations' and 'individual social and economic aggrandizement' often proved a fatal combination.[131] Dreyfus notes that, although 75% of the French Jews survived the war, 'all of the Jews were despoiled of their property: furniture and objects transiting through the camps in Paris were not automatically the ones of dead Jews.'[132] Especially in eastern Europe, Jews were often central to the local economy, with long-standing positions as tax collectors, innkeepers, or tradesmen. This classic middleman position meant that they were easy targets for locals who coveted their property or held personal grudges.[133] Not that most of the Jews were wealthy, but in this poor region of Europe, the promise of clothes, goods, and property being 'redistributed'—in a way that ensured the complicity of a wide cross-section of society—was a real spur to participation.[134]

Europe: World War II and its Aftermath, eds. István Deák, Gross and Tony Judt (Princeton: Princeton University Press, 2000), p. 25.

129. Rolf-Dieter Müller, *An der Seite der Wehrmacht: Hitlers ausländische Helfer beim 'Kreuzzug gegen den Bolschewismus', 1941–1945* (Berlin: Christoph Links, 2007). See also Per Anders Rudling, 'Historical Representation of the Wartime Accounts of the Activities of the OUN-UPA (Organization of Ukrainian Nationalists-Ukrainian Insurgent Army)', *East European Jewish Affairs*, 36, 2 (2006), pp. 163–89. From a military perspective, see Richard L. DiNardo, *Germany and the Axis Powers: From Coalition to Collapse* (Lawrence: University Press of Kansas, 2005).

130. Dean, 'Local Collaboration', p. 128.

131. Finder and Prusin, 'Collaboration in Eastern Galicia', p. 96.

132. Dreyfus, ' "Almost-Camps" ', p. 232.

133. See Yuri Slezkine, *The Jewish Century* (Princeton: Princeton University Press, 2004), on the Jews' historical position as middlemen.

134. Martin Dean, 'Jewish Property Seized in the Occupied Soviet Union in 1941 and 1942: The Records of the *Reichshauptkasse Beutestelle*', *HGS*, 14, 1 (2000), pp. 83–101; Yitzhak Arad, 'Plunder of Jewish Property in the Nazi-Occupied Areas of the Soviet Union', *YVS*, 29 (2001), pp. 109–48; Alex J. Kay, *Exploitation, Resettlement, Mass Murder: Political*

Nowhere was the distinction between the 'masses' and the Jews more pronounced than in Romania. Instead of seeing Jews as contributors to Romanian economic growth and socio-cultural development, in the age of post-imperial ethno-nationalism, Jews were instead targeted as aliens who were preventing Romanians from fulfilling their potential. Antisemitism in Romania went hand in hand with modernization. Antonescu knew perfectly well the importance of the Jews for the Romanian economy—'If we remove the Jews, this enormous void is created in the Romanian economy, which will produce a general, irreparable catastrophe for our state and its recovery will be impossible'—but that was insufficient to prevent their persecution.[135] In the circumstances of the war, then, the image of the Jews as parasites was easily radicalized; Antonescu described 'the parasite Jew' as an exploiter who had 'sucked, impoverished, speculated, and stopped the development of the people for several centuries'.[136] The element of *Rausch* ('rush' or ecstasy) that particularly characterizes the Holocaust in Romania can partly be explained by this 'competition-lust' and partly, as we have seen, by the legend of Judeo-Bolshevism.

Finally, there is the very simple fact that in 1942 the future seemed to be with Nazism. Fritzsche reminds us that 'until 1943 the German-dominated new order appeared to be permanent and German power invincible; antisemitism and fascist sympathies were contributing but secondary factors.'[137] Naturally, this claim needs more nuance: in Slovakia and Croatia, local authorities more than assisted the German hegemon in getting rid of the Jews, primarily because of Jew-hatred. By contrast, as the recent literature shows, in other cases—even in France, which is lumbered with the collaborationist label—local authorities at national and local levels lent greater or lesser support at different times, depending on the local and international, that is, war-related circumstances. Historians still need to respond to Kitson's challenge: 'Many Vichy police officers did ultimately make use of those zones of autonomy open to them, in spite of their government. The Resistance recognized this; why can't historians?'[138] But even taking that

and Economic Planning for German Occupation Policy in the Soviet Union, 1940–1941 (New York: Berghahn, 2006); *Confiscation of Jewish Property in Europe, 1933–1945: New Sources and Perspectives* (Washington, DC: Center for Advanced Holocaust Studies, United States Holocaust Memorial Museum, 2003).

135. Deletant, *Hitler's Forgotten Ally*, p. 107.
136. Antonescu cited in Benjamin, 'The Jew's Image', p. 124.
137. Fritzsche, *Life and Death*, p. 222.
138. Kitson, 'From Enthusiasm to Disenchantment', p. 390.

point into account, it is clear that enough people—from state officials to peasants—across Europe believed that they would benefit from the murder of the Jews at the very least to remain indifferent and at worst actively to assist or to take part in the murders.

In order to understand these phenomena it is necessary not to separate the Holocaust from World War II. The genocide of the Jews was part of a demographic project to reshape Europe along racial lines. It was the most pressing part, but only a part, of a long-term plan that would see mass murder committed against Slavic nations on a massive scale, reducing them to a helot population, and German colonists settle the Nazi empire east of the *Altreich*. Hence the idea of *Lebensraum* was inseparable from genocide, and the idea of 'Judeo-Bolshevism' explains not only why the invasion of the USSR was not a regular war but a racial crusade, and why this notion held wide appeal, especially to nations that had experienced Soviet occupation or feared Soviet expansionism.

'Aryanization'

Among the most interesting recent insights into the persecution of the Jews is the claim that the acquisition of Jewish property acted as a major spur. Historians have for many years investigated the economic aspects of German antisemitic persecution before 1939, with major studies by Helmut Genschel and Avraham Barkai.[139] Until very recently, though, the consensus has been that although certain individuals and businesses benefited from the expropriation of the Jews—'Aryanization', as the Nazis called it—this was not the main cause of the Holocaust. Economic benefits were considered a fortunate (for the perpetrators) by-product of the persecution, not its driving force. Although this view has not been overturned, a great deal of new information has been brought to light, allowing us to finesse the argument. The end of the Cold War was again significant in that new archival sources became accessible, but also, perhaps more important, the Europe-wide scale of the Holocaust has been increasingly acknowledged by historians, firms, and businesses, and official governmental inquiries from France to Latvia, which corroborate the findings discussed

139. Helmut Genschel, *Die Verdrängung der Juden aus der Wirtschaft im Dritten Reich* (Göttingen: Musterschmidt, 1966); Avraham Barkai, *From Boycott to Annihilation: The Economic Struggle of German Jews 1933–1945* (Hanover: University Press of New England, 1989).

above about extensive collaboration.[140] Two important conclusions, in particular, are worth noting. First, collaboration and bounty-hunting were far more widespread than historians had previously assumed. And second, although few historians would go so far as Götz Aly in arguing that economic considerations drove the persecution of the Jews, many would now agree that financial and material gain was, for many Germans and their collaborators, more than a side-effect of the Holocaust that kept the population complicit, particularly in eastern Europe.[141] When one considers the size of the looted goods from Auschwitz alone, one gets a sense of the scale of the plunder operation that the Nazis carried out.[142]

It is clear that this 'redistribution'—through the *Winterhilfswerk*, for example, or 'Jew markets' in Hamburg—ensured complicity.[143] But the

140. For a guide to these commissions, see the appendix in Avi Beker, 'Introduction: Unmasking National Myths—Europeans Challenge Their History' in *The Plunder of Jewish Property during the Holocaust*, ed. Beker (New York: New York University Press, 2001), pp. 22–9.

141. Götz Aly, *Hitlers Volksstaat*; cf. Aly, ed., *Volkes Stimme: Skepsis und Führervertrauen im Nationalsozialismus* (Frankfurt/M: Suhrkamp Taschenbuch Verlag, 2006), which offers a more nuanced account, indeed one that in places contradicts Aly's analysis in *Hitlers Volksstaat*. On *Hitlers Volksstaat*, see Adam Tooze, 'Economics, Ideology and Cohesion in the Third Reich: A Critique of Goetz Aly's *Hitlers Volksstaat*', *Dapim*, 20 (2006) and Frank Bajohr, 'Robbery, Ideology, and *Realpolitik*: Some Critical Remarks', YVS, 35, 1 (2007), pp. 179–91. However, note Aly's own response to his critics in the English edition, *Hitler's Beneficiaries: Plunder, Racial War, and the Nazi Welfare State* (New York: Metropolitan Books, 2006), pp. 327–32, as well as his very clear statement at the outset that 'it would be wrong to conclude that primary responsibility for the Holocaust or other Nazi crimes lay with the elite of the German bourgeoisie' (p. 1). In other words, Aly does not deny the significance of antisemitic ideology for the Third Reich's leaders (though the implication of his argument leads in that direction), but is arguing that the economic benefits of war and genocide kept the German population behind the regime until the end. For a critical analysis of the 'voluntaristic turn' see Geoff Eley, 'Hitler's Silent Majority? Conformity and Resistance under the Third Reich', *Michigan Quarterly Review*, 42, 2 (2003), pp. 550–83 (part 1) and 42, 3 (2003), pp. 389–425 (part 2); Neil Gregor, 'Nazism—A Political Religion? Rethinking the Voluntarist Turn' in *Nazism, War and Genocide: Essays in Honour of Jeremy Noakes* (Exeter: Exeter University Press, 2005), pp. 1–21; Richard Evans, 'Coercion and Consent in Nazi Germany', *Proceedings of the British Academy*, 151 (2007), pp. 53–81.

142. For the statistics see Andrzej Strzelecki, 'The Plunder of Victims and Their Corpses' in *Anatomy of the Auschwitz Death Camp*, eds. Gutman and Berenbaum, pp. 246–66.

143. Thomas E. de Witt, ' "The Struggle Against Hunger and Cold": Winter Relief in Germany, 1933–1939', *Canadian Journal of History*, 12, 3 (1978), pp. 361–81; Jean-Marc Dreyfus, 'The Looting of Jewish Property in Occupied Western Europe: A Comparative Study of Belgium, France, and the Netherlands' and Tatjana Tönsmeyer, 'The Robbery of Jewish Property in Eastern European States Allied with Nazi Germany', both in *Robbery and Restitution: The Conflict over Jewish Property in Europe*, eds. Martin Dean, Constantin Goschler, and Philipp Ther (New York: Berghahn, 2007), pp. 53–80 and 81–96; Irmtrud Wojak and Peter Hayes, eds., *'Arisierung' im Nationalsozialismus: Volksgemeinschaft, Raub und Gedächtnis* (Frankfurt/M: Campus, 2000); Frank Bajohr, *'Aryanization' in Hamburg: The Economic Exclusion of Jews and the Confiscation of Their Property in Nazi Germany* (New York: Berghahn, 2002).

economic aspects of the Holocaust also tell us a great deal about the nature of the Third Reich and its European empire. Scholars no longer see the structure of the Third Reich either in terms of omnipotent and terroristic dictatorship or as polycratic chaos. Competition between different institutions, for example, state bureaucracies and party agencies, tended to be competition towards the same goals. Ian Kershaw encapsulates this state of affairs most clearly in his phrase 'working towards the Führer', which suggests that the radicalization built into the system was a result of social Darwinistic competition, but within a constrained framework of obeisance to Hitler.[144] The Third Reich was a 'polycratic morass', but within parameters.[145] With respect to 'Aryanization', we see proof of Kershaw's model. Recent research has brought us back to the postwar notion of the Third Reich as a gangster regime, or to Hannah Arendt's claim that Nazism came 'from the gutter', though this time on the basis of solid empirical research. Just as Fritzsche has shown that the appeal of Nazism largely lay in its promise of an entrée into politics for those who were otherwise excluded by the comfortable club of the parliamentarians, so these arrivistes with no sense of commitment to the political process or the traditions of the neutral civil service, looted and stole as much as they could.[146] Frank Bajohr, Gerard Aalders, and Jonathan Petropoulos, among others, have argued that the Third Reich was a 'kleptocracy' run by bandits. Aalders documents the extraordinary extent to which the Dutch economy was fleeced by the Nazis—the equivalent of 14 billion guilders in today's money in Jewish-owned assets alone—and Petropoulos argues that 'the Nazis were not only the most notorious murderers in history but also the greatest thieves'.[147] Again, we see chaos and competition, but all

144. Ian Kershaw, ' "Working Towards the Führer": Reflections on the Nature of the Hitler Dictatorship' in his *Hitler, the Germans and the Final Solution* (New Haven: Yale University Press, 2008), ch. 1.
145. Michael Thad Allen, 'Introduction: A Bureaucratic Holocaust—Toward a New Consensus' in *Networks*, eds. Feldman and Seibel, p. 263.
146. Hannah Arendt, 'Fernsehgespräch mit Thilo Koch' in *Ich will verstehen: Selbstauskünfte zu Leben und Werk*, ed. Ursula Ludz (Munich: Piper, 1996), p. 36; Fritzsche, *Germans into Nazis*. For a discussion, see Peter Hayes, 'Polycracy and Policy in the Third Reich: The Case of the Economy' in *Reevaluating the Third Reich*, eds. Thomas Childers and Jane Caplan (New York: Holmes and Meier, 1993), pp. 190–210.
147. Jonathan Petropoulos, 'The Nazi Kleptocracy: Reflections on Avarice and the Holocaust'; Frank Bajohr, 'Cliques, Corruption, and Organized Self-Pity: The Nazi Movement and the Property of the Jews'; Gerard Aalders, ' "Lawful" Abuse of the Dutch Economy, 1940–1945', all in *Lessons and Legacies, Vol. 7: The Holocaust in International Perspective*, ed. Dagmar Herzog (Evanston: Northwestern University Press, 2006), pp. 29–38, 39–49, and

within the parameters set by the new regime. Whether in Germany or in occupied Europe, looting on a personal level, though officially forbidden, would be tolerated where it was carried out unobtrusively, and looting on a state-endorsed level was especially welcomed when it went hand in hand with the aim of hunting down the Jews. Individuals from Goering to lowly *Landser*, and Nazi units such as the *Einsatzstab Reichsleiter Rosenberg* (ERR, which stole artworks as well as basic items of clothing) show that corruption, plunder, and systematic persecution were entirely compatible, despite the bravado of Himmler's famous Posen speech where he condemned stealing among the SS. Indeed, Bajohr convincingly claims that the extent of corruption means that, contrary to those who emphasize dispassionate 'modernity' or bureaucracy in the murder process, the Holocaust 'cannot be reduced to the image of a state crime, organized coolly and objectively and implemented with bureaucratic precision'; rather, personal enrichment 'provided a motivational basis for many of those involved which should not be underestimated. "Base motives" such as greed also contributed to the Holocaust.'[148] These claims are borne out by the most thorough analysis of robbery of Jewish property yet published, Martin Dean's *Robbing the Jews*.[149]

Finally, this renewed emphasis on property and restitution reflects the place that the Holocaust has come to have in post-Cold War Europe, particularly since the Stockholm Forum of 2000, which officially enshrined the Holocaust into European memory, making it as central to European identity as it already was in Israel and the US. Particularly in eastern Europe, where discussions of private property were well-nigh impossible under the communist regimes, there has been a great deal of archive- and soul-searching since 1989. For Dan Diner, this is a natural process: there is an 'obvious, indeed organic interconnection between restituted private property rights and the evocation of past memories, or vice versa:

50–65 (Petropoulos quotation p. 34). See also Frank Bajohr, 'Expropriation and Expulsion' in *HH*, pp. 52–64; Bajohr, *Parvenüs und Profiteure: Korruption in der NS-Zeit* (Frankfurt/M: Fischer, 2001); Aalders, *Nazi Looting: The Plunder of Dutch Jewry during the Second World War* (Oxford: Berg, 2004).

148. Bajohr, 'Cliques, Corruption, and Organized Self-Pity', p. 47; Bajohr, 'The Holocaust and Corruption' in *Networks*, eds. Feldman and Seibel, p. 133, and the chapters in that volume by Dean and Petropoulos; Bajohr, 'The "Folk Community" and the Persecution of the Jews: German Society under National Socialist Dictatorship, 1933–1945', *HGS*, 20, 2 (2006), p. 193.

149. Martin Dean, *Robbing the Jews: The Confiscation of Jewish Property in the Holocaust, 1933–1945* (Cambridge: Cambridge University Press, 2008). See ch. 3.

Restitution of property as the result of recovered memory.'[150] By contrast, Lothar Probst takes the view that this process has been encouraged by political elites as much as by grassroots, 'organic' memories resurfacing after being placed in the communist freezer, and calls into question the value of the Holocaust as a 'founding myth' of Europe.[151] Yet both note the connection between Holocaust memory and the renewed emphasis on the question of Jewish property. The already large historiographies of business and industry in Nazi Germany, as well as that of the theft and restitution of Jewish property, will continue to be an area of intense scrutiny for the foreseeable future.[152]

As it already stands, the interest in business history is in itself quite a remarkable development in the historiography. From the 1930s onwards, and especially during the 1960s and 1970s, it was common on the left to assume that big business bankrolled Hitler, and that Nazism was a creation of capitalism in crisis. The link was pushed about as far as it could go by the East German regime, in communist historiography and, more memorably, in films such as *Der Rat der Götter* (The Council of the Gods, 1953) explicitly connecting big business with the gas chambers. However, in the same way that historians increasingly recognized that the working class—especially the unorganized elements of it—were not immune to Nazism's promises,[153] so they also came to acknowledge the weight of evidence that most industrialists did not give substantial financial backing to the Nazis and that the NSDAP (*Nationalsozialistische Deutsche Arbeiterpartei*/National Socialist German Workers' Party) was not the creature of 'capital'. Studies of big business were tarnished with the brush of vulgar Marxism and for several decades few historians paid much

---

150. Dan Diner, 'Restitution and Memory: The Holocaust in European Political Cultures', *New German Critique*, 90 (2003), p. 39. See also Diner, 'Memory and Restitution: World War II as a Foundational Event in a Uniting Europe' in *Restitution and Memory: Material Restoration in Europe*, eds. Diner and Gotthart Wunberg (New York: Berghahn, 2007), p. 13.

151. Lothar Probst, 'Founding Myths in Europe and the Role of the Holocaust', *New German Critique*, 90 (2003), pp. 45–58.

152. As well as books already mentioned, see Jürgen Lillteicher, *Raub, Recht und Restitution: Die Rückerstattung jüdischen Eigentums in der frühen Bundesrepublik* (Göttingen: Wallstein, 2007); Michael R. Marrus, *Some Measure of Justice: The Holocaust Era Restitution Campaign of the 1990s* (Madison: University of Wisconsin Press, 2009).

153. Tim Mason, *Sozialpolitik im Dritten Reich: Arbeiterklasse und Volksgemeinschaft* (Opladen: Westdeutscher Verlag, 1977); Mason, *Nazism, Fascism and the Working Class*, ed. Jane Caplan (Cambridge: Cambridge University Press, 1995); Henry Ashby Turner, Jr., *German Big Business and the Rise of Hitler* (Oxford: Oxford University Press, 1985).

interest to the question of Nazism and big business, even though the economic history of the Third Reich flourished.[154]

I will return to the question of economics and the Holocaust in Chapter 3, but in the context of this chapter, it is striking that the return to fashion of business history, though no longer encumbered with Cold War blinkers, tends to confirm many of the claims of those who several decades ago asserted that big business had quite a cosy relationship with the Third Reich, even if the latter was not the servant of the former. Since the end of the Cold War, the reopening of questions of collaboration has also extended to big business, the banking and clearing systems, insurance and international trade. The revelations in the 1990s about dormant Swiss bank accounts, stolen gold, and looted artworks, coupled with public debates about compensation for forced labourers, the establishment of national committees of inquiry across the world from Europe to Latin America, the opening up of major companies' archives to historians, and historical research into 'Jew markets' or the elite ERR, all added up to an explosion of interest in the sensitive topic of the financial implications of the persecution of the Jews.[155]

Since the 1970s, most western historians have rejected the argument that Hitler was a puppet of capitalists. But since the end of the Cold War, historians have reappraised the connections between business and Nazism. Few would subscribe to the 1960s' notion of 'fascism' which saw it as nothing more than 'crisis capitalism with a cudgel',[156] but many, on the basis of detailed empirical work in company archives, now believe that from the *Gleichschaltung* ('co-ordination' with the regime's requirements) of industry to the workings of the insurance and clearing systems, to the employment of forced labourers, many German (and international) firms were involved in the Holocaust to a far greater extent than postwar West German memory, which celebrated instead the *Wirtschaftswunder*

154. Notably R. J. Overy, *War and Economy in the Third Reich*, 2nd edn (Oxford: Clarendon Press, 1995).
155. Beker, ed., *The Plunder of Jewish Property*; *Confiscation of Jewish Property in Europe, 1933–1945: New Sources and Perspectives. Symposium Proceedings* (Washington, DC: United States Holocaust Memorial Museum, 2003); Helen Junz, 'Holocaust-Era Assets: Globalization of the Issue' in *Lessons and Legacies*, Vol. 6, ed. Diefendorf, pp. 431–46; Michael J. Bazyler, 'The Gray Zones of Holocaust Restitution: American Justice and Holocaust Morality' in *Gray Zones*, eds. Petropoulos and Roth, pp. 339–59.
156. Charles Maier, 'The Economics of Fascism and Nazism' in his *In Search of Stability: Explorations in Historical Political Economy* (Cambridge: Cambridge University Press, 1987), p. 71.

(economic miracle), admitted.[157] Studies of major German firms are detailed and thorough, and add up to a whole new sub-discipline of Holocaust historiography, daunting to non-specialists but important in presenting a nuanced picture of the intricate and sometimes troubled relationship between industry and Nazism.[158] Big business, whilst by no means the puppet master of communist mythology, was nevertheless deeply complicit with Nazi crimes and at least until the middle of the war was for the most part willing to go along with the demands made by the Nazi regime, since it benefited financially from doing so. Christopher Kobrak and Andrea H. Schneider sum up the complex nature of the historiography:

> for some companies profiting from the misery of human beings, at least at some points during the Nazi regime, was a matter of business as usual; other

157. S. Jonathan Wiesen, 'Public Relations as a Site of Memory: The Case of West German Industry and National Socialism' in *The Work of Memory: New Directions in the Study of German Society and Culture*, eds. Alon Confino and Peter Fritzsche (Urbana: University of Illinois Press, 2002), pp. 196–213; Volker R. Berghahn, 'Writing the History of Business in the Third Reich: Past Achievements and Future Directions' in *Business and Industry in Nazi Germany*, eds. Francis R. Nicosia and Jonathan Huener (New York: Berghahn, 2004), pp. 129–48.

158. To name only a few of the most representative publications: Peter Hayes, *Industry and Ideology: IG Farben in the Nazi Era* (Cambridge: Cambridge University Press, 1987); Hayes, *From Cooperation to Complicity: Degussa in the Third Reich* (Cambridge: Cambridge University Press, 2004); Harold James and Jakob Tanner, eds., *Enterprise in the Period of Fascism in Europe* (Aldershot: Ashgate, 2002); Harold James, *The Deutsche Bank* (London: Weidenfeld & Nicolson, 1995); James, *The Deutsche Bank and the Nazi Economic War Against the Jews* (Cambridge: Cambridge University Press, 2001); James, *The Nazi Dictatorship and the Deutsche Bank* (Cambridge: Cambridge University Press, 2004); Lothar Gall and Manfred Pohl, eds., *Unternehmen im Nationalsozialismus* (Munich: Beck, 1998); Lothar Gall et al., *Die Deutsche Bank, 1870–1995* (Munich: Beck, 1995); Jonathan Steinberg, *Die Deutsche Bank und ihre Goldtransaktionen während des Zweiten Weltkrieges* (Munich: Beck, 1999); Neil Gregor, *Daimler Benz in the Third Reich* (New Haven: Yale University Press, 1998); Hans Mommsen with Manfred Grieger, *Das Volkswagenwerk und seine Arbeiter im Dritten Reich* (Düsseldorf, ECON, 1996); Johannes Bähr, *Der Goldhandel der Dresdner Bank im Zweiten Weltkrieg* (Leipzig: Kiepenheuer, 1999); Christopher Kobrak, *National Cultures and International Competition: The Experience of Schering AG, 1851–1950* (Cambridge: Cambridge University Press, 2002); Gerald D. Feldman, *Allianz and the German Insurance Business, 1933–1945* (Cambridge: Cambridge University Press, 2001); Wilfried Feldenkirchen, *Siemens: Von der Werkstatt zum Weltunternehmen*, 2nd edn (Munich: Piper, 2003); Lothar Gall, ed., *Krupp im 20. Jahrhundert* (Berlin: Siedler, 2002); Saul Friedländer et al., *Bertelsmann im Dritten Reich*, 2 vols. (Munich: C. Bertelsmann, 2002); Stephan H. Lindner, *Inside IG Farben: Hoechst During the Third Reich* (Cambridge: Cambridge University Press, 2008); Simon Reich, 'Corporate Social Responsibility and the Issue of Compensation: The Case of Ford and Nazi Germany' in *Business and Industry*, eds. Nicosia and Huener, pp. 104–28; Reinhold Billstein et al., *Working for the Enemy: Ford, General Motors, and Forced Labor in Germany During the Second World War* (New York: Berghahn, 2000); Christoph Buchheim, ed., *German Industry in the Nazi Period* (Stuttgart: Franz Steiner, 2008). Christopher Kobrak and Andrea H. Schneider, 'Big Business and the Third Reich: An Appraisal of the Historical Arguments' in *HH*, pp. 141–72 offers a thorough survey.

firms preferred to keep their distance from what should have appeared to be an immoral activity that could only damage the firm's long-term international reputation. The studies also suggest that, even within firms, behaviour was not uniform. Progress in this area is blocked not so much by lack of evidence, but by the complexity of economic evaluation and questions about the role of intention, as opposed to result, and pain and suffering, as opposed to profit.

They end, however, with a clear statement: 'Although there are some isolated examples of company managers who strenuously resisted these trappings of power which helped the regime establish its position, col- lectively, business was eager to profit from Nazi economic salvation.'[159] In other words, the goals of the regime, as Gerald Feldman notes, 'were not determined by financial institutions or big business'. Nevertheless, the ultimate priority of politics over economics meant that 'what began as appeasement from the side of financial institutions inevitably ended up as collaboration and taking of profits such as they were, for as long as they lasted, and from wherever they came.'[160]

Finally, we should note that asking questions about collaboration only makes sense when one also asks about assistance and rescue. The history of the Holocaust on the ground is a mirror of complex social realities, and no single nation is composed only of evil or righteous individuals. Martin Dean notes that 'it would be a distortion to focus only on collaboration in the Holocaust, without also mentioning those who risked their lives to help Jews.'[161] Although his own research has focused primarily on collaborators, his point is correct. In France, for example, although 76,000 Jews lost their lives—mostly those without French citizenship—more than 250,000 survived, the highest survival rate of any Nazi-occupied country.[162] In Slovakia, after the Slovak National Uprising, some 10,000 Jews were rescued from deportation, often with the assistance of ordinary people.[163] In Ukraine and Belarus, as well as willing collaborators, there were those

---

159. Kobrak and Schneider, 'Big Business', pp. 161, 164.
160. Gerald D. Feldman, 'Financial Institutions in Nazi Germany: Reluctant or Willing Collab- orators?' in *Business and Industry*, eds. Nicosia and Huener, p. 39.
161. Dean, 'Local Collaboration', p. 130; cf. Melamed, 'Organized and Unsolicited Collabora- tion', p. 219.
162. Jeannine (Levana) Frank, *Righteous Among the Nations in France and Belgium: A Silent Resistance* (Jerusalem: Yad Vashem, 2008).
163. Ivan Kamenec, 'Changes in the Attitude of the Slovak Population to the So-Called "Solution to the Jewish Question" During the Period 1938–1945' in *Nazi Europe*, eds. Bankier and Gutman, p. 336.

who risked their lives to save Jews.[164] Sometimes, Jews were able to pay rescuers to help them.[165] Despite the battering that national mythologies have taken in Denmark, Italy, and Bulgaria, it remains the case that in those countries the wartime regimes did not participate in the Germans' murder plans to anything like the extent that Eichmann and his staff desired.[166] The same is true of the 'neutral' countries. Sweden and Switzerland have especially seen their reputations suffer, as the extent of their trading with the Third Reich or, in Switzerland's case, their poor record on taking in Jewish refugees, have been laid bare.[167] Nevertheless, such research does not seek simply to demolish national legends, but, done properly, raises important questions about international relations, national responsibilities, and ethics.[168] We should note the extensive size of the publications devoted to the 'righteous among the nations' who helped rescue Jews—even as we acknowledge the impossibility of ever satisfactorily defining the 'altruistic personality'—and bear in mind that even the vast majority who remained bystanders did so for the most part under extremely harsh conditions in which the very survival of their own families was at stake.[169] Especially in eastern Europe, where people paid with their lives and those of their families for sheltering Jews, one must be careful not to assume that lack of assistance was a reflection of sympathy for Nazi goals. The names of Lidice, Oradour-sur-Glane, and Sant'Anna di Stazzema are proof enough of how

164. Weiss, 'The Attitude of the Ukrainian Nationalist Groups', p. 269; Daniel Romanovsky, 'The Soviet Person as a Bystander of the Holocaust: The Case of Eastern Belorussia' in *Nazi Europe*, eds. Bankier and Gutman, pp. 305–6. For an unusual, moving example, see Norman Gershman, *Besa: A Code of Honor. Muslim Albanians Who Rescued Jews During the Holocaust* (Jerusalem: Yad Vashem, n.d.)
165. Jan Grabowski, *Rescue for Money: Paid Helpers in Poland, 1939–1945* (Jerusalem: Yad Vashem, 2008).
166. On Denmark, see Mette Bastholm Jensen and Steven L. B. Jensen, eds., *Denmark and the Holocaust* (Copenhagen: Institute for International Studies, 2003).
167. Neville Wylie, ed., *European Neutrals and Non-Belligerents During the Second World War* (Cambridge: Cambridge University Press, 2001); David Cesarani and Paul A. Levine, eds., *Bystanders to the Holocaust: A Re-Evaluation* (London: Frank Cass, 2002); Christian Leitz, *Nazi Germany and Neutral Europe During the Second World War* (Manchester: Manchester University Press, 2001).
168. Arne Ruth, 'Postwar Europe: The Capriciousness of Universal Values' in *A New Europe for the Old?*, ed. Stephen R. Graubard (New Brunswick: Transaction, 1999), pp. 241–76; Avi Beker, 'Introduction: Unmasking National Myths—Europeans Challenge Their History' in *The Plunder of Jewish Property*, ed. Beker, pp. 1–32; Junz, 'Holocaust-Era Assets'.
169. See the *Encyclopedias of the Righteous* published by Yad Vashem; see also the volumes in Wolfgang Benz and Juliane Wetzel, eds., *Solidarität und Hilfe für Juden während der NS-Zeit* (Berlin: Metropol, 1996–).

the Nazis treated those they suspected of being (or chose to believe were) resistors.[170]

Conclusion

This chapter began by considering whether we could talk of 'Holocausts' rather than 'the Holocaust'. If that is meant to indicate an interrelated series of independent schemes to murder the Jews, only loosely connected to German direction, then the answer is no. The only real case of a German ally acting independently to murder the Jews is Romania. Slovakia and Vichy France were regimes that pushed antisemitic legislation or action, but did not pursue state-directed mass murder on their own. Even the more extreme case of Croatia makes little sense without German control, for Independent Croatia, though it had plenty of room for manoeuvre (as the genocidal massacre of Serbs, not authorized by the Germans, shows) was ultimately a puppet state. Not that this conclusion exculpates those, particularly at the level of state agencies, who willingly collaborated with the Third Reich's murderous policies; it simply confirms what historians have always asserted: that the Holocaust could not have happened, even as a continent-wide project, without German leadership.

Nevertheless, the concept of 'Holocausts' does have value. The burgeoning historical research of the last two decades—which shows no signs of slowing—allows us to understand the murder of the Jews in extraordinary detail. But of course, by doing so, it also makes the picture more complicated. We can no longer talk of a smooth, systematic, murder operation; rather, the detailed local studies indicate contradiction, ad hoc decision-making, and conflict among the perpetrators. But they all also indicate one thing: the pursuit by these varied actors of a common aim,

---

170. On Lidice, Friedländer, *The Years of Extermination*, pp. 349–50; Heiner Lichtenstein, *Himmlers Grüne Helfer: Die Schutz- und Ordnungspolizei im 'Dritten Reich'* (Cologne: Bund Verlag, 1990), pp. 193–205; on Oradour, Sarah Farmer, *Martyred Village: Commemorating the 1944 Massacre at Oradour-sur-Glane* (Berkeley: University of California Press, 1999); on Sant'Anna, see the brochure *Sant'Anna di Stazzema: Parco Nazionale della Pace* (Stazzema: Centro regionale toscano della resistenza, 2001) and Francesca Cappelletto, 'Public Memories and Personal Stories: Recalling the Nazi–Fascist Massacres' in *Memory and World War II: An Ethnographic Approach*, ed. Cappelletto (Oxford: Berg, 2005), pp. 101–30. See also Peter Steinkamp, 'Lidice 1942', Ahlrich Meyer, 'Oradour 1944', and Carlo Gentile, 'Sant'Anna di Stazzema 1944' in *Orte des Grauens: Verbrechen im Zweiten Weltkrieg*, ed. Gerd R. Ueberschär (Darmstadt: Primus, 2003), pp. 126–35, 176–86, and 231–6.

the murder of the Jews, to the extent that this goal overrode all others, including disagreements over using Jewish labourers. Furthermore, they clarify the extent to which the plunder and murder of the Jews was genuinely a European undertaking, a fact which makes its institutionalization into European memory in recent years more comprehensible. In the next chapter, I will pursue this theme and ask whether the Holocaust was the result of a long-term plan or the outcome of unpredictable initiatives at the grassroots level of the occupation of Europe. I will show that, just as recent historiography has deepened our understanding of the Holocaust's European dimension, so the idea of a 'blueprint for genocide' makes little sense before late 1941. However, at the same time that historians have rejected the Nazis' self-image of a controlled, industrial operation, they have sought to show how all of these apparently discrete actions can be held together by Nazi ideology.

2

The Decision-Making Process in Context

I do not see our work as a separate project, as something that includes
only Jews, that is only about Jews, and that will interest only Jews.

Hersh Wasser, paraphrasing Emmanuel Ringelblum[1]

Introduction

The question of the decision-making process for the Final Solution
is one of the longest-running debates in Holocaust historiography.
Historians and educators have taken its centrality for granted—surely
we need to know how and when the Nazi leadership, especially Hitler,
embarked on this great crime?—but the complexity of the issue means that
very few historians really have the mastery of the archival sources necessary
to make reliable judgements about it. The debates have been most helpfully
summarized by Ian Kershaw and Christopher Browning, and those two
historians, along with Raul Hilberg, Saul Friedländer, Peter Longerich,
Philippe Burrin, Christian Gerlach, Dieter Pohl, and a few others have
dominated the debates.[2]

---

1. Hersh Wasser, 'A vort vegn Ringelblum Arkhiv', cited in Samuel D. Kassow, *Who Will Write
   Our History? Rediscovering a Hidden Archive from the Warsaw Ghetto* (London: Penguin, 2009),
   p. 387.
2. Ian Kershaw, *The Nazi Dictatorship: Problems and Perspectives of Interpretation*, 4th edn (London:
   Hodder Education, 2000), ch. 5; Christopher R. Browning, 'The Decision-Making Process'
   in *HH*, pp. 173–96.

In recent years, the historiography has taken a different turn. The original assumptions behind research on the decision-making process were that Hitler and the Nazi leadership initiated the murder process, and that with enough careful reconstruction of the intrigues and actions of the main protagonists—Hitler, Himmler and Heydrich as heads of the SS, Eichmann and his underlings (Wisliceny, Dannecker, and so on), Globocnik and the camp empire, the heads of the *Einsatzgruppen*, Hans Frank as head of the *Generalgouvernement*, Alfred Rosenberg as head of the Ministry for the Occupied Eastern Territories, and Goering as nominally in charge of the Jewish Question in the Third Reich—one can show, even on a day-by-day basis, how the Nazis decided to murder the Jews of Europe. These assumptions rested on the notion that the Final Solution was a systematic, German programme that, once decided on, could be executed using what Hilberg called 'the machinery of destruction', that is, all the resources of the German state. Yet, as the previous chapter showed, the reality of the Holocaust was far more complex. As it unfolded on the ground, the killing process required the considerable input of collaborating states, local institutions, and individuals. The timing of the killings, especially in 1941, suggests an ad hoc process, with policy being made on the hoof. Does it not, then, require a dependence on the Nazis' own self-estimation as orderly and of their actions and networks as *reibungslos* (smooth, frictionless) if we think of the Holocaust as a single project emanating from a clear line of order? Is the centrality of the question of the decision-making process less obvious once one examines the Holocaust as deriving from a radicalizing dynamic in a pan-European context? But does doing so not perhaps relegate the central actors in Berlin to a position of unjustified marginality?

In this chapter, I will first provide a brief survey of the historiography of this major debate. Then I will show how recent work on what Hans Mommsen first called 'cumulative radicalization' helps us to reconceptualize the emergence of a genocidal impulse in Nazi Europe.[3] Indeed, the term 'radicalization' is the guiding concept here, as the historiography clearly illustrates such a process, with respect to individuals and processes, and our task is to understand what this process of radicalization actually

---

3. Hans Mommsen, 'The Realization of the Unthinkable: the "Final Solution of the Jewish Question" in the Third Reich' in *The Policies of Genocide: Jews and Soviet Prisoners of War in Nazi Germany*, ed. Gerhard Hirschfeld (London: Allen & Unwin, 1986), pp. 97–144.

involved. The stress on 'radicalization' will, however, not be with the aim of reinstating Mommsen's ultra-functionalist account; 'neo-functionalist' studies from the 1990s that placed the burden of interpretation on events on the ground in the occupied eastern territories added realistic levels of complexity to the events, but tended to overlook or even omit altogether the Third Reich's leaders, as we will see. Instead, I will show how the competing networks of persecution 'worked towards the Führer', so that the decision-making process in Berlin and the events on the ground in Europe's occupied peripheries interacted, together giving rise to a policy of genocide. I will show how this conclusion can be reached by placing the historiography of the decision-making process in a wider context, showing how the radicalization of Nazi policy from Kristallnacht onwards helps us to understand where the impetus for the Holocaust came from. Studies such as Browning's magisterial work, *The Origins of the Final Solution* (2004), a worthy successor to Hilberg's *The Destruction of the European Jews* (1961), tend to focus on a narrower period; indeed, much research on the decision-making process has honed in on the second half of 1941 as the period most deserving intense scrutiny.

Having said all that, it is nevertheless worth bearing in mind Hermann Graml's claim that:

> The various stations along the path of National Socialist persecution of the Jews are thus by no means a process of radicalization; rather, they only constitute the process of maturation and revelation of an essentially radical conviction. . . . Concretely, what this means is that, although neither Hitler nor any other National Socialist would have been capable as early as 1933 of issuing the command for a mass murder of the Jews, such an order, which presupposed the requisite power for its issuance, was ineluctable at a later point in time.[4]

Whilst few historians would choose to use the language of 'ineluctability', Graml's important insight suggests that what we are talking about is a radicalization of confidence, assuredness, and determination under changing circumstances, not a radicalization in the functionalist sense that increasingly radical options emerged which had previously been unthinkable. It reminds us too, as does Alon Confino, that the dominance of the 'radicalization' paradigm can obscure the fact that a historical description that seems to be all about contingency and open possibilities actually risks becoming a

---

4. Hermann Graml, 'The Genesis of the Final Solution' in *November 1938: From 'Reichskristallnacht' to Genocide*, ed. Walter H. Pehle (New York: Berg, 1991), p. 175.

narrative of inevitability.[5] The idea that genocidal fantasies were present from the start may now be a common assumption even among the most empirically-minded historians. However, this is also not a revival of classic intentionalism, for the argument is neither that Hitler long had a plan to kill the Jews which he implemented at the first opportunity, nor that Nazi plans were *inevitably* radicalized as time went by. As Peter Fritzsche notes, the 'instrumental role' of Hitler and Himmler, as shown in recent historiography, goes hand in hand with the well-established functionalist insight into 'the dynamic role of circumstance in the formulation of Nazi anti-Jewish policies'.[6] But what these circumstances changed was a growing sense that what had existed as an incipient vision could actually be realized. There was no *plan* to murder the Jews in 1919, 1925, 1933, 1938, or even 1940; but at the heart of Nazism there was a *fantasy* of a world without Jews, and it was this always-existing fantasy and the dawning realization that it could be actualized that the changing circumstances radicalized.

The thrust of recent work suggests that it is impossible to pinpoint exactly when the decision was made to murder all the Jews of Europe, if, indeed, there was *a* decision. All the historians involved accept that there was probably no single *Führerbefehl*, the search for which was for some time a bogeyman of historical research. But the absence of such an order from Hitler (or rather, the absence of written evidence of such an order) does not mean that Hitler was uninvolved,[7] or that he merely sat on high giving vague instructions that he then left his subordinates to interpret. It might, for example, be reasonable to conclude, as Bogdan Musial does, that there were three or four major decisions that took the regime down a series of ever more murderous steps, from eliminating the Jewish men of the Soviet Union, then women and children too, to murdering the Jews of Poland, to the 'Final Solution' in all of Europe. Musial follows Christian Gerlach in arguing that Hitler gave one of his key orders after the US entered the war in December 1941, but he thinks that this order only concerned the Jews of the *Generalgouvernement*; only later, in spring 1942, according to Musial, was this

---

5. Alon Confino, 'A World Without Jews: Interpreting the Holocaust', *GH*, 27, 4 (2009), p. 546.
6. Peter Fritzsche, 'The Holocaust and the Knowledge of Murder', *JMH*, 80, 3 (2008), p. 594.
7. See Gerald Fleming, *Hitler and the Final Solution* (Oxford: Oxford University Press, 1986) and, most importantly, Peter Longerich, *The Unwritten Order: Hitler's Role in the Final Solution* (Stroud: Tempus, 2001). On this point all historians, from Friedländer to Mommsen are agreed.

decision extended to all of Europe's Jews.[8] In fact, as Longerich writes, 'the murder of the European Jews was not the outcome of a single order but the result of a policy pursued by the regime over a relatively long period of time, which was time and time again driven forward decisively by Hitler himself.'[9]

When one sees the radicalizing dynamic in a longer-term perspective, that includes Kristallnacht, the drive to create the *Volksgemeinschaft*, the so-called 'territorial solution', the creation of ghettos, the murder of asylum inmates in Poland and Jews in the early stages of the war against the Soviet Union, historians' fixation on the timing of the Final Solution seems less important than explaining the steady and (with hindsight) seemingly unstoppable drift towards full-scale mass murder. Hitler and, especially, the SS, retain their importance, but in terms of understanding how the Holocaust could happen, the paradigm turns to some extent away from a legalistic one of the search for incriminating documents and to a more anthropological one, which stresses the culture of racial fantasies that drove the Nazi regime. In the context of the war, these fantasies became more and more powerful, and one can trace their radicalization in such a way that the actions of the perpetrators become 'comprehensible' in the sense that one can see how the Nazis' world view, especially as the war progressed, led logically towards genocide.

Intentionalism and Functionalism

A detailed history of these historiographical 'schools' is hardly needed here, since it has been exhaustively covered elsewhere. Until the 1980s, most historians, with the notable exception of Hilberg, argued that the main cause of the Holocaust was Nazi antisemitism. This is an entirely understandable position—surely the murder of the Jews must have had something to do with hatred of Jews? Indeed, only with the emergence of a school of thought that doubted the correctness of this way of thinking—'functionalism' or 'structuralism'—could it be named at all, as 'intentionalism'.[10] Intentionalists, such as Lucy Dawidowicz, Eberhard

---

8. Bogdan Musial, 'The Origins of "Operation Reinhard": The Decision-Making Process for the Mass Murder of the Jews in the Generalgouvernement', *YVS*, 28 (2000), pp. 113–53.
9. Longerich, *The Unwritten Order*, p. 120.
10. The 'schools' are named in Tim Mason, 'Intention and Explanation', in *Der 'Führerstaat': Mythos und Realität*, eds. Gerhard Hirschfeld and Lothar Kettenacker (Stuttgart: Ernst Klett, 1981), pp. 23–42.

Jäckel, Andreas Hillgruber, Gerald Reitlinger, or Yehuda Bauer believed that Hitler had a plan to murder the Jews and that he implemented it at the earliest opportunity; this was the war, when amidst the confusion and widespread destruction a genocidal project could more easily be disguised. In the 1970s and 1980s, this interpretation increasingly came under pressure as historians discovered that the unfolding of the genocidal process was by no means straightforward; rather, the road to Auschwitz was, as one historian put it, 'twisted'.[11] If Hitler had always intended to murder the Jews, they argued, why was there a need for a gradual process of social exclusion, as occurred between 1933 and 1938? And after that date, why was the 'territorial solution' of deporting the Jews to Nisko in eastern Poland or to Madagascar dreamt up? Furthermore, historians began to argue that the ghettos were not initially established as 'holding pens' before deportation to killing centres, and they questioned the notion (rather paradoxical anyway, if there was always a plan) that the infamous Wannsee conference of 20 January 1942 played a pivotal role in the decision-making process.[12]

The debate was quite polarized, with some functionalist historians (Martin Broszat and Hans Mommsen) arguing not only that no single 'decision for the final solution' was ever taken by Hitler, but that there was no plan of any sort. For Mommsen, indeed, antisemitism was merely a rabble-rousing rhetorical device and the Holocaust a 'way out of a cul-de-sac' into which the Nazis had manoeuvred themselves during the war. Functionalists stressed that their claims drew attention away from only Hitler, Himmler, and Heydrich, and established the guilt of large sections of the German population and many sectors of the German state, from the *Reichsbahn* (the German railways) to the judiciary. Intentionalists, however, saw this argument as so wide a dissipation of guilt that the 'cumulative radicalization' that led to genocide occurred (the passive voice and the lack of agency are important) more or less by accident. This was a classic historiographical clash between those who see the world as driven by agency, and who therefore stress the role of individuals, and those who see social forces and structures as more important, since these direct and limit individual choice.[13]

---

11. Karl A. Schleunes, *The Twisted Road to Auschwitz: Nazi Policy Toward German Jews 1933–1939* (Urbana: University of Illinois Press, 1970). See also Uwe Dietrich Adam, *Judenpolitik im Dritten Reich* (Düsseldorf: Droste, 1972).

12. Mark Roseman, *The Villa, the Lake, the Meeting: Wannsee and the Final Solution* (London: Penguin, 2002).

13. For an excellent discussion see A. Dirk Moses, 'Structure and Agency in the Holocaust: Daniel J. Goldhagen and His Critics', *History and Theory*, 37, 2 (1998), 194–219. See also

By the early 1990s, the debate appeared to have died down. With Christopher Browning declaring himself a 'moderate functionalist' and Philippe Burrin naming himself a 'conditional intentionalist', a consensus appeared to have been reached. The former view accepted the premise that there was no pre-meditated plan for genocide, but saw Hitler as the driving force behind the decision-making process as it unfolded during the key months between September 1939 and October 1941.[14] The latter's position was not dissimilar, but placed greater emphasis on the role of Hitler: 'while the actual work of the Final Solution, directly and indirectly, was an anonymous business, cold and compartmentalized, one man, animated by intense convictions, played a pivotal role in bringing it to pass and sustaining its momentum. In matters of extermination, Hitler had the last word; he was the prime mover.'[15]

Debate was reignited thanks to the work of German historians who had visited the newly opened archives in the former communist countries of Europe. These historians argued in their 'regional' studies of Nazi occupation policies in eastern Europe, that the genocidal onslaught against the Jews certainly took place in an atmosphere fuelled by violent antisemitism, but that the immediate causes for the murders were to be found elsewhere, for example, food shortages in the region, or plans for urban and rural 'Germanization' drawn up by agronomists, statisticians, or nutritionists rapidly advancing their careers on the back of the occupation of eastern Europe. This 'neo-functionalism' convinces insofar as it is based on archival work, but tends to exaggerate the importance of the documents that underpin its conclusions: what the documents say does not necessarily conform to what happened. Merely because some young, careerist, mid-level technocrats who accompanied the occupation produced papers arguing that the Jews should be eliminated does not establish that this is the reason why such a thing took place. In fact, although they recognize the significance of antisemitism as the broad framework within which policy decisions were taken,

---

Nicolas Berg, *The Invention of 'Functionalism': Josef Wulf, Martin Broszat, and the Institute for Contemporary History (Munich) in the 1960s* (Jerusalem: Yad Vashem, 2003) for the claim that functionalism, by downgrading free will, recapitulated the claims of the Nazi criminals at Nuremberg. The argument, though not without merit, is one-sided and overlooks alternative sources of the functionalist position, especially the writings of émigré historians such as Franz Neumann (Hilberg's doctoral supervisor) and Ernst Fraenkel, who had no stake in repeating Nazi self-justifications.

14. Christopher R. Browning, *The Path to Genocide: Essays on Launching the Final Solution* (Cambridge: Cambridge University Press, 1992), esp. ch. 5.
15. Philippe Burrin, *Hitler and the Jews: The Genesis of the Holocaust* (London: Edward Arnold, 1994), p. 149.

these historians have remarkably little to say about the SS or about decisions being taken in Berlin. Nor does their work satisfactorily explain the western European dimension of the Holocaust. I will return to this topic later.

Thanks to the important questions asked by the 'neo-functionalists', and to the answers offered by their critics, most recently the historiography has been dominated by a 'return of ideology'. Where the academic consensus of the 1980s was a functionalist one, with the stress on 'industrial murder'—now the fascination with 'modernity', 'technology', or 'cumulative radicalization' has largely given way to a stress on violence, radical antisemitism, and fantasy.[16] This is not because of Goldhagen's *Hitler's Willing Executioners* (1996), which, if it had any positive effects, was to act as a catalyst for scholarship that was already under way, into, for example, SS ideological indoctrination, radical antisemitism in the Weimar Republic, and the extent to which 'race' structured and drove so many aspects of the Third Reich. Nevertheless, it is striking that there are now very few historians who would take either an extreme intentionalist or an extreme functionalist position, since most now recognize both that before 1941 or 1942 there was no clearly formulated blueprint for genocide *and* that a world view built on mystical race thinking, especially antisemitism, lay at the heart of the regime. The debate between Christopher Browning and Peter Longerich on the timing of the decision for the Final Solution illustrates this: both share many assumptions, but the former places more emphasis on the euphoria of early victories in the war against the Soviet Union in autumn 1941, and plays down the fact that the death camps did not begin operating until 1942, whereas the latter stresses a continuity in '*Judenpolitik*' that always sought to eliminate 'the Jew' but that only became fully genocidal in 1942.[17] How to reconcile these two points remains

16. Saul Friedländer, *Nazi Germany and the Jews: The Years of Persecution 1933–1939* (London: Weidenfeld & Nicolson, 1997), stresses 'redemptive antisemitism'; Armin Nolzen, 'The Nazi Party and Its Violence Against Jews, 1933–1939: Violence as a Historiographical Concept', *YVS*, 31 (2003), 245–85; Philippe Burrin, *Strands of Nazi Anti-Semitism* (Oxford: Europaeum, 2003); Burrin, *Nazi Anti-Semitism: From Prejudice to the Holocaust* (New York: The New Press, 2005); Alon Confino, 'Fantasies about the Jews: Cultural Reflections on the Holocaust', *History & Memory*, 17, 1/2 (2005), 296–322; Helmut Walser Smith, 'Anti-Semitic Violence as Reenactment: An Essay in Cultural History', *Rethinking History*, 11, 3 (2007), pp. 335–51.
17. Browning, 'The Decision-Making Process'; Browning with Jürgen Matthäus, *The Origins of the Final Solution: The Evolution of Nazi Jewish Policy 1939–1942* (London: William Heinemann, 2004); Peter Longerich, *Politik der Vernichtung: Eine Gesamtdarstellung der nationalsozialistischen Judenverfolgung* (Munich: Piper, 1998); Longerich, *The Unwritten Order*; Longerich, *Holocaust: The Nazi Persecution and Murder of the Jews* (Oxford: Oxford University Press, 2010). Florent Brayard argues that only in June 1942 did the 'Final Solution' become redefined according

unclear. Nor is it necessarily the most important question facing historians, all of whom agree on the determination of the leading Nazis to wipe out the Jews of Europe, though it remains perhaps the central plank of Holocaust historiography. After all, both Browning and Longerich agree that at the time of the invasion of the USSR, 'the *implied genocide* in the future of Jews on Soviet territory was not yet the Final Solution for all Soviet Jewry, much less the other Jews of Europe', that 'the decision-making process did not end in 1941', and that 'Only in May 1942 . . . was the mass murder of Reich Jews fully and unequivocally underway'.[18]

It would be mistaken then to assume that the fierce debates between intentionalists and functionalists of two decades ago have disappeared. It might be fair to say, as Christian Gerlach does, that they have subsided: 'historians no longer search for exclusive explanations—or the only true explanation—because the complexity of the roots of the Holocaust is more and more acknowledged. True, there are still different opinions, but present research is about elements of explanation and includes the attempt to actually understand the Holocaust as having had multiple causes.' Still, Gerlach goes on to admit that 'the question as to whether ideology was the prime cause of the Holocaust remains a major line of distinction between different understandings in historiography.'[19] Thus, among the 'multiple causes' Gerlach refers to, the same question that drove the earlier intentionalist/functionalist debate remains evident: the role of ideology on the one hand, and circumstances on the other, only now in a much broader, empirically rich, and analytically sophisticated historical context.

Before the Final Solution

One way that historians have broadened the context for understanding the decision-making process is by extending the chronology backwards. Few

to a plan drafted by Himmler to mean the immediate murder (as opposed to sterilization) of all of Europe's Jews (as opposed to proceeding on a country-by-country basis). See Brayard, *La 'solution finale de la question juive': La technique, le temps et les catégories de la décision* (Paris: Fayard, 2004); Brayard, 'To What Extent Was the "Final Solution" Planned?', *YVS*, 36, 1 (2008), pp. 73–109.

18. Christopher R. Browning, *Nazi Policy, Jewish Workers, German Killers* (Cambridge: Cambridge University Press, 2000), pp. 25, 31, 55.
19. Christian Gerlach, 'Some Recent Trends in German Holocaust Research', in *Lessons and Legacies, Vol. 6*, ed. Diefendorf, pp. 291, 292.

historians of the Holocaust have heeded Helmut Walser Smith's call to extend their explanatory quest back to the nineteenth century,[20] but the pre-1933 years have been subject to much greater scrutiny. For example, whilst there has been a long tradition—in the manner of George Mosse or Fritz Stern[21]—of looking at *völkisch* movements using a history of ideas perspective, surprisingly little was known about antisemitism in the Weimar Republic. Several works have now appeared which demonstrate that the occurrence of violent antisemitic acts increased during the Weimar years and, significantly, that over time the middle classes found such attacks more and more tolerable.[22] Nazi ideology has been examined from the founding of the NSDAP onwards, and the persecution of the Jews before 1939 has been analysed in detail, with volume one of Saul Friedländer's *Nazi Germany and the Jews* (1997) the culmination of that research.

Yet the immediate context of the war remains key to historical explanations of the origins of the Holocaust. For some time now, historians have detailed the interconnectedness of Operation Barbarossa and the 'Final Solution'.[23] They have argued too that the genocide of the Jews grew out

20. Helmut Walser Smith, 'The Vanishing Point of German History', *History & Memory*, 17, 1/2 (2005), pp. 269–95. See also Dirk Schumann, 'Europa, der Erste Weltkrieg und die Nachkriegszeit: eine Kontinuität der Gewalt?' and Piotr Wróbel, 'The Seeds of Violence: The Brutalization of an East European Region, 1917–1921', *Journal of Modern European History*, 1, 1 (2003), pp. 24–43 and 125–49; Benjamin Lieberman, *Terrible Fate: Ethnic Cleansing in the Making of Modern Europe* (Chicago: Ivan R. Dee, 2006); Cathie Carmichael, *Genocide Before the Holocaust* (New Haven: Yale University Press, 2009); Donald Bloxham, *The Final Solution: A Genocide* (Oxford: Oxford University Press, 2009), chs 1–3; and Timothy Snyder, *Bloodlands* (New York: Basic Books, 2010) for geographically wide-ranging pre-1933 contextualizations of the genocidal imagination.

21. George L. Mosse, *The Crisis of German Ideology: Intellectual Origins of the Third Reich* (London: Weidenfeld & Nicolson, 1970); Fritz Stern, *The Politics of Cultural Despair: A Study in the Rise of the Germanic Ideology* (Berkeley: University of California Press, 1974); more recently: Jost Hermand, *Old Dreams of a New Reich: Völkisch Utopias and National Socialism* (Bloomington: Indiana University Press, 1992); Uwe Puschner, *Die völkische Bewegung im wilhelminischen Kaiserreich: Sprache, Rasse, Religion* (Darmstadt: Wissenschaftliche Buchgesellschaft, 2001); Puschner, ' "One People, One Reich, One God": The *Völkische Weltanschauung* and Movement', *Bulletin of the German Historical Institute London*, 24, 1 (2002), pp. 5–28; Hubert Cancik and Uwe Puschner, *Antisemitismus, Paganismus, völkische Religion* (Munich: Saur, 2004).

22. Massimo Ferrari Zumbini, *Die Wurzeln des Bösen. Gründerjahre des Antisemitismus: Von der Bismarckzeit zu Hitler* (Frankfurt/M: Vittorio Klostermann, 2003); Dirk Walter, *Antisemitische Kriminalität und Gewalt: Judenfeindschaft in der Weimarer Republik* (Bonn: Dietz, 1999); Cornelia Hecht, *Deutsche Juden und Antisemitismus in der Weimarer Republik* (Bonn: Dietz, 2003); Michael Wildt, 'Violence Against the Jews in Germany 1933–1939', in *Probing the Depths of German Antisemitism: German Society and the Persecution of the Jews, 1933–1941*, ed. David Bankier (Jerusalem: Yad Vashem, 2000), pp. 181–209.

23. Christian Streit, *Keine Kameraden: Die Wehrmacht und die sowjetischen Kriegsgefangenen 1941–1945* (Bonn: Dietz, 1991 [1978]); Jürgen Förster, 'The Relation Between Operation Barbarossa as

of the Euthanasia programme, a theme that I will address in Chapter 4. Now they have also shown that the radical nature of the war in the Soviet Union was prefigured in the war against Poland.[24] As Richard Bessel notes, 'if the Polish campaign appeared a conventional war to the near-sighted, the nature of the German occupation quickly revealed itself as part of something far more sinister.'[25] Goebbels' diary reference to the Jews he saw in Łódź on his visit in November 1939—'These are not human beings, these are animals. Therefore it is not a humanitarian operation but a surgical one'—is widely cited, but major deportations took place not only of Jews (who at this stage were ghettoized and deported to the *Generalgouvernement*) but of Catholic Poles, hundreds of thousands of whom were deported. At the same time as he described Jews as animals, Goebbels summed up the Polish streets as 'Asia' and envisaged 'radical action against the Poles'.[26]

The experience of rapid victory in Poland—and, of course, in western Europe in 1940—shaped Nazi expectations vis-à-vis the Soviet Union. Poland in particular paved the way for what would happen further east, for it was in Poland that the *Einsatzgruppen* were first used, that Himmler (who was appointed Reich Commissar for the Strengthening of Germandom, RKFDV (*Reichskommisar für die Festigung deutschen Volkstums*), on 7 October 1939) really came to the fore in the Third Reich's internal struggle for power, that the newly created RSHA (forged out of the merger of the SD, SS, Gestapo, and Criminal Police), under Heydrich, began operating,

an Ideological War of Extermination and the Final Solution' in *The Final Solution: Origins and Implementation*, ed. David Cesarani (London: Routledge, 1994), pp. 85–102; Omer Bartov, *Hitler's Army: Soldiers, Nazis, and War in the Third Reich* (New York: Oxford University Press, 1991); Bartov, *Germany's War and the Holocaust: Disputed Histories* (Ithaca: Cornell University Press, 2003); Tobias Jersak, 'A Matter of Foreign Policy: "Final Solution" and "Final Victory" in Nazi Germany', *GH*, 21, 3 (2003), pp. 369–91; Richard Bessel, *Nazism and War* (London: Phoenix, 2005); Gerhard L. Weinberg, 'Two Separate Issues? Historiography of World War II and the Holocaust' in *Holocaust Historiography in Context: Emergence, Challenges, Polemics and Achievements*, eds. David Bankier and Dan Michman (Jerusalem: Yad Vashem, 2008), pp. 379–401.

24. Alexander B. Rossino, 'Destructive Impulses: German Soldiers and the Conquest of Poland', *HGS*, 11, 3 (1997), pp. 351–65; Rossino, *Hitler Strikes Poland: Blitzkrieg, Ideology, and Atrocity* (Lawrence: University Press of Kansas, 2003); Klaus-Michael Mallmann and Bogdan Musial, eds., *Genesis des Genozids: Polen 1939–1941* (Darmstadt: Wissenschaftliche Buchgesellschaft, 2004); Jochen Böhler, *Auftakt zum Vernichtungskrieg: Die Wehrmacht in Polen 1939* (Frankfurt/M: Suhrkamp, 2006); Doris L. Bergen, 'Instrumentalization of *Volksdeutschen* in German Propaganda in 1939: Replacing/Erasing Poles, Jews, and Other Victims', *German Studies Review*, 31, 3 (2008), pp. 447–70.

25. Bessel, *Nazism and War*, p. 91.

26. Joseph Goebbels, *Tagebücher 1924–1945*, ed. Ralf Georg Reuth (Munich: Piper, 1992), Vol. 3, p. 1340 (entry for 2 November 1939).

and that the euthanasia campaign was systematized. The concentration and ghettoization of Jews, which began immediately on the occupation of Poland, and the suppression and deportation of Catholic Poles, were vital waystations on the road to the 'war of annihilation' in the USSR.[27] The occupation of Poland opened up wider vistas for the creative visions of the SS. For the Wehrmacht too, a more sinister outlook became common: Rossino notes that 'Many German military personnel seem to have considered the Polish–German conflict a struggle between competing ethnic groups' and argues that this 'facilitated greater overall acceptance of the regime's definition of the war in racial–biological terms'. The result, he suggests, was that the war 'provided a fitting context for explosion of attitudes that had been deeply poisoned by prejudice, racism, and the exaltation of violence towards "others". In many ways, therefore, the viciousness of German soldiers in 1939 proved a foreshadowing of still greater violence to come, violence that provided a foundation for the "war of annihilation" and the genocide of the Jews.'[28]

These expanding visions are clearly visible in the plans for dealing with the Jews in the period before June 1941. In the almost two years between the signing of the Hitler–Stalin Pact and Operation Barbarossa, the furthest reach of the Nazi empire was the River San in southeast Poland. It was here that plans for a *Judenreservat* (Jewish reservation) were drawn up, its main manifestation the so-called Nisko Project—holding deported Jews at a transit camp in Nisko, near Lublin, before transferring them to an unspecified destination further east. The project failed for logistical reasons, but as with the later Madagascar Plan, this 'territorial solution' to the 'Jewish question' proved a significant milestone in the development of the Nazi genocidal imagination. It is clear that by the time of the invasion of the Soviet Union, Nazi Germany's leadership had already made some important mental leaps. The 'origins of the Holocaust', writes Fritzsche, 'lie in Germany's determination to fight a race war in Poland in September 1939'.[29] Bessel is even more explicit: 'The failure to realize these plans, combined with the rapid decomposition of normative

27. Phillip T. Rutherford, *Prelude to the Final Solution: The Nazi Program for Deporting Ethnic Poles, 1939–1941* (Lawrence: University Press of Kansas, 2007). Rutherford notes that when dealing with ethnic Poles in the Warthegau, economic rationality took precedence over genocidal ideology, a situation that was reversed in the case of the Jews. See also Michael Phayer, *The Catholic Church and the Holocaust, 1930–1965* (Bloomington: Indiana University Press, 2000), ch. 2.

28. Rossino, *Hitler Strikes Poland*, pp. 197, 226.   29. Fritzsche, *Life and Death*, p. 158.

behavioural constraints in the context of war and a growing belief among
the Nazi elite that anything was possible, would eventually open the gates
to Auschwitz.'[30]

Whilst scholars have described in detail the Nazi occupation of the
USSR, building on the earlier work of Robert Koehl, Alexander Dallin,
and others,[31] their arguments reveal that one cannot separate the war for
Lebensraum from the Holocaust. The destruction of 'Judeo-Bolshevism'
went hand in hand with grand schemes to expel Slavs in their tens of
millions to make way for the German paradise envisaged by Himmler. If it
was the thrill of rapid victory in Poland that gave a frisson of anticipation
to the racial fantasies of 1941, the discovery that the Soviet Union would
not capitulate quite so readily made the Nazis more ready to realize them,
as Fritzsche points out, reconciling Browning and Burrin:

> Both utter confidence in German victory and in the realization of grandiose
> imperial plans in the postwar period *and* the increasingly desperate mobiliza-
> tion against what became a worldwide coalition of enemies in December 1941
> shaped German policy. Euphoria encouraged the formation of increasingly
> radical anti-Jewish measures, while the prospect of defeat consolidated their
> murderous implementation.[32]

The key realization of the recent historiography of the build-up to the
'Final Solution' is thus not just to show that the territorial solution was
taken seriously by the Nazi leadership, a claim that made little sense when
an intentionalist viewpoint prevailed (when it had to be understood as
a way of diverting the Foreign Office's *Judenreferat* from discovering the
more radical steps being taken by the SS). Additionally—and here we
see empirical historians making an important leap of the imagination—the
consensus seems to be that one should not draw too much of a distinction
between earlier policies of deportation to 'reservations' and later policies of
extermination, since both were genocidal. Longerich, for example, writes
that the problem with making this distinction is that one thereby 'misses
the core of the plans of Nazi administrators of Jewish policy', because 'the
"territorial solution" was always conceived as a "final solution", for it was
ultimately directed at the physical destruction of the great majority of the

30. Bessel, *Nazism and War*, p. 93.
31. Robert Koehl, *RKFDV: German Resettlement and Population Policy 1939–1945. A History of
    the Reich Commission for the Strengthening of Germandom* (Cambridge, MA: Harvard University
    Press, 1957); Alexander Dallin, *German Rule in Russia 1941–1945: A Study of Occupation Policies*
    (London: Macmillan, 1957).
32. Fritzsche, *Life and Death*, p. 180.

Jews'.[33] Similarly, Browning writes that the Madagascar Plan, which, 'like a spectacular meteor . . . blazed across the sky of Nazi Jewish policy, only to burn out abruptly', was 'an important psychological step toward the road to the Final Solution'. Although the circumstances of the war—the failure to secure the sea routes across the Indian Ocean—meant that the plan died a rapid death, Browning notes that 'had the Nazis carried out the plan as they intended, it would have been a murderous operation'. As Himmler wrote, 'The very concept "Jew" I hope to see completely extinguished by creating the possibility of large-scale emigration of Jews to Africa or some other colony.'[34] What the Madagascar Plan reveals is the drive to find a quick solution to the 'Jewish question' in 1940; it was but a short step from a plan that was 'genocidal in its implications' to full-scale, continent-wide genocide.[35] What changed in 1941 was the overall conception of a genocidal plan rather than a more limited policy in which genocidal intent was still to some extent veiled, perhaps unconsciously.

Ghettos

In the light of this change in genocidal plan, Nazi ghettoization policy becomes clearer. Heydrich's infamous *Schnellbrief* (express letter) to the *Einsatzgruppen* chiefs of 21 September 1939, ordering the concentration of Jews in cities, preferably in the vicinity of rail junctions, is well known. He expressly noted that 'Distinction must be made between: 1. The final aim (which will require extended periods of time) and 2. The stages leading to the fulfilment of this final aim (which will be carried out in short periods).'[36] Tempting though it might be to hear in the words 'final goal' a euphemism for mass murder, it is highly unlikely that, in September 1939, anything other than deportation was meant. Besides, Heydrich left the arrangements for establishing ghettos to local authorities, and the result was that the process dragged on for months, with different results in the various locations involved. Nevertheless, given what historians now think about

33. Longerich, *Politik der Vernichtung*, p. 579.
34. Himmler, 'Denkschrift' (28 May 1940), in *Ursachen und Folgen*, eds. Herbert Michaelis and Ernst Schraepler (Berlin, n.d.), doc. 2879d.
35. Browning, *Origins*, pp. 88–89.
36. Yitzhak Arad, Yisrael Gutman and Abraham Margaliot, eds., *Documents on the Holocaust: Selected Sources on the Destruction of the Jews of Germany and Austria, Poland, and the Soviet Union*, 4th edn (Jerusalem: Yad Vashem, 1990), pp. 173–4.

the territorial solution, one might surmise that even if Heydrich could not have envisaged gas chambers or even mass shootings in 1939, a plan to deport Jews to an unspecified eastern destination should itself be regarded as murderous.[37] It seems then that when ghettos were first established in Poland, along with the destruction of small communities (under 500 people), the intention was that they should be temporary measures until the end of the war when the Jews would be deported 'to the East'. As Fritzsche suggests, the plans became more radical as the Nazis became bolder after each success, but the realization that the plans would not be fulfilled led to rage and a turn to mass murder. If the Nazi vision for a racially reshaped European empire could not be realized, at least their prime enemy would be dealt with. The ghettos then became holding pens, not for deportation 'east of the Urals', but to death.

But if the current historiographical consensus is that the ghettos of Poland were not established as part of a premeditated plan for mass murder, then neither were they incorporated into murderous policies because of local administrators' deliberate creation of untenable circumstances, with the intention of recommending ever more radical measures. Rather, as Browning demonstrates, ghettos were sites of struggles between 'attritionists' and 'productionists', with the victory of the latter only 'temporary and partial'. 'When Berlin finally opted for mass murder,' Browning writes, 'it found on the local level both eager attritionists who felt that their day had come, as well as exhausted productionists who either made no objection to being relieved of an intractable problem or quickly adapted to the new situation.'[38] In other words, whilst different groups of Nazis argued over the role of the ghettos in the short term, they were all Nazis who ultimately had no objection, or at least raised none, to the murder of the Jews. 'The economic rationale for keeping ghettos intact was not strong enough to reverse Nazi anti-Jewish policy from its most radical point of mass murder',

37. Dan Michman, 'Why Did Heydrich Write the *Schnellbrief*? A Remark on the Reason and on Its Significance', *YVS*, 32 (2004), p. 443, argues that the letter was not really intended for its addressees, the *Einsatzgruppen* leaders, since they already knew their tasks, but for the authorities that were outside of the SS who also received copies.
38. Christopher R. Browning, 'Before the "Final Solution": Nazi Ghettoization Policy in Poland (1940–1941)' in *Ghettos 1939–1945: New Research and Perspectives on Definition, Daily Life, and Survival: Symposium Presentations* (Washington, DC: Center for Advanced Holocaust Studies, United States Holocaust Memorial Museum, 2005), p. 4. Also Browning, 'Nazi Ghettoization Policy in Poland, 1939–1941' in his *The Path to Genocide: Essays on Launching the Final Solution* (Cambridge: Cambridge University Press, 1992), pp. 28–56; Browning, *Origins*, ch. 4.

writes Lower.[39] Her assertion is most clear in the case of Łódź, the longest-lasting of the ghettos because it was made to serve a 'productionist' purpose under the control of Arthur Greiser (and not, therefore, the RSHA, which would have taken a different view of such a large concentration of Jews on Reich territory). At the time of its establishment, when it was already clear that the Jews of the Warthegau would not immediately be expelled, *Regierungspräsident* Friedrich Uebelhoer noted that 'The creation of the ghetto is only a temporary measure. . . . The final goal in any case must be to burn out this plague boil.'[40]

The study of ghettos is the best example of the division in the historiography between those who study perpetrators and those who study victims. As we have seen, the former ask about the role of the ghettos in Nazi decision-making policies, with a particular focus on what to do with ghettos after the closing off of the territorial solution. The latter, drawing on the unusually large range of sources available (photographs, diaries, official transcripts of Jewish Council meetings, artefacts, and so on) examine the ghettos as social institutions in their own right. Their writings contribute to the growing scholarship on the victims' responses to their persecution and to the tendency to analyse the Holocaust as a chapter of Jewish history. Whilst the broader context is rarely forgotten, studies of the victims have tended to look at the ghettos as isolated worlds unto themselves, with detailed analyses of, for example, theatre or music, religion or study, smuggling or social conflict.[41] Questions about the role played by the *Judenräte* (Jewish Councils) and, in particular, the Jewish police, have long been painful and divisive, especially within Jewish communities.[42] And the

39. Wendy Lower, 'Facilitating Genocide: Nazi Ghettoization Practices in Occupied Ukraine, 1941–1942' in *Life in the Ghettos During the Holocaust*, ed. Eric J. Sterling (Syracuse: Syracuse University Press, 2005), p. 144. See also Helen Fein, 'Genocide by Attrition 1939–1993: The Warsaw Ghetto, Cambodia, and Sudan: Links Between Human Rights, Health, and Mass Death', *Health and Human Rights*, 2, 2 (1997), pp. 11–45.

40. Cited in Browning, 'Before the "Final Solution" ', p. 5.

41. See Corni, *Hitler's Ghettos*, ch. 6. In general on theatre, see Rebecca Rovit and Alvin Goldfarb, eds., *Theatrical Performance During the Holocaust: Texts, Documents, Memoirs* (Baltimore: Johns Hopkins University Press, 1999).

42. For an overview, see Dan Michman, 'Jewish Leadership *in Extremis*' in *HH*, pp. 319–40; Michman, *Holocaust Historiography: A Jewish Perspective. Conceptualizations, Terminology, Approaches and Fundamental Issues* (London: Vallentine Mitchell, 2003), pp. 159–75; Michman, 'On the Historical Interpretation of the *Judenräte* Issue: Between Intentionalism, Functionalism and the Integrationist Approach of the 1990s' and Yisrael Gutman, 'The Judenrat as a Leadership', both in *On Germans and Jews under the Nazi Regime: Essays by Three Generations of Historians*, ed. Moshe Zimmermann (Jerusalem: Hebrew University Magnes Press, 2006), pp. 385–97 and 313–35. For earlier discussions, see Philip Friedman, *Roads*

debate about resistance, although no longer as emotionally driven as it was immediately after World War II, is still hotly contested, and the historiography is large. Debates over definition continue, especially the question of whether one can compare 'spiritual' or 'cultural' resistance with the armed variety. Alternative concepts, such as *Resistenz* (as opposed to the standard German term *Widerstand*) or *Amidah*, a Hebrew word roughly meaning 'to take a stand', have been proposed to help clarify the conceptual differences between armed uprising and smaller, everyday forms of sabotage or survival.[43] The long-overlooked ZZW (*Żydowski Związek Wojskowy*, Jewish Military Organization) wing of the armed Jewish resistance in Warsaw, comprised mainly of revisionist Zionists and the Betar youth movement, has been recently investigated.[44] And the armed approach of the Warsaw fighters has been contrasted with the actions of the Minsk underground, which aimed at saving lives by enabling Jews to hide in the Belarussian forests rather than dying heroically.[45] The study of religious (including ultra-orthodox or *Haredi*) Jews—who made up a large percentage of the

to Extinction: Essays on the Holocaust (New York: Jewish Publication Society of America, 1980); Isaiah Trunk, *Judenrat: The Jewish Councils in Eastern Europe under Nazi Occupation* (Lincoln: University of Nebraska Press, 1996 [1972]); Raul Hilberg, 'The Ghetto as a Form of Government' in *Holocaust: Religious and Philosophical Implications*, eds. John K. Roth and Michael Berenbaum (New York: Paragon House, 1989), pp. 116–35; Randolph L. Braham, 'The Jewish Councils: An Overview' in *Unanswered Questions: Nazi Germany and the Genocide of the Jews*, ed. François Furet (New York: Schocken Books, 1989), pp. 252–74; Aharon Weiss, 'The Historiographical Controversy Concerning the Character and Function of the Judenrats' in *The Historiography of the Holocaust Period*, eds. Yisrael Gutman and Gideon Greif (Jerusalem: Yad Vashem, 1988), pp. 679–96; Yisrael Gutman and Cynthia Haft, eds., *Patterns of Jewish Leadership in Nazi Europe 1933–1945* (Jerusalem: Yad Vashem, 1979).

43. Robert Rozett, 'Jewish Resistance' in *HH*, pp. 341–63; Michael R. Marrus, 'Varieties of Jewish Resistance: Some Categories and Comparisons in Historiographical Perspective' in *Major Changes Within the Jewish People in the Wake of the Holocaust*, ed. Yisrael Gutman (Jerusalem: Yad Vashem, 1996), pp. 269–300; Marrus, 'Jewish Resistance to the Holocaust', *JCH*, 30, 1 (1995), pp. 83–110; Marrus, *The Holocaust in History*, ch. 7; Ruby Rohrlich, ed., *Resisting the Holocaust* (Oxford: Berg, 1998); Yehuda Bauer, *Rethinking the Holocaust* (New Haven: Yale University Press, 2001), pp. 119–66; James M. Glass, *Jewish Resistance During the Holocaust: Moral Uses of Violence and Will* (Basingstoke: Palgrave Macmillan, 2004).

44. Moshe Arens, 'The Warsaw Ghetto Uprising: A Reappraisal', *YVS*, 33 (2005), pp. 101–42; Arens, 'The Jewish Military Organization (ZZW) in the Warsaw Ghetto', *HGS*, 19, 2 (2005), pp. 201–25; Dariusz Libionka and Laurence Weinbaum, 'Deconstructing Memory and History: The Jewish Military Union (ZZW) and the Warsaw Ghetto Uprising', *Jewish Political Studies Review*, 18, 1/2 (2006); Libionka and Weinbaum, 'A New Look at the Betar "Idyll" in Hrubieszów', *YVS*, 37, 1 (2009), pp. 85–108.

45. Barbara Epstein, *The Minsk Ghetto, 1941–1943: Jewish Resistance and Soviet Internationalism* (Berkeley: University of California Press, 2008); also Hersh Smolar, *The Minsk Ghetto: Soviet–Jewish Partisans Against the Nazis* (New York: Holocaust Library, 1989).

Holocaust's victims, but have been neglected by historians—is an emerging field of considerable importance.[46]

The maturing of the historiography is reflected in the development of a broad consensus that the *Judenräte* ought not to be seen as 'traitors' or 'collaborators' as they sometimes were in the emotionally charged immediate postwar years.[47] Hilberg noted that the councils had to face the 'basic paradox inherent in their role as preservers of Jewish life in a framework of German destruction' which meant that 'Because of its compliance strategy, the *Judenrat* could be a dangerous organization precisely when it functioned most smoothly.'[48] Most historians, whilst they might not demur, prefer a somewhat less combative tone, and stress the fact that, as Braham says, 'whatever their mistakes and whatever the level of their cooperation and collaboration, one must never forget that the ultimate responsibility for the Holocaust must be borne almost exclusively by the Germans and their accomplices all over Europe.'[49] Braham's claim is backed up by the evidence. On 15 August 1942, Ephraim Barash, the energetic head of the Białystok *Judenrat*, addressed the council and, in response to a question as to whether 'the authorities' would agree to enlarge the ghetto with skilled workers, stated: 'The matter is difficult. The decisions will not after all be made by the Judenrat, nor by the Executive Board. The Germans will settle things. I knew this beforehand, but I

46. Dina Porat, ' "Amalek's Accomplices". Blaming Zionism for the Holocaust: Anti-Zionist Ultra-Orthodoxy in Israel During the 1980s', *JCH*, 27, 4 (1992), pp. 695–729; Dan Michman, 'Research on the Problems and Conditions of Religious Jewry under the Nazi Regime' in *The Historiography of the Holocaust Period*, eds. Gutman and Greif, pp. 737–48; Michman, 'The Impact of the Holocaust on Religious Jewry' in *Major Changes*, eds. Gutman and Saf, pp. 659–707; Michman, *Holocaust Historiography: A Jewish Perspective*, pp. 251–99; Thomas Rahe, 'Die Bedeutung von Religion und Religiosität in den nationalsozialistischen Konzentrationslagern' in *Die nationalsozialistischen Konzentrationslager*, eds. Ulrich Herbert, Karin Orth, and Christoph Dieckmann (Frankfurt/M: Fischer Taschenbuch Verlag, 2002), Vol. 2, pp. 1006–22; Gershon Greenberg, 'Ultra-Orthodox Reflections on the Holocaust: 1945 to the Present' in *Contemporary Responses to the Holocaust*, eds. Konrad Kwiet and Jürgen Matthäus (Westport: Praeger, 2004), pp. 87–121; Judith Baumel-Schwartz, 'Pioneers, Teachers, and Mothers: Ultra-Orthodox Women Among *She'erit Hapletah*', *YVS*, 36, 1 (2008), pp. 145–79; Havi Ben-Sasson et al., *Years Wherein We Have Seen Evil: Selected Aspects in the History of Religious Jewry During the Holocaust* (Jerusalem: Yad Vashem, 2003), 2 vols.
47. Michman, 'Jewish Leadership *in Extremis*', pp. 319–21; Dalia Ofer, 'The Strength of Remembrance: Commemorating the Holocaust During the First Decade of Israel', *Jewish Social Studies*, 6, 2 (2000), pp. 24–55, esp. 40–4; Roni Stauber, *The Holocaust in Israeli Public Debate in the 1950s: Ideology and Memory* (London: Vallentine Mitchell, 2007), ch. 5.
48. Hilberg, 'The Ghetto as a Form of Government', pp. 121, 122.
49. Braham, 'The Jewish Councils', p. 274.

considered it necessary to call it to the attention of the Judenrat.'[50] In one
of the most perceptive analyses of the *Judenräte*, Dan Diner is thus correct
to point out that the councils operated in a way that was rational given the
parameters of decision-making within which they were operating, but that,
thanks to Nazi control, these decisions ultimately acted *counter-rationally*
against the interests of the Jews. '[B]ereft of any other alternative', writes
Diner, the *Judenräte* 'directed the reversal of values engendered by the
Nazis—the value-ethics of ends and means, and the associated, generally
effective assumptions of rationality—against themselves, and against the
Jewish communities in the ghettos entrusted to their care.' The *Judenräte*,
Diner continues, 'were subservient to a reality in which the rationality of
action aimed at self-preservation was transformed to self-destruction as a
result of that reversal'.[51]

Despite the prevailing consensus that the *Judenräte* acted in the best
interests of the Jews in their care, historians also now recognize that there
was no single experience of ghettoization. Martin Dean points out that
there were over a thousand ghettos in Nazi-occupied eastern Europe, if
one includes what he calls the 'makeshift ghettos' that separated Jews from
their neighbours for a short period before their murder by mass shooting
in places such as Mar'ina Gorka, Pukhovichi, and Tal'ka in the vicinity
of Minsk. Soviet ghettos were generally short-lived affairs. Mordechai
Altshuler has examined 22 ghettos in five Soviet cities, finding that in five
of them all the Jews were killed in an average of 23 days following the
Nazi occupation; in nine, within 99 days; and in eight, in an average of
295 days. About many such places we know almost nothing, which is why
the USHMM has inaugurated a project to produce a vast seven-volume
encyclopedia of Nazi Europe's more than 20,000 camps and ghettos.[52]

50. 'From the Minute Book of the Bialystok Judenrat' in Lucy S. Dawidowicz, ed., *A Holocaust
    Reader* (West Orange: Behrman House, 1976), pp. 284–5.
51. Dan Diner, 'Historical Understanding and Counterrationality: The *Judenrat* as Epistemological
    Vantage' in *Probing the Limits of Representation: Nazism and the 'Final Solution'*, ed. Saul
    Friedländer (Cambridge, MA: Harvard University Press, 1992), p. 140.
52. Martin Dean, 'Life and Death in the "Gray Zone" of Jewish Ghettos in Nazi-Occupied
    Europe: The Unknown, the Ambiguous, and the Disappeared' in *Gray Zones: Ambiguity and
    Compromise in the Holocaust and Its Aftermath*, eds. Jonathan Petropoulos and John K. Roth
    (New York: Berghahn, 2005), pp. 205–21; Mordechai Altshuler, 'The Unique Features of
    the Holocaust in the Soviet Union' in *Jews and Jewish Life in Russia and the Soviet Union*,
    ed. Yaacov Ro'i (Portland: Frank Cass, 1995), p. 175; Geoffrey P. Megargee, ed., *The
    United States Holocaust Memorial Museum Encyclopedia of Camps and Ghettos 1933–1945*, 7 vols.
    (2009–).

By contrast, some countries, such as Germany, never experienced closed ghettos, and others, notably Hungary, did so only briefly. Hungary, indeed, stands apart from the mainstream history of the ghettos, since, as Tim Cole notes, there the ghettos existed only for a few weeks, and they were places for Jewish women, children, and the elderly, because Jewish men had been placed in labour battalions under the control of the Hungarian army. And in the Hungarian context, the ghetto in Budapest was, in Cole's words, 'exceptional'. First, there were several ghettos in Budapest, not one; and the Budapest ghettos 'were ultimately "liberated" rather than liquidated'.[53] In yet another case, Transnistria, ghettos were set up on the order of the Romanian authorities independently of the Germans. Tens of thousand of Jews died in them from typhus and starvation. Yet remarkably, many Jews survived the ghettos of Transnistria, thanks to the fact that, instead of being deported or shot, as they would have been had they been in German hands, after the summer of 1942 (when Antonescu reversed his policy regarding the Jews) they were for the most part left to fend for themselves. Remarkably, in February 1942, the Jews of Transnistria were able to set up an Aid Committee (*Comisiunea de Ajutorare*) which contributed enormously to the easing of conditions.[54] In France, Belgium, and the Netherlands, the Nazis established the equivalent of *Judenräte* (the *Union Générale des Israélites de France*, *Association des Juifs en Belgique*, and the *Joodsche Raad* respectively), but these were national bodies. Besides, as Michman points out, there are some important differences: although the *Joodsche Raad* was set up in Amsterdam in February 1941, in Belgium the German authorities did not establish the Association until a year and a half after the occupation, and referred to it not as a *Judenrat* but as the *Judenvereinigung* (Association of Jews).[55] In Germany itself, the year 1939 saw the Jews corralled into the *Reichsvereinigung der Juden in Deutschland* (Association of Jews in Germany). Where '*Vereinigungen*' rather than *Judenräte* existed, these proved less pliable

---

53. Tim Cole, 'Multiple and Changing Experiences of Ghettoization: Budapest, 1944' in *Life in the Ghettos*, ed. Sterling, pp. 146–7. See also Cole, *Holocaust City: The Making of a Jewish Ghetto* (New York: Routledge, 2003); Cole, 'Building and Breaching the Ghetto Boundary: A Brief History of the Ghetto Fence in Körmend, Hungary, 1944', *HGS*, 23, 1 (2009), pp. 54–75.
54. Dennis Deletant, 'Aspects of the Ghetto experience in Eastern Transnistria: The Ghettos and Labor Camp in the Town of Golta' in *Ghettos 1939–1945*, pp. 15–66.
55. Michman, 'Research on the Holocaust in Belgium and in General: History and Context' in *Belgium and the Holocaust: Jews, Belgians, Germans*, ed. Michman (Jerusalem: Yad Vashem, 1998), pp. 33–35.

and less ready to do the Germans' 'dirty work', as Michman puts it.[56] In western Europe, the Nazi-established councils competed with the existing Jewish organizations, which were not abolished, although their influence was much diminished. More research is needed on the *Consistoire Central* in Belgium and France, and the Dutch equivalents, which were split between the Sephardic and Ashkenazi communities, whereas for Germany much is already known about the *Reichsvertretung der deutschen Juden* (Reich Representation of German Jews), which was established in 1933.[57]

This need to differentiate is very clear too in the case of Poland. Apart from the fact that Warsaw and Łódź were very different,[58] major studies have now begun appearing on other ghettos, notably Minsk, Lublin, Białystok, Cracow, and Vilna. Most of the ghettos in the *Generalgouvernement* were actually established shortly before or after the invasion of the USSR, 'in order', as Sara Bender says, 'to facilitate implementation of the Final Solution to the Jewish Question and to facilitate the exploitation of Jewish skilled labour for the war effort'.[59] In Kielce, for example, the *Judenrat* was created in November 1939, as per Heydrich's order, but the ghetto was not set up until April 1941, along with those of the two other major cities of the Radom district of the *Generalgouvernement*, Radom and Częstochowa.[60] It

56. Michman, 'Research on the Holocaust in Belgium and in General', pp. 36–7.
57. For example, Otto Dov Kulka, *Deutsches Judentum unter dem Nationalsozialismus*, Vol. 1 (Tübingen: Mohr Siebeck, 1997); Jacques Adler, *The Jews of Paris and the Final Solution: Communal Response and Internal Conflicts, 1940–1944* (New York: Oxford University Press, 1989); Renée Poznanski, *Jews in France During World War II* (Waltham: Brandeis University Press, 2001); Michel Laffitte, *Un engrenage fatal: L'UGIF 1941–1944* (Paris: Liana Levi, 2003). A rare diary by a Jewish leader (of the UGIF in the 'Free Zone') has recently been published in English: Raymond-Raoul Lambert, *Diary of a Witness 1940–1943* (Chicago: Ivan R. Dee, 2007).
58. There have been fewer significant recent studies on Warsaw than on Łódź in English or German. The major exceptions are Kassow, *Who Will Write Our History?* and Barbara Engelking and Jacek Leociak, *The Warsaw Ghetto: A Guide to the Perished City* (New Haven: Yale University Press, 2009). See also Havi Ben-Sasson, ' "At the Present Time, Jewish Warsaw Is Like a Cemetery": Life in the Warsaw Ghetto During the Great Deportation' in *On Germans and Jews*, ed. Zimmermann, pp. 353–83; Michał Grynberg, *Words to Outlive Us: Eyewitness Accounts from the Warsaw Ghetto* (London: Granta, 2003); and the three articles on 'The Jews of Warsaw' in *YVS*, 33 (2005). For earlier studies, see especially Yisrael Gutman, *The Jews of Warsaw 1939–1943: Ghetto, Underground, Revolt* (Brighton: The Harvester Press, 1982) and the many published diaries and memoirs of ghetto inhabitants and fighters, from Adam Czerniaków to Marek Edelman. For discussion of recent works on Warsaw in Polish, see Stola, 'New Research on the Holocaust in Poland' and Pohl, 'War, Occupation and the Holocaust in Poland'.
59. Sara Bender, *The Jews of Białystok During World War II and the Holocaust* (Waltham: Brandeis University Press, 2009), p. 280.
60. Sara Bender, 'The Białystok and Kielce Ghettos: A Comparative Study' in *Ghettos 1939–1945*, pp. 85–6.

was a small, impoverished ghetto, continually living under fear of German harassment, and was liquidated suddenly in August 1942.[61] In Białystok, which had been part of Soviet-occupied Poland between September 1939 and June 1941, 7,000 of the city's 50,000 Jews were murdered and the rest were ghettoized within a month of the German invasion. Thanks to the efforts of Barash, the ghetto was located in an area of factories and acceptable housing, and Barash, like Jacob Gens in Vilna or Moshe Merin in Sosnowiec, set about trying to make the ghetto productive, thus—as he understandably saw things—ensuring its future. The strategy appeared to pay off, for the Białystok ghetto inhabitants learned in early 1943 that, whilst they were still alive, the Jews of the Białystok district (in, for example, Grajewo, Grodno, Łomża, Sokolovka, Sokółka, and Wolkowysk) had been sent to the death camps. Even after the *Aktion* of February 1943 which saw 10,000 Jews deported from the ghetto to Treblinka and Auschwitz, the Germans left 30,000 working. Even so, and despite the apparent logic of Barash's position—the ghetto was extremely productive—the Germans liquidated the Białystok ghetto without any warning in August 1943 in five days.[62] As Bender remarks, confirming Diner's analysis, 'Unfortunately, Barash found himself in a trap. He did not know, nor did he have any opportunity to learn, that German policy toward the Jews was not driven by utilitarian or rational considerations and that in the long run it had nothing to do with the inclinations or wishes of local German officials.'[63] Studies of the ghettos of Minsk, Cracow, and Grodno all also reveal differences, with important factors being the attitude of the *Judenrat* towards armed resistance, the esteem in which the *Judenrat* was held by the ghetto's inhabitants, and the strength of the local German authorities vis-à-vis the SS. Minsk, thanks to being surrounded by a barbed-wire fence rather than brick wall, and being guarded by patrols rather than fixed sentries, had a proportionately much higher rate of escape than other ghettos. The survival of these escapees was facilitated by good relations between the Jews from the ghetto and the local Belorussians, to the extent that Barbara Epstein argues that 'Minsk was the only city in which a substantial underground organization outside the ghetto worked with a ghetto underground toward this end'.[64]

61. Bender, 'Białystok and Kielce Ghettos', p. 90.
62. Bender, 'Białystok and Kielce Ghettos', pp. 90–1. See also Raul Hilberg, *Perpetrators, Victims, Bystanders: The Jewish Catastrophe 1933–1945* (New York: Secker & Warburg, 1995), pp. 181–2.
63. Bender, 'Białystok and Kielce Ghettos', p. 91.
64. Epstein, *The Minsk Ghetto*, pp. 41, 42.

But despite these differences, all the studies ultimately confirm Bender's and Diner's analyses, that the Jewish councils, even when they worked in what they thought were the best interests of the ghettos' inhabitants, were not ultimately in charge; they did not nor could they have been expected to understand the destructive logic of Nazism.[65]

The ghetto to which most attention has been paid is Łódź, about which a number of important publications have recently appeared. In some ways Łódź was an anomaly in the ghetto system, but for that very reason it is of tremendous importance, especially when one considers the large amount of evidence that survived its liquidation (both documentary and material).[66] The fact that Isaiah Trunk's seminal 1962 Yiddish study of the ghetto, which combined historical analysis with reproduction of key documents from the YIVO (Yiddish Scientific Institute) archives, has recently been published in English, indicates the strength of interest in Łódź, as do Peter Klein's study of the local German administration, which stresses perpetrator 'networks of persecution', and Andrzej Strzelecki's detailed study of the deportation of Jews from Łódź to Auschwitz in summer 1944, a book which Strzelecki explicitly regards as a kind of monument.[67] The part played by the Chairman of the *Judenrat*, Mordechai Chaim Rumkowski, remains especially contentious, for he exemplifies Primo Levi's 'vast zone of gray consciences that stands between the great men of evil and the pure victims'.[68] Most historians would probably now subscribe to Michal Unger's position that although Rumkowski was an unpleasant character, he was no traitor; his 'collaboration' was undertaken in the belief that it 'would best serve the Jewish interest'. Besides, the deportations would have occurred with or without him.[69]

65. Epstein, *The Minsk Ghetto*; recent Hebrew studies on Cracow (Yael Peled) and Grodno (Tikva Fatal Knaani) are discussed by Rozett, 'Jewish Resistance' in *HH*, p. 351.
66. Israel Gutman, 'The Distinctiveness of the Lodz Ghetto' in *The Last Ghetto: Life in the Lodz Ghetto 1940–1944*, ed. Michael Unger (Jerusalem: Yad Vashem, 1995), pp. 17–34.
67. Peter Klein, *Die 'Gettoverwaltung Litzmannstadt' 1940–1944: Eine Dienststelle im Spannungsfeld von Kommunalbürokratie und staatlicher Verfolgungspolitik* (Hamburg: Hamburger Edition, 2009); Andrzej Strzelecki, *The Deportation of Jews from the Łódź Ghetto to KL Auschwitz and Their Extermination: A Description of the Events and the Presentation of Historical Sources* (Oświęcim: Auschwitz-Birkenau State Museum, 2006); Isaiah Trunk, *Łódź Ghetto: A History* (Bloomington: Indiana University Press, 2006). See also the important documentary collections: Lucjan Dobroszycki, ed., *The Chronicle of the Łódź Ghetto 1941–1944* (New Haven: Yale University Press, 1984); Alan Adelson and Robert Lapides, eds., *Łódź Ghetto: Inside a Community under Siege* (New York: Viking, 1989).
68. Primo Levi, *Moments of Reprieve* (London: Abacus, 1987), p. 171. See also Levi, *The Drowned and the Saved* (London: Abacus, 1989), pp. 43–51.
69. Michal Unger, *Reassessment of the Image of Mordechai Chaim Rumkowski* (Jerusalem: Yad Vashem, 2004), p. 52; Richard L. Rubenstein, 'Gray into Black: The Case of Mordecai

Two books in particular stand out in the historiography of Łódź: Andrea Löw's and Gordon Horwitz's.[70] Both bring together perpetrator and victim histories in a powerful, affecting way. Horwitz brings out Rumkowski's arrogance and cites his conceited belief that 'no German would dare touch my prerogatives, and I shall never let any do so'. But he also demonstrates quite clearly that for the Germans, Rumkowski was 'a subordinate being, an instrument of German policy' and that the ghetto he governed 'would continue to exist only so long as his German superiors remained convinced that it served their interests'.[71] Horwitz's major innovation, along the lines of the 'regional studies' that I discuss below, is to show how the ghetto developed in the context of the city of Litzmannstadt, as Łódź was renamed in April 1940. Litzmannstadt was in the Warthegau, that is, the part of Poland that was incorporated into the Reich, and was thus in the process of being Germanized. What Rumkowski could not know was that, however useful his ghetto was to the German economy in the short term, future plans for the development of Litzmannstadt left no place for either the ghetto or the Jews.

Löw's monograph seeks to build on Friedländer's attempt in *Nazi Germany and the Jews* to present the Jewish victims 'not merely as an anonymous mass but individuals who had a history of their own until their deaths'. She brings Polish and Yiddish sources into consideration, quite an advance on general histories of the ghettos such as Gustavo Corni's (which nevertheless remains the best synthesis).[72] Her book thus focuses less on the usual debates—the role of the ghettos in the development of the killing process—but the reaction of the Jews to their ghettoization. On the other hand, Löw also intervenes in debates—dominated by Israeli historians—over the *Judenräte* and Jewish resistance. The result is that her book offers an unusually wide perspective on the ghetto, combining sensitivity to the everyday life of the ghetto's inhabitants with analyses of the documents concerning the Nazi administration and, under Greiser's command,

Chaim Rumkowski' in *Gray-Zones*, eds. Petropoulos and Roth, pp. 299–310, is more condemnatory; Shmuel Huppert, 'King of the Ghetto: Mordecai Haim Rumkowski, the Elder of Lodz Ghetto', *YVS*, 15 (1983), pp. 125–58.

70. Michal Unger's *Lodz: The Last Ghetto in Poland* (Jerusalem: Yad Vashem, 2005) is currently only in Hebrew. For a detailed review and comparison with Löw's book, see Samuel Kassow, 'The Case of Lodz: New Research on the Last Ghetto', *YVS*, 35, 2 (2008), pp. 245–266.

71. Gordon J. Horwitz, *Ghettostadt: Łódź and the Making of a Nazi City* (Cambridge, MA: Harvard University Press, 2008), pp. 127, 131.

72. Gustavo Corni, *Hitler's Ghettos: Voices from a Beleaguered Society 1939–1944* (London: Arnold, 2002).

liquidation of the ghetto. Löw discusses the surprisingly large number of people of all ages and classes who committed themselves to writing about the ghetto, and she explicitly joins with them in offering her book as a memento against forgetting and, in David Patterson's words, in opposition to the 'confusion of life and death' that the Nazi assault brought about.[73]

Many ghetto inhabitants turned to writing or other cultural activities, whether alone or in community organizations, to try to make sense of this confusion. Charting and understanding the responses of victims has thus been a large historiographical enterprise in its own right, from the Oneg Shabbat archive onwards, and especially in the postwar years in Israel.[74] Often cultural activities such as theatre or musical performances are considered as forms of resistance, as, often, are religious activities. As with armed resistance, the literature on culture in the ghetto has become far more sophisticated in the last twenty years. Few historians see cultural activities simply as resistance, not even necessarily as forms of 'spiritual resistance'. Historians have become much more alive to the possibility that the Nazis may have tolerated such cultural or educational activities as types of 'permitted dissent', making their rule easier.

Rebecca Rovit perceptively explains that there can be no 'all-encompassing explanation for such performances'. 'Art,' she notes, 'served many purposes; for example, some camp guards and officials misused art to benefit themselves or to humiliate prisoners. For some prisoners, performing theatre was a personal restorative or a mental escape. For others, it was a calculated means to extra rations or better housing.' Shirli Gilbert, in her book on music and the Holocaust, makes a similar point. Whilst it was certainly the case that in certain settings—the Vilna ghetto, for example—concertgoers experienced a temporary escape from a harsh reality (though one would be hard pushed to call this resistance), in others, such as Sachsenhausen, Jews were more likely to experience 'musical torture'.[75] Jewish camp inmates were often coerced into playing music, and in the ghettos, Gilbert notes, cultural activities may have been implicitly accepted. 'In an ironic inversion of the spiritual resistance

---

73. Andrea Löw, *Juden im Getto Litzmannstadt: Lebensbedingungen, Selbstwahrnehmung, Verhalten* (Göttingen: Wallstein, 2006); David Patterson, 'Death and Ghetto Death' in *Life in the Ghettos*, ed. Sterling, p. 164.

74. Ofer, 'The Strength of Remembrance'.

75. Rebecca Rovit, 'Cultural Ghettoization and Theater During the Holocaust: Performance as a Link to Community', *HGS*, 19, 3 (2005), p. 460; Shirli Gilbert, *Music in the Holocaust: Confronting Life in the Nazi Ghettos and Camps* (Oxford: Clarendon Press, 2005), p. 132.

argument', she writes of the Warsaw ghetto, 'it seems that music was one of many activities tolerated by the SS precisely because by diverting their attention from what was happening to them, it helped in deflecting any urge on the part of the victims to resist.'[76] Nevertheless, we should note that music and theatre were important elements in providing communal cohesion and, in certain circumstances—Czech-language reviews and cabarets in Theresienstadt, for example—could mock the Nazi authorities. Karel Švenk's revue, the Last Cyclist (1943), was a thinly veiled attack on a dictator who persecutes cyclists, only defeated by the brave actions of a surviving cyclist; although the Jewish Council of Elders banned it because its anti-Nazi allegory was so blatant, some of the songs crept into Švenk's next revue, The Same but Different.[77]

Musical and theatrical performances in the ghettos did not take place in a cultural vacuum but connected to familiar traditions. As Rovit reminds us, 'art did not arise simply as a response to being incarcerated. Cultural traditions did not disappear during the Holocaust years',[78] so we should perhaps not be surprised that the human urge to creativity expressed itself even in the most nightmarish settings. Although, as Christoph Daxelmüller writes, it seems inappropriate to speak of 'culture' in the concentration camps, nevertheless the evidence shows that one cannot simply dismiss the notion.[79] Holocaust diaries suggest, as Amos Goldberg notes, that 'Selfhood as identity, continuity, coherence, unity, and the capability of giving meaning to the world and to oneself hardly exists in these narratives';[80] yet the desire to find meaning—even if it was defeated—was always present.

Even though the ghettos do not mark the lowest point of the victims' experience of the Holocaust—some illusion of autonomous life was present in a way that was not true of the camps—we should hardly be shocked that ghetto reality crushed the Jews. Larissa Tiedens argues that the reason there was an uprising in Warsaw but not in Łódź is that residents in Warsaw lost any hope for the future whilst those in Łódź did not.[81] And Michael Marrus

76. Gilbert, Music in the Holocaust, p. 37.
77. Rovit, 'Cultural Ghettoization', p. 471. See also Anne D. Dutlinger, ed., Art, Music, and Education as Strategies for Survival: Theresienstadt, 1941–45 (New York: Herodias, 2000).
78. Rovit, 'Cultural Ghettoization', p. 462.
79. Christoph Daxelmüller, 'Kulturelle Formen und Aktivitäten als Teil der Überlebens- und Vernichtungsstrategie in den Konzentrationslagern' in Die nationalsozialistischen Konzentrationslager, eds. Herbert, Orth and Dieckmann, Vol. 2, pp. 983–1005.
80. Amos Goldberg, Holocaust Diaries as Life Stories (Jerusalem: Yad Vashem, 2004).
81. Larissa Z. Tiedens, 'Optimism and the Revolt of the Oppressed: A Comparison of Two Polish Jewish Ghettos of World War II', Political Psychology, 18, 1 (1997), pp. 45–69.

describes the arduousness of life in the ghettos through the pun of 'killing time'.[82] The ghettos are no longer only analysed as way-stations to death in the Nazis' decision-making process, but as phenomena in Jewish history, and the competing and co-existing realities that historians describe reveal complex societies, populated by real people, not just Nazi playthings. As Kassow writes of the Oneg Shabbat archive, it 'reminded posterity that in death, as in life, East European Jewry was a people, not a religious group or a community of martyrs. As a people it had its heroes and villains, its share of failures and successes.'[83] Ultimately though, the ghettos, of whatever sort, were united in one thing. As Bender writes, for all the differences between the ghettos that historians are now investigating, 'all the ghettos had one thing in common: they were all doomed to extinction'.[84]

Regional Studies

Referring to Ukraine, Brandon and Lower explain very neatly the reasons why it took so long to produce detailed local studies. Apart from the long-running intentionalist–functionalist debate, the main obstacle was what they term an 'Auschwitz syndrome':

> For understandable reasons, many historians, philosophers, and political scientists as well as the general public focused on the killing centers and the use of railroads to deport Jews to Auschwitz-Birkenau, as well as to Sobibor, Chelmno, Belzec, Majdanek, and Treblinka, where altogether as many as 3 million men, women, and children were gassed and cremated in the way a factory receives and processes raw materials and disposes of the remnants. A uniquely horrific and criminal invention on the part of Nazi Germany, Auschwitz became the central symbol of modernity derailed, the nadir of Western civilization. Almost inevitably, academic and public interest in one aspect was bound to lead to neglect elsewhere. Country and regional studies had to wait.[85]

Nevertheless, with some consensus in the earlier debate and the realization that a single Hitler order was unlikely to be found, and with the possibilities

82. Michael R. Marrus, 'Killing Time: Jewish Perceptions During the Holocaust' in *The Holocaust: History and Memory: Essays Presented in Honor of Israel Gutman*, eds. Shmuel Almog et al. (Jerusalem: Yad Vashem, 2001), pp. 10–38.
83. Kassow, *Who Will Write Our History?*, p. 386.   84. Bender, *The Jews of Białystok*, p. 293.
85. Ray Brandon and Wendy Lower, 'Introduction' in *The Shoah in Ukraine: History, Testimony, Memorialization*, eds. Brandon and Lower (Bloomington: Indiana University Press, 2008), p. 6.

of accessing new archival material, scholars could turn to more local studies.[86] From the research conducted since the end of the Cold War, then, we now have in-depth studies of the Holocaust in most regions of central and eastern Europe. Remarkably, until a decade or so ago, historians actually knew very little about the ways in which genocidal policies developed in the *Generalgouvernement*, in the Wartheland, in Ukraine, Belorussia, the Baltic States, or Romania. Now each of these places has at least one major study devoted to it.

These studies have mostly been carried out by German scholars, and many of them have been PhD or *Habilitation* (post-doctoral) theses. As a result, the level of empirical detail is very great (indeed, sometimes overwhelming). But what they tend to show is that local decision-making needs to be understood as very much part of the process by which the Jews came to be isolated and targeted. For example, in his study of the Wartheland, Michael Alberti shows that the decision to create ghettos in Łódź and elsewhere in the Gau in early 1940 was a result of the fact that earlier plans to deport the Jews to the *Generalgouvernement* had to be aborted, and that these decisions were made not in Berlin but by regional and local administrators. Only later, from summer 1941, once Jews from the *Altreich* and elsewhere were to be deported to Łódź, were the ghettos closed (with the exception of Łódź) and the Jews of the Warthegau were murdered at Chełmno.[87] By contrast, the Jews of the Radom district were murdered as part of Operation Reinhard

86. 'Regional studies' include: Walter Manoschek, *"Serbien ist Judenfrei"*: *Militärische Besatzungspolitik und Judenvernichtung in Serbien 1941–1942* (Munich: R. Oldenbourg, 1993); Christian Gerlach, *Kalkulierte Morde: Die deutsche Wirtschafts- und Vernichtungspolitik in Weißrußland 1941–1944* (Hamburg: Hamburger Edition, 1999); Dieter Pohl, *Nationalsozialistische Judenverfolgung in Ostgalizien 1941–1944: Organisation und Durchführung eines staatlichen Massenverbrechens* (Munich: R. Oldenbourg, 1997); Thomas Sandkühler, *'Endlösung' in Galizien: Der Judenmord in Ostpolen und die Rettungsinitiativen des Berthold Bietz* (Bonn: Dietz, 1996); Bernhard Chiari, *Alltag hinter der Front: Besatzung, Kollaboration und Widerstand in Weissrussland, 1941–1944* (Düsseldorf: Droste, 1998); Götz Aly, *'Final Solution': Nazi Population Policy and the Murder of the European Jews* (London: Arnold, 1999); Bogdan Musial, *Deutsche Zivilverwaltung und Judenverfolgung im Generalgouvernement: Eine Fallstudie zum Distrikt Lublin 1939–1944* (Wiesbaden: Harrasowitz, 1999); Christian Gerlach and Götz Aly, *Das letzte Kapitel: Realpolitik, Ideologie und der Mord an den ungarischen Juden 1944/45* (Stuttgart: DVA, 2002); Andrej Angrick and Peter Klein, *Die 'Endlösung' im Ghetto Riga: Ausbeutung und Vernichtung 1941–1944* (Darmstadt: Wissenschaftliche Buchgesellschaft, 2006); Chad Bryant, *Prague in Black: Nazi Rule and Czech Nationalism* (Cambridge, MA: Harvard University Press, 2007). See, for a summary, Ulrich Herbert, ed., *National Socialist Extermination Policies: Contemporary German Perspectives and Controversies* (New York: Berghahn, 2000).
87. Michael Alberti, *Die Verfolgung und Vernichtung der Juden im Reichsgau Wartheland 1939–1945* (Wiesbaden: Harrasowitz, 2006).

and the historian of the region places less stress on local decision-making, detailing instead the ways in which Himmler's orders were implemented by Globocnik and his staff, including Ukrainian 'Hiwis'.[88]

Finally, of course, as is clear from the above discussion, these studies are resolutely perpetrator-centric. This means that we are offered a detailed reconstruction of the unfolding of genocidal policies, as seen through the eyes of those organizing the occupation and carrying out the murders. Given the significant archival research involved, most of it carried out in eastern Europe, this achievement should not be disparaged. But it is, nevertheless, only part of the story. Historically speaking, the occupied populations barely appear, other than sometimes as collaborators, looters, or forced labourers. And psychologically, there is something about the German empirical tradition, with its total immersion in factual material, that can (but need not necessarily) act as a barrier to the horror of the events being described. Omer Bartov criticizes this sort of regional study, advocating a more detailed micro-analysis of inter-ethnic relations in particular localities (in his case, Buczacz, in eastern Galicia). It is worth citing him to get a flavour of the marked changes that are occurring in the historiography. Barely have the regional studies begun to make their presence felt (few have been translated into English), when they are being in some ways superseded by a new approach:

> Such works are helpful in providing the framework of the genocide but not very useful in depicting the reality on the ground for the populations involved—namely, the Jews targeted for extermination, on the one hand, and their neighbours, who not only suffered under foreign occupations but also, in part, profited from the killing of the Jews and the massacres and expulsions of other populations, on the other. Indeed, most of these studies do not make any use of testimonies, or utilize them only in a sketchy and anecdotal manner; they also rarely demonstrate any knowledge of the Jewish experience or of the relations between Jews and gentiles on the local level.[89]

What Bartov is calling for is a kind of 'thick description', to use anthropologist Clifford Geertz's famous term, an investigation that burrows deep down in the hope of illuminating wider questions, including the histories of racial hatred and inter-ethnic collaboration, of complex, multilingual and multiethnic regions, and of the part played by grey zones in which people

---

88. Jacek Andrzej Młynarczyk, *Judenmord in Zentralpolen: Der Distrikt Radom im Generalgouvernement 1939–1945* (Darmstadt: Wissenschaftliche Buchgesellschaft, 2007).
89. Omer Bartov, 'Eastern Europe as the Site of Genocide', *JMH*, 80, 3 (2008), p. 583.

could—in contrast to postwar communist or, indeed, many Jewish survivor narratives—be both victim and victimizer, suffer under a brutal occupation and steal property of murdered Jews. His aim is to integrate research on the Holocaust in eastern Europe with the broader historiography of the Holocaust, 'and at the same time linking the history of the Holocaust to local histories of East European countries'.[90] Examples already exist: Bartov's own work on Buczacz, Shimon Redlich on Brzeżany, John Czaplicka on Lviv, Holly Case on Cluj (Koloszvar/Klausenberg);[91] more are forthcoming. Where the regional studies tend to overstate the significance of the periphery for the decision-making process, such microhistories reveal that the local studies are the best way of understanding how war, occupation, and genocide were experienced by European, especially eastern European populations.

Both in the vein of the regional studies but also reacting against their (over)emphasis on the periphery, several historians have recently reasserted the centrality of Auschwitz and the culmination of the murder process in the gas chambers. The camp has never disappeared from the popular imagination, where it has become the iconic image of the Holocaust. But in the scholarly studies, the stress on the periphery, on the occupation of eastern Europe, on the face-to-face killings of 1941–42, and on the polycratic nature of the occupation regime have all conspired to place the emphasis elsewhere in recent years. One should note first, then, that Auschwitz (Oświęcim) lends itself particularly well to the 'regional studies' treatment; the camp was situated in *Ostoberschlesien* (East Upper Silesia), part of Poland that, after some deliberation, was annexed to the Reich, and thus the region was subjected to the full panoply of 'population management' measures in which the Nazis engaged. Not only Jews were dealt with—first shipped out of Oświęcim, a town with some 7,000–8,000 Jewish inhabitants before 1939 (with the largest kosher vodka factory in Poland)—and then brought back to be murdered in 1943 (relatively late, despite the proximity of the camp, because Jews in East Upper Silesia were used as forced labourers). Catholic Poles too were 'resettled' and Auschwitz

90. Bartov, 'Eastern Europe', p. 591.
91. Shimon Redlich, *Together and Apart in Brzezany: Poles, Jews, and Ukrainians, 1919–1945* (Bloomington: Indiana University Press, 2002); John Czaplicka, ed., *Lviv: A City in the Crosscurrents of Culture* (Cambridge, MA: Harvard University Press, 2005); Holly Case, *Between States: The Transylvanian Question and the European Idea During World War II* (Stanford: Stanford University Press, 2009).

was designated a 'model town' for ethnic German resettlement.[92] As Peter Hayes summarizes, Auschwitz became the emblematic camp because 'it became an ensemble of the main elements in Germanization policy in the conquered East: a concentration camp for the people displaced, a "model city" for those supplanting them, and a massive factory where both groups at least for a time, and on very different terms, would find employment.'[93]

These findings are important but, as Michael Thad Allen points out, a 'regional study' of Auschwitz also risks exaggerating the role played by peripheral actors. 'If', he writes, 'the first generation saw the Holocaust as a catastrophe of modern organized society, regional studies now imply the opposite.'[94] Allen in turn perhaps overstates the extent to which the regional studies stress discontinuities and ad hoc, local decision-making, but he asks an important question: 'did the Holocaust at Auschwitz result from the distinctive synthesis of modern technology, science, corporations and the state integral to the matrix of industrial societies? Or were the gas chambers merely an accident of "mission creep"?'[95] In asking this question, Allen does not imply that Lower and Brandon's 'Auschwitz syndrome' is not relevant; rather, that the detailed work on the context of the Holocaust in eastern Europe should not obscure the fact that Berlin was the place where real decision-making power resided, and that Auschwitz was indeed the culminating point of the Nazi genocide. Regional studies have displaced the somewhat clichéd image of industrial murder, but we should not forget that industrial murder was the final stage of the killing process. By examining the development of the design and production of the gas chambers, Allen shows that there was 'far more continuity of intention and design than the current consensus regarding Auschwitz

92. Robert Jan Van Pelt and Debórah Dwork, *Auschwitz 1270 to the Present* (New Haven: Yale University Press, 1996); Sybille Steinbacher, *'Musterstadt' Auschwitz: Germanisierungspolitik und Judenmord in Ostoberschlesien* (Munich: K. G. Saur, 2000); Steinbacher, *Auschwitz: A History* (London: Penguin, 2005); Steinbacher, 'In the Shadow of Auschwitz: The Murder of the Jews of East Upper Silesia' in *National Socialist Extermination Policies*, ed. Herbert, pp. 276–305; Franciszek Piper, 'Die Rolle des Lagers Auschwitz bei der Verwiklichung der nationalsozialistischen Ausrottungspolitik: Die doppelte Funktion von Auschwitz als Konzentrationslager und als Zentrum der Judenvernichtung' in *Die nationalsozialistischen Konzentrationslager*, eds. Herbert, Orth and Dieckmann, Vol. 1, pp. 390–414.

93. Peter Hayes, 'Auschwitz, Capital of the Holocaust', *HGS*, 17, 2 (2003), p. 343. Hayes believes that Steinbacher exaggerates the importance of short-term factors in the rise to prominence of the camp.

94. Michael Thad Allen, 'Not Just a "Dating Game": Origins of the Holocaust at Auschwitz in the Light of Witness Testimony', *GH*, 25, 2 (2007), p. 166, referring to work by Pohl and Sandkühler.

95. Allen, 'Not Just a "Dating Game" ', p. 167.

allows for'. Indeed, 'the tight coupling of central SS offices in Berlin with diverse locations in the occupied east as well as sub-contractors as far afield as Hamburg or Erfurt' presents a counter-image to that of fragmented command chains or 'cumulative radicalization'.[96] Allen's major finding is that the creation of the gas chambers destined for Auschwitz took place in October–November 1941, and thus that 'Auschwitz was not marginal during the origins of the Final Solution'. This does not overthrow the findings of the regional studies, but incorporates them into a broader narrative, one stressing '[c]ontinuity, interconnection, and coordination', and 'not spontaneous, disconnected, local initiative'.[97]

On the significance of the regional studies to the historiography of the Holocaust in general, perhaps the last word should go to Christopher Browning. In the light of his study of the centre-periphery question in the context of the occupation regime in Brest-Litovsk, Browning concludes:

> local initiatives that suited the purposes and policies of the regime—such as early killings by Police Battalion 309 and the Tilsit commando—were seized upon and institutionalized with alacrity. Local initiatives—such as the use of Jewish labour in Brest—that clashed with the long-term goals and policies of the regime were temporarily tolerated but brushed aside when the time came. But local initiatives that challenged the regime's policies in principle—such as Arwed Kempf's failure to ghettoize the Jews of Kovel—were crushed with draconic severity.[98]

In examining local initiative and scope for action, historians have taught us much about the timing, mechanics, and perpetration of the Holocaust that was unknown some twenty years ago. But ultimately, power resided in Berlin, as is confirmed by the now vast historiography of perpetrators, to which I now turn.

Perpetrators

In the early 1980s, historians could rightly say that 'No adequate study exists about the perpetrators of the Holocaust'.[99] Especially in Germany, *Täterforschung* (perpetrator research) has grown exponentially in the last

96. Allen, 'Not Just a "Dating Game" ', p. 179.
97. Allen, 'Not Just a "Dating Game" ', pp. 187, 188.
98. Browning, *Nazi Policy, Jewish Workers, German Killers*, p. 142.
99. Henry Friedlander, 'The Perpetrators' in *Genocide: Critical Issues of the Holocaust*, eds. Alex Grobman and Daniel Landes (Los Angeles: Simon Wiesenthal Center, 1983), p. 155.

decade, as the postwar generations finally began researching the questions that they had been afraid to ask their parents and grandparents.[100] From pioneering studies of individuals such as Ulrich Herbert's biography of Werner Best, one of the leaders of the Gestapo and later of occupied France and Denmark, to prosopographical studies of major institutions such as Christopher Browning on the Foreign Office and Michael Wildt on the SD, to photographic records of the *Weltanschauungskrieg* in eastern Europe,[101] a literature has emerged whose aim, in Peter Longerich's words, is 'to offer explanations for the crime of the century'.[102] In only a few years, we have reached a situation where ignorance and stereotypes have been replaced by such a wealth of detail that it is almost impossible to make any sort of general statements about perpetrators, so varied and heterogeneous do they appear. Thus, whilst explanations can be offered, no consensus prevails.

   The debate was kick-started by Browning's book *Ordinary Men* (1992), and developed in the context of the responses to Goldhagen's *Hitler's Willing Executioners* and the Wehrmacht exhibition after 1995. Browning depicted the activities of Order Police Battalion 101 in Poland, showing how a group of men who were not part of the SS and who came from ordinary backgrounds, developed into mass murderers, as part of the face-to-face killing process in occupied eastern Europe; he thus confirmed Raul Hilberg's earlier claim that 'Ordinary men were to perform extraordinary tasks.'[103] He did not deny that ideology was important, but showed that the men of Battalion 101 were not committed Nazi fanatics; rather, the

100. See Gerhard Paul, 'Von Psychopathen, Technokraten des Terrors und "ganz gewöhnlichen" Deutschen: Die Täter der Shoah im Spiegel der Forschung' in *Die Täter der Shoah: Fanatische Nationalsozialisten oder ganz normale Deutsche?*, ed. Paul (Göttingen: Wallstein, 2002), pp. 13–90.
101. Ulrich Herbert, *Best: Biographische Studien über Radikalismus, Weltanschauung und Vernunft, 1903–1989* (Bonn: Dietz, 1996); Christopher R. Browning, *The Final Solution and the German Foreign Office: A Study of Referat D III of Abteilung Deutschland 1940–43* (New York: Holmes & Meier, 1978); Michael Wildt, *Generation des Unbedingten: Das Führungskorps des Reichssicherheitshauptamtes* (Hamburg: Hamburger Edition, 2002); Wildt, *Generation of the Unbound: The Leadership Corps of the Reich Security Main Office* (Jerusalem: Yad Vashem, 2002); Klaus-Michael Mallmann, Volker Riess, and Wolfram Pyta, *Deutscher Osten 1939–1945: Der Weltanschauungskrieg in Photos und Texten* (Darmstadt: Wissenschaftliche Buchgesellschaft, 2003).
102. Peter Longerich, 'Tendenzen und Perspektiven der Täterforschung', *Aus Politik und Zeit-geschichte*, 14–15 (2 April 2007), p. 7.
103. Raul Hilberg, *The Destruction of the European Jews*, rev. edn (New Haven: Yale University Press, 1985), Vol. 3, p. 994.

men grew into their role for mundane reasons such as peer pressure, group dynamics, excessive alcohol consumption, and the brutalizing effects of the war. Browning concluded his study by noting: 'Within virtually every social collective, the peer group exerts tremendous pressure on behaviour and sets moral norms.' He then ended with the now famous question: 'If the men of Reserve Police Battalion 101 could become killers under such circumstances, what group of men cannot?'[104] Research on the question of perpetrators has since sought to answer that question by examining 'circumstances' and, especially, ideological motivation. The literature has been developed on the one hand by social psychologists, notably Harald Welzer, James Waller, and Steven K. Baum, and on the other hand by historians such as Jürgen Matthäus, Gerhard Paul, and Konrad Kwiet. The social psychological literature concludes, quite reasonably, that Holocaust perpetrators—and perpetrators of other genocides—are overwhelmingly not sadists, but 'normal' people in unusual situations.[105] This situationist account is probably accepted by most historians too by now, especially when examining lower-level perpetrators.[106]

What the historians add to the explanation are descriptions of the unusual situations and how they developed, that is to say, they bring the cultural and social factors into play that account for the situations in which perpetrators find themselves (or that they create for themselves). In particular, they have queried the notion of 'normal'; whilst many perpetrators may have been mentally stable, they for the most part lived through World War I and its aftermath and the crises of the Weimar years and, under Nazism, were subjected to or themselves promoted fierce antisemitic propaganda. As Andrej Angrick notes of the men of *Einsatzgruppe* D, 'Although it is speculative and, for the historian, risky, it can be claimed with some

104. Christopher R. Browning, *Ordinary Men: Reserve Police Battalion 101 and the Final Solution in Poland* (New York: HarperPerennial, 1993), p. 189.
105. James Waller, *Becoming Evil: How Ordinary People Commit Genocide and Mass Killing* (Oxford: Oxford University Press, 2002); Leonard S. Newman and Ralph Erber, eds., *Understanding Genocide: The Social Psychology of the Holocaust* (Oxford: Oxford University Press, 2002); Paul A. Roth, 'Hearts of Darkness: "Perpetrator History" and Why There Is No Why', *History of the Human Sciences*, 17, 2–3 (2004), pp. 211–51; Harald Welzer, *Täter: Wie aus ganz normalen Menschen Massenmörder werden* (Frankfurt/M: S. Fischer, 2005); Steven K. Baum, *The Psychology of Genocide: Perpetrators, Bystanders, and Rescuers* (Cambridge: Cambridge University Press, 2008).
106. Christian Gerlach, ed., *Durchschnittstäter: Handeln und Motivation* (Berlin: Assoziation Schwarze Risse Rote Straße, 2000).

justification that under a different system, a democratic one, the majority of perpetrators would never have become criminals.'[107] The other side of this coin is that, as Norman Naimark reminds us, with reference to German officers and soldiers: 'There were few "ordinary men" among them; or, better, ordinary German soldiers tended to have strong Nazi views, even if they were not Nazis themselves.'[108] The most striking proof of the perpetrators' 'ordinariness' (though it is perhaps more terrifying than if they were 'mad') is their mental stability after the war; as Konrad Kwiet notes, 'with few exceptions, the murderers were spared the lifelong symptoms of trauma that were and remain the dreadful legacy of the surviving victims'.[109]

This statement seems perfectly true of men like Best, Six, or Paul Werner Hoppe, the commandant of Stutthof, whom Orth identifies as the typical perpetrator: imbued with radical *völkisch* ideas and able to act according to objective, rational calculations; an ideal 'political soldier'.[110] The Camp SS, the Gestapo, and the '*Judenberater*' all conform to this model of educated men carrying out mass murder, as do the men on the next rung down the hierarchy, the SSPF and HSSPF (SS and Police Führer/Higher SS and Police Führer) like Erich von dem

107. Andrej Angrick, *Besatzungspolitik und Massenmord: Die Einsatzgruppe D in der südlichen Sowjetunion 1941–1943* (Hamburg: Hamburger Edition, 2003), p. 387. See also Angrick, 'The Men of *Einsatzgruppe D*: An Inside View of a State-Sanctioned Killing Unit in the "Third Reich" ' in *Ordinary People as Mass Murderers: Perpetrators in Comparative Perspective*, eds. Olaf Jensen and Claus-Christian Szejnmann (Basingstoke: Palgrave Macmillan, 2008), pp. 78–96; Angrick, 'Einsatzgruppe D' in Dieter Pohl and Andrej Angrick, *Einsatzgruppen C and D in the Invasion of the Soviet Union* (London: Holocaust Educational Trust, 2000), pp. 16–32.
108. Norman Naimark, 'War and Genocide on the Eastern Front, 1941–1945', *Contemporary European History*, 16, 2 (2007), p. 274. See also Michael Mann, 'Were the Perpetrators of Genocide "Ordinary Men" or "Real Nazis"? Results from Fifteen Hundred Biographies', *HGS*, 14, 3 (2000), pp. 331–66, and the discussion of Mann's work in Helmut Walser Smith, *The Continuities of German History: Nation, Religion, and Race across the Long Nineteenth Century* (Cambridge: Cambridge University Press, 2008), pp. 227–8.
109. Konrad Kwiet, 'Perpetrators and the Final Solution' in *The Memory of the Holocaust in the 21st Century: The Challenge for Education*, ed. Stephanie McMahon-Kaye (Jerusalem: Yad Vashem, 2001), p. 80. See also Klaus-Michael Mallmann and Andrej Angrick, eds., *Die Gestapo nach 1945: Karrieren, Konflikte, Konstruktionen* (Darmstadt: Wissenschaftliche Buchgesellschaft, 2009).
110. On Hoppe, see Karin Orth, *Die Konzentrationslager-SS: Sozialstrukturelle Analysen und biographische Studien* (Munich: Deutscher Taschenbuch Verlag, 2004), pp. 217–21. See also Orth's discussion of Hoppe in 'Die Kommandanten der nationalsozialistischen Konzentrationslager' in *Die nationalsozialistischen Konzentrationslager*, eds. Herbert, Orth, and Dieckmann, Vol. 2, pp. 755–86. It is worth noting Miroslav Kárný's comments in that volume's next chapter ('Waffen-SS und Konzentrationslager', pp. 787–99), that the ideal-type of 'political soldier' broke down into something altogether more shabby and brutal in the face of the reality of the camps—which these same 'political soldiers' created.

Bach-Zelewski, Friedrich Jeckeln, Friedrich-Wilhelm Krüger, Otto Ohlendorf, Fritz Rauter, and Odilo Globocnik.[111] Even the somewhat unusual Erich Koch, Gauleiter of East Prussia and Reich Commissar of Ukraine, more a highly competent administrator than a Nazi fanatic, followed a familiar trajectory of radicalization during World War I, the *Freikorps*, and the struggle for National Socialist dominance. His success in East Prussia meant that he was one of the very few leaders of the Third Reich whom Hitler was prepared to back against Himmler.[112] Not very many perpetrators fit the stereotypical bill, like Christian Wirth, who was described as a man 'who had no feelings or consideration, who treated people—whether Germans, Jews or Ukrainians—as numbers, or even worse', who had 'an exceptional talent for organization', who 'despised and abused people' and 'was a Jew-hater on an unimaginable scale'.[113]

Claudia Steur writes in her study of 'Eichmann's emissaries' that 'one can say that the *Judenberater*'s way of working was marked by an increasing radicalization and perfectionism'.[114] The emissaries can, according to Steur, be divided into two groups: those with close links to Eichmann and those without. Among the first group were Theodor Dannecker, Dieter Wisliceny, Alois Brunner, Fritz Boßhammer, and Franz Abromeit. In the second group were Kurt Asche, Wilhelm Zoepf, Heinz Röthke, Anton Burger, Gustav Richter, Hermann Krumey, and Otto Hunsche. All were born between 1905 and 1913, lived through World War I as children, and came to maturity in the postwar period. They constitute classic examples of those who had the ground pulled out from underneath their feet by the Weimar crises: 'Almost all the *Judenberater* came from the middle class, which had been especially hard hit by the crisis.' Most were businessmen who joined the NSDAP between 1930 and 1933. A combination of opportunism and craving for social status seems to have been central to their participation: 'The main reasons for their later participation in the murder of the Jews lie in their striving for power, respect and social

111. Ronald Smelser and Enrico Syring, eds., *Die SS: Elite unter dem Totenkopf. 30 Lebensläufe* (Paderborn: Schöningh, 2000) for some of these men.
112. Ralf Meindl, *Ostpreußens Gauleiter: Erich Koch—eine politische Biographie* (Osnabrück: Fibre, 2007).
113. Michael Tregenza, *Christian Wirth: Inspekteur des SS-Sonderkommandos 'Aktion Reinhard'* (1993, typescript held at Wiener Library, London), p. 1, citing Franz Suchomel.
114. Claudia Steur, 'Eichmanns Emissäre: Die "Judenberater" in Hitler's Europa' in *Die Gestapo im Zweiten Weltkrieg: 'Heimatfront' und besetztes Europe*, eds. Gerhard Paul and Klaus-Michael Mallmann (Darmstadt: Primus, 2000), pp. 403–36, here 431.

ascendancy.' Boßhammer, for example, found the measures being taken against the Jews 'terrible and inhuman' and was shocked that he 'should find himself employed in the *Judenreferate*'. But he still took the job: 'Only with "unconditional obedience" could one get the chance to rise to the position of *Regierungsrat*'. 'In the face of their superiors', writes Steur, 'these men made blind belief and obedience the order of the day and identified themselves completely with Hitler's state.'[115]

Globocnik, the subject of a recent biography, is perhaps exceptional, for he allowed his fanaticism to override any notion of dispassionate bureaucratic administration; indeed, it was his demotion from Gauleiter of Vienna (because of corruption) to SS Police Chief in Lublin that gave his violent antisemitic instincts free rein, as he became closely involved in the activities of the *Einsatzgruppen* in the USSR in 1941 and shortly afterwards the key figure in Operation Reinhard.[116] The empirical evidence provided by Orth, Herbert, Steur, and others seems to confirm the cliché of the perpetrators as 'cultured demons'. On the other hand, recent research takes us back to Browning's claim that not all perpetrators were radical ideologues; with reference to the *Einsatzgruppen*, for example, below the leadership level, and especially once conscription and local collaborators had to be used to bolster numbers, one sees a rather heterogeneous group.[117]

Recognizing perpetrator heterogeneity also means that historians are increasingly aware of the important role played by female perpetrators. Although there were only about 3,500 women camp guards (about 10% of the total), trained at Ravensbrück, little is known about most of them. Still, the literature has developed to the extent that there are now synthetic works dealing with female perpetrators, and a so-called *Historikerinnenstreit* (female historians' debate) has broken out in Germany over how female perpetrators should be understood: as victims of a male-oriented ideology, or as perpetrators able, even under Nazism, to act as free agents. Women, the latest research stresses, had multiple roles and considerable room for action.[118]

115. Steur, 'Eichmanns Emissäre', pp. 431, 432, 433, 434. On Dannecker, see Steur, *Theodor Dannecker: Ein Funktionär der 'Endlösung'* (Essen: Klartext, 1997).
116. Berndt Rieger, *Creator of Nazi Death Camps: The Life of Odilo Globocnik* (London: Vallentine Mitchell, 2007). Unfortunately, the author seems more interested in Globocnik's personal life than in the broader context necessary for a 'political biography'.
117. Klaus-Michael Mallmann, 'Menschenjagd und Massenmord: Das neue Instrument der Einsatzgruppen und—kommandos 1938–1945' in *Die Gestapo im Zweiten Weltkrieg*, eds. Mallmann and Paul, p. 304.
118. Among many publications, see for example: Kathrin Kompisch, *Täterinnen: Frauen im Nationalsozialismus* (Cologne: Böhlau, 2008); Christina Herkommer, 'Women under National

Current research, then, seeks to balance organizational and situational factors against ideological ones. But of course the two overlap, especially when an organization such as the police was heavily impregnated with ideological training. Still, most historians agree that an emphasis solely on ideology, as if it comes from nowhere and has no organizational setting, is inappropriate. Edward Westermann, for example, writing about Order Police battalions in occupied eastern Europe, writes that 'it is a grave oversight to dismiss the organizational culture of the Uniformed Police in a search for the motive force behind their participation in the conduct of genocide.' This argument—which is a clear criticism of Goldhagen—is based on two findings: the 'militarization' of the police since 1933 and the process of psychologically and physically 'merging' the uniformed police with the SS since June 1936, when Himmler assumed control of the unified police. These initiatives, Westermann assures us, 'go far to explain the manner in which individual policemen and the police battalions were shaped into instruments of annihilation'.[119] As head of the uniformed police, Kurt Daluege stated in September 1938: 'It can only be a question of time before the entire police coalesces with the SS corps into a permanent unit.'[120] And indeed, 'The police battalions that entered the Soviet Union in the summer of 1941 were led by officers and senior enlisted men whose backgrounds and training, as well as the organizational culture within the police, had prepared them for a war of extermination in the East.'[121] And they acquitted themselves appropriately, Daluege congratulating Himmler that 'For Adolf Hitler, this corps of the SS and the police represents his struggle for a greater Germany, Europe and the world. Its [the SS and police corps'] task is the annihilation of the eternal enemies of all *völkisch* and racially conscious nations.'[122] Westermann still arrives at the conclusion that ideology was important, but tries to present it as the outcome not of an innate national belief system but of deliberately organized institutional frameworks to which the men

Socialism: Women's Scope for Action and the Issue of Gender', and Irmtraud Heike, 'Female Concentration Camp Guards as Perpetrators: Three Case Studies', both in *Ordinary People as Mass Murderers*, eds. Jensen and Szejnmann, pp. 99–119 and 120–42; Susannah Heschel, 'Does Atrocity Have a Gender? Feminist Interpretations of Women in the SS' in *Lessons and Legacies, Vol. 6*, ed. Diefendorf, pp. 300–21.

119. Edward B. Westermann, 'Shaping the Police Soldier as an Instrument for Annihilation' in *The Impact of Nazism: New Perspectives on the Third Reich and Its Legacy*, eds. Alan E. Steinweis and Daniel E. Rogers (Lincoln: University of Nebraska Press, 2003), p. 131.
120. Cited in Westermann, 'Shaping', p. 137.   121. Westermann, 'Shaping', p. 144.
122. Daluege cited in Westermann, 'Shaping', p. 145.

willingly subscribed; he thus seeks to avoid 'focusing on the ideological forest at the expense of losing sight of the individual trees of human causation'.[123]

The same sense of complexity—and hence greater adherence to human behaviour—informs recent discussions of 'desk killers' versus 'active murderers'. The dominant image of the desk killer, prevalent from the 1960s until the 1990s, cohered largely with the functionalist notion of 'industrial genocide' and reluctance to confront the brutality of the events. We now know that the division is unjustified, for the men most often identified as 'desk killers'—Eichmann and his staff—were actively involved in implementing murderous policies on the ground throughout occupied Europe.[124] Similarly, according to the RSHA's policy of rotation, two-thirds of Gestapo leaders—with their middle-class upbringings, humanist schooling (almost half of them with doctorates in law) and narrow avoidance of military service in 1914–18, were 'actively involved as leaders of *Einsatzgruppen* and-*kommandos* as well as leaders of *Stapo-* and *Sipo*-posts in the mass murder of the Jewish population of the occupied regions'.[125] Clearly, it is wrong to focus only on bureaucratic efficiency or on radical racist passions when Nazism in action combined them so successfully. As George Browder neatly puts it: ' "Committed ideologue" versus "banal bureaucrat" may even be a false dichotomy; they are at best two extremes on a multidimensional spectrum of perpetrators.'[126]

This research, whilst placing greater stress than Browning on ideology, appears to confirm a neo-functionalist perspective for two reasons. First, it places considerable emphasis on decisions made at the periphery rather

---

123. Edward B. Westermann, ' "Ordinary Men" or "Ideological Soldiers"? Police Battalion 310 in Russia, 1942', *German Studies Review*, 21, 1 (1998), p. 42.
124. David Cesarani, *Eichmann: His Life and Crimes* (London: William Heinemann, 2004); Hans Safrian, *Die Eichmann-Männer* (Vienna: Europaverlag, 1993); Yaacov Lozowick, *Hitler's Bureaucrats: The Nazi Security Police and the Banality of Evil* (London: Continuum, 2002). Lozowick is somewhat out of step with most perpetrator research, seeing his subjects as 'monsters' in the manner of postwar stereotypes; see the review by George Browder, 'No Middle Ground for the *Eichmann Männer*?', *YVS*, 31 (2003), pp. 403–24. For an excellent example of a man who was both a desk killer and an actual murderer, see Jürgen Matthäus, 'Georg Heuser—Routinier des sicherheitspolizeilichen Osteinsatzes' in *Karrieren der Gewalt: Nationalsozialistische Täterbiographien*, eds. Klaus-Michael Mallmann and Gerhard Paul (Darmstadt: Wissenschaftliche Buchgesellschaft, 2004), pp. 115–25.
125. Paul, 'Von Psychopathen', p. 45. See also Steur, 'Eichmanns Emissäre' for similar comments on the '*Judenberater*', especially Dannecker and Brunner, who combined bureaucracy and ideological commitment with particular brutality.
126. George C. Browder, 'Perpetrator Character and Motivation: An Emerging Consensus?', *HGS*, 17, 3 (2003), p. 495.

than in Berlin. Second, it suggests that policy developed zig-zag fashion rather than following a pre-ordained blueprint. However, these points are counterbalanced by the fact that many of these studies strongly reassert the primacy of ideology, in that these heterogeneous 'ordinary men' (as well as the smaller number of less ordinary, committed careerist Nazis) operated in a framework suffused with antisemitism as a result of which their actions did not need to be directed, for it was already clear to them who their targets were. Whether they were committed ideologues or criminal '*Exzeßtäter*', their generational, social, religious, educational, and ideological heterogeneity did not get in the way of the production of a homogeneous victim group: 'In the final instance, the Shoah proved to be a collective deed carried out by division of labour on a European scale, to which the most varied perpetrator groups contributed with total devotion.'[127] Irrespective of the fact that the men of the *Einsatzgruppen* came from diverse backgrounds, 'Nevertheless, the Einsatzgruppe developed a horrifyingly "homogeneous" murderous effect, so that an end neither to their lust for conquest nor to the possibility of realizing it appeared foreseeable from a geopolitical or military standpoint in the winter of 1941–42.'[128] This is a conclusion at which Browning also arrives in a later study of the Order Police: 'Clearly the German Order Police was not monolithic', writes Browning, 'but in the end the diversity of attitudes and motives made little difference.'[129]

Perhaps this combination of 'neo-functionalism' and the 'return of ideology' is most fruitfully seen in detailed examinations of the development of the killing process as it occurred on the ground in occupied eastern Europe. Two terms, in particular, seem to sum up well the state of research: Wendy Lower's 'anticipatory obedience' and Jürgen Matthäus's 'controlled escalation'. Between them they capture the sense of the radicalization of policy brought about in the context of the 'war of annihilation', on the one hand, and the interplay between Berlin and the 'wild east', on the other.

In her case study of the *Generalbezirk* Zhytomyr, Lower builds on the 'regional studies' discussed above, to show that one should not go too far in stressing the importance of the periphery rather than the Berlin centre to the murder process. She notes that the regional studies tend to downplay the significance of Hitler, Himmler, and Heydrich, who

127. Paul, 'Von Psychopathen', p. 62.
128. Angrick, *Besatzungspolitik und Massenmord*, p. 450.
129. Browning, *Nazi Policy, Jewish Workers, German Killers*, p. 169.

appear there as shadowy background figures. Actual policy tends to be driven, in these works, by antisemitic and anti-Soviet violence emanating from the Wehrmacht and the occupation authorities more than by central directive. By contrast, Lower shows that, at least in the Zhytomyr region, an acceleration of violence followed visits to the area by Hitler, Himmler, and Jeckeln in the first months of the occupation. She notes several reasons for the escalation of anti-Jewish massacres: 'the direct involvement of Reich leaders who pressured their subordinates to kill more Jews, the accumulation and expansion of available killing forces in the region, and the collaboration of local commanders from the Wehrmacht and SS-Police, who proved to be efficient killers.'[130] Lower then demonstrates this interrelationship between centre and periphery, using examples such as the construction of Hitler's 'Werewolf' bunker just north of Vinnytsia and the close involvement of Hitler's personal SS escort, the Reich Security Service (RSD) under *SS-Gruppenführer* Hans Rattenhuber, in massacres of Jews in Vinnytsia, and Himmler's speech to senior SS and police leaders at his Hegewald compound in September 1942: 'Do not cling to your desk, instead make decisions in the field!'[131] Her conclusion, which even the term 'anticipatory obedience' understates to some extent, is that 'while German leaders at the periphery often acted independently, the highest Nazi leaders—whether physically present or indirectly involved—shaped events at the local level to a far greater extent than most authors of regional studies would accept.'[132] Peter Longerich's recent biography of Himmler confirms Lower's argument. After reviewing Himmler's activities in the occupied areas of the USSR after June 1941, Longerich concludes that Himmler's 'breathtaking travel schedule' in the first months after the invasion of the Soviet Union shows that he did everything possible to turn the mass execution of Soviet Jews into a comprehensive genocide, and that the transition to the systematic murder of the Jewish civilian population in the areas where his killing units were operating was brought about on his decisive initiative.[133]

More recently, Lower's viewpoint has received corroboration—and nuance—from a study of the first stages of Operation Barbarossa. Jürgen

130. Wendy Lower, ' "Anticipatory Obedience" and the Nazi Implementation of the Holocaust in the Ukraine: A Case Study of Central and Peripheral Forces in the Generalbezirk Zhytomyr, 1941–1944', *HGS*, 16, 1 (2002), pp. 4–5.
131. Lower, ' "Anticipatory Obedience" ', p. 13.
132. Lower, ' "Anticipatory Obedience" ', p. 13.
133. Peter Longerich, *Heinrich Himmler: Biographie* (Munich: Siedler, 2008), esp. pp. 543–58.

Matthäus's starting point is the opposite side of the coin from Lower's: he welcomes the regional studies since he thinks that most scholars have devoted too much time on the centre; but he agrees that more work is needed on the interplay between centre and periphery in order to understand the nature of the violence that was unleashed in the early stages of the war in the Soviet Union. Looking at the town of Garsden (Gargždai) in Lithuania, Matthäus shows how the local SS/SD leaders, Hans-Joachim Böhme and Werner Hersmann, spoke with Himmler and Heydrich, both of whom had been in the region. According to Böhme, the SS leaders 'received information from me on the measures initiated by the Stapostelle Tilsit and sanctioned them completely'. Most of the Lithuanian Jews were killed by *Einsatzkommando* 3, a sub-unit of *Einsatzgruppe* A, under Karl Jäger, but Böhme's men had still murdered 3,302 Jews by 18 July 1941. Matthäus's conclusion is that 'The beginnings of the Holocaust in Lithuania suggest that the push for these extreme "measures" came from officers in the field who at the time offered various justifications for their actions; references to specific orders are notably absent.'[134] Matthäus, then, places slightly more emphasis than Lower on the initiatives of the local leaders, but still notes the importance for them of having these actions legitimized by the centre and agrees with Lower that the presence of senior SS and police chiefs expedited the murder process and/or 'established this type of killing as standard operating procedure'.[135] Matthäus and Lower further agree on the vital role played by local collaborators, on the role of ideological indoctrination—'Himmler's indoctrination program and his men's eagerness to accept the leadership's legitimization of anti-Jewish violence mutually reinforced each other'[136]—and the importance of orders from the centre in radicalizing action on the ground. Matthäus cites Gestapo chief Heinrich Müller, from a speech of September 1941, to this effect: 'in the absence of written orders, they had to "get used to reading between the lines and acting accordingly"'.[137] Like Lower's 'anticipatory obedience', Matthäus's 'controlled escalation' is based on the claim that the Holocaust emerged neither from a top-down, order-driven approach, nor from grassroots initiatives alone that were then retrospectively endorsed by the

---

134. Jürgen Matthäus, 'Controlled Escalation: Himmler's Men in the Summer of 1941 and the Holocaust in the Occupied Soviet Territories', *HGS*, 21, 2 (2007), p. 223.
135. Matthäus, 'Controlled Escalation', p. 224.
136. Matthäus, 'Controlled Escalation', p. 229.
137. Matthäus, 'Controlled Escalation', p. 234.

leadership; rather, escalation was driven 'by the eagerness of subordinate officers to adopt new, more radical measures',[138] a process involving consensual negotiation between centre and periphery.

These studies confirm Ian Kershaw's claims concerning the onset of the Holocaust in the Wartheland.[139] They show how consensual decision-making was arrived at through a combination of top-down orders from the centre and initiative at the periphery, through improvization and experiment arriving at what subordinates thought was required of them. In other words, they illustrate what Kershaw means by 'working towards the Führer', creating in the process a 'community of violence' in which the perpetrators, from various social backgrounds and ideological positions, ended up at the same place: very few failed to fulfil the gruesome task they were set.[140] Thus, whilst, as Bloxham notes, historians may have exaggerated the extent to which division—even duplication—of labour in the Third Reich meant conflict among the 'polycracy' of competing agencies, it would be equally false to 'go to the opposite extreme and label the genocidal state as just another manifestation of the "network society" '.[141] Particularly when representatives of the Nazi leadership were present, the dynamic of genocide got a radicalizing boost; and in their absence, the different agents involved, in the context of the institutional frameworks of their various affiliations, acted to realize the 'Führer's will': ideological indoctrination, at the level of the Order Police and Wehrmacht as well as the SS/SD, was more significant than historians have realized, and 'High- and mid-ranking organizational men came together in a form of consensus politics that allowed subordinates to lead even as they followed.'[142]

The impact of these empirical studies is clear in the synthetic works. Scholars who have previously taken an intentionalist standpoint now modify their interpretations so as not to suggest that there is a simple link between idea and act. They insist on the importance of ideology, especially antisemitism, but note that ideology provided an overall framework within

---

138. Matthäus, 'Controlled Escalation', p. 233.
139. Ian Kershaw, 'Improvised Genocide? The Emergence of the "Final Solution" in the "Warthegau" ', *Transactions of the Royal Historical Society*, 6th Series (1992), pp. 51–78.
140. Alexander V. Prusin, 'A Community of Violence: The SiPo/SD and Its Role in the Nazi Terror System in Generalbezirk Kiew', *HGS*, 21, 1 (2007), pp. 1–30.
141. Donald Bloxham, 'Organized Mass Murder: Structure, Participation, and Motivation in Comparative Perspective', *HGS*, 22, 2 (2008), p. 218.
142. Jürgen Matthäus, 'An vorderster Front: Voraussetzungen für die Beteiligung der Ord- nungspolizei an der Shoah' in *Die Täter der Shoah*, ed. Paul, pp. 137–66; Bloxham, 'Organized Mass Murder', p. 212.

which policy could still be made on a reactive or ad hoc basis, depending on circumstances. Saul Friedländer provides the most thorough version of this approach, in his *The Years of Extermination* (2007). His explanatory framework of 'redemptive antisemitism' is put forward as the motor of Nazi policy, indeed of the Third Reich as a whole, but the development of *Judenpolitik* was nevertheless bound by broader geopolitical events and was, in his reading, by no means a straightforward implementation of a pre-conceived plan. As for the decision-making process, the nearest thing to a date that Friedländer is willing to offer is his assertion that 'The decision was taken sometime during the last three months of 1941'. The same is true in Peter Longerich's study, *Holocaust* (2010), in which circumstances are seen to radicalize an antisemitism that was always present, and which, in its inner logic, contained the seeds of genocide within itself from the start—on the level of the unconscious, or fantasy—and which developed as the regime faced new challenges, such as the Euthanasia problem and the changing fortunes of the war. As we have seen, the clearest example of this radicalization is the territorial solution, which, in Longerich's view, was genocidal from the outset, but which, in its failure, pointed the way to articulations of outright murder. Longerich also notes that with the changing circumstances of the war after 1942, and the efforts of the Jewish victims of Nazism to influence the perpetrators (through hiding, escape, or negotiation), one runs up against the limits of a pure *Täterforschung* that focuses only on the killers and their actions.[143] These two works represent, for the time being (and probably for some time to come) the pinnacle of the traditional historiography of the Holocaust.[144]

A good summary of what is meant by 'modified intentionalism' can be found in Doris Bergen's *War and Genocide* (2003), where she writes that Hitler 'could be flexible, pragmatic, and responsive to the situation "on the ground", but he took the initiative and provided much of the drive and the will that proved crucial in setting Germany on the path to war and genocide'.[145] But a particularly striking example of an intentionalist position struggling to incorporate neo-functionalist scholarship is to be

143. Longerich, 'Tendenzen und Perspektiven', p. 7.
144. Alon Confino, 'Narrative Form and Historical Sensation: On Saul Friedländer's *The Years of Extermination*', *History and Theory*, 48, 3 (2009), pp. 199–219; Paul Betts and Christian Wiese, eds., *Years of Persecution, Years of Extermination: Saul Friedländer and the Future of Holocaust Studies* (New York: Continuum, 2010).
145. Doris L. Bergen, *War and Genocide: A Concise History of the Holocaust* (Lanham: Rowman & Littlefield, 2003), p. 30.

found in Dan Diner's history of the twentieth century, *Cataclysms*. Diner's short narrative of how the Holocaust developed is a useful précis of the amalgamation of intentionalism with neo-functionalism. 'While the thrust of National Socialism's ideologically driven Jewish policy was towards annihilation,' he writes, 'this does not mean it was programmatically steered from the start.' Rather, the 'juncture between motive and circumstance points the way to the Holocaust'. Although it is 'doubtful whether a clear, administratively effective decision, traceable to specific officials, rests behind the killing process's sequential intensification', it is important for Diner to establish that this was no negligent or accidental slide into genocide: 'Even when what is at stake is a series of distinct but interrelated deeds rather than an elaborate plan driven by a declared will to act, intense deliberation and ideological motivation can be manifestly present.' Especially eye-catching is his use of the terms 'sequential intensification' and 'gliding escalation' to describe the unfolding of the genocidal decision-making process. Here Diner signifies his debt to Mommsen's 'cumulative radicalization', whilst not wishing to identify himself with Mommsen's ultra-functionalist position. Yet he is surprisingly close to Mommsen when he asserts that antisemitic ideology did not need to be pervasive but, as with all ideologies, operated by 'osmosis'. Thus, it was not necessary for all actors to be imbued with all-embracing antisemitism; rather, ideological conviction could remain in the background, and be brought to the fore at key points.[146] Here we see functionalism insofar as Diner permits a narrative that embraces inconsistency, confusion, and contingency, but intentionalism in that 'Despite the Nazi regime's institutional chaos, there was in fact little doubt about who was to be persecuted and finally subjected to "special treatment".' The perpetrators did not even need to hold a strong ideological conviction. 'What mattered far more', he concludes, 'was that they acted *as if* they were so motivated.'[147] Irrespective of the extent to which perpetrators subscribed to antisemitic propaganda, it is clear, in Mark Roseman's words, that 'the "intention", to follow the language of the older debate, was dispersed far more widely than historians once thought . . . we should treat antisemitism not as an abstract dogma, but

---

146. Dan Diner, *Cataclysms: A History of the Twentieth Century from Europe's Edge* (Madison: University of Wisconsin Press, 2008), pp. 166, 167, 176–9.
147. Diner, *Cataclysms*, p. 180. On the 'as if' in determining perpetrators' actions, see Arne Johan Vetlesen, *Evil and Human Agency: Understanding Collective Evildoing* (Cambridge: Cambridge University Press, 2005), pp. 87–89.

effectively as a lens that influenced the way other factors were perceived and evaluated.'[148]

Roseman's claim has clearly influenced the way historians are now thinking about perpetrators. As Michael Wildt suggests, irrespective of other motives, antisemitism seems to have served as the glue that held everything together:

> The prevailing motives may have been very varied: greed, envy and resentment might have driven those involved just as much as explicit hatred of Jews. And even the antisemitic motives may have included varied intentions. . . . But whatever intentions drove them to act, the violence was directed against Jews. . . . Antisemitic praxis allowed the unrestrained expression of all the feelings and resentments that were otherwise socially sanctioned.[149]

And the authors of a recent study of the German public and the Holocaust confirm the importance of an antisemitic consensus: 'the majority of the estimated 200,000 Holocaust perpetrators were not motivated by an internal, personal, desire to kill. . . . Without an implicit anti-Jewish consensus we cannot explain why the large majority of perpetrators accepted the appropriate concept of the enemy so consistently.'[150] Thus, even some notable contributors to the regional studies literature, such as Pohl, are coming to the conclusion that, whilst there is no simple link between ideology and action, the pervasive antisemitism that characterized the Third Reich provided a framework that allowed heterogeneous perpetrators and motives to come together.

What are the limits to such studies? Their achievement, which is their substantial empirical research, also explains their shortcomings. The paradigm is limited: each new study of another Nazi agency adds a wealth of empirical material to the scholarly literature but tends to reaffirm what we already know. Such studies tend to confirm the fears of critics, especially literary critics, who worry that the 'rational' exegesis that defines historical

148. Mark Roseman, 'Ideas, Contexts, and the Pursuit of Genocide, *Bulletin of the German Historical Institute London*, 25, 1 (2003), pp. 65, 83. Also Roseman, 'Beyond Conviction? Perpetrators, Ideas, and Action in the Holocaust in Historiographical Perspective' in *Conflict, Catastrophe, and Continuity: Essays on Modern German History*, eds. Frank Biess, Mark Roseman, and Hanna Schissler (New York: Berghahn, 2007), pp. 83–103.
149. Michael Wildt, 'Gewalt als Partizipation: Der Nationalsozialismus als Ermächtigungsregime' in *Staats-Gewalt: Ausnahmezustand und Sicherheitsregimes. Historische Perspektiven*, eds. Alf Lüdtke and Wildt (Göttingen: Wallstein, 2008), pp. 236–7, 238.
150. Frank Bajohr and Dieter Pohl, *Massenmord und schlechtes Gewissen: Die deutsche Bevölkerung, die NS-Führung und der Holocaust* (Frankfurt/M: Fischer Taschenbuch Verlag, 2008), p. 10.

study, somehow serves to hide the horror of what is being explained
and which motivated such scholarship in the first place. In the German
context, Jürgen Matthäus worries that the emphasis on *Täterforschung* might
unconsciously reflect and reinforce a trend towards *Opferforschung*, that is,
the notion of Germans as victims.[151] Furthermore, what this stressing of
networks, structures, and even ideology and propaganda can overlook,
with its focus on individual and collective biographies, is the question of
whether perpetrators enjoyed their tasks. This is of course a very sensitive
and difficult topic to address, and one can easily understand why the
'Auschwitz syndrome' was so successful. Yet a glance at the photographic
record suggests immediately that perpetrators saw themselves not simply
as bearers of a 'world-historical mission' which they had to undertake,
however distasteful they may have found it. One does not have to delve
very far to see smiling and laughing perpetrators. This is to argue neither
that the perpetrators were sadists nor that German men of this period
were somehow hard-wired to commit violence—the social psychological
literature utterly scotches such notions. But we do have to consider,
perhaps through an anthropologically inflected cultural history approach,
the suggestion that what Prusin calls a 'community of violence' was more
than just contingent. Suffice it here to say at this point that the extraordinary
transgression of 'normal' mores that we see in the Holocaust cannot be
satisfactorily explained by the interaction of structures and institutions.
Once again, this should not be seen as an attempt to impart some kind of
'demonic grandeur' to the events—as Arendt worried would be the case
if she spoke of radical evil in this context—for one of the achievements
of the functionalist literature has been to show how 'ordinary men' can
become genocidal killers. There is something chilling about the view that
genocide emerges out of social structures and actors that are recognizably
'normal'. Even so, this way of conceptualizing the murders can tend to
overlook the fact that placing the tools of the state at the disposal of mass
murder—what Hilberg termed the 'machinery of destruction'—is actually
rather uncommon, historically speaking.

Alon Confino notes that the massive accumulation of data that characterizes recent Holocaust historiography runs the risk of smothering the

---

151. Jürgen Matthäus, 'Agents of the Final Solution—Perpetration in Historical Perspective' in
Holocaust Historiography in Context, eds. Bankier and Michman, pp. 336–7; Bill Niven, ed.,
Germans as Victims: Remembering the Past in Contemporary Germany (Basingstoke: Palgrave
Macmillan, 2006).

horror, the sense of strangeness about the Holocaust that brought forth such interest amongst historians in the first place. The more complete the explanation, he also notes, the greater the danger of domestication, of losing that sense of strangeness.[152] Nevertheless, a striking sentence at the start of Peter Fritzsche's latest book seems to act as a challenge to those who study perpetrators: 'The violence of the Nazis was so excessive and their feeling of liberation from conventional morality so complete that any attempt at explanation falters. But a context of macabre premonitions of German death makes the mindset of perpetrators more comprehensible.'[153] Fritzsche's approach seems to offer a way of trying to understand the perpetrators historically whilst also heeding Confino's warning. For Confino believes that explanations which focus on German culture and sensibilities—and this is what Fritzsche seems to be proposing—can, if done sensitively, to some extent avoid the problem of smothering feeling in factual material. I will return to this question in Chapter 6.

Conclusion

It is now clearer than ever that the implementation of the Holocaust required negotiation between centre and periphery concerning the articulation and execution of orders. But even clearer is the fact that this negotiation took place in the context of clear orders delivered by Hitler and passed on primarily by Himmler. For all the achievements of the regional and local studies, we must ultimately come back to Berlin and to a very small group of German leaders in order to understand the decision-making process. As recent research shows, the Third Reich's leaders in Berlin were not responsible alone for the Holocaust, and one can no longer entertain the notion that the murder of the Jews followed a pre-conceived, detailed plan that was passed on through a clear chain of command. The perpetrators on the ground were not automatons who simply followed instructions from Berlin; they were much worse—active agents who drove the murder process forward at every stage. Yet without the leadership, the process is equally lacking in perspective. The regime's leaders' belief—increasingly widely shared as the war went on—that Germany's very existence was

152. Confino, 'Narrative Form'.
153. Peter Fritzsche, *Life and Death in the Third Reich* (Cambridge, MA: The Belknap Press of Harvard University Press, 2008), pp. 4–5.

threatened by the machinations of the 'international Jew'—drove the radicalization process, as is clear in their responses to their underlings and to the changing circumstances of the war. Hitler's words are key, as for example, this speech addressed to high officers of the Wehrmacht on 26 May 1944:

> By removing the Jew, I abolished the possibility of building up a revolutionary core or nucleus in Germany. Of course one might say to me, 'Yes, but couldn't you have solved this more simply—or not simply, since all other means would have been more complicated—but more humanely?' Gentlemen, fellow officers, we are engaged in a life-and-death struggle. If our opponents triumphed in this struggle, then the German people would be extirpated.[154]

What these studies also show is that the debate on the timing of the decision-making process for the Final Solution is not the be-all and end-all of historical research. Rather, the development of the radicalizing dynamic that ended in a continent-wide genocide against the Jews provides a broader canvas for understanding the unfolding of events. The various and sometimes competing efforts to understand this broad context will be explored in the next chapter.

154. Cited in Longerich, *The Unwritten Order*, pp. 122–3. On the perpetrators' sense of their own victimization see Robert Wolfe, 'Putative Threat to National Security as a Nuremberg Defense for Genocide', *Annals of the American Academy of Political and Social Science*, 450 (1980), pp. 46–67; Michael Geyer, 'Endkampf 1918 and 1945: German Nationalism, Annihilation, and Self-Destruction' in *No Man's Land of Violence: Extreme Wars in the Twentieth Century*, eds. Alf Lüdtke and Bernd Weisbrod (Göttingen: Wallstein, 2006), pp. 35–67; A. Dirk Moses, 'Empire, Colony, Genocide: Keywords and the Philosophy of History' in Moses, ed., *Empire, Colony, Genocide: Conquest, Occupation, and Subaltern Resistance in World History* (New York: Berghahn, 2008), pp. 3–54.

3

The Holocaust

Child of Modernity?

It is true that bureaucracy may turn into an anti-democratic force, but whether it does so or not will depend much more on the strength of the democratic forces than on its inner tendencies.

Franz Neumann[1]

Introduction

In the previous chapter I showed that situating the decision-making process for the Final Solution into a broader historical context helps explain how the genocidal process unfolded. But scholars have also sought philosophical or analytical explanations, offering frameworks that can aid our understanding of how such a thing was possible. It is now a cliché of Holocaust representation that, as George Steiner pointed out in the mid-1960s, the land of Goethe and Schiller could stoop so low, the implication being that there is something rotten in that civilization itself: 'we go on mouthing our hopes in culture', he wrote, recalling Eliot's *Waste Land*, 'as if it was not there to break our teeth'.[2] Thus, the very concept of modernity rapidly came into Holocaust historians' field of vision. As a result, debates about modernity have been some of the most productive in

---

1. Franz Neumann, *Behemoth: The Structure and Practice of National Socialism* (London: Victor Gollancz, 1943), p. 71.
2. George Steiner, *Language and Silence: Essays 1958–1966* (London: Penguin, 1969), p. 198.

Holocaust historiography, and they offer the best example of how large-scale explanatory frameworks shape the research strategies of historians and determine the kinds of questions that they ask.

In its most basic form, the 'modernity question' asks whether the Holocaust was brought about not by an atavistic irruption of 'medieval barbarism', a rejection of Enlightenment, but by the logic of modernity itself. This means, for example, that instead of seeing the Holocaust as a return to an earlier tradition of murderous Jew-hatred, as in the First Crusade, that the murder of the Jews stemmed from modern race science, with its notion of the essentially fixed nature of the human races, rejecting the long-held view that all peoples could emerge out of their primitive state and acquire the benefits of civilization. Or it could mean that the characteristics of modern society—bureaucracy, technology, state control over populations, the idea that nation-states should be homogeneous and are threatened by difference—gave rise to a genocide that could not have occurred under pre-modern conditions. Is there something inherent in the modern condition that leads to genocide?

These questions constitute a major challenge to Enlightenment notions of the value of science, rationality, and progress. The Enlightenment tradition, envisaged by thinkers such as Condorcet, foresaw the progressive release of humankind from superstition. But perhaps the scientific frame of mind itself ended by institutionalizing a form of rationality that was so divorced from morality that it ended with the total domination by some human beings—defined as superior—over others, defined as inferior or otherwise polluting or dangerous?

These questions are not new. In 1944, the émigré Frankfurt School philosophers Max Horkheimer and Theodor Adorno published their extraordinary book, *Dialectic of Enlightenment*. Their thesis was that the Enlightenment, which promised, in Kant's words, 'to release man from his self-incurred tutelage' and to bring about tolerance and open inquiry, had ended by becoming its own myth, with the result that human beings were being dominated by forces originally designed to liberate them. Instead, for example, of science, one had 'scientism', the belief that science *was* the answer, whatever the question might be. Instead of Enlightenment freeing human beings from superstition and ignorance, it had brought about their renewed enslavement: 'Men pay for the increase of their power with alienation from that over which they exercise their power. Enlightenment behaves toward things as a dictator toward men.' The very process of thinking was indicted by Horkheimer and Adorno for turning against itself: 'Thinking objectifies itself to become an automatic, self-serving process; an impersonation of the machine that it produces itself so that ultimately the machine can replace it. . . . Mathematical procedure became, so to speak, the ritual of thinking.'[3] For Horkheimer and Adorno, it was not inevitable that the Enlightenment would reach this impasse, although in *Negative Dialectics* (1966) Adorno came close to this position. Their description of the dialectic of Enlightenment followed Max Weber's claim that unintended consequences could emerge out of peculiar sets of circumstances, as with his famous claim that modern capitalism developed, unexpectedly, out of the world view promoted by the Protestant sects.[4] Horkheimer and Adorno's argument, that the rationalized structures of modern society had themselves become the focus of human affect, merged Weberian definitions of modernity with Marxist notions of coercion and discipline in order to arrive at a stark vision of the total domination over nature leading to totalitarianism, in a searing critique of the rational, Enlightenment project.

In more recent philosophical work, this bleak vision has been developed most fruitfully by the theorists of 'biopower', in particular Michel Foucault and Giorgio Agamben. They have seen in the Nazi state the apogee not only of racial thinking (a notion common in historiography for decades, as we will see in Chapter 4), but also of the racist constitution and illiberal nature of the nation-state *per se*.[5] But whereas Foucault saw Nazism as

3. Max Horkheimer and Theodor Adorno, *Dialectic of Enlightenment* (London: Verso, 1989), pp. 9, 25. The literature on Adorno and Horkheimer is vast, but for useful starting points in this context, see Michael Rothberg, *Traumatic Realism: The Demands of Holocaust Representation* (Minneapolis: University of Minnesota Press, 2000), ch. 1; Josh Cohen, *Interrupting Auschwitz: Art, Religion, Philosophy* (London: Continuum, 2003), ch. 2; Dana Villa, 'Genealogies of Total Domination: Arendt, Adorno, and Auschwitz', *New German Critique*, 100 (2007), pp. 1–45; Anson Rabinbach, ' "Why Were the Jews Sacrificed?" The Place of Antisemitism in Adorno and Horkheimer's *Dialectic of Enlightenment*' in *Adorno: A Critical Reader*, eds. Nigel Gibson and Andrew Rubin (Oxford: Blackwell, 2002), pp. 132–49.
4. Max Weber, *The Protestant Ethic and the Spirit of Capitalism* (London: George Allen & Unwin, 1976). For an excellent explication of Weber's notion of 'unintended consequences' and *Wahlverwandtschaften* (elective affinities)—one that rejects a deterministic link between Protestantism and capitalism—see Malcolm H. Mackinnon, 'The Longevity of the Thesis: A Critique of the Critics' in *Weber's Protestant Ethic: Origins, Evidence, Contexts*, eds. Hartmut Lehmann and Guenther Roth (Cambridge: Cambridge University Press, 1987), pp. 211–43.
5. Martin Stingelin, ed., *Biopolitik und Rassismus* (Frankfurt/M: Suhrkamp, 2003); Alan Milchman and Alan Rosenberg, 'Michel Foucault, Auschwitz, and the Destruction of the Body' in *Postmodernism and the Holocaust*, eds. Milchman and Rosenberg (Amsterdam: Rodopi, 1998), pp. 205–37.

the ultimate expression of modern biopolitics—the right of the state to determine the life and death of its populations—Agamben goes further and sees Nazism—in particular, the concentration camp—not only as exemplifying modern biopolitics but as 'the *nomos* of the modern' and 'the bare essence of politics as such'.[6] The Holocaust, in Agamben's reading, is the logical outcome of the modern world, by no means aberrant. Foucault's position might seem more appropriately cautious than Agamben's: although modern states have developed (and continue to develop) technologies for intervening at the level of the population, would it not be too reductive of the many ways in which modern state practices operate to claim that their intersection with genocide represents their logical or necessary end point?[7]

Aside from these philosophical origins, which one could call 'sociological' in inspiration, the argument about modernity stems from 'postmodern' distrust of grand narratives.[8] In other words, if one can show that the desire to create blueprints to shape the world leads inexorably to terror—those who do not fit or resist the implementation of the blueprint have to be 'removed' as 'backward' elements, standing in the way of the laws of history or nature[9]—then modernity as such becomes suspect, for modernity can be defined as the age that wishes to overcome itself: all that is solid melts into air to be replaced by a new vision of a purified society.[10] This is a claim that is identified with liberal 'postmodernists' on the one hand—Jean-François Lyotard, Jacques Derrida—and with conservative or free-market liberal thinkers on the other hand—Karl Popper, Friedrich Hayek, and Jacob Talmon—who, following Burke, argued that the notion that one could

6. Mark Mazower, 'Foucault, Agamben, Theory and the Nazis', *Boundary 2*, 35, 1 (2008), p. 34.
7. See especially Michel Foucault, *The History of Sexuality*, Vol. 1, *An Introduction* (London: Penguin, 1984); Giorgio Agamben, *Homo Sacer: Sovereign Power and Bare Life* (Stanford, CA: Stanford University Press, 1998). See Dan Stone, 'Biopower and Modern Genocide' in *History, Memory and Mass Atrocity: Essays on the Holocaust and Genocide* (London: Vallentine Mitchell, 2006), pp. 217–35, and A. Dirk Moses and Dan Stone, 'Eugenics and Genocide' in *The Oxford Handbook of the History of Eugenics*, eds. Alison Bashford and Philippa Levine (Oxford: Oxford University Press, 2010).
8. Jean-François Lyotard, *The Postmodern Condition: A Report on Knowledge* (Manchester: Manchester University Press, 1984), p. xxiv, defines postmodern as 'incredulity towards metanarratives'.
9. Tony Barta, 'On Pain of Extinction: Laws of Nature and History in Darwin, Marx, and Arendt' in *Hannah Arendt and the Uses of History: Imperialism, Nation, Race and Genocide*, eds. Richard H. King and Dan Stone (New York: Berghahn, 2007), pp. 87–105.
10. Marshall Berman, *All That is Solid Melts into Air: The Experience of Modernity* (London: Penguin, 1988); Roger Griffin, *Modernism and Fascism: The Sense of a Beginning under Mussolini and Hitler* (Basingstoke: Palgrave Macmillan, 2007).

radically alter society goes against human nature and leads only to violence and dictatorship.

Historians have taken these philosophical arguments and sought to provide empirical detail to back them up. They have focused on the role of bureaucracy or technology in the Holocaust, from railway timetables to Hollerith punch-card machines.[11] More recently, they have examined the role of organizations in the Holocaust, seeing it as a 'division-of-labour-based crime'. All of this literature is based on one important binary division: between Nazi ideology (especially antisemitism) on the one hand—as if ideology comes from nowhere—and structures or social setting on the other hand—as if these are created by no one. This distinction in the literature between ideology and context more or less replicates and maps onto the debate between intentionalists and functionalists. That debate is itself an expression of historians' fundamental starting points, depending on whether they see individuals and their ideas or the social contexts in which individuals exist—and which control them more than the reverse—as the most significant explanatory factor. In what follows, I will examine these debates, and assess their contribution to our understanding of the Holocaust.

If these quasi-philosophical discussions seem somewhat far removed from the concerns of historians, it suffices to recall the stunning insights of Zalman Gradowski. Whilst locked in the gas chamber and crematorium complex in Birkenau as a member of the *Sonderkommando*, Gradowski produced a text that adumbrates the *Dialectic of Enlightenment*—in fact, the two texts were written at about the same time, one in Birkenau, the other in California—and thus many of the questions that have been central to Holocaust historiography ever since. Speaking directly to his hoped-for reader, Gradowski wrote:

> Tell them that even if your heart turns to stone, your brain to a cold calculator and your eyes to camera lenses, even then, you will never again return to them. They would do better to seek you in the eternal forests, for you will have fled from the world inhabited by men, to seek comfort among the cruel beasts of the field, rather than live among cultured demons. For although

11. Raul Hilberg, 'German Railroads, Jewish Souls', *Society*, 14, 1 (1976), pp. 520–56; Hilberg, *Sonderzüge nach Auschwitz* (Mainz: Dumjahn, 1981); Alfred C. Mierzejewski, *The Most Valuable Asset of the Reich: A History of the German National Railway. Vol. 2: 1933–1945* (Chapel Hill: University of North Carolina Press, 2000); Mierzejewski, 'A Public Enterprise in the Service of Mass Murder: The Deutsche Reichsbahn and the Holocaust', *HGS*, 15, 1 (2001), pp. 33–46.

even animals have been restrained by civilization—their hooves have been
dulled and their cruelty greatly curbed—man has not, but has become a
beast. The more highly developed a culture, the more cruel its murderers, the
more civilized a society, the greater its barbarians; as development increases,
its deeds become more terrible.[12]

Modernity and the Holocaust: A Debate
of the 1980s and 1990s

Building on the historical debates of the 1960s, which turned on whether
or not Nazism was a 'developmental dictatorship', the question of Nazism's
relationship to 'modernity' was once again taken up in the 1980s, in the
wake of the advance of the structuralist argument.[13] Many historians debated
whether Nazism had contributed to the modernization of Germany;[14] but
the most significant in terms of the relationship of modernity and the
Holocaust were Detlev Peukert, Götz Aly and Susanne Heim, and the
sociologist Zygmunt Bauman. Prior to these historians, the most significant
in terms of this issue was Raul Hilberg, who had presented the Holocaust as
an 'administrative process'.[15] Famously, Hilberg wrote: 'When in the early
days of 1933 the first civil servant wrote the first definition of "non-Aryan"
into a civil service ordinance, the fate of European Jewry was sealed.'[16]
This is a strange claim for a historian to make, since it contravenes the
basic prohibition against reading the past backwards, making the events

12. Zalman Gradowski, 'Writings' in Ber Mark, *The Scrolls of Auschwitz* (Tel Aviv: Am Oved,
    1985), p. 175.
13. For the earlier works, see in particular David Schoenbaum, *Hitler's Social Revolution: Class
    and Status in Nazi Germany 1933–1939* (New York: Garden City, 1966) and Ralf Dahrendorf,
    Society and Democracy in Germany (London: Weidenfeld & Nicolson, 1968).
14. For example: Hans Mommsen, 'Nationalsozialismus als vorgetäuschte Modernisierung' in
    Der historische Ort des Nationalsozialismus: Annäherungen, ed. Walter H. Pehle (Frankfurt/M:
    Suhrkamp Taschenbuch Verlag, 1990), pp. 31–46; Norbert Frei, 'Wie modern war der
    Nationalsozialismus?', *Geschichte und Gesellschaft*, 19, 3 (1993), pp. 367–87; Axel Schildt,
    'NS-Regime, Modernisierung und Moderne: Anmerkungen zur Hochkonjunktur einer
    andauernden Diskussion', *Tel Aviver Jahrbuch für deutsche Geschichte*, 23 (1994), pp. 3–22;
    Mark Roseman, 'National Socialism and Modernization' in *Fascist Italy and Nazi Germany:
    Comparisons and Contrasts*, ed. Richard Bessel (Cambridge: Cambridge University Press,
    1996), pp. 197–229; Jan Philipp Reemtsma, 'Nationalsozialismus und Moderne' in *Die
    Gewalt spricht nicht: Drei Reden* (Stuttgart: Reclam, 2002), pp. 87–129.
15. Raul Hilberg, *The Destruction of the European Jews*, rev. edn (New Haven: Yale University
    Press, 1985), Vol. 1, p. 9.
16. Hilberg, *Destruction*, Vol. 3, p. 1044.

of the past appear pre-determined. But apart from the teleology, used by Hilberg for dramatic effect, the significance of Hilberg's approach is his stress on bureaucracy: 'With an unfailing sense of direction and with an uncanny pathfinding ability, the German bureaucracy found the shortest road to the final goal.'[17] With his descriptions of bureaucrats who adapted to the removal of restraints against persecution, and who became 'improvisors and innovators',[18] one can see Hilberg as the first structuralist in Holocaust historiography. Hence Saul Friedländer's comment that, despite *The Destruction of the European Jews* being 'on all counts the most important single study of the Holocaust', nevertheless, 'something essential was missing: a historical background that would explain the triggering of the bureaucratic wheels of destruction'.[19]

Following Hilberg's lead, Detlev Peukert sought to apply a Weberian analysis to the logic of the Holocaust. In English, Peukert's best known contribution to this debate is his essay, 'The Genesis of the "Final Solution" from the Spirit of Science', an article that began life as a chapter in a book on Weber. Peukert argues that, in modernity, science risks developing totalizing patterns of thought, and that this is exactly what happened in the run up to the 'Final Solution'. Rather than being an outburst of irrational fantasy, the aim of murdering the Jews grew out of a medical discourse that saw racial hygiene as the key to solving Germany's problems. Science, as Horkheimer and Adorno predicted, 'ideologized itself' and, under worsening socio-economic conditions, its schemes grew ever grander until the point at which the 'optimistic view, that scientific and industrial progress in principle removed the restrictions on the possible application of planning, education and social reform in everyday life, lost its last shreds of innocence when the National Socialists set about engineering their "brave

---

17. Hilberg, *Destruction*, Vol. 1, p. 9.   18. Hilberg, *Destruction*, Vol. 1, p. 15.
19. Saul Friedländer, 'Mosse's Influence on the Historiography of the Holocaust' in *What History Tells: George L. Mosse and the Culture of Modern Europe*, eds. Stanley G. Payne, David J. Sorkin, and John S. Tortorice (Madison: University of Wisconsin Press, 2004), p. 135. For an insightful assessment of Hilberg, see Federico Finchelstein, 'The Holocaust Canon: Rereading Raul Hilberg', *New German Critique*, 96 (2005), pp. 1–47. As Jeremy Noakes points out, many *Mischlinge* (mixed race) actually survived the war partly because of elements within the civil service: Lösener of the Interior Ministry and State Secretary Stuckart, both of whom collaborated with the murder of the Jews but were to some extent uncomfortable with the SS's demands to include the *Mischlinge* in the deportations. Noakes, 'The Development of Nazi Policy towards the German–Jewish "Mischlinge" 1933–1945', *Leo Baeck Institute Yearbook*, 34 (1989), pp. 352–3; Beate Meyer, *'Jüdische Mischlinge': Rassenpolitik und Verfolgungserfahrung 1933–1945* (Hamburg: Dölling und Galitz,1999).

new world" with compulsory sterilization, concentration camps and gas
chambers.'[20]

The most detailed attempt to explain not just how the bureaucracy
operated but also to analyse the Holocaust in terms of economic rationality
was Götz Aly and Susanne Heim's. In numerous studies, they sought to
prove that the Holocaust was carried out as a rational process following
cost–benefit analysis. 'Selection according to racist criteria', they wrote,
'did not stand in contradiction to economic calculation, but was an integral
component of it.'[21] Aly and Heim's contributions were the most empirically informed of the 'modernity' arguments, suggesting that the murder
process was driven forward by the planning of occupation functionaries
in eastern Europe: town planners, statisticians, nutritionists, demographers,
economists, and so on. On the basis of the research they conducted in
the newly available eastern European archives, Aly and Heim came to the
conclusion that the Holocaust was neither exceptional nor irrational but an
outcome of modern bureaucratic procedure. 'One can only understand the
dynamic of the annihilation and the actual decision-making process', they
write, 'if one sees the demographic–economic programme in the background.'[22] Furthermore, from a cost–benefit perspective, the Holocaust
made sense: in the *Generalgouvernement*, 'The death of the Jews provided
the simplest and most viable means of keeping down capital erosion and
of keeping open the possibility for an economic upswing in occupied
Poland.'[23] Hence the Final Solution can be understood in the rational terms
of political economy. The argument was most fully developed in *Vordenker
der Vernichtung* (1991), in which the murder of the Jews was situated in
a longer-term context of further mass murders of the local non-Jewish

20. Detlev Peukert, *Inside Nazi Germany: Conformity, Opposition and Racism in Everyday Life*
    (London: Penguin, 1989), p. 223. See also Peukert, *Max Webers Diagnose der Moderne*
    (Göttingen: Vandenhoeck und Ruprecht, 1989); 'Rassismus und "Endlösungs"-Utopie:
    Thesen zur Entwicklung und Struktur der nationalsozialistischen Vernichtungspolitik' in
    Nicht nur Hitlers Krieg: Der Zweite Weltkrieg und die Deutschen, ed. Christoph Kleßmann
    (Düsseldorf, Droste, 1989), pp. 71–81; *The Weimar Republic: The Crisis of Classical Modernism*
    (London: Penguin, 1991); 'The Genesis of the "Final Solution" from the Spirit of Science'
    in *Nazism and German Society, 1933–1945*, ed. David F. Crew (London: Routledge, 1994),
    pp. 274–99.
21. Susanne Heim and Götz Aly, 'Sozialplanung und Völkermord: Thesen zur Herrschaftsra-
    tionalität der nationalsozialistischen "Weltanschauung" ' in *'Vernichtungspolitik': Eine Debatte
    über den Zusammenhang von Sozialpolitik und Genozid im nationalsozialistischen Deutschland*, ed.
    Wolfgang Schneider (Hamburg: Junius, 1991), p. 22.
22. Aly and Heim, 'Sozialplanung und Völkermord', pp. 19–20.
23. Götz Aly and Susanne Heim, 'The Economics of the Final Solution: A Case Study from the
    General Government', *Simon Wiesenthal Center Annual*, 5 (1988), pp. 38–9.

population and the economic progress of the region. Economic considerations, they argue, made 'mass extermination into a "practical constraint", a prerequisite for long-term domination and economic subordination'.[24] Aly expanded on the argument about the relationship between the Holocaust and 'ethnic resettlement' in his 1995 book 'Final Solution', although most critics are not convinced that the murder of the Jews should be put down to the requirements of *Volkstumspolitik* (ethno-politics).[25]

Few books have generated so much discussion amongst Holocaust historians as Zygmunt Bauman's *Modernity and the Holocaust* (1989). Functionalism or structuralism had been gaining momentum for more than a decade and had become more or less an orthodox position amongst scholars, and Bauman's book represented that school's logical culmination. In some ways, Bauman's book is simply a more sociological version of Hilberg's *The Destruction of the European Jews*. Hilberg had already argued that the destruction of the Jews was 'the work of a far-flung administrative machine. This apparatus took each step in turn. The initiation as well as the implementation of decisions was largely in its hands.'[26] Bauman confirmed this analysis, setting the Holocaust into the context of the modern state.

Bauman's argument is that, far from being a throwback to pre-modern barbarism, the Holocaust represents an outcome of modernity itself: 'Without modern civilization and its most central essential achievements, there would be no Holocaust.'[27] He does not think that it was the *necessary* outcome of modernity, but one of modernity's 'hidden possibilities'.[28] Bauman characterizes modernity as 'an overwhelming urge to replace spontaneity, seen as meaningless and identified with chaos, by an order drawn by reason and constructed through a legislative and controlling effort.'[29] In the case of the Holocaust, this description is most clearly exemplified by

24. Götz Aly and Susanne Heim, *Vordenker der Vernichtung: Auschwitz und die deutschen Pläne für eine neue europäische Ordnung* (Frankfurt/M: Fischer Taschenbuch Verlag, 1993), p. 485.
25. Götz Aly, *'Final Solution': Nazi Population Policy and the Murder of the European Jews* (London: Arnold, 1999).
26. Hilberg, *Destruction*, Vol. I, p. 62. See also Browning, *The Path to Genocide*, pp. 125–44. The classic study of bureaucracy in the Third Reich is Hans Mommsen, *Beamtentum im Dritten Reich* (Stuttgart: Oldenbourg, 1966).
27. Zygmunt Bauman, *Modernity and the Holocaust* (Cambridge: Polity Press, 1989), p. 87.
28. Bauman, *Modernity*, p. 12.
29. Zygmunt Bauman, *Intimations of Postmodernity* (London: Routledge, 1992), p. 178. See, more recently, Bauman, *Wasted Lives: Modernity and its Outcasts* (Cambridge: Polity Press, 2003) and *Liquid Times: Living in an Age of Uncertainty* (Cambridge: Polity Press, 2007).

the bureaucratic administration, which sought, as per Weber's analysis, to divorce the technical from the moral. 'Bureaucracy is programmed to seek the optimal solution', he writes, arguing that, 'Once set in motion, the machinery of murder developed its own impetus.'[30]

Yet Bauman's position is not entirely clear. Does the bureaucracy fulfil tasks that are given it, or does the impetus for mass murder emerge out of bureaucratic culture itself? Very different understandings of modernity's dangers can be derived from these different versions, and Bauman seems to want to have it both ways. On the one hand, he argues that 'at no point of its long and tortuous *execution* did the Holocaust come in conflict with the principles of rationality', suggesting the weaker version of the claim. His assertion that this 'is not to suggest that the incidence of the Holocaust was determined by modern bureaucracy or the culture of instrumental rationality it epitomizes' implies that it is in the realization of an idea (which might itself not be rational) that the bureaucratic aspect of the Holocaust is most in evidence.[31] Yet, on the other hand, only a few sentences later, he writes that:

> the bureaucratic culture which prompts us to view society as an object of administration, as a collection of so many problems to be 'solved', as 'nature' to be 'controlled', 'mastered' and 'improved' or 'remade', as a legitimate target for 'social engineering', and in general a garden to be designed and kept in the planned shape by force (the gardening posture divides vegetation into 'cultured plants' to be taken care of, and weeds to be exterminated), *was the very atmosphere in which the idea of the Holocaust could be conceived.*[32]

This makes Weber's analysis work very hard. Although Bauman discusses antisemitism in the medieval world and anthropological concepts of fantasy and pollution, he vacillates on whether or not the drive to murder the Jews actually grew out of bureaucratic culture. But without such careful close analysis—as the works of Bauman's epigones reveals—the 'harder' argument is the one that seems to stick in the mind.[33]

---

30. Bauman, *Modernity*, pp. 104, 106.   31. Bauman, *Modernity*, pp. 17–18 (my emphasis).
32. Bauman, *Modernity*, p. 18 (my emphasis).
33. For example: Ronald J. Berger, 'The "Banality of Evil" Reframed: The Social Construction of the "Final Solution" to the "Jewish Problem" ', *The Sociological Quarterly*, 34, 4 (1993), pp. 597–618; Alan Milchman and Alan Rosenberg, 'The Unlearned Lessons of the Holocaust', *Modern Judaism*, 13, 2 (1993), pp. 177–90; Leon A. Jick, 'Method in Madness: An Examination of the Motivations for Nazi Mass Murder', *Modern Judaism*, 18, 2 (1998), pp. 153–72; Fred E. Katz, 'Implementation of the Holocaust: The Behavior of Nazi Officials', *Comparative Studies in Society and History*, 24, 3 (1982), pp. 510–29; Jay Weinstein and Nico Stehr, 'The Power of Knowledge: Race Science, Race Policy, and the Holocaust', *Social Epistemology*, 13,

Bauman's claims can be empirically falsified on many grounds. Nevertheless, in some ways, his argument does stand up to scrutiny. Social Darwinism and racial science were indeed key components of Nazi ideology.[34] Bureaucracy too was an essential characteristic of the Holocaust. The question is whether these were the driving forces of the Holocaust or whether they were frameworks or carriers for a prior position. Peter Fritzsche writes that what is frustrating about Peukert's and Bauman's 'pathbreaking analyses' is 'their insufficient appreciation of the fantastic vision of the National Socialists. The drive to renovate Europe along racial lines cannot be summed up either in the strict, delimiting terms of cost–benefit analysis or simply as one (horrible) version of the western ideal of self-cultivation.'[35] Unless one argues that bureaucracies can generate genocidal policy independently of the general cultural–political arena in which they operate, something, as Friedländer noted of Hilberg, is still missing.

Beyond empirical grounds, Bauman can be criticized for his sociological-theoretical presuppositions, in particular his reading of Weber, on which much of his argument depends. Bauman assumes that his definition of modernity as synonymous with bureaucracy, instrumental rationality, technology, and the honour of the civil servant, comes from Weber. Weber is indeed the pre-eminent theorist of bureaucratic rule, which he distinguished from charismatic rule and other forms of pre-modern legitimation.[36] But it is something of a caricature to sum Weber's thought up in his famous phrase of the 'iron cage' (*Gehäuse der Hörigkeit*) of rational modernity. Weber wrote that 'The fate of our times is characterized by rationalization and intellectualization and, above all, by the "disenchantment of the world" ', but when he predicted at the end of his remarkable 1918 lecture, 'Politics as a Vocation' that 'Not summer's bloom lies ahead of us, but rather a polar night of icy darkness and hardness, no matter which group may triumph externally now', he did not mean that this dark vision was the *necessary* outcome of rationalization.[37] Rather, scholars who have

1 (1999), pp. 3–35, for Bauman-like essays (not all, obviously, written after *Modernity and the Holocaust*).

34. Richard J. Evans, 'In Search of German Social Darwinism' in *Rereading German History 1800–1996: From Unification to Reunification* (London: Routledge, 1997), pp. 119–44.

35. Peter Fritzsche, 'Nazi Modern', *Modernism/Modernity*, 3, 1 (1996), p. 10.

36. Max Weber, 'Bureaucracy' in *From Max Weber: Essays in Sociology*, eds. H. H. Gerth and C. Wright Mills (London: Routledge, 1991), pp. 196–244.

37. *From Max Weber*, pp. 155, 128.

brought to light Weber's Nietzschean side—a side that has been neglected
in the Anglo-American tradition that regards Weber as the theorist of the
normative modern state—show that this dark vision reflected Weber's
belief that a rationalized world did not have the resources necessary to
meet people's needs.[38] The 'disenchantment of the world' is indeed a
Nietzschean moment, and the question is what will happen to re-enchant
the world. In Gerth and Mills's translation, Weber writes that 'Today the
routines of everyday life challenge religion. Many old gods ascend from
their graves; they are disenchanted and hence take the form of impersonal
forces. They strive to gain power over our lives and again they resume
their eternal struggle with one another.'[39] But in Weber's German, the first
sentence in this quotation reads '*Heute ist es religiöser Alltag*', that is, 'today
the everyday is religious', or 'today religion suffuses everyday life', in other
words, quite the opposite of Gerth and Mills's sense. Weber's point was
that, even in a rationalized world—perhaps especially in a rationalized and
disenchanted world—there was no such thing as a post-religious, secular
modernity.[40]

Where Weber sees the problem not as disenchantment *per se* but 'a
deranged, totalized rationalization which yields disenchantment',[41] Bauman
sees the Holocaust as the logical outcome of modernity. Where even
Horkheimer and Adorno describe a 'dialectic of Enlightenment', so that
Enlightenment only becomes totalizing and 'radiates disaster triumphant'
once it becomes its own myth, Bauman sees a line heading directly from
rationalization to genocide. Thus, downplaying the roles of charisma and
the non-rational facets of Nazism, Bauman provides a seductive, productive,
and provocative, but ultimately one-sided argument about the nature of
modernity and, as a consequence, about the origins of the Holocaust. Even
if it is by no means a sufficient explanation for the Holocaust, modernity,
however, remains a useful term of analysis.

38. See especially Bryan S. Turner, *For Weber: Essays on the Sociology of Fate*, 2nd edn (London:
    Sage, 1996); Lawrence A. Scaff, *Fleeing the Iron Cage: Culture, Politics, and Modernity in the
    Thought of Max Weber* (Berkeley: University of California Press, 1989); Mark E. Warren,
    'Nietzsche and Weber: When Does Reason Become Power?' in *The Barbarism of Reason:
    Max Weber and the Twilight of Enlightenment*, eds. Asher Horowitz and Terry Maley (Toronto:
    University of Toronto Press, 1994), pp. 68–96.
39. *From Max Weber*, p. 149.
40. Michael Ley, 'Apokalyptische Bewegungen in der Moderne' in *Der Nationalsozialismus als
    politische Religion*, eds. Michael Ley and Julius H. Schoeps (Bodenheim: Philo, 1997), p. 13.
41. Alkis Kontos, 'The World Disenchanted, and the Return of Gods and Demons' in *The
    Barbarism of Reason*, eds. Horowitz and Maley, p. 235.

Organization and Ideology

As we saw in Chapter 2, the most significant recent development in Holocaust historiography has been the 'return of ideology'. Many studies now exist that deal with individuals, research centres, the professions, and universities, Nazi institutions and agencies, propaganda, and so on that show the remarkably widespread and influential nature of Nazi ideology. From landscape planners to ethnographers, Nazi ideology was enthusiastically embraced and promoted by professionals.[42] Whilst this trend does not (always) constitute a return to a naïve form of intentionalism, it does reinforce the belief that the murder of the Jews was driven primarily by the Nazis' paranoid conspiracy theory view of the world, even if the actual process by which this ideology was actualized was often ad hoc, reactive, and disorganized, and driven more by inter-agency competition than by coherent administration.

To this end, recent research that deals directly with ideology contributes helpfully to the ongoing discussions about perpetrator motivation. It is one thing to show that Nazi propaganda was suffused with antisemitic imagery, but the question of what drove individuals to take part in genocide remains, of course, an open one. For example, Jürgen Matthäus's and Edward Westermann's essays on ideological indoctrination and organizational culture in the SS and the Order Police show how the broad *Haltung* (state of mind) of the SS and police structured and legitimized murderous antisemitism even when the Jewish question was not explicitly mentioned.[43] These findings are of a piece with work on collaboration and the eastern front discussed in Chapter 1.

Beyond the studies of individual perpetrator motivation, an outpouring of works devoted to understanding the workings of perpetrator institutions

---

42. See, for example, Joachim Wolschke-Bulmahn, 'Violence as the Basis of National Socialist Landscape Planning in the "Annexed Eastern Areas" ' in *How Green Were the Nazis? Nature, Environment, and Nation in the Third Reich*, eds. Franz-Josef Brüggemeier, Mark Cioc, and Thomas Zeller (Athens: Ohio University Press, 2005), pp. 243–56; Ingo Haar and Michael Fahlbusch, eds., *German Scholars and Ethnic Cleansing, 1919–1945* (New York: Berghahn, 2005); Margit Szöllösi-Janze, ed., *Science in the Third Reich* (Oxford: Berg, 2001).

43. Jürgen Matthäus, 'Anti-Semitism as an Offer: The Function of Ideological Indoctrination in the SS and Police Corps During the Holocaust' and Edward Westermann, 'Ideology and Organizational Culture: Creating the Police Soldier', both in *Lessons and Legacies, Vol. 7: The Holocaust in International Perspective*, ed. Dagmar Herzog (Evanston: Northwestern University Press, 2006), pp. 116–28 and 129–41.

has recently appeared. In terms of the debate about modernity, what these studies tend to demonstrate, if only implicitly, is that modernity was less the driving force of the Holocaust than the setting for it. That is to say, when one examines the workings of these agencies and the operational presumptions of those who ran them, their individual capabilities as bureaucrats and institutional efficiency based on procedural regulations varied considerably. But what they all had in common was a commitment to targeting the Jews. To be sure, they often disagreed about how this aim was to be achieved, and some were playing a longer-term game than others (some in the SD, for example, were willing temporarily to exploit Jewish labour, especially in the later years of the war), but overall their ideological ambition was shared. This picture of Nazi institutions constitutes a weak version of the 'modernity' argument: that modernity in Bauman's or Peukert's sense as the predominance of bureaucratization, instrumental thinking, and rationalization was not the motor of the Holocaust but simply the conduit through which it was channelled. Thus, as I noted above, even if Bauman were right to say that 'At no point in its long and tortuous execution did the Holocaust come in conflict with the principles of rationality' (and this is certainly open to question), the statement leaves unanswered the question about the origin of the idea.[44] Historians have explained the execution of the Holocaust in great detail—and, as we have seen, largely dismissed the claim that it was an entirely smooth and rational process—but the problem of where the idea to murder the Jews came from is by no means dealt with in the same explanation. Empirical studies back up the weaker version of Bauman's assertion that modernity was the setting for the Holocaust and that bureaucratic involvement was necessary and considerable; but not that the bureaucracy was the place where the idea for the Holocaust first developed.

Let us examine some of the major studies of Nazi agencies and institutions and consider what their findings tell us about 'modernity'. This necessarily means some discussion of the internal structure of the Third Reich, but I will keep the focus on what this body of literature tells us about the Holocaust. Already some 25 years ago, studies of the structure of the Third Reich were building in a sophisticated way on the pioneering research of Hans Buchheim, Martin Broszat, Karl Dietrich Bracher, and others. A 1986 collection edited by Dieter Rebentisch and Karl Teppe showed

---

44. Bauman, *Modernity*, p. 17.

that the Third Reich was characterized by a wide variety of administrative institutions, from existing state bureaucracies to the panoply of new Party agencies, such as the Gauleiters, the Führer's Chancellery, or the SS's WVHA (*Wirtschafts-Verwaltungshauptamt*/Economic Administrative Main Office).[45] Whether one looks at the civil service or the Order Police, one sees a state and a regime with a polycratic character, that is to say, a multiplicity of agencies competing for control of policy and vying with each other for the ear of the Führer. This phenomenon has been observed for many years and in different contexts, from the Foreign Office to the occupied eastern territories to communal administration in Germany.[46] It has also been modified to some extent by historians who argue that 'polycracy' has become synonymous with 'inefficiency' and who want instead to stress that institutional competition meant the loss neither of bureaucratic efficiency nor of a shared overall goal.[47] The question here is what these insights tell us about the 'modernity' of the Holocaust. In surveying much of the literature, I suggest that Nazi polycracy—even when it was not mutually exclusive of efficiency—does not conform to

45. Dieter Rebentisch and Karl Teppe, eds., *Verwaltung contra Menschenführung im Staat Hitlers: Studium zur politisch-administrativen Systems* (Göttingen: Vandenhoeck & Ruprecht, 1986). On the Gau system, see also Gerhard Kratzsch, *Der Gauwirtschaftsapparat der NSDAP: Menschenführung, 'Arisierung', Wehrwirtschaft im Gau Westfalen-Süd. Eine Studie zur Herrschaftspraxis im totalitären Staat* (Münster: Aschendorff, 1989); Jürgen John, Horst Müller and Thomas Schaarschmidt, eds., *Die NS Gaue: regionale Mittelinstanzen im zentralistischen 'Führerstaat'* (Munich: R. Oldenbourg, 2007).

46. For example, Dieter Rebentisch writes that Rosenberg's *Ostministerium* was a classic example of 'a multi-headed and polymorphous, "polycratic" administrative organization, whose individual branches, each focused on carrying out "Führer-issued tasks", and working partly side by side but frequently against each other, created incessant conflicts of authority'. *Führerstaat und Verwaltung im Zweiten Weltkrieg: Verfassungsentwicklung und Verwaltungspolitik 1939–1945* (Stuttgart: Franz Steiner, 1989), p. 310. On polycracy, see Jane Caplan, *Government Without Administration: State and Civil Service in Weimar and Nazi Germany* (Oxford: Clarendon Press, 1989); Peter Hayes, 'Polycracy and Policy in the Third Reich: The Case of the Economy' in *Reevaluating the Third Reich*, eds. Thomas Childers and Jane Caplan (New York: Holmes and Meier, 1993), pp. 190–210; Peter Hüttenberger, 'Nationalsozialistische Polykratie', *Geschichte und Gesellschaft*, 2 (1976), pp. 417–42. For local administration: Bernhard Gotto, *Nationalsozialistische Kommunalpolitik: Administrative Normalität und Systemstabilisierung durch die Augsburger Stadtverwaltung 1933–1945* (Munich: R. Oldenbourg, 2006).

47. Wolf Gruner and Armin Nolzen, eds., *Bürokratien: Initiative und Effizienz* (Berlin: Assoziation A, 2001); Bernhard Gotto, 'Polykratische Selbststabilisierung: Mittel- und Unterinstanzen in der NS-Diktatur' in *Hitlers Kommissare: Sondergewalten in der nationalsozialistischen Diktatur*, eds. Rüdiger Hachtmann and Winfried Süß (Göttingen: Wallstein, 2006), pp. 28–50. Cf. Dan P. Silverman, 'Nazification of the German Bureaucracy Reconsidered: A Case Study', *JMH*, 60, 3 (1988), pp. 496–539, which shows how the Reich Institution for Placement and Unemployment Insurance was destroyed in the attempt to Nazify it.

the notion of the Weberian state as set out by Bauman, nor to the leading Nazis' self-conception as a rational, 'ice-cold' elite.

Take, for example, the Order Police, the branch of the German police made familiar by Browning's and Goldhagen's work on Battalion 101. Bernd Hüppauf rightly noted that the significance of the title of Browning's book was that it brought unimaginable mass murder into the realm of the imaginable and real: 'It did not lose its horror. But the horror lost its strangeness. This new proximity made the images of extermination more menacing.'[48] The many studies that have appeared since then provide detailed reconstructions of the nature of some of the most significant institutions operating during the Third Reich. But even before Browning, Heiner Lichtenstein's study of 1990 aimed to show that not only the SS but even the ordinary police had been involved in atrocities. Once Himmler took control of the whole security and police apparatus across the Reich (1936), police roles were mixed, so that the distinction between the 'criminal' SS and the 'decent' Order Police was nothing more than a postwar myth. As Lichtenstein says, had the Allied judges at Nuremberg examined the internal structure of the SS, they would rapidly have announced that the Order Police, like the SS, was a criminal organization.[49]

As with individual perpetrators, studies of institutions reveal that ideological commitment tended to run deep. The closer they were to the centre of the Nazi Party the more this holds true. With respect to the Gestapo, for example, once historians turned in the 1980s and 1990s away from institutional histories and looked instead at the Gestapo's actual operations and actions, they made several important discoveries. Not only did the Gestapo rely heavily on support from the German public—in making denunciations, for example—since it was far less omnipotent that its own propaganda (and postwar historiography) suggested; furthermore, 'the National Socialist "Prerogative State" (*Maßnahmenstaat*) was certainly no thoroughly rationalized mechanism of repression.'[50] Since the bulk of the

---

48. Hüppauf cited in Paul, 'Von Psychopathen', p. 42.
49. Heiner Lichtenstein, *Himmlers Grüne Helfer: Die Schutz- und Ordnungspolizei im 'Dritten Reich'* (Cologne: Bund Verlag, 1990), p. 27.
50. Klaus-Michael Mallmann and Gerhard Paul, 'Omniscient, Omnipotent, Omnipresent? Gestapo, Society and Resistance' in *Nazism and German Society*, ed. Crew, pp. 173–4. The reference is to Ernst Fraenkel's distinction between the 'normative state' (*Normenstaat*) and the 'prerogative state' (*Maßnahmenstaat*), concepts first put forward in his 1941 work *The Dual State*. These concepts, which help explain why the split between state and party is too simplistic to encompass the complexity of the Third Reich's inner workings (see,

Gestapo was formed from the Political Department of the Weimar police, committed ideologues were usually to be found only at the top levels; as Mallmann and Paul note, in 1939 only 3,000 of roughly 20,000 employees held an SS rank.[51] This was not an efficient organization, and it relied on 'professional and amateur helpers', of whom there were a substantial number.[52]

By contrast, the SS, which certainly had its organizational difficulties, was more thoroughly suffused with Nazi ideology. Here we see that ideology is not necessarily incompatible with efficiency and bureaucracy; nevertheless, organizational competence was clearly not the driving force behind the SS's promotion of Nazi genocidal policies. As most recent histories show, or at least imply, SS bureaucracies did not invent the idea of mass murder because they were bureaucracies.

Studies of the SS have always been prominent in the historiography of the Third Reich. In the last twenty years, that research has tended to reflect the broader trends of the historiography, moving from a functionalist perspective—including debates about polycracy or total control—to the 'return of ideology'. Published at the high point of the functionalist consensus, Herbert Ziegler's *Nazi Germany's New Aristocracy* drew on social-science models to analyse the make-up of the SS's leaders; he concluded that the SS constituted a ' "test-tube revolution" in elite recruitment and advancement'.[53] Jens Banach's prosopography of the officer corps of the SiPo (*Sicherheitspolizei*/security police) and SD arrives at a similar conclusion, as do George Browder's and Jan Erik Schulte's analyses of the SD and WVHA (see below). Although the leadership of the SD tended to come from 'respectable' strata of society, mid-level SD functionaries were more likely to have been promoted on the basis of merit, since

for example, Neumann, *Behemoth*, p. 72: 'We are confronted by two simultaneous trends: enormous growth of the public bureaucracy in number and function; and an ideological campaign of denunciation waged against the bureaucracy, accompanied by a campaign to aggrandize the party'), are tested in Gruner and Nolzen, eds., *Bürokratien*.

51. Mallmann and Paul, 'Omniscient, Omnipotent, Omnipresent?', p. 176.

52. Robert Gellately, *The Gestapo and German Society: Enforcing Racial Policy 1933–1945* (Oxford: Clarendon Press, 1991), p. 72; also Gellately, 'The Gestapo and German Society: Political Denunciation in the Gestapo Case Files', *JMH*, 60, 4 (1988), pp. 654–94; Eric A. Johnson, *Nazi Terror: The Gestapo, Jews, and Ordinary Germans* (New York: Basic Books, 1999).

53. Herbert F. Ziegler, *Nazi Germany's New Aristocracy: The SS Leadership, 1925–1939* (Princeton: Princeton University Press, 1989), p. 148, citing Leonard Krieger, 'Nazism: Highway or Byway?', *CEH*, 11, 1 (1978), p. 15. See also Bernd Wegner, 'The "Aristocracy of National Socialism": The Role of the SS in National Socialist Germany' in *Aspects of the Third Reich*, ed. H. W. Koch (Basingstoke: Macmillan, 1985), pp. 430–50.

their 'personality structure—bureaucratic pedantry, ambition, and lust for power—corresponded with the SD-atmosphere of mysteriousness and exceptionality'.[54] These are the men described by Wildt as the 'unbound generation'. As for the leaders of the SS, they are the men most associated with terror and mass murder on the one hand and 'ruthless efficiency' on the other. Smelser and Syring sum up the dualism:

> In spite of a strong anti-modern and ruralist ideological component, the SS depicted itself as a modern, corporate structure of international caliber. In an age of secularization, it embodied for the 'true believers' among its members a kind of 'priesthood' analogous to the medieval knights' orders, opening an outlet for a kind of secular religiosity for them.[55]

More recently, and by striking contrast with Ziegler's social-science methodology, Martin Cüppers shows that the Waffen-SS—the militarized wing of the SS—displayed a high degree of ideological affinity with Nazism and that it was heavily involved with the ghettoization and forced labour processes in Poland and then the murder of the Jews in the Soviet Union.[56] The extent of the Waffen-SS's ideological commitment is summed up in a passage where Cüppers breaks with the historian's customary sober tone. After citing the words of an SS-Junker in 1944 to the effect that Germany would win the war because of its racial superiority, Cüppers writes: 'For half-way rational people, Germany's military defeat was abundantly clear by the summer of 1944. By contrast, the young SS-Junker's hallucinatory National Socialist victory points to the SS's widely-held belief, at the war's final stages, in a fanatical "final victory mentality" that was totally divorced from reality.'[57]

Some parts of the SS were of course devoted to racial–ideological questions, most notably the *Rasse- und Siedlungshauptamt* (RuSHA, Race and Resettlement Head Office), which has been investigated by Isabel Heinemann. The RuSHA was founded in 1932 and constituted one of the three oldest 'pillars' of the SS. Originally set up to assess the racial selection

54. Jens Banach, *Heydrichs Elite: Das Führungskorps der Sicherheitspolizei und des SD 1936–1945* (Paderborn: Schöningh, 1998), p. 19. Cf. Browder, *Hitler's Enforcers: The Gestapo and the SS Security Service in the Nazi Revolution* (New York: Oxford University Press, 1996).
55. Ronald Smelser and Enrico Syring, 'Annäherungen an die "Elite unter dem Totenkopf" ' in *Die SS: Elite unter dem Totenkopf. 30 Lebensläufe*, eds. Smelser and Syring (Paderborn: Schöningh, 2000), p. 10.
56. Martin Cüppers, *Wegbereiter der Shoah: Die Waffen-SS, der Kommandostab Reichsführer-SS und die Judenvernichtung 1939–1945* (Darmstadt: Wissenschaftliche Buchgesellschaft, 2005).
57. Cüppers, *Wegbereiter*, p. 107.

of SS candidates and their wives, its remit expanded enormously during the war. Under its leader Otto Hofmann, and some 500 'race experts', the RuSHA sought to provide German policies of conquest, annihilation, and Germanization with a racial 'soul'. The fact that many of the RuSHA men belonged to Hans F. K. Günther's Nordic Ring, one of the most passionate of the pre-1933 *völkisch* organizations, is instructive, for it demonstrates the seriousness with which the agency regarded racial anthropology and its significance for the 'Germanic race'. The RuSHA was responsible for organizing the expulsion of ethnic Poles from the annexed regions of western Poland, for replacing them with *Volksdeutsche* and settlers from the Reich, and for assessing the racial value of huge populations. Those deemed 'racially valuable' or 'regermanizable' were locally employed or sent to work in Germany where they would aid the war economy and be 'returned to Germandom', and those deemed 'racially inferior' were to be 'removed', either by deportation 'to the east' or by being murdered on the spot. Plans for deportation extended to 31 million people from Poland, the Baltic, and the Soviet Union. Only the Jews were not required to pass through this process of racial assessment, for they were to be deported and murdered without exception.

Heinemann shows that the genocide of the Jews was bound up with racial policies that sought to reshape the demography of the whole continent. For whilst most Jews and many Poles and Romanies were being murdered, those of 'average racial value' were set to work, and those labelled 'racially valuable' from eastern and western Europe were subjected to a process of forced Germanization. As Heinemann points out, what is striking is not that the RuSHA extended its operation across occupied Europe, from Oslo to Kiev, but that in its work one can see the way in which selection and breeding ideals originally designed for the elite order of the SS were extended to the populations of conquered regions. She shows that Nazi population policy as a whole, which includes the murder of the Jews, can only be understood on the basis of racial presuppositions. All occupation agencies—and here the RuSHA is paradigmatic—worked within a shared racist framework: 'Without a precisely executed sorting of people according to "racial criteria", the planned population movements, the "removal" of the "unrequired" and the promotion of "regermanizables" would have lacked foundations.'[58]

---

58. Isabel Heinemann, *'Rasse, Siedlung, deutsches Blut': Das Rasse- und Siedlungshauptamt der SS und die rassenpolitische Neuordnung Europas* (Göttingen: Wallstein, 2003), p. 38.

It is likely that Heinemann overstates the importance of the RuSHA to the SS *Volkstums*-apparatus; the RuSHA did not have the resources to assess the racial characteristics of the whole population of the western Polish regions or Alsace-Lorraine.[59] Nor should we see the Holocaust solely as a by-product of the 'sorting' of eastern-European populations. But in terms of what the RuSHA tells us about the organization of Nazi racial policies, and the supposed opposition between 'modernity' and non-rational ideology, Heinemann rightly sees them as intertwined. Numerous agencies were involved in the racial purification of the occupied eastern territories apart from the RSHA: 'race experts from the RuSHA, police forces, labour office officials, farmers and representatives of the Gau administrations'. Her conclusion backs up the claim of Gruner and Nolzen that 'polycracy' should not be understood as synonymous with chaos: 'The cooperation of various different offices must have greatly facilitated the smooth functioning of each one, since the participants viewed themselves as firmly integrated into an objective administrative process. The implementation and radicalization of the "redistribution of population", the evacuations and settlements in occupied Western Poland, are best explained with the help of a double perspective of racist ideology and cooperative practice.'[60]

Similarly, the Interior Ministry agency, the *Reichssippenamt* (RSA, Reich Kinship Office), was, by the mid-1930s, the 'sole administrative body for processing complicated cases of descent in the population at large'.[61] Although not part of the SS—indeed, increasingly in competition with it—the RSA reveals the extent to which racial thought was administered by a bureaucratic apparatus devoted to creating the Aryan people's community. Its task was to adjudicate in cases of disputed racial ancestry and to issue *Ariernachweise* (racial certificates) on the basis of racial examinations,

59. Heinemann, '*Rasse, Siedlung, deutsches Blut*', pp. 601–2 n8 for figures. For an emphasis on the relatively small numbers of Polish forced labourers who underwent 'racial selection', see Gerhard Wolf, 'Rassistische Utopien und ökonomischen Zwänge: die rassischen Selektionen polnischer Arbeitskräfte durch die SS in den Lagern der Umwandererzentralstelle' in *Nationalsozialistische Lager: Neue Beiträge zur NS-Verfolgungs- und Vernichtungspolitik und zur Gedenkstättenpädagogik*, eds. Akim Jah, Christoph Kopke, Alexander Korb, and Alexa Stiller (Münster: Klemm & Oelschläger, 2006), pp. 125–48.
60. Isabel Heinemann, ' "Ethnic Resettlement" and Inter-Agency Cooperation in the Occupied Eastern Territories' in *Networks of Nazi Persecution*, eds. Feldman and Seibel, p. 229. See also Heinemann, ' "Another Type of Perpetrator": SS Racial Experts and Forced Population Movements in the Occupied Regions', *HGS*, 15, 3 (2001), pp. 387–411.
61. Thomas Pegelow, 'Determining "People of German Blood", "Jews" and "*Mischlinge*": The Reich Kinship Office and the Competing Discourses and Powers of Nazism, 1941–1943', *Contemporary European History*, 15, 1 (2006), p. 45.

which were often carried out with the assistance of the Kaiser-Wilhelm Institute for Anthropology. Thomas Pegelow shows how the practices of the RSA changed over time, as interpretations of who counted as a *Mischling* developed. He shows too that different officials within the agency interpreted the rules differently, with the result that disputes sometimes arose over who was a 'Jew'. By 1943, as the RSA was coming under the political influence of the SS, the regulations hardened and the earlier flexibility in decision-making was somewhat eroded. The SS wanted to end the equivocation over the definition of *Mischlinge* and to do so in a way that was not beneficial to them, that is, not to classify them as 'German'. They intervened more and more in the work of the RSA with the aim of clarifying the distinction between 'German' and 'Jew' in a radical way.[62] Indeed, at the end of the war, plans were afoot to incorporate the RSA into the RuSHA.

Following Heinemann's comments on the RuSHA and Pegelow's on the RSA, it is clear that, although inter-agency competition existed, that fact did not prevent working towards a shared goal. In his study of the RSA, Eric Ehrenreich confirms this impression:

> The Genealogical Authority files support the view of Nazi Germany as a polycracy: numerous agencies, without clear lines of authority, competed with each other for increased power. The authority itself was in a constant state of tension between the maintenance and delegation of its authority. Yet despite the ongoing conflict over questions of power and resources, in no instance did I note in any other institution's dealings with the Genealogical Authority even a hint of doubt as to the propriety of the ancestral proof requirement. Again, all—whether party, state, or private—acted as if having to prove one's racial suitability was a completely natural practice.[63]

Here we see polycracy, in the sense of shared ambition in the context of bureaucratic competition. However, bureaucracy was not driving the process; rather, it was fulfilling the requirements of a radical regime that had at its disposal the tools of a modern state.

If one turns to an organization that was more remote from the centre of the SS's power, such as the *Volksdeutsche Mittelstelle* (VoMi, Ethnic German

---

62. Pegelow, 'Determining', p. 63.
63. Eric Ehrenreich, *The Nazi Ancestral Proof: Genealogy, Racial Science, and the Final Solution* (Bloomington: Indiana University Press, 2007), pp. 83–84. Ehrenreich refers to the 'Reich Genealogical Authority' to describe the various incarnations of the body that eventually became the RSA. See also Diana Schulle, *Das Reichssippenamt: Eine Institution nationalsozialistischer Rassenpolitik* (Berlin: Logos, 2001).

Liaison Office), set up in 1935 to act as an interface between the Reich and the *Volksdeutsche* living outside it, one sees a similar picture: polycratic disorganization, but the commitment to a racial politics that usually managed to transcend intra-SS sectarian interests. Notorious *Volksdeutsche* regiments such as the Prinz Eugen Division in Yugoslavia are only the best known of such units, and by some reckonings there were more *Volksdeutsche* than Reich Germans in the Waffen-SS by the end of the war.[64]

What is significant is that the more such studies appear, the more the 'race paradigm' is understood less as a free-floating signifier than as a contested set of practices and beliefs that were sites of negotiation and competition over definition and action. This does not devalue the importance of 'race', but suggests that individuals in the Third Reich might have engaged with the regime's 'racializing' demands for a number of reasons. Where early scholars of the Third Reich like Fraenkel identified a 'dual state', so much of the recent literature stresses the cynical, 'nation-building' aspect of Nazism over its ideological commitments. The notion of the Third Reich as a gangster regime is apparent in studies of looting, for example, or in the operation of the various levels of bureaucracy in the state, for example, in the failure of the civil authorities to rein in Party organizations in the occupied east, where, as Rebentisch writes, 'The surviving files and witness testimonies unanimously report that in the occupied eastern territories, organs of the traditional state administration and elements of the Führer's executive, as well as senior party members and their organizations, and all sorts of semi-official agencies wrestled with each other for decision-making power, admittedly in a relationship which was much more favourable for the NSDAP's political leadership than in the *Altreich*.'[65]

Yet the race paradigm, even if its omnipresence can be overstated, still holds considerable importance. Whatever their reason for subscribing to it, it is striking how quickly and easily the majority of the German population adapted themselves to its requirements. A good example is Cornelia Essner's study of the Nuremberg Laws, or, as she subtitles her book, 'the administration of racial madness'. The juxtaposition of 'administration' and 'racial madness' provides a salutary reminder that paranoid racial theories did not exist solely in a world of fantasy but were indeed administered by the

---

64. Valdis O. Lumans, *Himmler's Auxiliaries: The Volksdeutsche Mittelstelle and the German National Minorities of Europe, 1933–1945* (Chapel Hill: University of North Carolina Press, 1993), p. 216.
65. Rebentisch, *Führerstaat und Verwaltung*, p. 325.

modern state; and that the emphasis on the state—which tends to be bound up with ideas of rational, or means–ends bureaucratic procedures—can all too easily overlook the specific 'non-rational' dynamic that drove the process. A fundamentally non-rational belief in the existence of a threat posed by Jewish blood was judicially organized, legislated against, and administered. Essner notes that the debate over who counted as a Jew was especially fierce among the SS after December 1943—precisely when the majority of Jews killed in the Final Solution were already dead. As Essner writes, Himmler's belief in the 'dominance of Jewish blood' meant that debates over what to do with *Mischlinge* and how to limit the spread of 'Jewish blood' outlasted the genocide itself.[66] Rebentisch too concludes that 'polycracy was the particular method of rule of an irrationally-led ideological movement, which conducted a radical war against state and society'; he further claims that the National Socialist Führer-state was not a brutal variant of the authoritarian state but 'an anachronistic system of personal loyalties [*Personenverband*] centred on Hitler's tyranny'.[67]

But probably the most revealing example for a discussion of modernity and ideology is the *Wirtschafts-Verwaltungshauptamt* (WVHA, Economic Administrative Main Office), since this was the agency within the SS that above all others sought to embody the principles of productivity, efficiency, and technocratic business management. Led by Oswald Pohl, the WVHA was founded in 1942 out of the former *SS-Verwaltungs- und Wirtschaftsorganisation*. As of March 1942, the WVHA controlled the concentration camps and managed a massive economic empire whose more than 40,000 employees oversaw more than half a million concentration camp inmates in 1,200 *Nebenlager* (auxiliary camps). As Schulte points out, the WVHA uniquely combined bureaucratic procedures and legal norms with control over the concentration camps, the 'extra-normative terror instrument of the National Socialist "prerogative state" '.[68]

After Himmler and Heydrich, Pohl was the third most powerful man in the SS; yet he argued in Nuremberg that 'his rational management

66. Cornelia Essner, *Die 'Nürnberger Gesetze' oder Die Verwaltung des Rassenwahns 1933–1945* (Paderborn: Schöningh, 2002), p. 444.
67. Rebentisch, *Führerstaat und Verwaltung*, pp. 552–3.
68. Jan Erik Schulte, 'Die Konvergenz von Normen- und Maßnahmenstaat: Das Beispiel SS-Wirtschafts-Verwaltungshauptamt, 1925–1945' in *Bürokratien*, eds. Gruner and Nolzen, p. 152. For the most detailed study of the SS economy, see Hermann Kaienburg, *Die Wirtschaft der SS* (Berlin: Metropol, 2003).

of a "modern" administration relieved him of any direct responsibility
for crimes against humanity'. He was, however, responsible for no fewer
murders than Heydrich or Eichmann.[69] Indeed, in his important study
on the WVHA, Jan Erik Schulte characterizes Pohl as 'an ideologically-
motivated careerist'.[70] Majdanek (KL Lublin) was conceived as the centre
of a reservoir of forced labour for the settlement of the eastern territories
and Jewish slave labour was also organized under the aegis of the WVHA.
As Schulte shows, slave labour did not contradict the extermination policy:
'The goal was not the execution of a particular task, but the murder of
the people concerned.'[71] Economic rationality was not much in evidence:
'economic thinking dominated SS concerns for only a few years'.[72]

Donald Bloxham reminds us that 'extermination through labour' is a
term that needs to be unpacked, and that there was no single rule for
the treatment of groups, which changed over time. Wolf Gruner concurs,
demonstrating that as many as one million Jews were used as labourers in
camps run not by the SS but by civil administrations, tens of thousands
of whom survived the war as a result. Gruner is quite right to assert
that 'The fact that hundreds of special forced labor camps existed for
German, Austrian, and Polish Jews, entirely independently of the SS-
administered concentration camp system, is scarcely known even today',
and he argues that historians' focus on the *Generalgouvernement* has distorted
the wider picture by generalizing from what was 'a regional or local
phenomenon'. Yet even if 'ideology did not always in all sectors totally
govern the treatment of the Jews: economics sometimes played a role',
neither Gruner's nor Bloxham's research overturns the general rule, which
is that, for the most part, Jews were to perish irrespective of economic need
or rational calculation.[73]

69. Michael Allen, 'Oswald Pohl: Chef der SS-Wirtschaftsunternehmen' in *Die SS*, eds. Smelser
    and Syring, p. 394.
70. Jan Erik Schulte, *Zwangsarbeit und Vernichtung: Das Wirtschaftsimperium der SS. Oswald Pohl und
    das SS-Wirtschafts-Verwaltungshauptamt 1933–1945* (Paderborn: Schöningh, 2001), pp. 32–45.
71. Schulte, *Zwangsarbeit und Vernichtung*, p. 364.
72. Schulte, *Zwangsarbeit und Vernichtung*, p. 439.
73. Donald Bloxham, *'Extermination Through Work': Jewish Slave Labour under the Third Reich*
    (London: Holocaust Educational Trust, 1999), p. 1; Bloxham, *The Final Solution: A Geno-
    cide* (Oxford: Oxford University Press, 2009); Wolf Gruner, *Jewish Forced Labor under the
    Nazis: Economic Needs and Racial Aims, 1938–1944* (Cambridge: Cambridge University Press,
    2006), p. xiv; Gruner, 'Jewish Forced Labor as a Basic Element of Nazi Persecution:
    Germany, Austria, and the Occupied Polish Territories (1938–1943)' in *Forced and Slave
    Labor in Nazi-Dominated Europe: Symposium Presentations* (Washington, DC: United States
    Holocaust Memorial Museum, 2004), p. 43. See also Nikolaus Wachsmann, ' "Annihilation

For the Jewish slave labourers at IG Farben, for example, 'work' was not a way of escaping death; rather, it constituted an alternative way to die. As Bernd Wagner notes, 'It was apparently of no concern to the SS how inmates lost their lives. The "annihilation through labour" system, established with the help of IG, met the tasks set by the RSHA planners just as well as gassing—with the additional "advantage" that the Reich made something from its victims.'[74] At *Ostindustrie*, an SS enterprise founded by Pohl in March 1943 that lasted only eight months but in that time operated some sixteen different plants and operations, Jewish labour was not a route to salvation, but, according to Schulte, was 'merely a synonym for a longer death.'[75] Economically speaking, the result of this mistreatment of the slave labourers was that productivity was poor and there was no meaningful armaments production. Even though some Jews were put to work, no effort was made (or was successful on the part of those who tried) to improve the inmates' living conditions and thus their ability to work. 'For the inmates', writes Schulte, 'the camps remained places solely of terror and murder. That did not prevent Himmler and Pohl, who ignored the real conditions in the camps, from seeing the inmates above all as a potential workforce for their armaments factories.'[76]

The WVHA, then, shows the limits of rationality in the SS empire. Although there were those who were frustrated by the inability of Pohl and Himmler to adjust their short-term thinking and to use the potential productivity of the Jews at least for the time needed to win the war, the camps remained conducive only to murder. The history of *Ostindustrie* shows 'how varied the SS's actions were, and how independently

Through Labor": The Killing of State Prisoners in the Third Reich', *JMH*, 71, 3 (1999), pp. 624–59; Mark Spoerer, *Zwangsarbeit unter dem Hakenkreuz: Ausländische Zivilarbeiter, Kriegsgefangene und Häftlinge im Dritten Reich und im besetzten Europa 1939–1945* (Stuttgart: Deutsche Verlags-Anstalt, 2001); Mark Spoerer and Jochen Fleischhacker, 'Forced Laborers in Nazi Germany: Categories, Numbers, and Survivors', *Journal of Interdisciplinary History*, 33, 2 (2002), pp. 169–204; Ulrich Herbert, *Hitler's Foreign Workers* (Cambridge: Cambridge University Press, 1997). It is worth bearing in mind Hilberg's claim (*Destruction*, Vol. 2, p. 542) that 'The Polish Jews were annihilated in a process in which economic factors were truly secondary'.

74. Bernd C. Wagner, 'Gerüchte, Wissen, Verdrängung: Die IG Auschwitz und das Vernichtungslager Birkenau' in *Ausbeutung, Vernichtung, Öffentlichkeit: Neue Studien zur nationalsozialistischen Lagerpolitik*, eds. Norbert Frei, Sybille Steinbacher and Bernd C. Wagner (Munich: K. G. Saur, 2000), p. 238. See also Wagner, *IG Auschwitz: Zwangsarbeit und Vernichtung von Häftlingen des Lagers Monowitz 1941–1945* (Munich: K. G. Saur, 2000).
75. Jan Erik Schulte, 'Zwangsarbeit für die SS: Juden in der Ostindustrie GmbH' in *Ausbeutung, Vernichtung, Öffentlichkeit*, eds. Herbert et al., p. 43.
76. Schulte, 'Zwangsarbeit für die SS', p. 73.

different authorities could act, as long as Himmler did not personally intervene'. Furthermore, whilst *Ostindustrie* reveals that the murder of the Jews played a part in the SS's economic considerations, it clearly indicates that 'modern' rational thinking did not prevail over ideological interest.[77]

Although his stress on 'modernization' distinguishes his approach from Schulte's, the assertion that 'rational' thinking did not prevail is confirmed by Michael Thad Allen. Although they are terms that Schulte would reject, Allen argues that for the SS managers, 'productivism' and 'modernization' went hand in hand with notions of racial supremacy and the creation of the 'New Order' in Europe. But the ideological enthusiasm came first, with the result that, with few exceptions, the WVHA's enterprises were badly managed. A good example is the *Deutsche Erd- und Steinwerke* (DESt, German Earth and Stone Works), where outside expert Erduin Schondorff introduced modern machinery and managerial methods following his appointment by Pohl. The continued use of unskilled concentration camp labourers meant that Schondorff's initiatives came to naught. By contrast, *Textil- und Lederverwertung GmbH* (TexLed, Textile and Leather Utilization Ltd) proved successful, thanks to the combination of good management (under committed Nazis Fritz Lechler and Felix Krug) and the fact that the labour-intensive work lent itself to the use of Ravensbrück's female slave labourers. The success of TexLed proves, says Allen, that 'there is no inherent contradiction between modern business organization, slavery, and barbaric ideology'.[78] But the only truly impressive WVHA success, according to Allen, was Hans Kammler, who headed the SS's construction corps after 1941. Kammler 'saw no contradiction between notions of blood and soil and the methods of modern organization and technology. He wished to place the best means of modern organization at the disposal of National Socialism; and among National Socialism's ideals was the glorification of modern means in the name of productivism.'[79] He went on to earn a formidable reputation for being able to push through major civil engineering works, making use of modern equipment where available and

---

77. Schulte, 'Zwangsarbeit für die SS', p. 74. See also Schulte, 'Die Konvergenz von Normen- und Maßnahmenstaat', pp. 179–80.

78. Michael Thad Allen, *The Business of Genocide: The SS, Slave Labor, and the Concentration Camps* (Chapel Hill: University of North Carolina Press, 2002), p. 71. On DESt, see especially Paul Jaskot, *The Architecture of Oppression: The SS, Forced Labor, and the Nazi Monumental Building Economy* (London: Routledge, 2000).

79. Allen, *Business*, p. 55.

brutally bringing in slave labourers where necessary, for example, in the construction of underground factories.[80]

Allen's evidence confirms Paul Jaskot's claim that the distinction between productive forced labour and oppression is not clear-cut.[81] It also shows that TexLed and Kammler were exceptions and that on the whole Pohl could not recruit men with the ability to combine modern managerial methods with a commitment to the Nazi world view. The IKL (*Inspektion der Konzentrationslager*), for example, remained impervious to modernization. Thus, if 'modernity' is equated, à la Bauman, with technology and rational means–end thinking and bureaucratization, then the WVHA only partly meets the definition. Allen himself notes that 'we can understand the SS's modernization drive only if we do not conflate "modernity" with "rationality" and "pure" technocratic instrumentalism, or insist that modernization necessarily leads to a democratic polity, or the full flowering of the Enlightenment'.[82] Although Allen replicates this way of thinking to some extent in his study—the implication seems to be that where managerial efficiency was absent, so too was 'modernity'—he is theoretically astute in asserting that the SS, especially the WVHA, can still be seen as 'modern', as long as one does not simply equate 'modernity' with 'rationality' and 'technocracy'. In other words, 'The Nazis' vision of modernity was only one among many that demonstrate how irrational belief in modernization can be.'[83]

We now have a significant historiography of the agencies and institutions that made up the administrative apparatus of the Third Reich. Whether one looks at the police apparatus or more specific agencies such as the *Einsatzstab Reichsleiter Rosenberg*, responsible for coordinating art theft across Europe,[84] or the RSA, the administration of the NSDAP, or civil and military administrative structures in the *Altreich* or the occupied territories, one sees

80. Allen, *Business*, p. 206.
81. Paul Jaskot, 'Concentration Camps and Cultural Policy: Rethinking the Development of the Camp System, 1936–41' in *Lessons and Legacies, Vol. 6*, ed. Diefendorf, p. 7.
82. Allen, *Business*, p. 272.
83. Allen, *Business*, p. 272. See also Allen, 'The Business of Genocide: The SS, Slavery, and the Concentration Camps' in *Business and Industry*, eds. Nicosia and Huener, pp. 81–103, and the subtle discussion of Schulte and Allen in Nikolaus Wachsmann, 'Looking into the Abyss: Historians and the Nazi Concentration Camps', *European History Quarterly*, 36, 2 (2006), pp. 258–61.
84. On the ERR, see Jonathan Petropoulos, 'The Polycratic Nature of Art Looting: The Dynamic Balance of the Third Reich' in *Networks*, eds. Feldman and Seibel, pp. 103–17; Petropoulos, *Art as Politics in the Third Reich* (Chapel Hill: University of North Carolina Press, 1996).

certain factors in common: competition and rivalry, certainly, but also some things taken for granted, to the fulfilment of which the various agencies were dedicated. Most notable here is Jewish policy; subject to bureaucratic administration in many cases and 'initiative' in others, all the competing agencies of the Nazi regime subscribed—some more enthusiastically than others—to the aim of eradicating the Jewish population from Europe.[85] This is true at the local level in Nazi Germany, as the flowering of regional history is bringing to light.[86] What determined this involvement was not the degree of bureaucratization; rather, bureaucracy was placed at the service of the realization of the Nazi world view.

Beyond analyses of Nazi agencies and institutions, there has also been an important intrusion of economic history into the debate about modernity and the Holocaust. In particular, apart from the issue of forced and slave labour, the question of food supply is linked by some historians to the history of the unfolding of Nazi genocide, against not just the Jews but the occupied populations of eastern Europe in general. Christian Gerlach and Christoph Dieckmann have argued that the immediate catalyst for murder was the problem of feeding the Wehrmacht in eastern Europe, and that this helps explain the realization of the pre-existing plan to starve the urban (and largely Jewish) populations of Belorussia and Lithuania. Both stress the fact that murderous attitudes to Jews were already in place, but see economic considerations as the spark that brought that potential to life.[87] Gerlach in particular has developed the link between

---

85. Rebentisch and Teppe, eds., *Verwaltung contra Menschenführung*; Gruner and Nolzen, eds., *'Bürokratien'*; Armin Nolzen, 'Charismatic Legitimation and Bureaucratic Rule: The NSDAP in the Third Reich, 1933–1945', *GH*, 23, 4 (2005), pp. 494–518; Bogdan Musial, *Deutsche Zivilverwaltung und Judenverfolgung im Generalgouvernement: Eine Fallstudie zum Distrikt Lublin 1939–1944* (Wiesbaden: Harrasowitz, 1999). Hilberg (*Destruction*, Vol. 1, p. 56) pointed this out long ago: 'In spite of the different historical origins of these four bureaucracies [civil service, military, industry and the Nazi Party] and in spite of their different interests, all four could agree on the destruction of the Jews.'

86. Wolf Gruner, 'Local Initiatives, Central Coordination: German Municipal Administration and the Holocaust' in *Networks*, eds. Feldman and Seibel, pp. 269–94; Gruner, 'The German Council of Municipalities (*Deutscher Gemeindetag*) and the Coordination of Anti-Jewish Local Politics in the Nazi State', *HGS*, 13, 2 (1999), pp. 171–99; Panikos Panayi, *Life and Death in a German Town: Osnabrück from the Weimar Republic to World War II and Beyond* (London: I. B. Tauris, 2007); Andrew Bergerson, *Ordinary Germans in Extraordinary Times: The Nazi Revolution in Hildesheim* (Bloomington: Indiana University Press, 2004); Claus-Christian W. Szejnmann, *Nazism in Central Germany: The Brown Shirts in Red Saxony* (New York: Berghahn, 1999); and the references in Peter Longerich, *'Davon haben wir nichts gewusst!' Die Deutschen und die Judenverfolgung 1933–1945* (Munich: Siedler, 2006).

87. Christian Gerlach, 'German Economic Interests, Occupation Policy, and the Murder of the Jews in Belorussia, 1941/43' and Christoph Dieckmann, 'The War and the Killing of

food and genocide. He sees food policy as the key factor linking the terrorization of the Poles, Ukrainians, and Jews, and argues that economic problems in the *Generalgouvernement*—from the point of view of the German occupiers—expedited the decision to murder Jews 'incapable of work' in order to feed the non-Jewish population. From the start of the occupation, it was 'clear that the Jews' rations were even less able to sustain life than those of the Belorussians and Poles. What aggravated matters were the Germans' random halts in supply or decreases in allocations.'[88] When the food situation worsened, in August–September 1942, so Gerlach claims, the decision was made to kill all Jews in the *Generalgouvernement*, including workers. Some were temporarily saved by the intervention of the armaments industry, but hundreds of thousands were killed. A similar scenario unfolded in Volhynia-Podolia, according to Gerlach.[89] Gerlach has been criticized along similar lines as Aly and Heim, that is to say, the nature of the genocide cannot be understood through the lenses of nutrition policy. But Gerlach does not deny the significance of pre-existing racial ideas for understanding the Nazis; rather, he seeks to show how these ideas interacted with economic realities on the ground during the occupation of eastern Europe.[90] 'Food policy', he argues, 'was by no means merely an auxiliary factor which disguised the "real" goal, the extermination of the Jews.'[91] Most historians would not disagree; the question is one of tone and the relative weight to be placed on the occupiers' perception of economic circumstances and Nazi antisemitism. The 'rational' decision to save food by killing the Jews presupposes an already existing antisemitic world view.

Trying to reconcile these factors has become a productive way of understanding the context in which the decision-making process unfolded. Adam Tooze, in his study of the Third Reich's economy, relies heavily on Gerlach in his chapter on labour, food, and genocide. Noting that, in general,

the Lithuanian Jews', both in *National Socialist Extermination Policies: Contemporary German Perspectives and Controversies*, ed. Ulrich Herbert (New York: Berghahn, 1999), pp. 210–39 and 240–75. See also Gerlach, 'Failure of Plans for an SS Extermination Camp in Mogilev, Belorussia', *HGS*, 11, 1 (1997), pp. 60–78.

88. Gerlach, *Kalkulierte Morde: Die deutsche Wirtschafts- und Vernichtungspolitik in Weißrußland 1941 bis 1944* (Hamburg: Hamburger Edition, 1999), p. 672.

89. Christian Gerlach, *Krieg, Ernährung, Völkermord: Forschungen zur deutschen Vernichtungspolitik im Zweiten Weltkrieg* (Hamburg: Hamburger Edition, 1998), pp. 168–9.

90. Cüppers, for example (*Wegbereiter*, p. 13), claims with explicit reference to Gerlach that the actions of the Waffen-SS in Belorussia cannot be understood in these terms.

91. Gerlach, *Krieg, Ernährung, Völkermord*, p. 251.

ideology trumped labour requirements where the murder of the Jews was concerned, Tooze correctly observes that focusing only on labour means that one overlooks the question of food, a question that 'in 1941 had been an independent and powerful "economic" imperative for mass murder'.[92] He follows Gerlach in focusing especially on the *Generalgouvernement*, where Minister of Food and Agriculture Herbert Backe (who had taken over from his former boss, the increasingly marginalized Walther Darré) promoted radical policies aimed at ensuring the German food supply, the failure of which during World War I had been a source of great discontent on the home front. Backe, writes Tooze, 'predicated his demands specifically on the elimination of the Polish Jews from the food chain'.[93] The integration of labour and food supply questions into the decision-making process adds considerably to our understanding of the functions and roles of the different bureaucratic agencies involved in occupation administration and genocide (Backe-Himmler-Goering, Gauleiter Sauckel as general plenipotentiary for labour mobilization, and Albert Speer); but, where the interaction of the Hunger Plan and the Holocaust is concerned, have these historians described anything more than a coincidence of wants? As Gesine Gerhard notes, the documents prove that Backe was responsible for mass murder, 'but they do not prove that food policy was the driving force behind the Final Solution'.[94]

*

All of the above suggests a kind of neo-functionalist approach or organization-theory approach, stressing 'network interactions' as key. But what is it really the key to? The 'networks' approach might help us understand the functioning of the polycratic bureaucracy that administered the Holocaust, but not the origin of the murderous idea, unless one accepts the claim—as few historians do—that the idea came from within the bureaucracy itself. The broader context of ideology and indoctrination, and the perpetrators' 'self-creation' as 'world-historical actors', as 'bearers of secrets' (*Geheimnisträger*) with their '*Ostrausch*' and sense of 'mission' should

---

92. Adam Tooze, *The Wages of Destruction: The Making and Breaking of the Nazi Economy* (London: Penguin, 2007), p. 538.
93. Tooze, *Wages*, p. 545.
94. Gesine Gerhard, 'Food and Genocide: Nazi Agrarian Politics in the Occupied Territories of the Soviet Union', *Contemporary European History*, 18, 1 (2009), p. 60; see also Uwe Mai, *Rasse und Raum: Agrarpolitik, Sozial- und Raumplanung im NS-Staat* (Paderborn: Schöningh, 2002).

not be forgotten in this context. Michael Thad Allen succinctly sets out the problematic:

> bureaucracies under National Socialism were not so much instrumental in overcoming 'resistance' to the Holocaust among 'ordinary Germans'; nor did they foster the 'banality of evil'; rather, they served to channel and recombine the enthusiasm of local functionaries. . . . The absence of concrete programmatic substance only enhanced the division of labor within the Nazi regime by spurring multiple initiatives, which could be understood, in the eyes of ambitious white-collar workers, as so many virtuous iterations of the 'Führer's' will. It is a tragic but conspicuous fact that the centralized bureaucracies of the Holocaust never lacked initiatives to choose from.[95]

Apart from Allen, perhaps the most insightful of the 'organization' scholars is Wolfgang Seibel, who in a number of articles depicts the interaction of ideological and organizational factors, arguing that whilst utilitarian motives were necessary for bringing in perpetrators, yet the whole enterprise was still based around a basic antisemitic premise:

> The very universalism of utilitarian motives triggered the mobilization of human resources for mass crime under a great variety of circumstances in German controlled Europe to a degree that never could have emanated from the particularism of anti-Semitic ideology. Utilitarian motivation of institutional actors was, presumably, the main source of radicalization. Anti-Semitism and state coercion, nonetheless, remained the constitutive basis of persecution. . . . [A]nti-Semitism represented a kind of convertible currency. Whatever the personal Weltanschauung, as soon as peripheral actors had something to offer the 'center' that fitted the anti-Semitic agenda they could expect advantages in exchange.[96]

Seibel thus confirms Pohl's and Matthäus's notion of an antisemitic consensus amongst perpetrators, even if for Seibel this was a state-directed position to which peripheral perpetrators subscribed less out of conviction than knowledge that doing so would bring them some reward.

In other words, the empirical historiography shows that the distinction between the normative and prerogative state is too clearly drawn, as is Weber's distinction between bureaucratic and charismatic legitimation of

95. Michael Thad Allen, 'A Bureaucratic Holocaust—Toward a New Consensus' in *Networks*, eds. Feldman and Seibel, p. 266.
96. Wolfgang Seibel, 'A Market for Mass Crime? Inter-Institutional Competition and the Initiation of the Holocaust in France, 1940–1942', *International Journal of Organization Theory and Behavior*, 5, 3&4 (2002), p. 236.

rule, at least as applied to the way that the Third Reich operated.[97] The emphasis on modernity in Bauman's terms ends by telling us nothing more than the *reductio ad absurdum* that the Holocaust occurred in the modern age. The studies of Nazi institutions based on concepts of organization, networks, and division of labour, borrowed from management theory, sometimes tend to the same circular argument, but they have the merit of explaining that modern bureaucratic structures and a supposedly anti-modern, non-rational *Weltanschauung* were compatible. If this seems to be stating the obvious, one might bear in mind that, in the popular imagination, it is apparently still hard to accept that Nazism was anything other than an atavistic throwback. The Holocaust was not simply the logical outcome of the organization society but nor was it simply a denial of modernity and Enlightenment. The idea for the Holocaust can only be understood in the context of centuries of anti-Jewish hatred and the short-term factors of imperial rivalry, World War I, the Great Depression, and the German interwar crisis. Yet this was still a modern idea in the sense that it was part of a revolt against modernity that is by necessity thoroughly modern (one can only be anti-modern if modernity exists). In Chapter 6 I will examine this dialectic in greater detail, and show how cultural history is helping us to understand the fatal juxtaposition of rationality and hatred that underpinned the Third Reich and its drive to destruction. But now let us turn to the one institution that typifies Nazi rule and that, for many scholars, exemplifies the intersection between modernity and genocide: the camp.

The Nazi Camps

What do studies of camps tell us about this debate? A mainstay of the historiography is the claim that the death camps marked a new and historically unprecedented stage in the genocidal process. The transition to gas chambers indicates to most historians that something specifically modern was taking place:

97. Frank Bajohr, 'The Holocaust and Corruption' in *Networks*, eds. Feldman and Seibel, pp. 133; Nolzen, 'Charismatic Legitimation', pp. 514–5; Wildt, *Generation des Unbedingten*, p. 858; Wildt, 'The Political Order of the Volksgemeinschaft: Ernst Fraenkel's Dual State Revisited' in *On Germans and Jews under the Nazi Regime: Essays by Three Generations of German Historians*, ed. Moshe Zimmermann (Jerusalem: Hebrew University Magnes Press, 2006), pp. 143–60.

The erection of extermination camps signified the decisive step in the history of the genocide's development. Killing by mobile shooting squads always had the character of a massacre. Planned and rationally-organized murder at centralized sites, at which a particular technique, operated by specialized personnel, was employed (gas chambers), made the genocide a quasi-industrial crime, whose dimensions had never been seen before, as was the case with the methodical realization of the intention.[98]

The camps then serve as perfect illustrations of the problem of talking about the relationship between 'organization' and 'ideology' in the perpetration of the Holocaust.

Of course, apart from this analytical or explanatory debate, recent research is important in its own right in filling many gaps in the historiography. For example, historians have begun exploring issues such as forced prostitution in the camps, seeing it as a form of slave labour and not, as in earlier sensationalist literature, a post for which 'asocial' women with loose morals volunteered.[99] Elsewhere they have discussed lesser known transit and auxiliary camps' place in the camp system, or the role played by *Volksdeutsche* as guards.[100] There exists a rather unappealing sub-genre concerning the technology of the gas chambers,[101] and debate continues over whether the Allies could or should have bombed Auschwitz.[102] Surprisingly, despite

98. Wolfgang Benz, 'Nationalsozialistische Zwangslager: Ein Überblick' in *Der Ort des Terrors: Geschichte der nationalsozialistischen Konzentrationslager. Vol. 1: Die Organisation des Terrors*, eds. Wolfgang Benz and Barbara Distel (Munich: Beck, 2005), pp. 24–5.

99. Robert Sommer, 'Die Häftlingsbordelle im KZ-Komplex Auschwitz-Birkenau: Sexzwangsarbeit im Spannungsfeld der NS-"Rassenpolitik" und der Bekämpfung von Geschlechtskrankheiten' in *Nationalsozialistische Lager*, eds. Jah et al., pp. 81–103; Christa Schikorra, 'Forced Prostitution in the Nazi Concentration Camps' and Doris L. Bergen, 'Sexual Violence in the Holocaust: Unique and Typical?', both in *Lessons and Legacies, Vol. 7*, ed. Herzog, pp. 169–78 and 179–200; Zoë Waxman, 'Testimony and Silence: Sexual Violence in the Holocaust' in *Feminism, Literature and Rape Narratives: Violence and Violation*, eds. Zoe Brigley and Sorcha Gunne (London: Routledge, 2010).

100. For example, Alexa Stiller, 'Zwischen Zwangsgermanisierung und "Fünfter Kolonne": "Volksdeutsche" als Häftlinge und Bewacher in den Konzentrationslagern' in *Nationalsozialistische Lager*, eds. Jah et al., pp. 104–24; *Dachauer Hefte, 5: Die vergessenen Lager* (Munich: Deutscher Taschenbuch Verlag, 1994).

101. Jean-Claude Pressac, *Auschwitz: Technique and Operation of the Gas Chambers* (New York: The Beate Klarsfeld Foundation, 1989); Michael Thad Allen, 'The Devil in the Details: The Gas Chambers of Birkenau, October 1941', *HGS*, 16, 2 (2002), pp. 189–216; Robert Jan van Pelt, *The Case for Auschwitz: Evidence from the Irving Trial* (Bloomington: Indiana University Press, 2002).

102. Richard Levy, 'The Bombing of Auschwitz: A Critical Analysis', *HGS*, 10, 3 (1996), pp. 267–98; Michael J. Neufeld and Michael Berenbaum, eds., *The Bombing of Auschwitz: Should the Allies Have Attempted It?* (New York: St Martin's Press, 2000); Edward B. Westermann, 'The Royal Air Force and the Bombing of Auschwitz: First Deliberations, January 1941', *HGS*, 15, 1 (2001), pp. 70–85; Jeffrey Herf, 'The Nazi Extermination Camps

the well-known images from the camps, drawn from film footage (such as the liberation of Auschwitz or Majdanek), reportage or testimonies, the historiography of the Nazi camps is relatively small, at least in comparison with other areas of Holocaust historiography, and the focus has been firmly on the camps inside Germany (Dachau, Sachsenhausen, Ravensbrück, Neuengamme, Bergen-Belsen, and Buchenwald, most prominently), which were statistically less significant than the killing centres in 'the east'. That situation is starting to change, especially with the appearance of multivolume studies of the camp system, but it is striking that there is still only one monograph on the Operation Reinhard camps, that the literature on Chełmno and Majdanek is vanishingly small, that a historiography on camps outside of the Reich and occupied Poland is still emerging,[103] that the experience of deportation has received so little attention,[104] and that there is not more on Auschwitz, given its predominant status in the scholarly and popular imagination.

Even theoretically, there has been surprisingly little work, although there is quite a large literature in 'memory studies' about the musealization of the camps and the changing roles they have played in memory culture since the end of the war.[105] The most significant sociological study of the camp system

and the Ally to the East: Could the Red Army and Air Force Have Stopped or Slowed the Final Solution?', *Kritika: Explorations in Russian and Eurasian History*, 4, 4 (2003), pp. 913–30.

103. For example, Monique-Lise Cohen and Eric Malo, *Les camps du sud-ouest de la France, 1933–1944: exclusion, internement et déportation* (Toulouse: Éditions Privat, 1994); Detlef Hoffmann and Volkhard Knigge, 'Die Südfranzösischen Lager' in *Das Gedächtnis der Dinge: KZ-Relikte und KZ-Denkmäler 1945–1995*, ed. Detlef Hoffmann (Frankfurt/M: Campus, 1998), pp. 206–23; Denis Peschanski, *La France des camps: L'internement 1938–1946* (Paris: Gallimard, 2002); Wolfgang Benz and Barbara Distel, eds., *Terror im Westen: Nationalsozialistische Lager in den Niederlanden, Belgien und Luxemburg 1940–1945* (Berlin: Metropol, 2004); Marğers Vestermanis, 'Die nationalsozialistischen Haftstätten und Todeslager im okkupierten Lettland 1941–1945' and Michael Wildt, 'Die Lager im Osten: Kommentierende Bemerkungen', both in *Die nationalsozialistischen Konzentrationslager*, Vol. 1, eds. Herbert, Orth, and Dieckmann, pp. 472–92 and 508–20.
104. Simone Gigliotti, *The Train Journey: Transit, Captivity, and Witnessing in the Holocaust* (New York: Berghahn, 2009).
105. For example: Hoffmann, ed., *Das Gedächtnis der Dinge*; Harald Marcuse, *Legacies of Dachau: The Uses and Abuses of a Concentration Camp 1933–2001* (Cambridge: Cambridge University Press, 2001); Robin Ostow, 'Reimagining Ravensbrück', *Journal of European Area Studies*, 9, 1 (2001), pp. 107–23; Sarah Farmer, 'Symbols that Face Two Ways: Commemorating the Victims of Nazism and Stalinism at Buchenwald and Sachsenhausen', *Representations*, 49 (1995), pp. 97–119; Chris Keil, 'Sightseeing in the Mansions of the Dead', *Social & Cultural Geography*, 6, 4 (2005), pp. 479–94; Barbara Buntman, 'Tourism and Tragedy: The Memorial at Belzec, Poland', *International Journal of Heritage Studies*, 14, 5 (2008), pp. 422–48; Andrew Charlesworth, 'The Topography of Genocide' in *HH*, pp. 216–52; Charlesworth and Michael Addis, 'Memorialization and the Ecological Landscapes of Holocaust Sites: The

is Wolfgang Sofsky's *The Order of Terror*.[106] Sofsky's argument is in some respects in the Bauman mould. He emphasizes the complex bureaucracy of the camp administration, controlled by the SS Death's Head units, which were taken over by the Waffen-SS in 1940, leaving the *Inspektion der Konzentrationslager* (IKL) as a separate agency under Theodor Eicke; he stresses the rigidly hierarchical structure of command on the one hand and the deliberately cultivated camaraderie of the camp SS on the other.[107] And he regards the reality of what happened in the camps as separate from Nazi ideology, that is to say, the drive to 'excessive power' took on a dynamic of its own.[108] In this reference to 'excessive power', Sofsky distinguishes his position from an argument that sees what happened in the camps as an outcome of bureaucracy. Rather, the 'absolute power' that characterized the camps was 'not a means to an end, but an end in itself'.[109] In contradistinction to Aly and Heim, Sofsky argues that this absolute power meant that excessive violence became an everyday occurrence, an occurrence without a goal, not driven by ideological imperatives: 'Excess is violent force for its own sake: terror per se.'[110] And he leaves the Baumanesque world of rational calculation behind when he talks of a 'political economy of waste' which 'cannot be comprehended by following the principles of calculation and value enhancement'.[111]

So, on the one hand, Sofsky does not see the camps as a classic bureaucratic organization, governed by rules and strategic rationality. Yet by rejecting the role of Nazi ideology—'The camp SS was anything but an ideologically schooled unit'[112]—as well as any sort of intentionalism—'The frictionless operation of the terroristic function supplanted the intentions and decisions of the individual'[113]—his claims about 'excessive power' and

Cases of Plaszow and Auschwitz-Birkenau', *Landscape Research*, 27, 3 (2002), pp. 229–51; Claudia Koonz, 'Between Memory and Oblivion: Concentration Camps in German Memory' in *Commemorations: The Politics of National Identity*, ed. John R. Gillis (Princeton: Princeton University Press, 1994), pp. 258–80; Reinhard Matz, *Die unsichtbaren Lager: Das Verschwinden der Vergangenheit im Gedenken* (Reinbek: Rowohlt, 1993).

106. Wolfgang Sofsky, *The Order of Terror: The Concentration Camp* (Princeton: Princeton University Press, 1997).
107. Sofsky, *Order*, p. 104.   108. Sofsky, *Order*, p. 20.
109. Sofsky, *Order*, p. 21.   110. Sofsky, *Order*, p. 224.
111. Sofsky, *Order*, p. 280. By contrast, Bauman says: 'Unlike so many other acts of mass cruelty that mark human history, the camps were cruelty *with a purpose*, means to an end. The camps—senseless in every other respect—had their own, sinister *rationality*.' Bauman, 'The Camps, Eastern, Western, Modern' in *The Fate of the European Jews, 1939–1945: Fate or Contingency*, ed. Jonathan Frankel (New York: Oxford University Press, 1997), p. 35.
112. Sofsky, *Order*, p. 20.   113. Sofsky, *Order*, p. 225.

the 'political economy of waste' take on a strongly functionalist flavour. Sofsky suggests that, as well as being unmotivated by ideology, the camp SS engaged in brutality not because they were driven by aggression or blood lust but because they were operating in a structure that demanded it: 'Cruelty was more a methodical mode of behaviour with a complex configuration of power than an eruption of uninhibited physical urges on the part of an individual.'[114] By putting the violence of the camps down to 'competition in brutality' arising from 'a group structure where it was expected that members exceed the limits of normal violence', Sofsky goes so far as to suggest that the composition of the groups of perpetrators and victims was unimportant: 'In this atmosphere, the atrocities involved are not even directed primarily against the victims. . . . This had nothing to do with anger, hatred, or rage. The identity of the victim was totally immaterial.'[115] Nowhere is this clearer than in the 'death factory'. Here we see the smooth operation of mass murder, though Sofsky stresses that it 'was less the mechanization of violence, as it is sometimes maintained, than the high degree of organization of the process of killing that made the death factories into such an unprecedented and unparalleled machinery for extermination'.[116] Sofsky is not interested in the reasons why Jews and other victims ended up in the camps, but merely in the operation of the camps once they were there.

How far does research confirm Sofsky's claims? As with Bauman, the evidence does not overturn them completely, but suggests that something is missing that necessitates a de-emphasis on the purely functionalist aspects of the story. Much work is currently being done on the establishment and development of concentration camps in the years 1933–39, but here I will keep the focus on the Holocaust, that is, the expansion of the camps after Kristallnacht and the building of death camps.[117]

Among the foremost historians of the camps is Karin Orth. She provides a history of the early camps and of the expansion of the camp system in the early stages of the war; she then discusses mass killings of disabled inmates,

---

114. Sofsky, *Order*, p. 225.   115. Sofsky, *Order*, pp. 228–9.
116. Sofsky, *Order*, p. 263.
117. Wolfgang Benz and Barbara Distel, eds., *Terror ohne System: Die ersten Konzentrationslager im Nationalsozialismus 1933–1935* (Berlin: Metropol, 2001); Jane Caplan and Nikolaus Wachsmann, eds., *Concentration Camps in Nazi Germany: The New Histories* (London: Routledge, 2010); Geoffrey P. Megargee, ed., *The United States Holocaust Memorial Museum Encyclopedia of Camps and Ghettos 1933–1945*, 7 volumes (2009–).

'political commissars', and medical experiments in the camps before turning to slave labour and genocide. Orth has little to say about Chełmno—the first site where the Nazis used gas for the mass murder of Jews and the place where most of the Jews of the Warthegau were murdered—or the Operation Reinhard annihilation sites, since they were independent of the IKL-administered camp system.[118] She gives a brief history of the development of the gassing process at Birkenau and Majdanek, noting the camps' changing functions at different stages of the war. As well as being one of the largest concentration camps, Majdanek was also the headquarters of Operation Reinhard and the central store for the belongings taken from the victims of the Reinhard camps. Following 'Operation Harvest Festival' on 3–4 November 1943 (when the SS murdered the vast majority of the 40,000–43,000 Jews still alive in the Lublin district), after which, as Orth notes, the recently completed agreement between the SS and *Ostindustrie* on the use of slave labour suddenly became irrelevant as all the workers had been killed, Majdanek became an execution site for Polish civilians and disabled camp inmates.[119] In other camps, such as Mauthausen, Dachau, and Neuengamme, the death rate slowed in 1943 as the SS sought to make use of slave labour, but 'one cannot speak of a general improvement of inmates' conditions'.[120] Indeed, like Schulte, Orth sees labour and genocide as two sides of the same coin.

118. Karin Orth, *Das System der nationalsozialistischen Konzentrationslager: Eine politische Organisationsgeschichte* (Zürich: Pendo, 2002), p. 199. Orth distinguishes between 'concentration camps' and 'extermination sites' since Chełmno and the Operation Reinhard sites were not really camps in the strict sense, other than for a very small number of 'prisoner functionaries'. On Chełmno, there is only one scholarly monograph: Shmuel Krakowski, *Das Todeslager Chełmno/Kulmhof: Der Beginn der 'Endlösung'* (Göttingen: Wallstein, 2007) and a useful document selection in Eugen Kogon, Hermann Langbein, and Adalbert Rückerl, eds., *Nationalsozialistische Massentötungen durch Giftgas: Eine Dokumentation* (Frankfurt/M: Suhrkamp Taschenbuch Verlag, 1986), pp. 110–45.
119. Orth, *Das System*, pp. 211–12. On Majdanek in the context of the Holocaust, see Barbara Schwindt, *Das Konzentrations- und Vernichtungslager Majdanek: Funktionswandel im Kontext der 'Endlösung'* (Würzburg: Königshausen und Neumann, 2005); Tomasz Kranz, *Extermination of Jews at the Majdanek Concentration Camp* (Lublin: Państwowe Muzeum na Majdanku, 2007); Kranz, 'Between Planning and Implementation: The Lublin District and Majdanek Camp in Nazi Policy' in *Lessons and Legacies, Vol. 4: Reflections on Religion, Justice, Sexuality, and Genocide*, ed. Larry V. Thompson (Evanston: Northwestern University Press, 2003), pp. 215–35; Wolfgang Scheffler, 'Chelmno, Sobibór, Bełzec und Majdanek' in *Der Mord an den Juden im Zweiten Weltkrieg: Entschlußbildung und Verwirklichung*, eds. Eberhard Jäckel and Jürgen Rohwer (Stuttgart: Deutsche Verlags-Anstalt, 1985), pp. 145–51.
120. Orth, *Das System*, pp. 219. On the changing functions of camps in the Third Reich, see the essays in *Die nationalsozialistischen Konzentrationslager*, Vol. 2, eds. Herbert, Orth, and Dieckmann.

This multi-functionality of the camps is generally true, but is of less relevance to the history of the Holocaust than to the history of the general camp system in Nazi Germany. Auschwitz and Majdanek had various functions and their uses changed over time; the Operation Reinhard camps differ, however, from the standard camp histories since they were erected especially for murder and were dismantled once that role had been performed. There are many basic facts about the Reinhard camps that remain unknown; for example, we do not know when Himmler ordered Globocnik, the SS Police Chief (SSPF) in Lublin, to murder the Jews of occupied Poland. But the purpose of the camps is clear, even given the lack of detail; and, as Timothy Snyder recently reminded us, 'An adequate vision of the Holocaust would place Operation Reinhardt, the murder of the Polish Jews in 1942, at the centre of its history.'[121] Yitzhak Arad's book remains the only monograph on Operation Reinhard as a whole, although the collection of essays edited by Bogdan Musial adds much useful detail.[122] Jens Hoffmann's recent work on 'Aktion 1005'—the squad set up in 1943 to eradicate traces of mass murder in eastern Europe—provides both a summary of Operation Reinhard and the most detailed account available of the end of the camps, when Jewish slave labourers were given the appalling task of exhuming and burning corpses of the camps' murdered victims.[123]

The chapters on the Reinhard camps in Wolfgang Benz and Barbara Distel's multivolume work on the Nazi camps provide useful overviews. Robert Kuwałek stresses the role played by Globocnik in fulfilling Himmler's decision of July 1941 to 'cleanse' the Lublin region of its Jewish population, as well as the expertise and availability of the SS men involved in the T4 project, which was officially coming to an end at the same time. Bełżec was chosen primarily on logistical grounds as the site of the Nazis'

121. Timothy Snyder, 'Holocaust: The Ignored Reality', *New York Review of Books*, 56, 12 (16 July 2009).
122. Yitzhak Arad, *Belzec, Sobibor, Treblinka: The Operation Reinhard Death Camps* (Bloomington: Indiana University Press, 1987); Bogdan Musial, ed., *'Aktion Reinhardt': Der Völkermord an den Juden im Generalgouvernement 1941–1944* (Osnabrück: Fibre, 2004), esp. Dieter Pohl, 'Die "Aktion Reinhard" im Licht der Historiographie', pp. 15–47, who highlights the difference between our knowledge of the Holocaust in western Europe and Operation Reinhard.
123. Jens Hoffmann, *'Das kann man nicht erzählen'. 'Aktion 1005': Wie die Nazis die Spuren ihrer Massenmorde in Osteuropa beseitigten* (Hamburg: Konkret, 2008), esp. pp. 35–49 (Operation Reinhard) and 223–59.

first extermination camp to be fitted with fixed gassing installations.[124] These gas chambers, Kuwałek reports, were made from wood and were 'very primitive'.[125] The deportees came from the Lublin region and Galicia. The date of the last transport to the camp is not known, but in December 1942, after operating for nine months, Bełżec was closed. The corpses were exhumed and burned, and in mid-1943 the camp was totally dismantled. A document in the Public Record Office in London, released in 2000, suggests that the number of Jews killed at Bełżec was 434,508; additionally, an unknown number of Catholic Poles and Romanies were murdered there.[126]

The history of Sobibór is quite similar. Construction began on the camp in March 1942, and it operated from April until December 1943, during which period between 150,000 and 250,000 Jews were murdered there (a precise figure cannot be arrived at because all the files were destroyed). Apart from Jewish Poles, the victims also came from Holland, France, Germany, Czechoslovakia, Belorussia, and the Baltic states. Perhaps the most well-known fact about Sobibór is the revolt of 14 October 1943, which was led with the military expertise of Red Army Lieutenant Alexander Petchersky, and which has been most brilliantly explored artistically in Claude Lanzmann's film *Sobibór*. The revolt led Himmler to decide to close the camp and raze it to the ground.[127]

Treblinka was the largest and 'most perfectly organized' of the three Operation Reinhard camps. In existence from July 1942 until August 1943, following the uprising from which about 60 of the 700 participants survived, some 900,000 Jews and several thousand Romanies were killed there. Were it not for the fact that the camp was dismantled, it would probably be as well known as Auschwitz. Benz stresses the continuities between T4 and Treblinka, the key role played by Globocnik and the growing expertise of the SS in the techniques of mass murder.[128] All three of the Reinhard

124. Robert Kuwałek, 'Bełżec' in *Der Ort des Terrors: Geschichte der nationalsozialistischen Konzentrationslager*, Vol. 8, eds. Wolfgang Benz and Barbara Distel (Munich: C. H. Beck, 2008), pp. 331–71. Also Kuwałek, *Obóz Zagłady w Bełżcu* (Lublin: Państwowe Muzeum na Majdanku, 2005).
125. Kuwałek, 'Bełżec', p. 334.
126. Kuwałek, 'Bełżec', pp. 358–9; Peter Witte and Stephen Tyas, 'A New Document on the Deportation and Murder of Jews During "Einsatz Reinhardt" ', *HGS*, 14, 3 (2001), pp. 468–86.
127. Barbara Distel, 'Sobibór' in *Der Ort des Terrors*, eds. Benz and Distel, pp. 375–404.
128. Wolfgang Benz, 'Treblinka' in *Der Ort des Terrors*, eds. Benz and Distel, pp. 407–43.

camps were overseen by more Ukrainian 'Trawnikis' than SS men (most of whom were transferred from the T4 project[129]), and historians have not overlooked this fact.[130]

There are now also monographs on each of these camps, though none is by any means the last word on the subject. Because the Nazis demolished the camps, and as a result of the fact that there were so few surviving eye-witnesses (only two Jews survived Bełżec, for example), writing the history of these murder sites is extremely challenging. Apart from a few well-known documents, such as Rudolf Reder's 1946 deposition on Bełżec, Thomas Toivi Blatt's memoir of Sobibór, and Richard Glazar's of Treblinka, and Kurt Gerstein's famous report, historians have relied on archaeological and architectural evidence as well as Nazi files.[131]

Of the three Reinhard camps, Bełżec has been and Sobibór is currently being archaeologically investigated. The digs in Bełżec upset some orthodox Jewish groups, for whom the site's sacred status as a graveyard was violated by drilling and reports that the corpses have transformed over time into 'wax-fat mass'.[132] The work of Andrzej Kola and Robin O'Neil confirms

129. Dieter Pohl, 'Die Stellung des Distrikts Lublin in der "Endlösung der Judenfrage" ' in 'Aktion Reinhardt', ed. Musial, pp. 96–7; Patricia Heberer, 'Eine Kontinuität der Tötungsoperationen: T4 Täter und die "Aktion Reinhard" ' in 'Aktion Reinhardt', ed. Musial, pp. 285–308; Michael Tregenza, Christian Wirth and the First Phase of 'Einsatz Reinhard' (1991, typescript held in Wiener Library, London); Tregenza, Christian Wirth: Inspekteur der SS-Sonderkommandos 'Aktion Reinhard' (1993, typescript held in Wiener Library, London).

130. Peter Black, 'Die Trawniki-Männer und die "Aktion Reinhard" ' in 'Aktion Reinhardt', ed. Musial, pp. 309–52.

131. Rudolf Reder, 'Bełżec', Polin: Studies in Polish Jewry, 13 (2000), pp. 268–89; Thomas Toivi Blatt, From the Ashes of Sobibor: A Story of Survival (Evanston: Northwestern University Press, 1997); Richard Glazar, Trap with a Green Fence: Survival in Treblinka (Evanston: Northwestern University Press, 1995); Gitta Sereny, Into that Darkness: From Mercy Killing to Mass Murder (London: Pimlico, 1995); Alexander Donat, ed., The Death Camp Treblinka: A Documentary (New York: Holocaust Library, 1979); Ernst Klee, Willi Dressen, and Volker Riess, eds., 'Those Were the Days': The Holocaust as Seen by the Perpetrators and Bystanders (London: Hamish Hamilton, 1991), pp. 211–49; Tuwiah Friedman, ed., Sobibór: Ein NS-Vernichtungslager im Rahmen der 'Aktion Reinhard' (Haifa: Institute of Documentation in Israel for the Investigation of Nazi War Crimes, 1998); Friedman, ed., NS-Vernichtungslager Bełżec: Dokumenten-Sammlung (Haifa: Institute of Documentation in Israel for the Investigation of Nazi War Crimes, 1995); Gerstein's report, written on 26 May 1945 shortly before his suicide, is in Noakes and Pridham, Nazism 1919–1945, Vol. 3, pp. 1149–53.

132. Andrzej Kola, Bełżec: The Nazi Camp for Jews in the Light of Archaeological Sources. Excavations 1997–1999 (Warsaw/Washington, DC: The Council for the Protection of Memory of Combat and Martyrdom/United States Holocaust Memorial Museum, 2000), p. 20. Chełmno too has been excavated; see Łucja Pawlicka-Nowak, ed., Chełmno Witnesses Speak (Konin: The Council for the Protection of Memory of Combat and Martyrdom in Warsaw, 2004), pp. 42–67.

the statistics of death—which were not in doubt in any case—and mean that Bełżec is no longer 'the forgotten camp' to the extent that was the case a few years ago.[133] O'Neil's book is written in the style of a forensic report, and further work remains to be done to integrate Bełżec more firmly into narrative accounts of the Holocaust.

Julius Schelvis's book *Sobibor* is the work of one of the few survivors of the camp, and was first published in Dutch in 1993. However, it is not a survivor testimony—Schelvis was in Sobibór for only a few hours before being sent on to a labour camp at Dorohucza—although Schelvis cites his own memoir. Providing the most thorough survey yet of the origins and operations of the camp—as well as a prosopography of the survivors and perpetrators—Schelvis shows how far removed from any ideal-type of industrial-style genocide Sobibór really was. Instead a gruesome history of extreme brutality, filth, and primitive technology prevails.[134] The same picture emerges in Witold Chrostowski's study of Treblinka: trains took far longer to reach the camp than was necessary; they had to wait for hours before being unloaded; the terrified victims were beaten and abused as soon as the train doors were opened.[135] Certainly the gas chamber could kill 2,000 people in 30–40 minutes; but any talk of 'industrial genocide' shields us from the brutality of the whole operation.

Chełmno and the Reinhard camps are depicted in recent historiography, as in the few testimonies, as brutal and violent places. Although the victims were murdered in gas vans or chambers with carbon dioxide gas produced by petrol engines, any talk of 'modernity' in the smooth, bureaucratic sense seems more a way of hiding the reality of the horror from ourselves than a faithful description.[136] Chrostowski notes that the Germans hid their main weakness—their tiny numbers—by engaging in 'wildly brutal and cruel behaviour towards the victims arriving in transports and the Jewish workers'. Furthermore, 'It often happened that the engine

133. Robin O'Neil, 'Bełżec—The "Forgotten" Death Camp', *East European Jewish Affairs*, 28, 2 (1998), pp. 49–62; O'Neil, 'Bełżec: A Reassessment of the Number of Victims', *East European Jewish Affairs*, 29, 1&2 (1999), pp. 85–118; O'Neil, *Bełżec: Stepping Stone to Genocide* (New York: JewishGen, 2008).

134. Jules Schelvis, *Sobibor: A History of a Nazi Death Camp* (Oxford: Berg, 2007), especially the appalling details of ch. 7.

135. Witold Chrostowski, *Extermination Camp Treblinka* (London: Vallentine Mitchell, 2004), pp. 58–60. Chrostowski's recreation of a gassing in the same chapter is, to my mind, rather distasteful.

136. Jacek Andrzej Młynarczyk, 'Treblinka—ein Todeslager der "Aktion Reinhard" ' in *'Aktion Reinhardt'*, ed. Musial, p. 260.

malfunctioned, which prolonged the agonies of the tightly-enclosed victims in an unimaginable manner',[137] or arrivals were shot en masse because the gas chambers were not ready.

It appears to be true then, that 'Closer analysis of the camps in the "east" shows that the widely-held view of a bureaucratic, division-of-labour-based, and anonymous SS rule is false.'[138] But does this statement apply when we turn to Auschwitz, the place that has become synonymous with Nazi genocidal crimes? If the concept of modern, industrial genocide applies anywhere, then surely it is here? The term is not entirely inappropriate; but it applies most convincingly only to the short period of spring 1944 when the Hungarian Jews were deported to Birkenau. That is the period that provides us with our images of the selection and murder process, from the famous *Auschwitz Album*; it is the period that saw the building of the infamous ramp inside Birkenau (prior to 1944 selections took place at the side of the railway tracks in Auschwitz station); and it is the period of the extraordinary *Sonderkommando* photographs, the four images taken by members of the resistance to be smuggled out to the Polish underground in Cracow.[139] In other words, the point at which the killing process became most streamlined was an exception within the history of the Holocaust, since by 1944 most of the victims of the Holocaust were already dead.

Despite the large number of testimonies and artistic representations, and the fact that 'Auschwitz' does duty as shorthand for the Holocaust as a whole, the historiography has only recently developed in detail. From the calendar of events to memorial books providing lists of deportees, to studies of the early history of Auschwitz as a camp for political prisoners to resistance, the operation of the gas chambers and the final days of the camp, many aspects of the three main Auschwitz sites and the many satellite camps have now been minutely examined.[140] Most of these studies

137. Chrostowski, *Extermination Camp Treblinka*, p. 40; Młynarczyk, 'Treblinka', p. 263.
138. Wildt, 'Die Lager im Osten', p. 520.
139. Dan Stone, 'The Sonderkommando Photographs' in *History, Memory and Mass Atrocity*, pp. 15–30; Georges Didi-Huberman, *Images malgré tout* (Paris: Les Éditions de Minuit, 2003).
140. Danuta Czech, *Auschwitz Chronicle 1939–1945* (New York: Henry Holt, 1990); Yisrael Gutman and Michael Berenbaum, eds., *Anatomy of the Auschwitz Death Camp* (Bloomington: Indiana University Press, 1994); Wacław Długoborski and Franciszek Piper, eds., *Auschwitz 1940–1945: Central Issues in the History of the Camp* (Oświęcim: Auschwitz Birkenau State Museum, 2000), 5 vols; Andrzej Strzelecki, *The Evacuation, Dismantling and Liberation of KL Auschwitz* (Oświęcim: Auschwitz Birkenau State Museum, 2001).

deal with issues internal to the camp's history, whilst the most debated issues concern the place of Auschwitz in the wider narrative of the Holocaust.

In that wider context, two books stand out: Debórah Dwork and Robert Jan Van Pelt's *Auschwitz 1270 to the Present* and Sybille Steinbacher's *'Musterstadt' Auschwitz*. Unlike the essay collections, these have overarching conceptual frameworks and attempt to provide a coherent explanation of the origins and development of the camp. Dwork and Van Pelt offer a *longue durée* analysis of Auschwitz, and with their innovative maps and drawings they provide a rich and detailed account. Like Aly and Heim, they stress the interconnectedness of genocide and German settlement policy: 'The creation of the camp at Birkenau, which by the end of 1942 had become a major center for the annihilation of Europe's Jews, was directly connected to Himmler's program to transform Auschwitz [the town] into a paradigm of German settlement in the East.'[141] Interestingly, though, they reach this conclusion without stressing rational, economic factors; instead their emphasis is more firmly on ideological factors, to the extent that their decision to highlight 'blood and soil' over economic rationality overlooks the moments when *Volkstumspolitik* was also a matter of expediency.[142] Steinbacher, by contrast, is much more firmly in the 'neo-functionalist' camp and aligns herself with the authors of the regional studies. She focuses more on the town than on the camp, and she emphasizes the connections between the expulsion of Catholic Poles, the resettlement of ethnic Germans in the 'model city' of Auschwitz, and the extermination of the Jews.[143] These links are persuasive; but none of them fully explains the choice of Auschwitz as the central killing centre for the 'Final Solution', and thus they do not explain why Auschwitz became, in Peter Hayes's phrase, the 'capital of the Holocaust'. As he pointed out several years ago, the recent research provides 'very valuable building blocks for a comprehensive, well-synthesized *history* of Auschwitz, but not yet the

---

141. Debórah Dwork and Robert Jan van Pelt, *Auschwitz 1270 to the Present* (New Haven: Yale University Press, 1996), p. 254.
142. For example, on p. 145 they refer to the issue of Baltic Germans whose inclusion in the resettlement plans clearly owed a good deal to the realities of the Hitler–Stalin pact.
143. Sybille Steinbacher, *'Musterstadt' Auschwitz: Germanisierungspolitik und Judenmord in Ostober-schlesien* (Munich: K. G. Saur, 2000); the book is the second in a four-volume set that also includes an edition of the Auschwitz Command Orders and Post Orders, a study of Monowitz and a collection of essays on aspects of labour and extermination policy; see note 74 above.

thing itself'.[144] Therefore, probably one of the most pressing requirements in the whole of Holocaust historiography remains a one-volume history that combines detailed histories of the various camps making up the Auschwitz complex with the questions of demographic engineering, race-thinking, and, often overlooked in recent studies, the victims themselves.

We have already encountered Michael Thad Allen's argument that the plans for erecting gas chambers in Auschwitz can be dated to October–November 1941, and thus that Auschwitz was not marginal in the development of the Final Solution.[145] In appalling detail, he cites the architects, engineers, and even prisoner-functionaries/technicians who designed the camps and the gas chambers, most of whom knew what they were for. Clearly, a pride in technological excellence and a problem-solving attitude dominated their work. But, even if his argument about the origins of Auschwitz-Birkenau is right,[146] as Allen notes, this is not the whole story. 'What is so frightful', he writes, 'is the straightforward, seemingly uncritical admission that these men counted the murder of harmless Jews as just another necessity of war.'[147] In other words, bureaucratic rationality, polycratic competition, division of labour, and technology alone cannot

144. Peter Hayes, 'Auschwitz, Capital of the Holocaust', *HGS*, 17, 2 (2003), p. 348. See also Michael R. Marrus, 'Auschwitz: New Perspectives on the Final Solution' in *The Fate of the European Jews*, ed. Frankel, pp. 74–83.
145. Michael Thad Allen, 'Not Just a "Dating Game": Origins of the Holocaust at Auschwitz in the Light of Witness Testimony', *GH*, 25, 2 (2007), pp. 162–91.
146. Allen's *GH* article developed out of a rather bad-tempered exchange with Jan Erik Schulte concerning Auschwitz-Birkenau's role in the origins of the Holocaust. Schulte ('Vom Arbeits- zum Vernichtungslager: Zur Entstehungsgeschichte von Auschwitz-Birkenau, 1941/42', *VfZ*, 50, 1 (2002), pp. 41–69) argued that Himmler and Pohl had originally (i.e., September 1941) envisaged Auschwitz as 'a huge forced labour camp for the "*Ostsiedlung*" ' (p. 68) and that only after May 1942 did systematic murder start taking place there, with Birkenau becoming the centre for the murder of the Jews of western and south-eastern Europe only after July 1942. Allen ('Anfänge der Menschenvernichtung in Auschwitz, Oktober 1941: Eine Erwiderung auf Jan Erik Schulte', *VfZ*, 51, 4 (2003), pp. 565–73) responded by arguing that extermination had always been part of the camp's role. In his reply, Schulte ('Auschwitz und der Holocaust 1941/42: Eine kurze Antwort auf Michael Thad Allen', *VfZ*, 52, 3 (2004), pp. 569–72), not unreasonably, suggested that the two were talking past each other. Schulte's claims are more in line with Longerich's argument that only by the spring of July 1942 was the 'Final Solution' in full swing, and that 'experimental gassings' of Soviet POWs in September 1941 do not prove that the European Jews were to be murdered, but Allen's claims need to be considered; after all, it is clear that the building of a site such as Birkenau requires planning, probably driven by the centre and not only by local initiative. See also Rainer Fröbe, 'Bauen und Vernichten: Die Zentralbauleitung Auschwitz und die "Endlösung" ' in *Durchschnittstäter: Handeln und Motivation*, ed. Christian Gerlach (Berlin: Assoziation Schwarze Risse Rote Straße, 2000), pp. 155–209, which lends credence to Schulte's position.
147. Allen, 'Not Just a "Dating Game" ', p. 187.

account for the emergence of a death camp at Auschwitz; the mission to kill the Jews was the prerequisite for this massive effort, not a product of it.

*

What the historiography of the camps brings to light, apart from the inter-agency competition and power struggles that characterized the complex bureaucracy, is that rather than a rationalized, efficient, cost–benefit-driven system that regulated forced labour in the interests of the war economy and carried out genocide in a cool, methodical, industrial fashion, the camps represent the interaction of a non-rational world view and the modern means of realizing it. In terms of architecture, technology, and the state infrastructure—especially the use of the railways—the camp system was 'modern', and many of its operatives styled themselves as 'managers', an image that was later repeated by East German historians who tried to make the camps fit their vision of 'fascism' as a tool of big business: 'Eichmann was really nothing more than a manager—not of an individual concern, but of the whole of German monopoly capital', as one historian put it.[148] But what they were doing cannot be—or can only partly be—grasped in terms of rational calculation. The inmates of the camps, despite the efforts of a few SD technocrats, were not kept in a condition that promoted productivity, and the murder of the Jews and the Romanies is very hard to fit into a framework based on economic rationality. Even if one accepts Aly and Heim's or Steinbacher's claims that the murder of the eastern European Jews makes sense as part of a grander vision of demographic engineering, this does not explain the trouble that the Nazis went to in hunting down and deporting the Jews of Rhodes, Crete, or the south of France. Nor is a focus on 'rationality' easily reconciled with the terror and brutality that pervade survivor testimonies.

Conclusion

An emphasis on networks or organization theory, though useful in many ways, cannot on its own explain the origins of the Holocaust. Neither can a focus solely on ideology, unless it is placed in a context where actors and institutions develop and operationalize it. It is thus necessary

---

148. Jürgen Kuczysnki, 'Die Barbarei', *Zeitschrift für Geschichtswissenschaft*, 9, 7 (1961), p. 1485.

to bring together the two previously competing schools of thought rather than replace them altogether with a new one in a 'weak *Aufhebung*', showing how the 'modern' and 'non-rational' aspects of the Holocaust were conjoined in the perpetrators' institutions and behaviour. In the same way that food policy, slave labour, and genocide could simultaneously co-exist as part of SS policy, so we should interpret these phenomena through a multiplicity of analytical frameworks.

Frank Bajohr argues that 'the mass murder of the European Jews would not have been possible in its vast dimensions without the institutions of a modern bureaucratic state. To describe the actions of these institutions under the rubric of classical "bureaucratic" behaviour, however, conceals the actual character of many of the participating institutions, whose substructure was characterized by a network of personal relationships and cliquelike structures.' Bajohr, following Dieter Pohl, describes this phenomenon as a 'totalitarian colonial administration'.[149] But the 'bureaucratic model' is not only flawed as a description of the operation of Nazi administration, especially in occupied eastern Europe. The empirical studies of Nazi agencies and camps show that the trappings of modernity—bureaucracy, organization, and technology—were vital to the implementation of the Holocaust. But they do not account for the origin of the idea to murder the Jews. The Third Reich was certainly a state characterized by high degrees of efficiency and technological sophistication—findings not at odds with seeing polycracy in the regime's administrative structures, where 'polycracy' does not mean chaos but rather a spur to radicalization. As many have noted, this efficiency and all-embracing regulation must have been the case; otherwise, how to account for the fact that the Third Reich held out against the military forces of most of the developed world for so long? Yet this efficiency was placed at the service of a 'non-rational' idea, that of Aryan racial supremacy and the need to eradicate from the face of the earth the major threat to Aryan supremacy—'the Jew'—and other 'polluting' races that stood in the way of the acquisition of a purified Lebensraum: Poles, Russians, Ukrainians, Roma and Sinti, 'diseased' Aryans. As David Lindenfeld puts it, 'To be sure, the execution of the Holocaust required massive amounts of planning and organization on the part of the state and

149. Bajohr, 'The Holocaust and Corruption', p. 133.

parts of the private sector as well. But this was pursuant to decisions that had been made by other, nonrational means.'[150]

Even more explicitly, Norbert Frei argues that 'the concept of modernity loses all meaning in the context of Hitler's *Weltanschauung*'.[151] Thus, the opposition that is set up in much of the historiography between 'modernity' on the one hand and the 'irrational' on the other is unsustainable. There are no grounds for surprise that modernity, under certain specific, unusual conditions, could be the setting for a rapid coming-together of in many ways quite common ideas to produce a world view that was fundamentally non-rational. Nor should we be surprised that this non-rationality was realized and put into practice using the tools of the modern state.[152] As Fritzsche recognizes, 'What scholars have long recognized as apocalyptic features in the National Socialist world view, which invalidated the predictable "story line" of historical development since 1789 and postulated the commencement of "new time", rested on a thoroughly modernist sensitivity to the discontinuous punctuation of crisis and opportunity.'[153] Modernity and barbarism go hand in hand, not because of the logic of the Enlightenment but because modernity creates the desire to overcome itself and provides the technological means with which to do so. Whilst these statements may seem obvious, few historians have developed them, preferring to focus on the 'modern' on the one hand or the irrational on the other. As we will see in the next chapter, this dichotomy is represented most clearly—and is most in need of critique—in the historiography of racial science in the Third Reich.

150. David F. Lindenfeld, 'The Prevalence of Irrational Thinking in the Third Reich: Notes Toward the Reconstruction of Modern Value Rationality', *CEH*, 30, 3 (1997), pp. 376–7.
151. Frei, 'Wie modern war der Nationalsozialismus?', p. 386.
152. Dan Stone, 'Modernity and Violence: Theoretical Reflections on the Einsatzgruppen', *JGR*, 1, 3 (1999), pp. 367–78; A. Dirk Moses, 'Genocide and Modernity' in *HG*, pp. 156–93.
153. Fritzsche, 'Nazi Modern', p. 16; cf. Paul Betts, 'The New Fascination with Fascism: The Case of Nazi Modernism', *JCH*, 37, 4 (2002), pp. 541–58.

4

Race Science

The Basis of the Nazi World View?

Blood transmits a propensity for heart diseases; if it also transmits a propensity for treason, no one has ever been able to prove it.

Lieutenant Dr Voss to Max Aue, in Jonathan Littell, The Kindly Ones[1]

After all, the Nazis were not interested in the 'Jewish nose'. They were concerned with the 'Jewish influence.'

Raul Hilberg[2]

Introduction

At a party rally on 6 September 1938, Hitler described National Socialism as 'a cool doctrine of reality based on the most incisive scientific knowledge and its theoretical elucidation'. He went on to say that 'in opening the heart of the nation to this doctrine we do not wish to fill it with a mysticism which is external to the purpose and goal of our doctrine'.[3] What was this doctrine and was Hitler speaking truthfully when he said that it provided the basis of Nazism? Was mysticism really banished from the party, and only science permitted to inform the Nazis' world view? And what role did 'race' play in the Holocaust?

1. Jonathan Littell, *The Kindly Ones: A Novel* (London: Chatto & Windus, 2009), pp. 302–3.
2. Raul Hilberg, *The Destruction of the European Jews*, rev. edn (New Haven: Yale University Press, 1985), Vol. 1, p. 68.
3. Hitler, speech of 6 September 1938, in *Nazism 1919–1945: A Documentary Reader. Vol. 4: The German Home Front in World War II*, eds. J. Noakes and G. Pridham (Exeter: Exeter University Press, 1998), p. 108.

In a stimulating article, Alan Beyerchen argues that the Nazis employed rational means, but used them towards an end that cannot be considered rational. This distinction, he argues, is the key weakness of arguments such as Bauman's:

> There is no doubt that the Nazis manipulated the means/ends calculations of instrumental rationality, that they fostered euphemisms that sounded as if a solution were proposed to a specific problem or 'question', that they often relied upon their opponents and victims to reach a rationalized position that was actually weaker than an emotionally charged fight, or that they mobilized the institutions in German society to accomplish their purposes. Yet to what end?[4]

It is the question also left begging by Hilberg's description of the German railway's involvement in genocide. Hilberg brilliantly sums up the process by which many agencies contributed to realizing the 'Final Solution':

> The Jews could not be destroyed by one Führer or one order. That unprecedented event was a product of multiple initiatives, as well as lengthy negotiations and repeated adjustments among separate power structures, which differed from one another in their traditions and customs but which were united in their unfathomable will to push the Nazi regime to the limits of its destructive potential.[5]

But where did the will come from and what made it seem a goal worth pursuing? The answer to that question cannot be found in the timetables of the *Sonderzüge* (special trains).

No better way into this debate exists than the question of the role played by 'race' in Nazi Germany. 'Race' is a modern concept, and the proponents of racial antisemitism vigorously distinguished their world view from that of the religious Jew-haters of previous centuries. But in making 'race' the key to understanding Nazism as a philosophy and the Third Reich as a regime, do historians necessarily take as given a set of concepts—technology, bureaucracy, surveillance, in short, modernity—that, as we have seen in Chapter 3, only accounts for half of the horror of the Holocaust?

For some years now, the idea of the Third Reich as a 'racial state' has been common currency. In previous decades, historians stressed terror or totalitarianism, chaos or polycracy, or the primacy of foreign policy as the defining characteristic of the regime; now the emphasis is firmly on race.

4. Alan Beyerchen, 'Rational Means and Irrational Ends: Thoughts on the Technology of Racism in the Third Reich', *CEH*, 30, 3 (1997), p. 388.
5. Raul Hilberg, 'German Railroads/Jewish Souls', *Society*, 35, 2 (1998), p. 174.

The 'return of ideology' to the historiography of the Third Reich and the Holocaust is most visible in the sphere of Nazi racism and the way in which Nazism sought to racialize the everyday lives of the Germans, both those who were part of the *Volksgemeinschaft* and those who were excluded from it. The most recent and all-encompassing statement to this effect comes from Peter Fritzsche: 'For the Nazis, biology was the key to the destiny of the German people. It offered a completely new understanding of human existence, rearranging what was necessary and possible, what was enduring and ephemeral, what was virtuous and dangerous. By thinking in biological terms, the Nazis recast politics in an exceptionally vivid way.'[6] Furthermore, in a classic statement of the 'voluntaristic turn' in the study of the Third Reich, Fritzsche argues that this racialized world view was one that millions of Germans enthusiastically entertained: 'The degree to which Germans accepted the Nazi world view, recognized themselves as Aryans, and endeavored to racially groom themselves is startling given the limited period in which these developments took place.'[7] Few historians dispute the significance of race to Nazi Germany, although some are starting to question whether we have exaggerated the consistence and intellectual coherence of its application; perhaps in some cases, a racial discourse merely overlay older traditions, in social or foreign policy, for example? It suffices to recall Martin Dean's argument that 'the widespread participation of the local population as beneficiaries from Jewish property served to spread complicity', with the result that 'the Nazis and their collaborators were able to mobilize society in support of Nazi racial policies to a greater extent than the spread of racial antisemitism alone would have permitted'.[8]

Apart from the fact that the study of race science in the Third Reich has blossomed since the mid-1980s and therefore deserves a historiographical overview, it also constitutes a prime example of how the 'modernity' paradigm has influenced historians' understanding of the period. In this chapter, I will examine the historiography of German eugenics and racial hygiene insofar as it contributed to the Nazi world view. I will then

6. Peter Fritzsche, *Life and Death in the Third Reich* (Cambridge, MA: The Belknap Press of Harvard University Press, 2008), p. 84.
7. Fritzsche, *Life and Death*, p. 83. See also John Weiss, *Ideology of Death: Why the Holocaust Happened in Germany* (Chicago: Ivan R. Dee, 1996); Klaus P. Fischer, *The History of an Obsession: German Judeophobia and the Holocaust* (London: Constable, 1998).
8. Martin Dean, *Robbing the Jews: The Confiscation of Jewish Property in the Holocaust, 1933–1945* (Cambridge: Cambridge University Press, 2008), p. 15.

examine the debates among historians over whether the 'Euthanasia pro-gramme'—the Nazis' first foray into mass murder—should be conceptually linked with the Holocaust or whether they constituted separate projects. I will look at recent work on race scientists in the broadest sense to include doctors and other professionals in the Third Reich, and consider historians' claims for their influence in the regime. Finally, I will compare the focus on race science with a very different strand of the historiography, one that connects with an older tradition which sees Nazism essentially as a variety of romanticism and explains Nazi antisemitism as a variety of racial mysticism. I will ask whether it is possible (or desirable) to reconcile these two ways of conceiving Nazi antisemitism, one tied to the 'modernity' paradigm, with its stress on bureaucracies, technology, networks, and the complicity of wide swathes of the German state and society, and one more to a 'Nazism as aber-ration' paradigm, with its view of Nazism as a rejection of modernity. First, however, I will briefly examine the historiography of the Third Reich as a 'racial state', examining how the 'race paradigm' has come to dominate the field, and asking what that means for our understanding of the Holocaust.

Before doing so, it is necessary to set out some preparatory thoughts. First, what did the Nazis actually mean by 'race'? Did they believe what they said? In order to answer those questions, we need to distinguish between racism and race thinking. The former can, as Christian Delacampagne writes, only exist with the support of reason, for it is 'nothing but *biologism*, that is, a face—extreme, exaggerated as much as you like, but a face all the same—of modern scientific reason'. Racism, as Delacampagne neatly puts it, 'is the reduction of the cultural to the biological, the attempt to make the first dependent on the second'.[9] This is the sort of racism that we see in race science, of which there was no shortage in Nazi Germany. But there is another sort of race thinking, one that is more mystical and—although drawing on scientific claims—based not on reason but on non-rational assumptions about the world, such as that the Jews are engaged in a conspiracy to destroy the Aryan race.

For example, Richard M. Lerner argues that biological determinism—in particular the danger posed by miscegenation with genetically defective

9. Christian Delacampagne, 'Racism and the West: From Praxis to Logos' in *Anatomy of Racism*, ed. David Theo Goldberg (Minneapolis: University of Minnesota Press, 1990), pp. 85, 87. Historians have, however, demonstrated that the idea of race long predated the modern age; see, for example, Lisa Lampert, 'Race, Periodicity, and the (Neo-) Middle Ages', *Modern Language Quarterly*, 65, 3 (2004), pp. 391–421.

peoples—paved the way from prejudice to genocide. Yet he reveals that this biological determinism rested less on science than on belief in the superiority of the German *Volk* and the threat posed to it by 'the Jew', referring to the belief in 'the genetic superiority of the German Volk' as a 'mystical or transcendental vision'. To this end he cites Hitler's definition of the *Volk*, seeing *Volk* as synonymous with 'race'; *Volk*, in this definition, means:

> the union of a group of people with a transcendental 'essence' . . . [which] might be called 'nature' or 'cosmos' or 'mythos', but in each instance . . . was fused to man's innermost nature, and represented the source of his creativity, his depth of feeling, his individuality, and his unity with other members of the Volk. Here we may say that Volk came to embody an immortalizing connection with eternal racial and cultural substances.[10]

Race science in the strict sense here gives way to a mystical vision of a racially ordered world.

When the Nazis talked about race they switched, often unconsciously, between the two registers of race science and race mysticism. Although Hitler claimed to be bound by science, his 'science' served thoroughly non-rational ends. There is no doubt, as we will see, that the leading Nazis believed in what Beyerchen calls the 'aesthetic-cultic' elements of their world view, understanding world history as a struggle between Aryan and non-Aryan forces. This Nazi philosophy of history, which we can understand as an 'Aryan salvation history', saw History coming to its end upon the defeat of 'the Jew' and the creation of a racially harmonious *Volksgemeinschaft*.[11] That does not mean that we should underestimate the contribution made by race scientists either to the legitimacy of the Third Reich or to its genocidal crimes; as Beyerchen notes, although the intended end of purifying the German people was not rational, 'Means were certainly open to suggestions, measures of efficiency, and participation by specialists, professionals, academics, and other rationally motivated experts.'[12] But it does mean that we should question whether a straight line runs from eugenics to Auschwitz, or 'from Darwin to Hitler', as some historians advocate. Just as bureaucracy was essential to the realization of the Holocaust

10. Richard M. Lerner, *Final Solutions: Biology, Prejudice, and Genocide* (University Park: Pennsylvania State University Press, 1992), pp. 22–3; implying that this is a quotation from Hitler, Lerner attributes the citation to Robert Jay Lifton, *The Nazi Doctors: Medical Killing and the Psychology of Genocide* (New York: Basic Books, 1986), p. 14, but Lifton is in turn citing George L. Mosse, *The Crisis of German Ideology: Intellectual Origins of the Third Reich* (London: Weidenfeld & Nicolson, 1970), p. 4.
11. Beyerchen, 'Rational Means', p. 392.   12. Beyerchen, 'Rational Means', pp. 390–1.

but was not the setting where the idea for the 'Final Solution' originated, so race science was crucial for the legitimacy and self-image of the Nazi regime and race scientists participated in the Holocaust; but the decision to murder the Jews emerged from the Nazi leadership's interactions with its functionaries on the ground in occupied Europe and not from the dissection tables of anthropologists. Race thinking—from notions such as the *Volkskörper* to belief in the threat posed by 'the international Jew'—is a *sine qua non* of the Holocaust, but that race thinking should not be understood as synonymous with racial science.

This distinction between racial science and race mysticism is helpfully summarized by a digression into fiction. In his remarkable novel *The Kindly Ones*, Jonathan Littell has his protagonist, the intelligent and aberrant SD man Max Aue engage in numerous debates. These intellectual contests are among the best passages in Littell's book, and the most impressive is the showdown in Nalchik between Aue, a fanatical Nazi and Leutnant Dr Voss, a university researcher drafted to serve the *Abwehr* (military intelligence) as an expert on Caucasian linguistics. Voss brings his academic expertise to bear on Aue's race mysticism, and provides one of the most compelling demolitions of Nazi racial thinking that one can find in fiction or history. When Aue states that dealing with local populations is 'quite simply a racial problem', Voss challenges him to define 'race', because for him 'that's a concept that is scientifically indefinable and hence without any scientific value'. Aue retorts that German racial anthropologists have proven that race exists, whereupon Voss explodes into a remarkable tirade:

> This *philosophy of veterinarians*, as Herder called it, has stolen all its ideas from linguistics, the only social science to this day that has a scientifically valid theoretical basis. . . . Racial anthropology, by contrast, has no theory. It postulates races, without being able to define them, then posits hierarchies, without the slightest criteria. All the attempts to define races biologically have failed. Cranial anthropometry was a total flop: after decades of measurements and compilations of tables, based on the most far-fetched indices or angles, we still can't tell a Jewish skull from a German skull with any degree of certainty. As for Mendelian genetics, it gives good results for simple organisms, but aside from the Habsburg chin, we're still far from being able to apply it to man. All this is so much the case that in order to write our famous racial laws, we were forced to use the grandparents' religion as a basis! It was postulated that the Jews of the last century were racially pure, but that's absolutely arbitrary. Even you have to see that. As for what constitutes a racially pure German, no one knows, whatever your Reichsführer-SS may say. So racial

anthropology, incapable of defining anything, was simply built on the so much more demonstrable categories of linguistics.[13]

What Aue likes to think of as the scientific basis of his thinking, Voss exposes as pure ideology, as the former implicitly admits when he responds that Voss underestimates 'some of the idealistic notions that form our *Weltanschauung*'.[14] The distinction between race science and racial mysticism is important, for it goes to the heart of whether historians see the Holocaust as emerging primarily from rational processes of technique and means–ends thinking or from paranoid political conspiracy theories that owe very little to science and instrumental rationality. We know (as Voss knows too in Littell's novel) that racial science is itself a kind of mysticism, insofar as 'race' is a biologically meaningless category and its devotees had to make a leap of faith to accept basic presuppositions (such as the existence of human 'races') before they could conduct their scientific research. Nevertheless, even though the tools were at hand before World War I to discredit eugenics on scientific grounds, Europe's racial scientists were regarded not as cranks but as cutting-edge scientists.[15] Although we can now dismiss all serious attempts to understand the world through the lenses of race theory as 'pseudoscience' or mysticism, it makes more sense for understanding the Holocaust to hold on to the distinction. Not so that 'science' can be exculpated, for the complicity of scientists went too deep for that, but so that a fuller understanding of the variety of ideas that fed into the Nazis' genocidal mindset can be appreciated.

The Racial State

Although the transformation of Germany into the 'racial state' was justified at every turn by appeals to science—popular magazines and school

---

13. Littell, *The Kindly Ones*, pp. 300–2.
14. Littell, *The Kindly Ones*, p. 303. In light of this passage, we should note Christopher M. Hutton's words (*Race and the Third Reich: Linguistics, Racial Anthropology and Genetics in the Dialectic of* Volk (Cambridge: Polity, 2005), p. 100): 'The notion that Nazism involved a confusion of language and racism is an extended red herring, as is the notion that the evils of Nazism can be traced back primarily to modern theories of anthropological race.' Rather, Hutton argues that scholarly theories were steadily displaced by Nazi racial propaganda, as it became clear that racial science was incompatible with the Nazis' vision of racial reordering in Europe.
15. Diane B. Paul and Hamish G. Spencer, 'Did Eugenics Rest on an Elementary Mistake?' in Paul, *The Politics of Heredity: Essays on Eugenics, Biomedicine, and the Nature–Nurture Debate* (Albany: State University of New York Press, 1998), pp. 117–32.

textbooks always asserted that the Nazis' claims were backed by the latest research—historians have tended to overlook the fact that, in the end, even the science rested on non-rational presuppositions. If the goal was the removal of the Jews, then the scientists provided reasons to justify that end, and not vice versa. Furthermore, as we will see, the regime needed the scientists far less than the scientists needed the regime. In this section, I will not go into detail, as I will pick up the question of the creation of the *Volksgemeinschaft* as the counterpart to genocide in Chapter 6. But I want briefly to indicate here how in recent years historians have changed our understanding of the Third Reich from a society ruled by terror and administrative chaos to a 'consensus dictatorship' with Nazi rule backed by popular support for the sweeping-away of the degenerate Weimar 'system' and the creation of an orderly, racially homogeneous *Schicksalsgemeinschaft* (community of fate).

Among the most notable of the historians of antisemitism is Shulamit Volkov. Volkov argues that, although there were continuities between traditional Jew-hatred and the racial and political antisemitism that developed from the 1880s onwards, Nazism must be understood as more than an extension of pre-1914 race theory:

> Racism, as a biologically founded social theory, claiming the support of modern science, was indeed a novelty of these years, but its importance for the development of contemporary anti-Semitism was overestimated. . . . [Racism] was no more than a useful instrument for them, an additional weapon in their arsenal of anti-Jewish arguments—a convenient but not indispensable substitute for the outdated categories of religion.[16]

As in the case of Richard Wagner, it was possible to be an extreme antisemite but 'not a true racist' in Delacampagne's sense. Nazism's origins, in this reading, lie partly in the *völkisch* movements of the late nineteenth century but more 'in a fuller and better understanding of its total present'.[17]

Volkov's claim is lent credence once one examines the content of this new racialized public sphere. Claudia Koonz, for example, notes that racial studies (*Rassenkunde*) 'became a required part of the curriculum in many disciplines and produced a market for new textbooks untainted by

16. Shulamit Volkov, 'The Written Matter and the Spoken Word: On the Gap Between Pre-1914 and Nazi Anti-Semitism' in *Unanswered Questions: Nazi Germany and the Genocide of the Jews*, ed. François Furet (New York: Schocken, 1989), pp. 39, 40.
17. Volkov, 'The Written Matter', pp. 40, 37. See Volkov, *Germans, Jews, and Antisemites: Trials in Emancipation* (Cambridge: Cambridge University Press, 2006) for more detail.

outmoded humanist values'. Racial research was promoted and, 'Backed by state and party, scholars constructed a simulacrum of a thriving academic endeavour. But', Koonz notes, 'a close look reveals that this so-called research served merely to endow traditional Christian stereotypes about "the Jew" with the cachet of modern scholarship. . . . Blood and race became master metaphors for the corrosive modernist spirit that had almost destroyed ethnic spiritual health in Weimar Germany.'[18]

This 'master metaphor' certainly provided a powerful organizing function in the Third Reich. As we have seen in Chapter 3, the 'Nazi ancestral proof' became a sought-after document, with millions of people necessarily engaging with the racial requirements of the regime in order to acquire one. In schools, biological racism penetrated into every part of the curriculum, from mathematics to children's fiction. The whole of the public sphere in the Third Reich was effectively racialized; one could not avoid the racial propaganda in the state-controlled press or on the ubiquitous wall posters, nor could one listen to the radio or go to the cinema without being confronted with racial rhetoric and instruction. Eugenics exhibitions, art galleries, church sermons, and Nazi organizations from the Hitler Youth to *Kraft durch Freude* meetings that largely replaced pre-existing societies, trade unions, and leisure activities, were all suffused with Nazi race theories. As Ehrenreich notes, such popular success indicates that, despite the 'irrational foundations of racial scientific claims', 'a great many Germans *wanted* to believe that racist ideas had been scientifically proven'.[19] This role played by race was malleable, and could bend in accordance with labour or military needs,[20] but as an overarching framework it gave new meaning to Germans that helped to explain what the National Socialist 'revolution' was all about.

As Fritzsche writes, 'National Socialism added up to an extraordinary endeavour to establish a new racial morality, one that pulled Germans at all levels further and further into active, self-willed complicity with Nazi projects.'[21] To use corporate-speak, what the historiography reveals is the extent to which the Nazis achieved 'buy-in', by making the bulk of the population identify with its world view. Koonz also argues that the

18. Claudia Koonz, *The Nazi Conscience* (Cambridge, MA: The Belknap Press of Harvard University Press, 2003), p. 200.
19. Eric Ehrenreich, *The Nazi Ancestral Proof: Genealogy, Racial Science, and the Final Solution* (Bloomington: Indiana University Press, 2007), p. xii.
20. Aristotle A. Kallis, 'Race, "Value" and the Hierarchy of Human Life: Ideological and Structural Determinants of National Socialist Policy-Making', *JGR*, 7, 1 (2005), pp. 5–29.
21. Peter Fritzsche, 'The Holocaust and the Knowledge of Murder', *JMH*, 80, 3 (2008), p. 596.

realization of genocide was made possible by the relentless racial propaganda of the pre-1939 years. Both for the direct perpetrators and those in the *Volksgemeinschaft*, racial propaganda was of fundamental importance. 'The focus on either battlefield conditions or on ancient hatreds', she writes with respect to the first group, 'obscures a crucial stage in the formation of a genocidal consensus. From 1933 through 1939—the so-called peaceful years—racial warriors underwent mental training that prepared them for their subsequent tasks.'[22] In particular, *Der Stürmer's* use of 'Words like "extermination" (*Ausrottung*), "purging" (*Säuberung*), and "elimination" (*Vernichtung*) stocked the imaginations of hardcore antisemites long before World War II created a context in which mass murder of Jews could become a reality.'[23] And with respect to the latter group—those responsible for 'racial war at home'—Koonz claims: 'What haunts us is not only the ease with which soldiers slaughtered helpless civilians in occupied territories but the specter of a state so popular that it could mobilize individual consciences of a broad cross-section of citizens in the service of moral catastrophe.'[24] The Third Reich was indeed a 'racial state', one created as much by the broad population's willingness to take on board the regime's ideas as by the threat of terror and exclusion.[25]

Race Science

Race science was a complex field, one which the Nazi leadership sought to simplify. It developed from the natural sciences of the eighteenth century, when Buffon, Linnaeus, Blumenbach, and others attempted to typologize nature and to situate human beings into the animal world.[26] But the

22. Koonz, *The Nazi Conscience*, p. 221. 'Battlefield conditions' is a reference, above all, to Omer Bartov, *Hitler's Army: Soldiers, Nazis and War in the Third Reich* (New York: Oxford University Press, 1992). On ideological indoctrination in the SS, see Jürgen Matthäus, Konrad Kwiet, Jürgen Förster, and Richard Breitman, *Ausbildungsziel Judenmord? 'Weltanschauliche Erziehung' von SS, Polizei und Waffen-SS im Rahmen der 'Endlösung'* (Frankfurt/M: Suhrkamp Taschenbuch Verlag, 2003). As Matthäus puts it (pp. 40–1): 'In the end, "ideological education" helped to produce "a certain mentality", precisely because of the breadth of its content and themes, and this in turn made it easier for Himmler's men to carry out the "Final Solution of the Jewish Question." '

23. Koonz, *The Nazi Conscience*, p. 230.   24. Koonz, *The Nazi Conscience*, p. 272.

25. Michael Burleigh and Wolfgang Wippermann, *The Racial State: Germany 1933–1945* (Cambridge: Cambridge University Press, 1991).

26. Among the massive literature see, for example: David Bindman, *Ape to Apollo: Aesthetics and the Idea of Race in the 18th Century* (London: Reaktion, 2002); Hannah Franziska Augstein,

harder, hereditarian form of race science, indeed the professionalization of race science, is really a phenomenon of the post-Darwinian late nineteenth century. The mix of race science and social Darwinism was to prove a potent one for aiding the spread of a racialized understanding of the world.[27] In the German context, where Darwin's theory of evolution was initially less well received than elsewhere, racial anthropology developed with no less rapidity than in Britain or the US. In the early twentieth century, the major manifestation of race science was eugenics, the science of 'improving' the human race. Based on fear—of the poor, of the racially inferior—as much as on belief in white racial superiority, eugenics offered scientific solutions to some of the major social problems of the day and proposed inexorable laws to explain the 'disappearance' of 'backward races'.[28] Negative eugenics—the attempt to get rid of undesirable traits—went hand in hand with positive eugenics—the attempt to select desirable ones.[29] Eugenics was by no means only an ideology of the Right, for it appealed to technocratically-minded social engineers of the Left to a great extent.[30] There were also some well-known Jewish eugenicists,

ed., *Race: The Origins of an Idea, 1760–1850* (Bristol: Thoemmes Press, 1996); Emmanuel Chukwudi Eze, *Race and the Enlightenment: A Reader* (Oxford: Blackwell, 1997); Ivan Hannford, *Race: The History of an Idea in the West* (Washington, DC: Woodrow Wilson Center Press, 1996).

27. Lee D. Baker, *From Savage to Negro: Anthropology and the Construction of Race, 1896–1954* (Berkeley: University of California Press, 1998); John S. Haller, Jr., *Outcasts from Evolution: Scientific Attitudes of Racial Inferiority 1859–1900*, 2nd edn (Carbondale: Southern Illinois University Press, 1995); Mike Hawkins, *Social Darwinism in European and American Thought 1860–1945: Nature as Model and Nature as Threat* (Cambridge: Cambridge University Press, 1997); George W. Stocking, Jr., 'The Turn-of-the-Century Concept of Race', *Modernism/Modernity*, 1, 1 (1994), pp. 4–16. It should be noted that eugenics and social Darwinism were by no means synonymous; indeed, they were often at odds with one another.

28. Patrick Brantlinger, *Dark Vanishings: Discourse on the Extinction of Primitive Races, 1800–1930* (Ithaca: Cornell University Press, 2003); Russell McGregor, *Imagined Destinies: Aboriginal Australians and the Doomed Race Theory, 1880–1939* (Carlton South: Melbourne University Press, 1997).

29. Dan Stone, *Breeding Superman: Nietzsche, Race and Eugenics in Edwardian and Interwar Britain* (Liverpool: Liverpool University Press, 2002).

30. Veronique Mottier and Natalia Gerodetti, 'Eugenics and Social Democracy: Or, How the European Left Tried to Eliminate the "Weeds" from its National Gardens', *New Formations*, 60 (2006–07), pp. 35–49; Kevin Repp, ' "More Corporeal, More Concrete": Liberal Humanism, Eugenics, and German Progressives at the Last Fin de Siècle', *JMH*, 72, 3 (2000), pp. 683–730; Reinhard Mocek, 'The Program of Proletarian *Rassenhygiene*', *Science in Context*, 11, 3/4 (1998), pp. 609–17; Diane B. Paul, 'Eugenics and the Left', *Journal of the History of Ideas*, 45, 4 (1984), pp. 567–90; Michael Freeden, 'Eugenics and Progressive Thought: A Study in Ideological Affinity', *Historical Journal*, 22, 3 (1979), pp. 645–71.

and the topics of Jewish 'racial purity' and 'racial survival' exercised both Jewish and non-Jewish race scientists for decades.[31]

The history of eugenics has been dealt with many times, and this book is not the place to reprise it, but some background is necessary. 'Eugenics' was a term coined by Francis Galton, the Victorian renaissance man and cousin of Charles Darwin. The historiography of eugenics has for a long time focused on Britain and the US as the major centres of eugenics, with Germany as something of an anomaly because of the rise of Nazism when 'mainstream eugenics' was allegedly on the decline in the Anglophone world. But eugenics was a worldwide enterprise, and eugenics societies existed in most countries of Europe—in eastern Europe they often went hand in hand with ethnic nationalism[32]—and beyond, with active eugenics movements throughout the world, including, as historians now recognize, in colonial settings such as the 'white settler colonies' of Australia, New Zealand, Canada, and South Africa, as well as parts of the French, Dutch, and American empires.[33]

Where the history of German eugenics differs from the histories of eugenics in most other settings is in its continued radicalization during the interwar years and in becoming official state policy under the Nazis. This is by no means an absolute difference: in the 1920s, Fritz Lenz observed that the 'Anglo-Saxons have an advantage in the field of eugenic legislation',[34] and eugenic sterilizations took place in the US, Canada, and the Scandinavian states until the 1970s; historians, especially of Britain and the US, have tended to exaggerate the extent to which eugenic ideas fell from favour in the 1930s. In fact, eugenics persisted throughout

---

31. Raphael Falk, 'Eugenics and the Jews' in *The Oxford Handbook of the History of Eugenics*, eds. Alison Bashford and Philippa Levine (Oxford: Oxford University Press, 2010); John M. Efron, *Defenders of the Race: Jewish Doctors and Race Scientists in Fin-de-Siècle Europe* (New Haven: Yale University Press, 1994); Dan Stone, 'Of Peas, Potatoes and Jews: Redcliffe N. Salaman and the British Debate over Jewish Racial Origins', *Simon Dubnow Institute Yearbook*, 3 (2004), pp. 221–40.
32. Marius Turda and Paul J. Weindling, eds., *Blood and Homeland: Eugenics and Racial Nationalism in Central and Southeast Europe 1900–1940* (Budapest: Central European University Press, 2007).
33. For the most up-to-date research on eugenics in a global context, see Bashford and Levine, eds., *The Oxford Handbook of the History of Eugenics*. On German race science in an international context, see Andrew Zimmerman, *Anthropology and Antihumanism in Imperial Germany* (Chicago: University of Chicago Press, 2001); H. Glenn Penny and Matti Bunzl, eds., *Worldly Provincialism: German Anthropology in the Age of Empire* (Ann Arbor: University of Michigan Press, 2003).
34. Fritz Lenz, 'Eugenics in Germany', *The Journal of Heredity*, 15, 5 (1924), p. 231.

the post-1945 period and, according to some, remains with us today, albeit in a different guise.[35] Furthermore, there was such a thing as the 'eugenics international', with renowned scientists sharing ideas at international conferences, in scholarly journals, and in popularizing efforts. Eugenics was funded on an international basis, with big business interests such as Rockefeller, Carnegie, and Kellogg all providing large sums of money to researchers to prove that social problems had not socio-economic but hereditary causes. The Rockefeller Foundation, in particular, gave German eugenicists enormous sums of money until well into the Nazi period. The Germans reciprocated in kind, with Harry Laughlin, one of America's most noted and influential eugenicists, being awarded an honorary MD by the University of Heidelberg in 1936 for being, in the words of the citation, 'a successful pioneer of practical eugenics and the far-seeing representative of racial policy in America'.[36]

Whether or not there was a *Sonderweg* of German eugenics, where it was known as *Rassenhygiene* (racial hygiene), encompassing race theory and a hygienic-welfare focus, it remains the case that only in Nazi Germany did eugenic ideas rest at the heart of state policy.[37] As many historians have pointed out, the views of Alfred Ploetz, Hermann Muckermann, Wilhelm Schallmeyer, Ludwig Woltmann, Rudolf Virchow, Otto Ammon, Felix von Luschan, Otmar von Verschuer, Ernst Rüdin, Eugen Fischer, Erwin

35. Gavin Schaffer, *Racial Science and British Society, 1930–62* (Basingstoke: Palgrave Macmillan, 2008); Troy Duster, *Backdoor to Eugenics*, 2nd edn (New York: Routledge, 2003); Alan H. Goodman, Deborah Heath, and M. Susan Lindee, eds., *Genetic Nature/Culture: Anthropology and Science Beyond the Two-Culture Divide* (Berkeley: University of California Press, 2003); Peter Weingart, 'The Thin Line between Eugenics and Preventive Medicine' in *Identity and Intolerance: Nationalism, Racism, and Xenophobia in Germany and the United States*, eds. Norbert Finzsch and Dietmar Schirmer (Cambridge: Cambridge University Press, 1998), pp. 397–412.

36. Garland E. Allen, 'The Ideology of Annihilation: American and German Eugenics, 1900–1945' in *Medicine and Medical Ethics in Nazi Germany: Origins, Practices, Legacies*, eds. Francis R. Nicosia and Jonathan Huener (New York: Berghahn, 2002), p. 32. See also Stefan Kühl, *The Nazi Connection: Eugenics, American Racism, and German National Socialism* (New York: Oxford University Press, 1994); Diane B. Paul, 'The Rockefeller Foundation and the Origins of Behavior Genetics' in *The Politics of Heredity: Essays on Eugenics, Biomedicine, and the Nature–Nurture Debate* (Albany: State University of New York Press, 1998), pp. 53–79; Paul Crook, 'American Eugenics and the Nazis: Recent Historiography', *The European Legacy*, 7, 3 (2002), pp. 363–81.

37. Paul Weindling, 'The "Sonderweg" of German Eugenics: Nationalism and Scientific Internationalism', *British Journal of the History of Science*, 22, 3 (1989), pp. 321–33. On *Rassenhygiene*, see Marius Turda, 'Race, Science and Eugenics in the Twentieth Century' and Paul Weindling, 'German Eugenics and the Wider World: Beyond the Racial State', both in *The Oxford Handbook of the History of Eugenics*, eds. Bashford and Levine.

Baur, Fritz Lenz, and many other eugenicists and race scientists received official praise after the Nazi ascent to power, and most of the scientists were only too glad to be of service.[38]

Eugenic and race hygienic concepts were most obviously applicable with respect to those considered by the Nazis to be 'disabled', 'outsiders', or 'asocials'. The key text in the history of German eugenic legislation is usually held to be Karl Binding and Alfred Hoche's 1920 work, *Authorization of the Destruction of Life Unworthy of Life* (*Freigabe der Vernichtung lebensunwerten Lebens*), which advocated voluntary euthanasia for the terminally ill. The tract did not mention race, and it is clear that their economic, social, and ethical arguments were focused on the well-being of the German population. Hence, many of the Nazis' earliest measures targeted the disabled, 'habitual criminals', prostitutes, homosexuals, vagrants, and 'Gypsies', now, of course, without the voluntary element.[39] Yet it is important to remember that the race hygiene movement was very varied, and an advocate of sterilization would not necessarily endorse the killing of disabled patients.

Apart from universities, the most important institutional setting for the race scientists' ideas was the Kaiser Wilhelm Society (KWG, *Kaiser-Wilhelm-Gesellschaft*), a highly-regarded umbrella organization that ran a number of different research institutes, for example, for botany, brain research, metallurgy, fluid dynamics, law, physics, psychiatry and biology, as well as, most pertinent in this context, the Kaiser Wilhelm Institute for Anthropology, Human Heredity and Eugenics (KWIA), based in Berlin, to which Fischer, Lenz, and Verschuer all belonged. In the mid-1980s, Benno Müller-Hill first put Mengele's relationship with Verschuer into the public

38. For the standard histories of German race hygiene, see Peter Weingart, Jürgen Kroll, and Kurt Bayertz, *Rasse, Blut und Gene: Geschichte der Eugenik und Rassenhygiene in Deutschland* (Frankfurt/M: Suhrkamp, 1988); Paul Weindling, *Health, Race and German Politics between National Unification and Nazism 1870–1945* (Cambridge: Cambridge University Press, 1989). See also Robert Proctor, 'From *Anthropologie* to *Rassenkunde* in the German Anthropological Tradition' in *Bones, Bodies, Behavior: Essays on Physical Anthropology*, ed. George W. Stocking, Jr (Madison: University of Wisconsin Press, 1988), pp. 138–79; Benoît Massin, 'From Virchow to Fischer: Physical Anthropology and "Modern Race Theories" in Wilhelmine Germany' in *Volksgeist as Method and Ethic: Essays on Boasian Ethnography and the German Anthropological Tradition*, ed. George W. Stocking, Jr (Madison: University of Wisconsin Press, 1996), pp. 79–154; and the excellent exhibition catalogue *Deadly Medicine: Creating the Master Race*, ed. Dieter Kuntz (Washington, DC: United States Holocaust Memorial Museum, 2004).
39. The topic is very broad; see, as starting points, Michael Berenbaum, ed., *A Mosaic of Victims: Non-Jews Persecuted and Murdered by the Nazis* (London: I. B. Tauris, 1990); Robert Gellately and Nathan Stoltzfus, eds., *Social Outsiders in Nazi Germany* (Princeton: Princeton University Press, 2001).

sphere, and in 2000, William Seidelman accused the KWG's successor, the Max Planck Society, one of the world's foremost research institutes, of suffering from 'disordered memory', for failing to address its own history.[40] Since then, a great deal has changed.

First, a number of scholars have analysed the role played by the KWIA in Nazi Germany which all reveal that, under Fischer's leadership, the institute sought to make itself indispensable to the regime. By providing scientific backing for racial legislation and providing expert testimonials for use in the Reich Genetic Health Courts, the KWIA engaged in a programme of training a generation of racial 'experts' who furthered the 'deadly symbiosis' between science and Nazism.[41] More significant, following a speech by Hubert Markl, the President of the Max Planck Society in June 2001, to mark the opening of a symposium on the links between the KWG and Nazism, the society has now produced an impressive set of studies on its own past. Carola Sachse edited the volume based on that 2001 symposium, Hans-Walter Schmuhl edited another on racial research at the KWG and, most important, authored a large volume on the history of the KWIA between its founding in 1927 and 1945.[42] A summary of this research (and on the KWG more generally) has recently been published in an English-language collection.[43] Although there was no straightforward continuity between the KWIA's activities before and after 1933, serious science was certainly considered important by many leading Nazis; Bernhard Rust, for

40. Benno Müller-Hill, *Murderous Science: Elimination by Scientific Selection of Jews, Gypsies, and Others, Germany 1933–1945* (New York: Oxford University Press, 1988); Seidelman, 'Pathology of Memory: German Medical Science and the Crimes of the Third Reich' in *Medicine and Medical Ethics*, eds. Nicosia and Huener, pp. 104–7.
41. Thomas M. Berez and Sheila Faith Weiss, 'The Nazi Symbiosis: Politics and Human Genetics at the Kaiser Wilhelm Institute', *Endeavour*, 28, 4 (2004), pp. 172–7; see also Weiss, 'Human Genetics and Politics as Mutually Beneficial Resources: The Case of the Kaiser Wilhelm Institute for Anthropology, Human Heredity and Eugenics During the Third Reich', *Journal of the History of Biology*, 39, 1 (2006), pp. 41–88; Kristie Macrakis, *Surviving the Swastika: Scientific Research in Nazi Germany* (New York: Oxford University Press, 1993).
42. Carola Sachse, ed., *Die Verbindung nach Auschwitz: Biowissenschaften und Menschenversuche an Kaiser-Wilhelm-Instituten. Dokumentation eines Symposiums im Juni 2001* (Göttingen: Wallstein, 2004); Hans-Walter Schmuhl, ed., *Rassenforschung an Kaiser-Wilhelm-Instituten vor und nach 1933* (Göttingen: Wallstein, 2003); Schmuhl, *Grenzüberschreitungen: Das Kaiser-Wilhelm-Institut für Anthropologie, menschliche Erblehre und Eugenik 1927–1945* (Göttingen: Wallstein, 2005). The Wallstein series 'Geschichte der Kaiser-Wilhelm-Gesellschaft im Nationalsozialismus', currently stands at 17 volumes.
43. Susanne Heim, Carola Sachse, and Mark Walter, eds., *The Kaiser Wilhelm Society under National Socialism* (Cambridge: Cambridge University Press, 2009). See also Carola Sachse and Mark Walker, eds., *Politics and Science in Wartime: Comparative International Perspectives on the Kaiser Wilhelm Institute* (Chicago: University of Chicago Press, 2005).

example, the Minister of Education, went to some lengths to persuade Fritz
von Wettstein, a non-party member considered the best plant geneticist
in Germany, to take up the post of head of the KWI for Biology in
Berlin.[44] Scientists of all varieties were, as historians have shown, deeply
in the pocket of the Nazi regime, although that does not mean that the
regime had full control over what scientists were doing.[45] Whether they
were biologists, chemists, physicists, landscape planners, nutritionists, or
criminologists, as exiled physicist Lise Meitner wrote to her friend and
former colleague Otto Hahn in Berlin in the immediate aftermath of the
war, 'All of you also worked for Nazi Germany . . . you let millions of
innocent humans be murdered and no protest was raised.'[46]

Yet it is well to remember that 'race' in Germany meant not only race
science as it was being conducted by *Rassenhygieniker*, much of whose work
did not concern the 'Jewish question' directly. The regime also encouraged
the growth of *Erforschung der Judenfrage* ('research into the Jewish question',
abbreviated to *Judenforschung*), both in universities and in 'independent'
research institutes, and historians have recently unearthed much interesting
material concerning their activities.[47] Alan Steinweis argues that the scholars
and experts engaged in this research—an interdisciplinary approach that
drew on history, linguistics, theology, economics, and other areas in the
humanities and social sciences—were committed to realizing Hitler's goal
of an 'antisemitism of reason', though he also states that such work 'occupied

44. Cf. Paul Weindling, 'Weimar Eugenics: The Kaiser Wilhelm Institute for Anthropology,
    Human Heredity and Eugenics in Social Context', *Annals of Science*, 42, 3 (1985), p. 315 with
    Ute Deichmann and Benno Müller-Hill, 'Biological Research at Universities and Kaiser
    Wilhelm Institutes in Nazi Germany' in *Science, Technology and National Socialism*, eds. Monika
    Renneberg and Mark Walter (Cambridge: Cambridge University Press, 1994), p. 175.
45. See, for example, Helmuth Trischler, 'Aeronautical Research under National Socialism: Big
    Science or Small Science?' in *Science in the Third Reich*, ed. Margit Szöllösi-Janze (Oxford:
    Berg, 2001), pp. 79–110.
46. Ute Deichmann, *Biologists under Hitler* (Cambridge, MA: Harvard University Press, 1996),
    p. 334 (Meitner); Szöllösi-Janze, ed., *Science in the Third Reich*; Konrad H. Jarausch, *The Unfree
    Professions: German Lawyers, Teachers, and Engineers, 1900–1950* (Oxford: Oxford University
    Press, 1990); Richard Wetzell, *Inventing the Criminal: A History of German Criminology,
    1880–1945* (Chapel Hill: University of North Carolina Press, 2000); Michael Berkowitz, *The
    Crime of My Very Existence: Nazism and the Myth of Jewish Criminality* (Berkeley: University
    of California Press, 2007); Nicole Rafter, 'Criminology's Darkest Hour: Biocriminology in
    Nazi Germany', *Australian and New Zealand Journal of Criminology*, 41, 2 (2008), pp. 287–306.
47. On universities in general, see Jeremy Noakes, 'The Ivory Tower under Siege: German
    Universities in the Third Reich', *Journal of European Studies*, 23, 4 (1993), pp. 371–407;
    Michael Grüttner, 'Die deutschen Universitäten unter dem Hakenkreuz' in *Universitäten in
    den Diktaturen des 20. Jahrhunderts: Zwischen Autonomie und Anpassung*, eds. John Connelly and
    Michael Grüttner (Paderborn: Schöningh, 2003), pp. 67–100.

a grey zone between scholarship and propaganda'.[48] The scholars built on earlier, perfectly respectable research into Jewish history and culture, often by Jewish social scientists,[49] and made it into a showpiece of Nazified academia.

Among the most important institutions for *Judenforschung* were the Institute for Research on the Jewish Question, established in Frankfurt am Main in 1941, whose centrepiece was Frankfurt city library's Hebraica collection, and the Department of Research on the Jewish Question of the Reich Institute for the History of the New Germany, set up in 1936 in Munich.[50] These institutes expanded abroad and new ones were founded as Germany occupied more of Europe. As Dirk Rupnow writes, this sort of institute, despite being outside of the traditional university system, represented 'by no means an isolated branch of scholarship; it was firmly rooted in the academic landscape of the time'.[51] He agrees with Steinweis about the nature of such research, saying that even though the researchers sought to dissociate themselves publicly from politics so as to protect their scholarly credentials, 'propaganda, politics and scholarship were in fact almost indistinguishable in the field of Nazi Jewish Studies'. Indeed, their supposed 'theoretical neutrality' (what Proctor calls 'neutral racism'[52]) did not lead the *Judenforscher* 'to embrace a model of tolerance and plurality but rather one of solidarity with the National Socialist ideology and with the German volk'.[53] Significantly, Rupnow notes that *Judenforschung* was far from synonymous with race science or physical anthropology. Since Jewishness was to be identified in terms of the 'Jewish spirit' or the 'Jewish

48. Alan E. Steinweis, *Studying the Jew: Scholarly Antisemitism in Nazi Germany* (Cambridge, MA: Harvard University Press, 2006), ch. 1 and p. 157.
49. Mitchell B. Hart, ' "Let the Numbers Speak!" On the Appropriation of Jewish Social Science by Nazi Scholars', *Simon Dubnow Institute Yearbook*, 5 (2006), pp. 281–99.
50. On the former, see Patricia von Papen-Bodek, 'Anti-Jewish Research of the Institut zur Erforschung der Judenfrage in Frankfurt am Main between 1939 and 1945' in *Lessons and Legacies, Vol. 6: New Currents in Holocaust Research*, ed. Jeffrey M. Diefendorf (Evanston: Northwestern University Press, 2004), pp. 155–89; Dieter Schiefelbein, 'Das "Institut zur Erforschung der Judenfrage Frankfurt am Main": Antisemitismus als Karrieresprungbrett im NS-Staat' in *'Beseitigung des jüdischen Einflusses . . . ' Antisemitische Forschung, Eliten und Karrieren im Nationalsozialismus*, ed. Fritz Bauer Institut (Frankfurt/M: Campus, 1999), pp. 43–71; on the latter, von Papen, 'Schützenhilfe nationalsozialistischer Judenpolitik: Die "Judenforschung" des "Reichsinstituts für Geschichte des neuen Deutschland" 1935–1945' in *'Beseitigung des jüdischen Einflusses . . . '*, ed. Fritz Bauer Institut, pp. 17–42. See also Claudia Koonz, 'Respectable Racism: State-Sponsored Anti-Jewish Research 1935–1940', *Simon Dubnow Institute Yearbook*, 5 (2006), pp. 399–423.
51. Dirk Rupnow, 'Racializing Historiography: Anti-Jewish Scholarship in the Third Reich', *Patterns of Prejudice*, 42, 1 (2008), p. 32.
52. Proctor, *Racial Hygiene*, ch. 2.   53. Rupnow, 'Racializing Historiography', p. 36.

mind', the 'Jewish question' had to be approached from many angles, not just racial anthropology.[54]

In recognition of the fact that many scholars involved in *Judenforschung* were historians, contemporary German historians have, belatedly, also finally begun investigating their forerunners' involvement with the regime. Theodor Schieder, Werner Conze, and Karl-Dietrich Erdmann, three of West Germany's most influential historians, have come under particularly intense scrutiny. Konrad Jarausch asserts that 'it is clear that the proponents of *Volksgeschichte* zealously contributed to a climate of opinion and a store of information that facilitated the racial projects of the SS', though he questions the extent to which their writings actually influenced decision-making on the part of the SS.[55] What all of these studies of *Judenforschung* show—perhaps unsurprisingly, given that they deal with racial research institutes—is that, as Steinweis puts it: 'Race, rather than religion or political orientation, lay at the core of the most fundamental policy decisions regarding membership in the so-called German "community of the people" (*Volksgemeinschaft*).'[56] They thus confirm the 'racial state' analysis. But this is not to say that such scholars—with a few exceptions, such as the economist Peter-Heinz Seraphim[57]—were directly involved in genocide, though they certainly benefited from expropriation (of libraries, for example) and, like the race scientists, provided the regime with scholarly legitimacy; Steinweis summarizes the contribution made by the *Judenforscher* by saying that they 'did not so much determine the main contours of Nazi anti-Jewish policy

---

54. Rupnow, 'Racializing Historiography', pp. 39–45.
55. Konrad H. Jarausch, 'Unasked Questions: The Controversy about Nazi Collaboration Among German Historians' in *Lessons and Legacies*, Vol. 6, ed. Diefendorf, p. 193; see also Karen Schönwälder, *Historiker und Politik: Geschichtswissenschaft im Nationalsozialismus* (Frankfurt/M: Campus, 1992); Schönwälder, ' "Taking Their Place in the Front-line" (?): German Historians during Nazism and War', *Tel Aviver Jahrbuch für deutsche Geschichte*, 25 (1996), pp. 205–17; Schönwälder, 'The Fascination of Power: Historical Scholarship in Nazi Germany', *History Workshop Journal*, 43 (1997), pp. 133–53; Peter Schöttler, ed., *Geschichts-schreibung als Legitimationswissenschaft 1918–1945* (Frankfurt/M: Suhrkamp Taschenbuch Verlag, 1997); Winfried Schulze and Otto Gerhard Oexle, eds., *Deutsche Historiker im Nationalsozialismus* (Frankfurt/M: Suhrkamp Taschenbuch Verlag, 1999); Ingo Haar, 'Die Genesis der "Endlösung" aus dem Geiste der Wissenschaften: Volksgeschichte und Bevölkerungspolitik im Nationalsozialismus', *Zeitschrift für Geschichtswissenschaft*, 49, 1 (2001), pp. 13–31; Alan E. Steinweis, 'Nazi Historical Scholarship on the "Jewish Question" ' in *Nazi Germany and the Humanities*, eds. Wolfgang Bialas and Anson Rabinbach (Oxford: Oneworld, 2007), pp. 399–412.
56. Steinweis, *Studying the Jew*, p. 24.
57. See Steinweis, *Studying the Jew*, pp. 142–51; Aly and Heim, *Vordenker der Vernichtung*; Hans-Christian Petersen, 'Ein "Judenforscher" danach—Zur Karriere Peter-Heinz Seraphims in Westdeutschland', *Simon Dubnow Institute Yearbook*, 5 (2006), pp. 515–35.

as they contributed to decision-making by helping to define and articulate the alleged "problem", generating concrete information about Jewish communities, recommending a range of possible solutions, and providing arguments that could be invoked by Nazi leaders seeking to justify one policy or another.'[58]

One cannot understand Germany's specific trajectory, then, solely through the history of eugenics. It was equally a result of the popu-larity in the first half of the twentieth century of race mystics of the nineteenth, such as Gobineau, Chamberlain, and Vacher de Lapouge, whose ideas underpinned the scientific search for Jewish racial markers. I will discuss these ideas in more detail below, but it is worth bearing in mind Weindling's simple and effective statement: 'There were inherent contradictions between variants of völkisch and scientific racism.'[59] In the next section, we will examine how these ideas about human betterment and racial regeneration were put into practice.

Sterilization and Euthanasia

Doctors were the most highly represented professional group in Nazi struc-tures, with nearly 45% joining the NSDAP, a quarter the SA, and 7% the SS. This is considerably higher than the next most Nazified profession, lawyers, 25% of whom belonged to the party.[60] Yet it is perhaps unsurprising, given the promotion of health and 'body-culture' during the Weimar years, which became central to the state's concerns after 1933.[61] The National Socialist Physicians League (NS-Ärztebund) set up by former Freikorps lead-er Dr Gerhard Wagner in 1929, was a key legitimizing institution, lending the regime establishment credibility. Indeed, along with lawyers, medics were at the heart of the regime, with Reich Health Leader Leonardo Conti (who succeeded Wagner on the latter's death in 1938), Hitler's doctor Karl Brandt, Gerhard Bohne and Herbert Linden of the Reich Ministry

58. Steinweis, Studying the Jew, p. 18.
59. Paul Weindling, 'Compulsory Sterilisation in National Socialist Germany', GH, 5 (1987), p. 19.
60. Michael H. Kater, 'Criminal Physicians in the Third Reich' in Medicine and Medical Ethics, eds. Nicosia and Huener, p. 79. For more detail, see Kater, Doctors under Hitler (Chapel Hill: University of North Carolina Press, 1989), pp. 54–74.
61. Hugh Gregory Gallagher, By Trust Betrayed: Patients, Physicians, and the License to Kill in the Third Reich, rev. edn (Arlington: Vandamere Press, 1995), p. 152.

of the Interior, and many other senior leaders with medical backgrounds being responsible for the sterilization and Euthanasia programmes.

The Nazis' first eugenically-inspired legislation was the so-called 'sterilization law', the Law for the Prevention of Hereditarily-Diseased Offspring, announced on 14 July 1933 and taking effect on 1 January 1934. Before targeting the 'racially foreign', it was imperative in the Nazi world view to repair the Aryan race. Many other countries had already introduced laws permitting compulsory sterilization, but none exercised it with comparable vigour. By the start of the war, some 300,000 people had been sterilized, with a further 100,000 by May 1945—one percent of the German population aged between 14 and 50.[62] The figure includes 30,000 women who underwent eugenic abortions with compulsory sterilization.[63] Paul Weindling suggests, on the basis of these figures, that with the drift from sterilization to 'euthanasia', and the gradual targeting of ethnic groups rather than genetically tainted 'Aryans', 'medicine became part of genocidal policies of extermination and resettlement'.[64]

With the onset of the children's euthanasia campaign in September 1939 (Hitler's signed authorization was backdated to 1 September), and then with the expansion of the programme to involve the murder of adult patients in the six killing centres (Grafeneck, Brandenburg, Hartheim, Sonnenstein, Bernburg, and Hadamar), eugenically-inspired Nazi policies entered a new, more radical phase.[65] Hitler appointed his personal physician—and, as one of his 'commissars' outside of the party or state bureaucracies, one of the most powerful men in the Reich—Karl Brandt, and Philipp Bouhler,

62. Gisela Bock, 'Nazi Sterilization and Reproductive Policies' in *Deadly Medicine*, ed. Kuntz, p. 62. For more detail, see Bock, *Zwangssterilisation im Nationalsozialismus: Studien zur Rassenpolitik und Frauenpolitik* (Opladen: Westdeutscher Verlag, 1986); Bock, 'Racism and Sexism in Nazi Germany: Motherhood, Compulsory Sterilization, and the State' in *When Biology Became Destiny: Women in Weimar and Nazi Germany*, eds. Renate Bridenthal, Atina Grossmann, and Marion Kaplan (New York: Monthly Review Press, 1984), pp. 271–96.

63. Bock, 'Nazi Sterilization and Reproductive Policies', p. 80. See also Henry P. David, Jochen Fleischhacker, and Charlotte Hohn, 'Abortion and Eugenics in Nazi Germany', *Population and Development Review*, 14, 1 (1988), pp. 81–112; Gunther Link, *Eugenische Zwangssterilisationen und Schwangerschaftsabbrüche im Nationalsozialismus: Dargestellt am Beispiel der Universitätsfrauenklinik Freiburg* (Frankfurt/M: Peter Lang, 1999).

64. Paul Weindling, 'International Eugenics: Swedish Sterilisation in Context', *Scandinavian Journal of History*, 24, 2 (1999), p. 192. See also Claudia Koonz, 'Eugenics, Gender and Ethics in Nazi Germany: The Debate about Involuntary Sterilization 1933–1936' in *Reevaluating the Third Reich*, eds. Thomas Childers and Jane Caplan (New York: Holmes & Meier, 1993), pp. 66–85; Margret Hamm, ed., *Lebensunwert—zerstörte Leben: Zwangssterilisation und 'Euthanasie'* (Frankfurt/M: VAS, 2005).

65. See Ulf Schmidt, 'Reassessing the Beginning of the "Euthanasia" Programme', *GH*, 17, 4 (1999), pp. 543–50, which shows the significance of the start of the war.

chief of the Führer's Chancellery (KdF) to run the operation. Bouhler appointed Victor Brack, the head of the KdF's Office II, to take charge of the day-to-day running of the programme. The children's Euthanasia programme, whose origins are usually ascribed to the case of the 'Knauer child', whose parents wrote to Hitler requesting that their baby be granted a 'mercy death', soon mutated into the adult programme, at which point the starvation of children was replaced with the gassing of adults. By the time of the official halt in 1941, over 70,000 patients had been murdered and, in an illustration of how the Nazis viewed the action in cost–benefit terms, a statistician calculated that RM 885,439,980 had been saved over ten years by these 70,000 'disinfections'.[66]

A recent study of Brandt details not only how the Euthanasia programme operated, but reveals it to have been a microcosm of the way in which the Third Reich functioned in general.[67] With the range of agencies involved and the hands-off approach taken by Hitler and Brandt, who modelled his leadership style on him, there was ample scope for both radicalization and dissembling. Brandt and Bouhler faced competition from Conti and others, who wanted to take charge of the programme, though Brandt, until late in 1944, remained in control. Brandt, who had been a mediocre medical student but was a fanatical Nazi, was deeply committed to the T4 project, in the interests of purifying the race, but later claimed at Nuremberg not to have had any knowledge of the murder of the Jews. The claim is not to be entertained, but it shows how the T4 project and the Holocaust could be conceptualized as separate enterprises. Ulf Schmidt notes that Brandt could proudly claim at Nuremberg that he 'genuinely believed in the rightness of the killing operation' but still go to great lengths to distance himself from the murder of the Jews.[68]

Apart from the T4 physicians and nurses,[69] racial anthropologists were active in many other ways in Nazi Germany, including the racial profiling

66. Henry Friedlander, 'From "Euthanasia" to the "Final Solution" ' in *Deadly Medicine*, ed. Kuntz, p. 167. The case of the 'Knauer child' has generated quite a controversy amongst historians trying to identify it. See Udo Benzenhöfer, *Der Fall Leipzig (alias 'Fall Kind Knauer')* *und die Planung der NS-'Kindereuthanasie'* (Münster: Klemm und Oelschläger, 2008) and Ulf Schmidt, *Karl Brandt: Medicine and Power in the Third Reich* (London: Hambledon Continuum, 2007), pp. 117–20, who names the child as Gerhard Herbert Kretschmar. It is likely that the decision for the Euthanasia programme had in any case been taken before the letter reached the KdF.
67. Schmidt, *Karl Brandt*, p. 209.   68. Schmidt, *Karl Brandt*, p. 380.
69. On nurses, see Bronwyn R. McFarland-Icke, *Nurses in Nazi Germany: Moral Choices in History* (Princeton: Princeton University Press, 1999).

of individuals in the Reich and occupied populations, conducting medical experiments in camps, and carrying out anthropological examinations on the remains of murdered victims, some of whom were murdered specially for the purpose (most famously the 86 Jews sent from Auschwitz to Natzweiler-Struthof in Alsace, where they were killed in the specially-built gas chamber and their bodies sent for analysis to Professor August Hirt at the University of Strasbourg; their identities have been recovered after thorough research by Hans-Joachim Lang[70]). Recent research shows in depressing detail just how deeply this participation went. Gretchen Schafft shows how anthropologists Dora Kahlisch and Elfriede Fliethmann undertook physical measurements among the Jews of the Tarnów ghetto in 1942, revealing the combination of precision and 'nonsense' that made up the research; they concluded, even though the Jews of the ghetto were 'a mix of various races', that 'one can always tell a Jew by appearance'.[71] Schafft also recreates the research of the *Institut für deutsche Ostarbeit* (IDO, Institute for German Work in the East), a body connected to the University of Vienna. She concludes: 'The research of the anthropologists at the IDO was totally meaningless. For all the measurements taken and the villages studied, there was little analysis, nor could there be. There were no standards by which to judge Jewishness, so no conclusions ever could have been drawn from the morphological measurements. Even had it been possible from the data, the anthropologists themselves did not know how to do the simplest statistical procedures.'[72] Ethnographers and experts on ethnic Germans, Georg Leibbrandt and Karl Stumpp were, respectively, a high official in Rosenberg's Ministry for the Occupied Eastern Territories and attendee at the Wannsee Conference; and in charge of an 80-man *Sonderkommando* in western Ukraine that may have been involved in some killing

---

70. Hans-Joachim Lang, *Die Namen der Nummern: Wie es gelang, die 86 Opfer eines NS-Verbrechen zu identifizieren* (Hamburg: Hoffman und Campe, 2004). See also Angelika Uhlmann, 'Die medizinische Fakultät der Reichsuniversität Straßburg und die Menschenversuche im KZ Natzweiler-Struthof' in *Medizin im Nationalsozialismus und das System der Konzentrationslager: Beiträge eines interdisziplinäre Symposiums*, eds. Judith Hahn, Silvija Kavčič, and Christoph Kopke (Frankfurt/M: Mabuse Verlag, 2005), pp. 165–87. Cf. Steinweis, *Studying the Jew*, pp. 60–3.

71. Gretchen E. Schafft, *From Racism to Genocide: Anthropology in the Third Reich* (Urbana: University of Illinois Press, 2004), pp. 23–4; see also Schafft, 'Scientific Racism in the Service of the Reich: German Anthropologists in the Nazi Era' in *Annihilating Difference: The Anthropology of Genocide*, ed. Alexander Laban Hinton (Berkeley: University of California Press, 2002), pp. 117–34.

72. Schafft, *From Racism to Genocide*, p. 32.

operations.[73] Numerous scholars were involved in varieties of *Ostforschung*, some of whose work contributed to the occupation policies, particularly *Volkstumspolitik*.[74]

The most notorious of all the Auschwitz doctors is Josef Mengele, and the literature on him is voluminous. Most stresses his medical background and his desire to become a famous scientist; his fame now rests primarily on his role in the 'selection' process on the ramp at Auschwitz and in his gruesome medical experiments, primarily on twins (twin research having long been promoted by his mentor, Verschuer). In Mengele's opinion, as Klee writes, the gas chambers at Auschwitz served the purpose of improving the species.[75] Mengele is the key link between medicine and genocide, showing how the former could be put to the service of the latter:

> Medicine in the Nazi period meant always and above all selection. The biologically inferior were to be eliminated from the organic body of the *Volk* [*Volkskörper*], always with the promise of a better biological future for the *Volk*. The individual did not count, he was mercilessly sterilized, euthanized, medically executed. Auschwitz is the culmination of medical selection, not a departure from it. That is why doctors stood on the ramp, selecting men older than 50 and women older than 45 for the gas chamber. No one was seen more frequently on the ramp than Josef Mengele. He is the symbol of German medical selection.[76]

No wonder then, that some historians, like Benoît Massin, claim that 'Not only did these scientists help the regime, sometimes they directly inspired its murderous policies.'[77]

The 'Euthanasia Programme' and the Link with the Holocaust

The reason why the historiography of race science is so significant in this context—and why it can be quite neatly mapped onto the 'modernity'

73. Eric J. Schmaltz and Samuel D. Sinner, 'The Nazi Ethnographic Research of Georg Leibbrandt and Karl Stumpp in Ukraine, and Its North American Legacy' in *German Scholars and Ethnic Cleansing, 1919–1945*, eds. Ingo Haar and Michael Fahlbusch (New York: Berghahn, 2005), pp. 51–85.
74. Michael Burleigh, *Germany Turns Eastwards: A Study of Ostforschung in the Third Reich* (Cambridge: Cambridge University Press, 1988).
75. Ernst Klee, *Auschwitz, die NS-Medizin und ihre Opfer* (Frankfurt/M: S. Fischer, 1997), p. 461.
76. Klee, *Auschwitz, die NS-Medizin*, p. 470.
77. Benoît Massin, 'The "Science of Race" ' in *Deadly Medicine*, ed. Kuntz, p. 125.

paradigm—is that many historians take it for granted that the Holocaust was the logical outcome of racial science, especially eugenics/racial hygiene. For example, Michael Kater writes: 'Auschwitz was the logical extension of sterilization and "euthanasia"; it became the racial clinic par excellence.' The reason? It 'was the exclusive prerogative of physicians to make selections for the gas chambers and to decide who among the Jewish prisoners was physically fit enough to continue living or ill enough to die.'[78] William Seidelman is even more far-reaching in his assessment:

> The extermination process of the 'final solution' evolved from eugenic sterilization and medical 'euthanasia'. . . . The infamous selection process on the ramp at Auschwitz was a medical selection made by physicians responsible for determining who was fit for slave labour and who would die in the gas chamber. The infamous gas chamber arose from the T4 'euthanasia' medical killing program. The turning on of the gas in the 'euthanasia' program was deemed to be a medical act assigned to a physician.[79]

And Ernst Klee states that 'What began with the eradication of the sick, aged and handicapped, who were allegedly unworthy of life, ended with the holocaust. The murderers of the sick provided not only the staff, but above all the method—gas chambers disguised as shower rooms. Everything that happened in the "extermination of the Jews" had been copied from the murder of the sick.'[80]

The systematic murder process under the auspices of Hitler's authorization began in occupied Poland, with the murder of mental patients in asylums in Pomerania, East Prussia, Danzig-West Prussia, and the Posen region.[81] It continued in many occupied countries, including tens of thousands of mental patients murdered in Ukraine.[82] And clearly, with the

---

78. Kater, *Doctors under Hitler*, p. 182.
79. Seidelman, 'Pathology of Memory' in *Medicine and Medical Ethics*, eds. Nicosia and Huener, p. 95. See also Seidelman, 'Medical Selection: Auschwitz Antecedents and Effluent', *HGS*, 4, 4 (1989), pp. 435–48, e.g., p. 436: 'The great therapy performed on behalf of the state in the "central hospital" of Auschwitz was the elimination of the disease known as the Jews.'
80. Ernst Klee, ' "Turning the Tap On Was No Big Deal"—The Gassing Doctors During the Nazi Period and Afterwards', *Dachau Review*, 2 (1990), p. 52.
81. Saul Friedländer, *The Years of Extermination: Nazi Germany and the Jews 1939–1945* (London: HarperCollins, 2007), pp. 14–16; Hans-Walter Schmuhl, *Rassenhygiene, Nationalsozialismus, Euthanasie: Von der Verhütung zur Vernichtung 'lebensunwerten Lebens', 1890–1945* (Göttingen: Vandenhoeck & Ruprecht, 1987), pp. 240–7; Volker Rieß, *Die Anfänge der Vernichtung 'lebensunwerten Lebens' in den Reichsgauen Danzig-Westpreußen und Wartheland 1939/40* (Frankfurt/M: Peter Lang, 1995).
82. Vasyl Dogusov and Svitlana Rusalov'ska, 'The Massacre of Mental Patients in Ukraine, 1941–1943', *International Journal of Mental Health*, 36, 1 (2007), pp. 105–11; see also the articles in the same issue and in 35, 4 (2006–07) on eugenic sterilization and euthanasia

transfer of T4 personnel to Chełmno and the Reinhard camps, we see important strands of continuity. Under the command of Christian Wirth (himself under the command of Globocnik), and still on the T4 payroll, these men were responsible for constructing a gas chamber at Bełżec in December 1941; the commandant of Sobibór, and later Treblinka, Franz Stangl, also came from T4, as did Treblinka's later commandant, Irmfried Eberl, the only T4 physician to be assigned to the Reinhard camps.[83]

This transfer from T4 to Operation Reinhard occurred after the Euthanasia programme was officially stopped. But with Operation 14f13 (named after the numbers of the bureaus responsible at the IKL), the SS and the T4 personnel worked together to eradicate concentration camp inmates no longer able to work, with a strong emphasis on Jews and Romanies. Proctor puts it neatly when he writes: 'Operation 14f13 represents the transition from the systematic destruction of the handicapped and the mentally ill to the systematic destruction of the ethnically and culturally marginal.'[84] Historians have in recent years investigated 'wild euthanasia'—the unofficial continuation of the T4 campaign after 1941—in greater detail, including the continued killing of children (which had never used gas chambers); they have also produced individual and group studies of perpetrator medics and of 'euthanasia' in the last phase of the war.[85]

throughout Europe during World War II, sometimes carried out with very little German involvement, as in the case of Norway, or sometimes hardly taking place at all, as in Estonia.

83. Paul Weindling, *Epidemics and Genocide in Eastern Europe, 1890–1945* (Oxford: Oxford University Press, 2000), p. 297. Weindling argues (p. 298) that 'Racialised anti-typhus measures accelerated and extended the Nazi genocide', though he later admits (p. 313) that 'What remains unclear is the transition from normal delousing to mass killing.' On Eberl, see Michael Grabher, *Irmfried Eberl: 'Euthanasie'-Arzt und Kommandant von Treblinka*, 2nd edn (Frankfurt/M: Peter Lang, 2006) and Patricia Heberer, 'Eine Kontinuität der Tötungsoperationen: T4–Täter und die "Aktion Reinhard" ' in *'Aktion Reinhardt': Der Völkermord an den Juden im Generalgouvernement 1941–1944*, ed. Bogdan Musial (Osnabrück: Fibre, 2004), pp. 298–301.

84. Proctor, *Racial Hygiene*, p. 208. See also Henry Friedlander, *The Origins of Nazi Genocide: From Euthanasia to the Final Solution* (Chapel Hill: University of North Carolina Press, 1995), pp. 142–50; Ute Hoffmann, 'Von der "Euthanasie" zum Holocaust: Die "Sonderbehandlung 14f13" am Beispiel der "Euthanasie"-Anstalt Bernburg' in *Lebensunwert—zerstörte Leben*, ed. Hamm, pp. 158–67.

85. Udo Benzenhöfer, *'Kinderfachabteilungen' und 'NS-Kindereuthanasie'* (Wetzlar: GWAB-Verlag, 2000); Mary V. Seeman, 'What Happened After T4? Starvation of Psychiatric Patients in Nazi Germany', *International Journal of Mental Health*, 35, 4 (2006–07), pp. 5–10; Michael Wunder, *Euthanasie in den letzten Kriegsjahren: Die Jahre 1944 und 1945 in der Heil- und Pflegeanstalt Hamburg-Langenhorn* (Husum: Matthiesen, 1992); Schmidt, *Karl Brandt*; Walter Kohl, *'Ich fühle mich nicht schuldig': Georg Renno, Euthanasiearzt* (Vienna: Paul Zsolnay, 2000); Hans Hesse, *Augen aus Auschwitz: Ein Lehrstück über nationalsozialistischen Rassenwahn und medizinische Forschungen. Der Fall Dr. Karin Magnussen* (Essen: Klartext, 2001), the last

Apart from general studies of the Euthanasia programme, German historians have been very active in producing local studies of Euthanasia institutions, including asylums and hospitals and not just the six killing centres. There is not the space here for a detailed discussion, but the phenomenon is noteworthy as it forms a counterpart to the very many local studies that attempt to recreate the lives of German Jews.[86] The number of self-taught historians, often from the medical profession, involved in these enterprises is noteworthy; they were instrumental in bucking the resistance of the postwar West German medical establishment, bravely seeking to reveal the truth about their teachers' crimes.[87] And 'resistance' to the Euthanasia programme has also been investigated, although its absence remains the most noteworthy fact, for this demonstrated to Hitler that the regime could put into practice genocidal schemes.[88]

The most compelling statement of the continuity thesis is Henry Friedlander's book, *The Origins of Nazi Genocide* (1995) whose subtitle, *From Euthanasia to the Final Solution*, makes his position clear. Along with Klee,

mentioned on Verschuer's assistant, whose investigations into heterochromia used eyes from Sinti and Roma victims, specially killed for the purpose by Mengele in Auschwitz.

86. The literature is large; examples include: Petra Fuchs, Maike Rotzoll, Ulrich Müller, Paul Richter, and Gerrit Hohendorf, *'Das Vergessen der Vernichtung ist Teil der Vernichtung selbst': Lebensgeschichten von Opfern der nationalsozialistischen 'Euthanasie'* (Göttingen: Wallstein, 2007); Waltraud Häupl, *Die ermordeten Kinder vom Spiegelgrund: Gedenkdokumentation für die Opfer der NS-Kindereuthanasie in Wien* (Vienna: Böhlau, 2006); Jan Nikolas Dicke, *Eugenik und Rassenhygiene in Münster* (Berlin: Weissensee Verlag, 2004); Herwig Czech, *Erfassung, Selektion und 'Ausmerze': Das wiener Gesundheitsamt und die Umsetzung der nationalsozialistischen 'Erbgesundheitspolitik' 1938 bis 1945* (Vienna: Deuticke, 2003); Christoph Braß, *Zwangssterilisation und 'Euthanasie' im Saarland 1935–1945* (Paderborn: Schöningh, 2004); Carola Einhaus, *Zwangssterilisation in Bonn (1934–1945): Die medizinischen Sachverständigen vor dem Erbgesundheitsgericht* (Vienna: Böhlau, 2006); Eberhard Gabriel and Wolfgang Neugebauer, *NS-Euthanasie in Wien* (Vienna: Böhlau, 2000); Wolfgang Freidl and Werner Sauer, eds., *NS-Wissenschaft als Vernichtungsinstrument: Rassenhygiene, Zwangssterilisation, Menschenversuche und NS-Euthanasie in der Steiermark* (Vienna: Facultas, 2004); Johannes Neuhauser and Michaela Pfaffenwimmer, *Hartheim wohin unbekannt: Briefe und Dokumente* (Weitra: Bibliothek der Provinz, 1992); Thomas Schilter, *Unmenschliches Ermessen: Die nationalsozialistische 'Euthanasie'-Tötungsanstalt Pirna-Sonnenstein 1940/41* (Leipzig: Kiepenheuer, 1999); Matthias Meusch, 'Hadamar: A German Psychiatric Treatment Center in World War II', *Biomolecular Engineering*, 17, 1 (2001), 65–9. See also Annette Hinz-Wessels, Petra Fuchs, Gerrit Hohendorf, and Maike Rotzoll, 'Zur bürokratischen Abwicklung eines Massenmords: Die "Euthanasie"-Aktion im Spiegel neuer Dokumente', *VfZ*, 53, 1 (2005), pp. 79–107.

87. Including Klaus Dörner, Ernst Klee, Benno Müller-Hill, and Karl-Heinz Roth.

88. Claudia Koonz, 'Ethical Dilemmas and Nazi Eugenics: Single-Issue Dissent in Religious Contexts', *JMH*, 64, 4 (1992), supplement pp. 9–31; Michael Burleigh, *Ethics and Extermination: Reflections on Nazi Genocide* (Cambridge: Cambridge University Press, 1997), ch. 5; Beth Griech-Polelle, 'Image of a Churchman Resister: Bishop von Galen, the Euthanasia Project and the Sermons of Summer 1941', *JCH*, 36, 1 (2001), pp. 41–57; Proctor, *Racial Hygiene*, ch. 9; Friedländer, *The Years of Extermination*, pp. 185–6.

Schmuhl, and Burleigh, Friedlander offers the most detailed history of the
T4 programme, and explains the links between the killing of handicapped
children and adults, Romanies, and Jews both in terms of the wider orders
for the Final Solution (Goering, Hitler, and Heydrich) and the experience
of the T4 killers: 'The murder of the handicapped preceded the murder
of Jews and Gypsies', he writes, 'and it is therefore reasonable to conclude
that T4's killing operation served as a model for the final solution.'[89] Hence
he concludes that the connection between the killing of the handicapped,
the Romanies, and the Jews was 'ideological, based on the belief in human
inequality and on the determination to cleanse the gene pool of the German
nation'.[90] Elsewhere he writes: 'Obviously, antisemitism as a cause is too
restrictive when applied to men who started their killing careers murdering
non-Jews. Instead we must point to the larger eugenic and racial ideology
of the Nazis, one that included hostility towards the handicapped as inferior ("minderwertig") and towards Jews and Gypsies as aliens.'[91] Thanks
to the work of Friedlander, Klee, and others, we now have a profound
understanding of the connections between T4 and the Holocaust.

There is a good argument to be made, therefore, that the 'Final Solution'
emerged, in Peukert's words, 'from the spirit of science'; certainly, doctors,
anthropologists, and other scientists eagerly availed themselves of the
opportunities presented by the regime and contributed to its success. Apart
from the technological and personnel connections, then, many historians
see a direct line of ideas from early eugenics and racial hygiene to Auschwitz.
Peukert argues against the central importance of antisemitism, instead seeing
the Final Solution as resulting 'from a fatal racist dynamic present within the
human and social sciences'. The 'general crisis of modernization in German
society and the economy' exacerbated trends that were visible elsewhere

89. Friedlander, *Origins*, p. 284. See also Ernst Klee, *'Euthanasie' im NS-Staat: Die 'Vernichtung
    lebensunwerten Lebens'* (Frankfurt/M: Fischer Taschenbuch Verlag, 2001); Müller-Hill, *Mur-
    derous Science*; Schmuhl, *Rassenhygiene, Nationalsozialismus, Euthanasie*; and Michael Burleigh,
    Death and Deliverance: 'Euthanasia' in Germany, c.1900–1945 (Cambridge: Cambridge Univer-
    sity Press, 1994) for general overviews of T4. In 1985, it was not unreasonable for Klee to
    write (p. 373) that 'The role played by T4 in the "solution of the Jewish question" has, until
    now . . . been underestimated.' See also Klee, 'Von der "T4" zur Judenvernichtung: Der
    "Aktion Reinhard" in den Vernichtungslagern Belzec, Sobibor und Treblinka' in *Aktion T4
    1939–1945: Die 'Euthanasie'-Zentrale in der Tiergartenstraße 4*, ed. Götz Aly (Berlin: Edition
    Hentrich, 1989), pp. 147–52.
90. Friedlander, *Origins*, p. 295.
91. Henry Friedlander, 'The T4 Killers: Berlin, Lublin, San Sabba' in *The Holocaust and History:
    The Known, the Unknown, the Disputed, and the Reexamined*, eds. Michael Berenbaum and
    Abraham J. Peck (Bloomington: Indiana University Press, 1998), p. 246.

and transformed Nazism's radical utopianism into a negative scheme to eradicate those without value.[92] Stefan Kühl puts forward a similar argument, and André Mineau boldly states: 'The Holocaust happened as the consequence of the unchecked development of social hygiene as political common sense of twentieth century European culture.'[93]

Others put forward more modest claims, discussing continuities in eugenic thought and Nazi legislation. Most notable is Richard Weikart's argument that Hitler's world view derived from Darwinism, which justified the extinction of 'inferior races' and gave grounds for believing in racial improvement for the 'superior'. Although he does not discuss the Holocaust in any detail, the implication is that the murder of the Jews should also be understood as deriving from this social Darwinist ethic.[94] 'Of course', he says, 'there was no direct path from Darwinism to the Nazis' mass extermination'; then continues: 'but surely Sheila Faith Weiss is right when she asserts that "to categorize people as 'valuable' and 'valueless', to view people as little more than variables amenable to manipulation for some 'higher end', as Schallmayer and all German eugenicists did, was to embrace an outlook that led, after many twists and turns, to the slave-labour and death camps of Auschwitz." '[95]

Yet, as Christian Pross points out, 'racism was not the only source of the disaster'. Pross cites Alexander Mitscherlich, the official delegate of the West German Chamber of Physicians at the Nuremberg doctors' trial, who wrote: 'Before such monstrous deeds and thoughts could shape everyday

92. Detlev J. K. Peukert, 'The Genesis of the "Final Solution" from the Spirit of Science' in *Nazism and German Society, 1933–1945*, ed. David F. Crew (London: Routledge, 1994), pp. 278, 292.
93. Kühl, 'The Relationship between Eugenics and the so-called "Euthanasia-Action" in Nazi Germany: A Eugenically Motivated Peace Policy and the Killing of the Mentally Handicapped during the Second World War' in *Science in the Third Reich*, ed. Szöllösi-Janze, pp. 185–210; André Mineau, 'Social Hygiene and the Holocaust', *The European Legacy*, 12, 7 (2007), p. 802.
94. Richard Weikart, *From Darwin to Hitler: Evolutionary Ethics, Eugenics, and Racism in Germany* (New York: Palgrave Macmillan, 2004); also *Hitler's Ethic: The Nazi Pursuit of Evolutionary Progress* (Basingstoke: Palgrave Macmillan, 2009).
95. Richard Weikart, 'Darwinism and Death: Devaluing Human Life in Germany 1859–1920', *Journal of the History of Ideas*, 63, 2 (2002), pp. 343–4, citing Weiss, *Race Hygiene and National Efficiency: The Eugenics of Wilhelm Schallmayer* (Berkeley: University of California Press, 1987), p. 158. In her useful survey of German eugenics: 'The Race Hygiene Movement in Germany', *Osiris*, 2nd series, 3 (1987), pp. 193–236, Weiss unambiguously states (p. 234): 'While there are ideological links between race hygiene and the destruction of unwanted "racial groups", it would be inaccurate to assume that individual German eugenicists or German race hygiene as a whole was directly responsible for the Holocaust.' For a clear statement of Weikart's position, see 'Does Darwinism Devalue Human Life?' at: http://www.csustan.edu/History/faculty/Weikart/DarDevalue.htm (accessed 1 July 2009).

routine and real life, the disaster must have originated from many sources. Only in the crossing of two currents could the doctor turn into a licensed killer and publicly employed torturer: at the point where his aggressive search for the truth met with the ideology of the dictatorship.'[96] Thus, Kater notes of Verschuer that he 'became more susceptible to irrational currents, and characteristically, it was his own prefigured racism that propelled him into the camp of the ideological fanatics . . . his unsavory racism was even more radicalized when in 1944 he acknowledged that Germany was waging a "racial war" against "World Jewry" and demanded as a "political priority of the present, a new, total solution to the Jewish problem." '[97] Similarly, Eric Ehrenreich distinguishes between Verschuer's scientific work—for example, on hereditary disposition to tuberculosis—and his racial claims, especially about the 'hereditary danger' posed to Germans by Jews, 'the existence of which was least grounded in any sort of rigorous scientific methodology'.[98] Mengele too 'continued to mingle the rational with the irrational'; in the case of his experiments on twins in Auschwitz, for example, he 'pushed an already questionable methodology into the dual realm of falsely scientific and the irrational, for in their case, that which was to be proven, their racial insufficiency (an irrational presumption), was already preordained (a methodic fallacy).'[99] And even Proctor, after charting

96. Christian Pross, 'Introduction' to Götz Aly, Peter Chroust, and Christian Pross, *Cleansing the Fatherland: Nazi Medicine and Racial Hygiene* (Baltimore: Johns Hopkins University Press, 1994), p. 2. See also Karl Kessler, 'Physicians and the Nazi Euthanasia Program', *International Journal of Mental Health*, 36, 1 (2007), pp. 4–16, on the need for racist assumptions to 'fill in the gaps' of scientific knowledge.

97. Kater, *Doctors under Hitler*, pp. 232–3, citing Verschuer, 'Bevölkerungs- und Rassenfragen in Europa', *Europäischer Wissenschaftsdienst*, 1 (1944), p. 11.

98. Eric Ehrenreich, 'Otmar von Verschuer and the "Scientific" Legitimization of Nazi Anti-Jewish Policy', *HGS*, 21, 2 (2007), pp. 56, 58. On Verschuer, see also Weindling, *Health, Race and German Politics*, pp. 559–63. Massin ('The "Science of Race" ', p. 111), notes that although the 'Jewish question' was omnipresent during the Third Reich, 'the number of published investigations did not increase dramatically' and that 'new research was rare', but does not say why; presumably, it was because there was no way of identifying Jewishness either genetically or through physical anthropological measurements. See also Pauline M. H. Mazumdar, 'Blood and Soil: The Serology of the Aryan Racial State', *Bulletin of the History of Medicine*, 64, 2 (1990), pp. 187–219, which notes at the outset (p. 187) that investigations into the relationship between race and blood groups legitimated racial discrimination but that 'little or no direct official use seems to have been made of the work of the blood group researchers for any of the race examinations required by Nazi policies'.

99. Kater, *Doctors under Hitler*, pp. 234–5. See also Lifton, *The Nazi Doctors*, ch. 17. Lifton's well-known arguments about doctors having to engage in what he calls 'doubling' to be able to participate in Nazi crimes is now widely contested; see, for instance, James M. Glass, *'Life Unworthy of Life': Racial Phobia and Mass Murder in Hitler's Germany* (New York: Basic Books, 1997), pp. 105–7.

race scientists' involvement in the genetic health courts (which adjudicated on sterilization cases), in advising the *Reichssippenamt* and working with the RuSHA, states that ultimately 'The Nazis supported anthropology—but perhaps only because so many anthropologists were so eager and willing to support the Nazis.'[100]

Practically too the link was not necessary and is soon revealed as circumstantial rather than analytically meaningful. It is correct to note that the technology for the gassing process was first developed in the context of the T4 programme and that the 'Brack method' (the gas chamber) proved just as 'successful' when applied to Jews. But, as Weindling notes, by 1945 supplies of Zyklon B were being disrupted 'and victims (sometimes alive, sometimes after being shot) were pushed into mass open pits for burning'. Thus, even 'Without the lethal technology, the system of mass murder continued to be implemented.'[101] And as Friedlander points out, although some physicians who had been involved in T4 were assigned to the Operation Reinhard camps, there they 'did not operate, as did their colleagues in the killing wards, with the deceptive trappings of medicine'. This fact by no means hindered the programme: 'After Eberl's departure, no physician remained in any of the camps of Operation Reinhard. Obviously, the extermination camps of the east functioned well despite the absence of physicians.'[102] Indeed, he criticizes those who see the killings at Birkenau as 'medicalized', and plainly states that 'Physicians were not essential . . . for the smooth operation of a killing centre'. In Birkenau, the presence of physicians at 'selections' merely 'reflected a normal bureaucratic division of labour'; the 'idea that SS physicians were employed because they brought to the task special skills as race scientists did not apply. As Müller-Hill has pointed out, even though the SS physicians were the students of the race scientists, it was not necessary to be an anthropologist "to select old people, mothers, and children." '[103]

100. Proctor, 'From *Anthropologie* to *Rassenkunde*', pp. 160–1, 166.
101. Weindling, *Epidemics and Genocide*, p. 320.
102. Friedlander, 'Physicians as Killers in Nazi Germany: Hadamar, Treblinka, and Auschwitz' in *Medicine and Medical Ethics*, eds. Nicosia and Huener, pp. 62, 66.
103. Friedlander, *Origins*, pp. 301, 302, citing Müller-Hill, 'Selektion: Die Wissenschaft von der biologischen Auslese des Menschen durch Menschen' in *Medizin und Gesundheitspolitik in der NS-Zeit*, ed. Norbert Frei (Munich: Oldenbourg, 1991), pp. 151–2. See also Friedlander, 'Die Entwicklung der Mordtechnik: Von der "Euthanasie" zu den Vernichtungslagern der "Endlösung" ' in *Die nationalsozialistischen Konzentrationslager*, eds. Herbert, Orth, and Dieckmann, pp. 493–507, esp. p. 503.

We now know far more about the role played by doctors, biologists, and anthropologists in the Holocaust than we did two decades ago. The evidence points to widespread complicity and overwhelming support for the regime's genocidal policies among these groups. Kater is right to dismiss the claim that the German medical profession was basically sound, but infected by a few atypical evildoers.[104] But what remains contentious is the extent to which the idea of murdering the Jews of Europe was developed and promoted by these race scientists. Weikart, in particular, sees no conceptual distinction between the murder of the disabled in the T4 programme and the murder of the Jews in the 'Final Solution', ascribing them both to the Nazis' belief that Darwinism provided them with the laws of evolutionary progress; by eliminating the 'unfit' who would die out anyway, the Nazis believed that they were simply expediting the inevitable.[105]

The studies of Schafft, Weikart, and others irrefutably demonstrate the profound involvement of physicians and scientists in racial selections, medical experiments, and other criminal activities.[106] But in taking the scientists as their subject of study, historians tend to overlook the prime movers of the Holocaust: Hitler, Himmler, and Heydrich, and the higher- and middle-level perpetrators: the SS's *Judenberater*, the SD intellectuals, the *Einsatzgruppen*, and the camp SS. These men turned to the 'Brack method' because of the psychological strains of mass murder faced by the *Einsatzgruppen*. The exception—in contrast to the historiography of the Nazi camps—is Operation Reinhard, which receives considerable attention insofar as it reveals continuities in ideas, personnel, and technology from the T4 operation. Many historians tend to be seduced by the claims of the race scientists, claims that they made in order to ingratiate themselves

104. Kater, *Doctors under Hitler*, pp. 222–3. See also Peter Weingart, 'German Eugenics between Science and Politics', *Osiris*, 2nd series, 5 (1989), p. 280.
105. Weikart, *From Darwin to Hitler*, p. 227.
106. On medical experiments, see Alfred Pasternak, *Inhuman Research: Medical Experiments in German Concentration Camps* (Budapest: Akadémiai Kiadó, 2006); Naomi Baumslag, *Murderous Medicine: Nazi Doctors, Human Experimentation, and Typhus* (Westport: Praeger, 2005); Paul Weindling, 'Genetik und Menschenversuche in Deutschland, 1940–1950: Hans Nachtsheim, die Kaninchen von Dahlem und die Kinder von Bullenhuser Damm' in *Rassenforschung*, ed. Schmuhl, pp. 245–74; Astrid Ley and Marion Maria Ruisinger, eds., *Gewissenlos—gewissenhaft: Menschenversuche im Konzentrationslager* (Erlangen: Specht, 2001); Freya Klier, *Die Kaninchen von Ravensbrück: Medizinische Versuche an Frauen in der NS-Zeit* (Munich: Knauer, 1994). See also Y. Michael Barilan, 'Medicine Through the Artist's Eyes: Before, During, and After the Holocaust', *Perspectives in Biology and Medicine*, 47, 1 (2004), pp. 110–34.

with those in power. They are seduced too by the very technology that they condemn, when in fact it is clear that the murder process worked with or without correctly-functioning technology. By focusing on doctors and race scientists, they overstate the extent to which the Holocaust was conceived as a 'medical' procedure, and thus end by contradicting their own arguments when they admit—as the above quotations show—that the origins of the genocidal idea lay more in fantasies of Jewish world power than in scientifically corroborated claims about defective Jewish genes. The importance of racial-scientific ideas is much clearer in Nazi sterilization and 'euthanasia' programmes than in the decision-making process that culminated in the systematic murder of Europe's Jews, for the Holocaust was an outcome of racial fantasy far more than of race science.

Yet in one respect there was a vital link between the Euthanasia programme and the Holocaust. As Aly points out, the most important connection, more significant than continuities in institutions or personnel:

> was the discovery made by its organizers that all levels of German adminis-
> tration, as well as the German people in general, were willing to accept such
> a procedure. Occasional remonstrance or resistance remained rare enough
> to permit a state policy of mass murder of people who had already been
> marginalized in various ways. The significance of Operation T-4 as a pre-
> lude to the gas chambers of Belzec and Auschwitz lies not so much in its
> developments of techniques of camouflage and murder as in its undeniable
> political success—in the overt as well as tacit acceptance of the murder of
> marginalized, defenceless people by the overwhelming majority of sectors of
> the population. It is thus hardly surprising that the national leadership drew
> the obvious conclusions, continuing its extermination policy and trusting that
> Germans would silently consent to this policy.[107]

What the Euthanasia programme did—like the Madagascar Plan or the occupation of Poland in 1939–41—was to encourage the development of a genocidal mindset. Historians disagree as to whether the 'origins of Nazi genocide' really should be sought in the Euthanasia programme, or whether the term 'Holocaust' should encompass the murder of the disabled carried out under that campaign. But there is no disagreement about the fact that the 'success' of the T4 programme helped to pave the way for the later, more far-reaching genocide of the Jews. 'If', as Aly points out, 'people did

---

107. Götz Aly, 'Medicine Against the Useless' in Aly, Chroust, and Pross, *Cleansing the Fatherland*,
     pp. 92–3. In Aly's early work on T4 one can see the origins of his later studies of Nazism
     as a 'welfare dictatorship' and a '*Gefälligkeitsdiktatur*'.

not protest even when their own relatives were being murdered, they could hardly be expected to object to the murder of Jews, Gypsies, Russians, and Poles.'[108]

Race and Antisemitism in the Nazi World View

As we have seen, it is commonplace to assert that Nazi racism developed out of a combination of antisemitism and eugenics. Weikart, for example, says that 'many of Hitler's ideas derived ultimately from respectable scientists and scholars who were grappling with the implications of Darwinism for ethics and society'.[109] But as Massimo Zumbini reminds us, this conjunction was not inevitable, but was a result of 'careful "selection" ' and the cross-fertilization of ideas throughout the complex development of antisemitism and eugenics, a process to which writers such as Theodor Fritsch contributed.[110] Indeed, Weindling readily grants that, 'In contrast to the sophisticated genetics of the Kaiser Wilhelm Institute, Hitler's racial biology was scientifically antiquated, and much more closely linked to currents of mystic Germanic and Nordic racial purity.'[111] It is true, as Geoff Eley points out, that, if one looks to *völkisch* origins, there is a risk that 'an overemphasis on the long run or deep-historical perspective on Nazi antisemitism occludes the complex specificities of experience under the Third Reich itself' and 'distorts the earlier nineteenth-century contexts of antisemitism as well'.[112] But recent historiography that stresses the centrality of racial fantasy is not simply reprising the earlier works of George Mosse, Fritz Stern, Norman Cohn, or Joshua Trachtenberg. That is to say, rather than seeking to join up the dots in an intellectual history running from Gobineau to Hitler (which would be as one-sided as the 'Darwin to Hitler' approach), the recent focus on racial fantasy tries to show how those fantasies were part of the immediate context in which the Third Reich constituted itself and carried the German people along.

108. Aly, 'Medicine Against the Useless', p. 93.
109. Weikart, *From Darwin to Hitler*, p. 8.
110. Massimo Ferrari Zumbini, *Die Wurzeln des Bösen. Gründerjahre des Antisemitismus: Von der Bismarckzeit zu Hitler* (Frankfurt/M: Vittorio Klostermann, 2003), pp. 403–4.
111. Weindling, 'Understanding Nazi Racism', p. 73.
112. Geoff Eley, 'What are the Contexts for German Antisemitism?' in *The Fate of the European Jews, 1939–1945: Fate or Contingency*, ed. Jonathan Frankel (New York: Oxford University Press, 1997), p. 113.

Instead of 'an extraordinarily strong teleology of origins' or assuming that antisemitism was particularly common in Germany,[113] the focus on race mysticism in the last decade presents it not simply as a necessary precursor to the rise of Nazism after 1918, but shows how it was operationalized in the specific contexts of the late 1920s and 1930s. It is thus necessary to juxtapose the historiography on race science with the historiography of race mysticism.

The geneticist-historian Benno Müller-Hill has written that 'the most popular German books about race were not written by scientists but by authors lacking a genetic education, such as the racial psychologist Ludwig Clauss and the Nordic propagandist Hans F. K. Günther, among others.'[114] These others included, most notably, Ludwig Klages, Alfred Bäumler, and Ernst Krieck, earlier theorists such as Gobineau, Houston Stewart Chamberlain, Julius Langbehn, Paul de Lagarde, Oswald Spengler, the inventor of 'anthroposociology' Georges Vacher de Lapouge,[115] the theorists of *Geopolitik*, Friedrich Ratzel and Karl Haushofer, as well as leading Nazis with philosophical pretensions, such as Rosenberg and Darré.[116] Historians, especially intellectual historians, have recently turned their attention to these figures again, reassessing their contributions to Nazism in the light of the historiography of perpetrators. Michael Biddiss, for example, argues that it was the liaison between 'an explicit, if quite undiscriminating, recognition of the claims of science (especially in the biological sphere)' and 'an even more evident addiction to crude irrationalism' that formed Nazism.[117] The republication of Uriel Tal's essays from the 1970s and 1980s, with their focus on myth, ritual, and the sacred in Nazi ideology, reminds historians that in order to understand Nazi race thinking, the non-rational basis of

113. Eley, 'What are the Contexts', pp. 113–4.
114. Benno Müller-Hill, 'Reflections of a German Scientist' in *Deadly Medicine*, ed. Kuntz, p. 196.
115. Michael Biddiss, 'Myths of the Blood', *Patterns of Prejudice*, 9, 5 (1975), pp. 11–19; Biddiss, 'History as Destiny: Gobineau, H. S. Chamberlain and Spengler', *Transactions of the Royal Historical Society*, 6th series, 7 (1997), pp. 73–100; Jennifer Michael Hecht, 'Vacher de Lapouge and the Rise of Nazi Science', *Journal of the History of Ideas*, 61, 2 (2000), pp. 285–304.
116. Gesine Gerhard, 'Breeding Pigs and People for the Third Reich: Richard Walther Darré's Agrarian Ideology' in *How Green Were the Nazis?*, eds. Brüggemeier, Cioc, and Zeller, pp. 129–46; on Rosenberg, see Robert Cecil, *The Myth of the Master Race: Alfred Rosenberg and Nazi Ideology* (London: B. T. Batsford, 1972); Reinhard Bollmus, *Das Amt Rosenberg und seine Gegner: Studien zum Machtkampf im nationalsozialistischen Deutschland* (Stuttgart: Deutsche Verlagsanstalt, 1970), which was republished in 2006; Ernst Piper, *Alfred Rosenberg: Hitlers Chefideologe* (Munich: Karl Blessing, 2005).
117. Biddiss, 'History as Destiny', p. 99.

Nazi scientism must be taken into account.[118] It would be quite wrong to see these thinkers as presenting a united front; studies of *Geopolitiker*, in particular, have noted the discord between the advocates of racial and geographical determinism.[119] But what they had in common was their emphasis on a science that would confirm existing beliefs: the need for *Lebensraum*, the superiority of the Aryan race, the threat posed by the Jews. It is, as Bassin says, 'highly indicative' that Ernst Haeckel, the man who conceived of the scientific study of ecology, was an early advocate of the *völkisch* movement. 'Race', he explains, 'was the formative factor in this process [of the *Volk* imprinting its character on the natural environment], and the cultural landscape acquired significance as a sort of materialization and visual embodiment of an encoded racial essence.'[120]

Klages and Bäumler are famous as advocates of 'heroic realism',[121] but both were considered to be formidable philosophers in their own right, by Walter Benjamin, for example. These foremost proponents of *Lebensphilosophie*—with its focus on *Rausch* (intoxication or ecstasy) and animal drives—differed considerably, Bäumler being more restrained in his methodology than Klages, who gave fuller rein to aesthetic, 'biocentric' radicalism.[122] Bäumler, however, was politically more radical, and was appointed to head the science office at the Centre of Nazi Pedagogy, a position which made him 'responsible for the "Nazification" of the German academic world'.[123] In this position he committed himself, as Tal states, to the 'attainment of irrational goals by rational means'.[124]

Ernst Krieck, though more anti-intellectual than Klages or Bäumler, played a key role in promoting the 'total educational state'.[125] He provides

118. Uriel Tal, *Religion, Politics and Ideology in the Third Reich: Selected Essays* (London: Routledge, 2004).
119. Mark Bassin, 'Blood or Soil? The *Völkisch* Movement, the Nazis, and the Legacy of Geopolitik' in *How Green Were the Nazis?*, eds. Brüggemeier, Cioc, and Zeller, pp. 204–42; Dan Diner, 'Knowledge of Expansion: On the Geopolitics of Karl Haushofer' in *Beyond the Conceivable: Studies on Germany, Nazism, and the Holocaust* (Berkeley: University of California Press, 2000), pp. 26–48.
120. Bassin, 'Blood or Soil?', pp. 206, 229. On Haeckel, see Daniel Gasman, *Haeckel's Monism and the Birth of Fascist Ideology* (New York: Peter Lang, 1998).
121. Max Whyte, 'The Uses and Abuses of Nietzsche in the Third Reich: Alfred Baeumler's "Heroic Realism" ', *JCH*, 43, 2 (2008), pp. 171–94. See also David Pan, 'Revising the Dialectic of Enlightenment: Alfred Baeumler and the Nazi Appropriation of Myth', *New German Critique*, 84 (2001), pp. 37–52.
122. Nitzan Lebovic, 'The Beauty and Terror of *Lebensphilosophie*: Ludwig Klages, Walter Benjamin, and Alfred Baeumler', *South Central Review*, 23, 1 (2006), pp. 23–39.
123. Lebovic, 'The Beauty', p. 33.   124. Tal, *Religion, Politics and Ideology*, p. 89.
125. Koonz, *The Nazi Conscience*, p. 136.

an excellent example of the way in which science was subordinated to Nazi race mysticism:

> The scientific system of Eugen Fischer, according to which hereditary characteristics should be considered the motive force of history, is the key to understanding the value of the individual. And there are scientists in the world rising to disagree with the possibility of proving the existence of race scientifically. However we have learned from Chamberlain's and especially from the Führer's teachings that the verification of the existence of race, and perhaps of existence in general, does not require artificial scientific tools. . . . The fact of the existence of race is not doubtful, because man carries it in his heart, his spirit, his soul, or because man wants race to become a fact.[126]

But apart from the race mystics, sometimes even the internationally respected scientists explained their support for Nazism in different terms, as, in this case, Eugen Fischer:

> It is a rare and special good fortune for a theoretical science to flourish at a time when the prevailing ideology welcomes it, and its findings can immediately serve the policy of the state. The study of human heredity was already sufficiently mature to provide this, when years ago National Socialism was recasting not only the state but also our ways of thinking and feeling. Not that National Socialism needed a 'scientific' foundation as proof that it was right, ideologies are formed through practical experience and struggle rather than through laborious scientific theorizing. However the results of the study of human heredity become absolutely indispensable as a basis for the important laws and regulations created by the new state.[127]

Fischer was no opportunist, but had been working on giving race research and racial politics a solid scientific basis since before World War I; the Nazi state helped him to realize this ambition.[128] As Aurel Kolnai wrote in his remarkable 1938 study of Nazi thinking, *The War Against the West*, 'The desideratum of racial *purity* belongs mainly to the mystical side'.[129]

126. Krieck, 'Die Intellektuellen und das Dritte Reich', cited in Tal, *Religion, Politics and Ideology*, p. 9.
127. Fischer, 'Erbe als Schicksal', *Deutsche Allgemeine Zeitung* (28 March 1943), cited in Müller-Hill, 'Reflections of a German Scientist', p. 196.
128. Benoît Massin, 'Rasse und Vererbung als Beruf: Die Hauptforschungsrichtungen am Kaiser-Wilhelm-Institut für Anthropologie, menschliche Erblehre und Eugenik im Nationalsozialismus' in *Rassenforschung*, ed. Schmuhl, pp. 190–244, here p. 243. Massin also cites the Fischer passage quoted here.
129. Aurel Kolnai, *The War Against the West* (London: Victor Gollancz, 1938), p. 443. On Kolnai's book, one of the very few to take Nazi thinkers seriously, see my *Responses to Nazism in Britain, 1933–1939: Before War and Holocaust* (Basingstoke: Palgrave Macmillan, 2003), pp. 26–34.

This race mysticism was embodied most clearly in the SS. Although the intellectuals of the SD regarded Rosenberg and Darré as superannuated cranks, their own 'rationality'—which focused on 'action' based on economic and ethnological statistics—was no less founded on non-rational assumptions about race, in particular the need to save Germany by getting rid of the Jews. As Peter Reichel notes: 'This National Socialist organization was the most contradictory "synthesis of the primeval and the most modern". More than any other it seemed to be a community of the elect and the extraordinary. A "mysticism beyond morality" was created. Atheistic "men of action" propagated and organized the "deification of the irrational".'[130]

A good example of what Reichel means is provided by Gordon Horwitz's description of the discourse of disease at the time of the construction of the Łódź ghetto. Here we see a clear case of rational science being underpinned by non-rational racial fantasy, and a clear link between these racial fantasies and the Holocaust. That Jews were carriers of typhus was an 'unquestioned assumption' among the German medical establishment. One medical officer wrote that strict intervention was necessary to keep Jews from infecting the rest of the population: 'In this state of affairs the sole remaining hygienic measure promising success in combating the epidemic must be to avoid under all circumstances any contact with the Jews, for, as far as anyone can judge, only in this way is the transmission of lice to be ruled out.' Isolating the Jews, then, would 'hermetically' seal off 'all paths which scientific experience indicates the epidemic could take'.[131] Planners noted that in order to make the situation effective, there would have to be a neutral zone around the ghetto, a hospital staffed exclusively by ghetto medics would have to be built, medicines would have to be available at the four ghetto pharmacies, latrine facilities would need to be expanded, water taps would need to be provided at the edge of the ghetto, and the burial of the dead would take place in the old Jewish cemetery located within the ghetto. The result would be that the city's inhabitants could look forward to 'the well-founded prospect of limiting spotted fever in Lodsch to its source and in so doing protect the general public from the spread of the epidemic'.[132]

130. Peter Reichel, 'Festival and Cult: Masculine and Militaristic Mechanisms of National Socialism' in Shaping the Superman: Fascist Body as Political Icon—Aryan Fascism, ed. J. A. Mangan (London: Frank Cass, 1999), p. 166.
131. Wilhelm Hallbauer, 'Denkschrift über die Notwendigkeit der Einrichtung eines Ghettos in Lodsch', 1 February 1940, cited in Gordon J. Horwitz, Ghettostadt: Łódź and the Making of a Nazi City (Cambridge, MA: Harvard University Press, 2008), p. 37.
132. Hallbauer, 'Denkschrift', cited in Horwitz, Ghettostadt, p. 39.

On the face of it, what we see here is an eminently modern, scientific understanding of the spread and containment of disease—of the role of lice, and the measures required to limit the spread of disease and to prevent contact with those infected. But the whole project—which in its framework is no different from any other attempt to control the spread of disease—rested on a faulty assumption: the claim that the Jews were the main carriers. As Horwitz writes: 'In regard to their own assumptions about the concentration and spread of tuberculosis, however, authorities were confronted with the need to explain the inconvenient anomaly that local rates of infection and mortality for this disease were actually lower among the Jews than among the gentile population.' To get around this problem, the authorities argued that the lower rates of infection among Jews resulted from the Jews being heavily underrepresented in the numbers of physical labourers, the section of the population which bore the brunt of the disease.[133] As rich parasites, they had unjustly escaped the scourge of the illness. 'Left unmentioned', Horwitz points out, 'was why it was then judged a matter of the common good to uproot those Jews whose superior occupations and living standards had so clearly contributed to their better health in order to crowd them as well into a ghetto where conditions would more closely resemble those decried by the planners as so favourable to the spread of disease.'[134] Where at first glance we see a modern, scientific, rational discourse applying the findings of modern medicine to the eradication of a social scourge such as typhus or tuberculosis, a deeper analysis reveals that this discourse is overlaid upon a 'non-rational' belief that Jews carry diseases. Horwitz's discussion of the emergence of the Łódź ghetto therefore encapsulates and highlights the place held by race science in the Third Reich: a 'scientific' discourse, and often the application of science, on top of a theory of race that did not derive from science, even though it utilized science for justification.

The fact is that the Nazis were driven primarily by racial phobias rather than an 'antisemitism of reason'; similarly, race scientists' underlying assumptions rather than scientific objectivity were more significant in

133. Horwitz, *Ghettostadt*, pp. 39–40.
134. Horwitz, *Ghettostadt*, p. 40. On the long-established idea that Jews were resistant to tuberculosis, see: Mitchell B. Hart, *The Healthy Jew: The Symbiosis of Judaism and Modern Medicine* (New York: Cambridge University Press, 2007), ch. 5; Todd Samuel Presner, *Muscular Judaism: The Jewish Body and the Politics of Regeneration* (London: Routledge, 2007); Veronika Lipphardt, *Biologie der Juden: Jüdische Wissenschaftler über 'Rasse' und Vererbung 1900–1935* (Göttingen: Vandenhoeck & Ruprecht, 2008).

shaping their ideas. A comparison between Franz Boas, the most significant anthropologist of the early twentieth century and the 'father' of modern cultural anthropology, and Hans F. K. Günther proves the point. Both were products of the relatively liberal late nineteenth-century German anthropological tradition, with its opposition to evolutionism. Both accepted the fundamental presuppositions of racial anthropology and believed that modern populations were heavily racially mixed. Yet before World War I, Boas developed a devastating critique of racial anthropology through his examination of the change in head shapes from one generation of Italian immigrants to the US to the next, whilst Günther became one of the most infamous race obsessives in Nazi Germany, and a favourite of the regime, thanks to his simple racial schemes.[135]

Thus, what we see ultimately is race thinking driven less by scientific rationalism than by obsessive mysticism, fear, and paranoia, 'thinking with the blood'. Hence the reorientation of racial policy by Hitler after 1935, after it had become evident that a scientific definition of 'Jewishness' would not be forthcoming: 'From that point on, cultural stereotypes about Jewish character displaced physical traits in the hunt for sources of Jewishness, and the burden of proof shifted away from the natural sciences to the social sciences and the humanities.'[136]

Whilst some advocates, such as Walter Gross, continued to value the popular validation of Nazi thinking that racial science brought the regime, the turn to 'racial instinct' rather than racial science was clear. Hutton is even more explicit; in his detailed survey—in fact, the only sustained one available—of academic debates in Nazi racial science, he writes that 'there was never any question of the Party and state authorities yielding their final authority in such matters to purely scholarly criteria. In any case, the scholars themselves, for all their bluster, did not have coherent or convincing answers to offer. The regime increasingly sought to keep academic and scholarly discussion of race separate from race propaganda in the public

135. Franz Boas, 'Changes of Bodily Form of Descendants of Immigrants' in *Race, Language and Culture* (Chicago: University of Chicago Press, 1982 [1940]), pp. 60–75; Amos Morris-Reich, 'Race, Ideas, and Ideals: A Comparison of Franz Boas and Hans F. K. Günther', *History of European Ideas*, 32, 3 (2006), pp. 313–32; see also Julia E. Liss, 'Diasporic Identities: The Science and Politics of Race in the Work of Franz Boas and W. E. B. Du Bois, 1894–1919', *Cultural Anthropology*, 13, 2 (1998), pp. 127–66. A good deal has been written about Günther; for a useful starting point, see Steinweis, *Studying the Jew*, pp. 25–41.
136. Koonz, *The Nazi Conscience*, p. 197. See also Allyson D. Polsky, 'Blood, Race, and National Identity: Scientific and Popular Discourses', *Journal of Medical Humanities*, 23, 3/4 (2002), pp. 171–86.

sphere.'[137] This was most obviously the case where the discussion turned to the racial unity of the German population, where scholarly findings would not be allowed to stand in the way of the regime's racial message. With respect to the Holocaust, Hutton shows that scientists cannot be let off the hook: 'Racial anthropologists were key personnel in the state's profiling of its population, and in the preparation of racial evaluations of individuals and groups.' But they were neither the originators of the 'Final Solution' nor were they central to Nazism's presentation of the German *Volk*'s essential unity: 'Racial anthropologists had shown their usefulness in making clear that Jews and other undesirable elements were not part of the *Volk*, and in clarifying that the *Volk* could not be defined purely in linguistic terms, but they had no coherent answer to offer in relation to the positive definition of the German *Volk*.'[138] Earlier notions of a 'Nordic race' were displaced in favour of the unifying and suitably vague concept of the German *Volk*, which avoided academic hair-splitting and permitted the easy creation of ingroups and outgroups. Nazi anthropologists knew, as did anthropologists the world over, that all populations were racially mixed, including the German; this is why their views had to be politically neutralized. A study of Nazi race propaganda proves the point: even when most of the Jews killed in the Holocaust were already dead, Goebbels' propaganda machine kept insisting on the need to defend Germany from the Jewish international conspiracy.[139] No wonder, then, that Müller-Hill, one of the pioneer historians of genetics under the Nazis, concludes that eugenics was the 'science and religion of the Nazis'.[140]

Conclusion

'The struggle to renovate and arm the national *Volkskörper* was in no way incompatible with the spirit of modernism or the technocratic practice of scientists', writes Fritzsche.[141] Thus, we are not dealing here with a question of exculpating 'modernity' or 'science'; but the Nazi 'war against the Jews'

137. Hutton, *Race and the Third Reich*, p. 139.   138. Hutton, *Race and the Third Reich*, p. 167.
139. Herf, *The Jewish Enemy*.
140. Benno Müller-Hill, 'Eugenics: The Science and Religion of the Nazis' in *When Biology Went Mad: Bioethics and the Holocaust*, ed. Arthur L. Caplan (Totowa: Humana Press, 1992), pp. 43–52. See also André Mineau, *The Making of the Holocaust: Ideology and Ethics in the Systems Perspective* (Amsterdam: Rodopi, 1999), pp. 81–8.
141. Peter Fritzsche, 'Nazi Modern', *Modernism/Modernity*, 3, 1 (1996), p. 16.

preceded the technocracy and made use of it, for the Holocaust did not emerge 'from the spirit of science'. The Third Reich was a racial state, but one based more on race mysticism than on racial science. This claim helps us to understand the relative weight to be ascribed to 'rational' factors in the Holocaust; the debate about 'race' in the Holocaust is thus the archetypal case for dissecting the larger debate about modernity. By understanding the Holocaust as a policy emanating from the centre of the Nazi regime and nuanced by the centre's interactions with the occupying forces—as the mainstream historiography of the decision-making process does—we can see that whilst race scientists serviced the Third Reich and played a significant role in creating a racially profiled *Volksgemeinschaft*, scientific ideas *per se* were more valuable for initiating the Euthanasia campaign than the 'Final Solution of the Jewish Question'.

The thrust of this chapter's assessment of the historiography of race science in Nazi Germany should not be misread as an exculpation of scientists' involvement in the criminal acts of the regime, which most enthusiastically supported. As Ehrenreich notes, research institutes might not actually have been the setting for the origins of the Holocaust, but many scientists justified their positions in the Third Reich by claiming that this was in fact the case:

> While Verschuer and others offered only feeble 'scientific' reasoning in support of Nazi anti-Jewish policies, during the Third Reich these same scientists boldly declaimed the 'scientific necessity' for such measures. Thus even if most race scientists never worked in a death camp as did Verschuer's protégé Mengele, they nevertheless played a key role in the implementation of policies justified by the regime.[142]

Race scientists and physicians were prominent in the drawing-up and implementation of the sterilization and Euthanasia programmes—which can be understood as 'medical procedures' far more easily than the Holocaust—and they worked with the regime in assessing individuals for 'Aryan passes' or their potential to be 'regermanized'. Hence, their critics of the 1980s onwards have been right to highlight the scandalous cases of criminally implicated doctors continuing to work after 1945, and of institutions failing to address their brown pasts.[143]

142. Ehrenreich, 'Otmar von Verschuer', p. 66.
143. For example, Michael H. Kater, 'The Burden of the Past: Problems of a Modern Historiography of Physicians and Medicine in Nazi Germany', *German Studies Review*, 10, 1 (1987), pp. 31–56.

Nonetheless, the Holocaust cannot be seen in an unproblematic way as the outcome of racial science. Most historians of race science look at some point to the non-rational presuppositions that underpinned the science and, more important, one should not overstate the importance of the race scientists to the Nazi leaders, who actually made the decisions pertaining to the 'final solution'. The race scientists needed the regime far more than the regime needed them. What one needs to consider is whether the Holocaust would or could have happened without the race scientists' input.

Historiographically, the focus on race science should be understood as part of the broader 'modernity' paradigm of the 1980s and 1990s. It fits the 'modernity' perspective nicely to understand the Holocaust as emerging from the 'spirit of science', with its emphasis on technical fixes, means–ends rationality and bureaucratically administered inhumanity. Thus, the developing criticisms, such as Ehrenreich's or Hutton's, can be seen as of a piece with the wider phenomenon of the 'return of ideology' and a more careful, in-depth analysis of the content and function of the Nazi world view. Their work by no means dismisses the findings of the last twenty years, nor does it return us to a naïve intentionalism; but it does confirm that the leading Nazis rather than the race scientists were the prime movers in the creation and implementation of *Judenpolitik*.

Finally, what are the philosophical implications of Lindenfeld's claims that the non-rational preceded the rational or the 'modern'? Given the scientists' ready involvement in the Holocaust, we can and should still critique the Enlightenment tradition for its potential to throw up drives towards total domination. But given the fact that the Holocaust cannot be explained by science alone, it is also the case that such a critique should not lead to a celebration of the irrational, without which the 'modern' aspects of the German state would not have been placed in the service of genocide. As is often noted of Bauman, modern bureaucracies make unemployment and child benefit payments, and do not all end in genocide, even in our more surveillant, technocratic states of today.[144] Rather, the implication is that a better version of the Enlightenment be found, one based not on totalizing blueprints (this is in any case a caricature of Enlightenment thought) but on 'epistemological modesty', as Lindenfeld puts it.[145] Or, as Hutton remarks: 'Bizarrely, the idea of Enlightenment modernity as "Nazi"

144. Edward Ross Dickinson, 'Biopolitics, Fascism, Democracy: Some Reflections on Our Discourse about "Modernity" ', *CEH*, 37, 1 (2004), pp. 1–48.
145. Lindenfeld, 'The Prevalence of Irrational Thinking', p. 385.

is the mirror image of the idea of the Enlightenment as "Jewish", with the Nazis, instead of the Jews, understood as destructive of racio-cultural difference within modernity.'[146] This links postmodern understandings of history to the liberal tradition, in the promotion of variety, plurality, and tolerance: precisely the things that Nazi racial policy sought to eradicate.

146. Hutton, *Race and the Third Reich*, p. 16.

5

Genocide, the Holocaust, and the History of Colonialism

Yes, it would be worthwhile to study clinically, in detail, the steps taken by Hitler and to reveal to the very distinguished, very humanistic, very Christian bourgeois of the twentieth century that without his being aware of it, he has a Hitler inside him, that Hitler *inhabits* him, that Hitler is his *demon*, that if he rails against him, he is being inconsistent and that, at bottom, what he cannot forgive Hitler for is not *crime* in itself, *the crime against man*, it is not *the humiliation of man as such*, it is the crime against the white man, the humiliation of the white man, and the fact that he applied to Europe colonialist procedures which until then had been reserved exclusively for the Arabs of Algeria, the coolies of India, and the blacks of Africa.

Aimé Césaire, *Discourse on Colonialism*[1]

Introduction

In the previous chapter, I suggested that antisemitism as a mystical world view was a more proximate cause of the Holocaust than race science or the 'antisemitism of reason', although the latter certainly legitimized and aided the former to a very great extent. But it would be a circular argument simply to appeal to antisemitism as the cause of the Holocaust. The weakness of the intentionalist argument—even the 'modified' intentionalist

---

1. Aimé Césaire, *Discourse on Colonialism* (New York: Monthly Review Press, 1972 [1955]), p. 14.

argument—is that it does not explain how antisemitism, which, after all, was hardly unique to Germany, was made the basis of state policy. To find an answer to that question, one has to bear in mind Helmut Walser Smith's and Geoff Eley's point, that a longer-term contextualization is necessary. We know in extraordinary detail what happened between autumn 1939 and spring 1942, in terms of the decision-making process for the 'Final Solution'. But only an ultra-structuralist perspective which puts everything down to contingency would be satisfied with that as an explanation, as opposed to a description of the Holocaust's unfolding. If we take seriously the previous chapter's argument about the importance of race mysticism, then we need to ask: where did that mystical antisemitism come from?

That question has mostly been answered with reference to nineteenth-century German history. Since Eley and Blackbourn's devastating critique, *Sonderweg*-style arguments have no longer been fashionable. But in explaining the emergence of Nazism, immediate causes—such as the Great Depression—still need longer-term contextualization if they are to be meaningful.[2] For without examining the similarities between what happened in Germany and what happened in Britain or France (the classic countries of comparison in *Sonderweg* debates), the differences cannot be understood. Similarities, as we saw in Chapter 4, are easily found in race thinking, social Darwinism, and eugenics, phenomena by no means confined to Germany. Even the violent antisemitism of the Weimar years, recently the subject of historical inquiry, does not mark Germany as different from many other European countries.

This focus on German domestic history has recently been challenged by the resurgence of interest in imperial and colonial history in general, and the German overseas empire in particular. Formal German colonial settlement took place over a very short period, from the 1880s until 1919, when Germany was stripped of its colonies in the post-Great war settlements. Is the German colonial experience in any way relevant for understanding the rise of Nazism or, more specifically, the Holocaust? For many historians, the question is instinctively absurd, for it is obvious to them that the causal

2. David Blackbourn and Geoff Eley, *The Peculiarities of German History: Bourgeois Society and Politics in Nineteenth-Century Germany* (Oxford: Oxford University Press, 1984); Helmut Walser Smith, *The Continuities of German History* (Cambridge: Cambridge University Press, 2008); Walser Smith, 'When the *Sonderweg* Debate Left Us', *German Studies Review*, 31, 2 (2008), pp. 225–40; see also the forum on 'The Long Nineteenth Century', *GH*, 26, 1 (2008), pp. 72–91.

nexus that gave rise to the Holocaust is dominated by World War I and its after-effects, and the crises of the interwar years. But, in the last decade, the claim that colonialism can tell us something important about the origins of the Holocaust has inspired a large historiography that now constitutes a major analytical challenge to established explanations because it adds to our store of long-term explanations for the Holocaust.

In this chapter, I will situate this debate about German colonialism and the Holocaust into the context of the earlier debate concerning the 'uniqueness' of the Holocaust. This debate, whose high watermark was the West German *Historikerstreit* (historians' debate) of the mid-1980s, is informative for an understanding of Holocaust historiography insofar as it marks a change in the discourse surrounding the genocide of the Jews, opening up questions of a comparative nature: does the Holocaust have features in common with Stalinist terror? Is 'genocide' a useful term for understanding the Holocaust? Can the Holocaust usefully be compared with other cases of genocide, such as the colonial settlement of North America or Australia, the Ottoman destruction of the Armenians in 1915–16, the Khmer Rouge's devastation of Cambodia in 1975–79, or the annihilation of Tutsis in Rwanda in 1994? I begin with an analysis of the 'uniqueness' debate, then turn to an examination of the emergence of the new field of 'genocide studies', and ask how they help us to conceptualize the Holocaust. Finally, I look at the recent, ongoing debates about the relationship between colonialism and the Holocaust.

Many historians now accept the fact that the German occupation of Europe during World War II was a colonial enterprise; the treatment of 'indigenous peoples' such as the Ukrainians and Russians shares many commonalities with European overseas practices. But when it comes to understanding the genocide of the Jews, many scholars doubt that a colonial paradigm can be of service. Here I ask whether this distinction between the treatment of Slavs and Jews by the Nazis is conceptually defensible, and whether the Holocaust stands alone in the Nazis' grand project to reshape Europe's population along racial lines. Common to all of these questions is the relationship between 'race' and 'space'; where these were intertwined in previous cases of colonial genocide, in the Holocaust the question of 'space' appears to be less significant, for the conquering of territory for German settlement necessitated the removal of huge numbers of Slavs, but not Jews, who were a minority population (albeit, in Poland, a large one). In what ways, then, can the Holocaust be seen as part of a historical trajectory encompassing earlier European practices such as slavery, colonial settlement, and imperial 'population control'? And, if there is a difference between the treatment of the Jews and other population groups under Nazi control, does this mean that a 'new *Sonderweg*' is creeping into the historiography, a special German path 'from Africa to Auschwitz'?

The Uniqueness of the Holocaust

The notion that the Holocaust is unique is a long-standing one in Holocaust historiography and, especially, in the popular imagination. In the 1960s and 1970s the claim served the important function of countering the relative inattention paid to the Holocaust in the postwar world; by the 1980s, it was commonplace and historians could make the claim for uniqueness without being controversial. The horror of the Nazis' attempt to destroy a people for no other reason than their birth as Jews (or 'Jews' as the Nazis defined them, for of course, many of those persecuted by the Nazis were Christians, irreligious, or not aware of their Jewish descent[3]) made the claim seem unobjectionable. Elie Wiesel wrote that 'the fundamental uniqueness was the plan, the intention of the enemy, to obliterate a whole people down to the last person.'[4] Lucy Dawidowicz wrote: 'The murder of the 6 million Jews stands apart from the deaths of the other millions, not because of any distinctive fate that the individual victims endured, but because of the differentiative intent of the murderers and the unique effect of the murders.'[5] And Eberhard Jäckel, in a famous quotation that encapsulates the uniqueness argument, argued that 'the National-Socialist murder of the Jews was unique because never before had a nation with the authority of its leader decided and announced that it would kill off as completely as possible a particular group of humans, including old people, women, children, and infants and actually put this decision into practice, using all the means of governmental power at its disposal.'[6] Whilst for most

3. James F. Tent, *In the Shadow of the Holocaust: Nazi Persecution of Jewish-Christian Germans* (Kansas: University Press of Kansas, 2003).
4. Jorge Semprun and Elie Wiesel, *Schweigen ist unmöglich* (Frankfurt/M: Suhrkamp, 1997), p. 35.
5. Lucy S. Dawidowicz, *The Holocaust and the Historians* (Cambridge, MA: Harvard University Press, 1981), p. 14.
6. Eberhard Jäckel, 'The Impoverished Practice of Insinuation: The Singular Aspect of National-Socialist Crimes Cannot be Denied' in *Forever in the Shadow of Hitler? Original Documents of the Historikerstreit, the Controversy Concerning the Singularity of the Holocaust*, eds. James Knowlton and Truett Cates (Atlantic Highlands: Humanities Press, 1993), p. 76.

historians, Nazi intent provided sufficient grounds for uniqueness, some
took the claim even further, claiming that the Holocaust somehow stood
outside of historical comprehension. Nora Levin, for example, stated that
'The world of Auschwitz was, in truth, a new planet'; Gunnar Heinsohn
asserts that the Holocaust was a 'uniquely unique genocide' by virtue of
its attempt to overthrow the basic tenets of Judeo-Christian civilization;
and Stephen Eric Bronner argues that 'Never before or since has genocide
been launched against humanity itself. The holocaust is made unique by
its genocidal dynamic.'[7] Others even made the claim the basis of a *Verbot*,
suggesting that to question the idea of uniqueness was tantamount to
Holocaust denial.[8]

The first major challenge to the uniqueness argument came with the
Historikerstreit, when conservative historians, notably Ernst Nolte and Chan-
cellor Kohl's speech-writer Michael Stürmer, started arguing that the time
had come to historicize Nazism and its crimes just like any other period
in history. Their argument was bolstered by the comparative claim that
the Holocaust was in essence no different from the crimes committed by
Stalin's regime. In the context of West Germany at this time, this argument
was obviously an attempt to reestablish a stronger sense of German national
identity than had been permissible in the postwar period. Thus, conser-
vatives argued in favour of comparability and liberals, most notably the
philosopher Jürgen Habermas, vigorously defended the uniqueness claim.
When Nolte wrote, rather scandalously, that 'the so-called annihilation of
the Jews by the Third Reich was a reaction or distorted copy [of the Gulag]
and not a first act or an original', he made his aims very clear, and offended
many in the process.[9] Habermas's argument, that West German stability
and identity depended on maintaining a sense of what Dirk Moses calls
'redemptive republicanism', which required upholding the Holocaust's
uniqueness, seemed to win the day, as did Saul Friedländer's argument
in his famous exchange with Martin Broszat on the historicization of
the Holocaust. But the question of comparison was now firmly on the

7. Nora Levin, *The Holocaust: The Destruction of European Jewry 1933–1945* (New York: Thomas
   Y. Crowell Company, 1968), p. xii; Gunnar Heinsohn, 'What Makes the Holocaust a
   Uniquely Unique Genocide?', *JGR*, 2, 3 (2000), pp. 411–30; Stephen Eric Bronner, 'Making
   Sense of Hell: Three Meditations on the Holocaust', *Political Studies*, 47, 2 (1999), p. 323.
8. Deborah E. Lipstadt, *Denying the Holocaust: The Growing Assault on Memory and Truth* (London:
   Penguin, 1994), p. 213.
9. Ernst Nolte, 'Between Historical Legend and Revisionism? The Third Reich from the
   Perspective of the 1980s' in *Forever in the Shadow of Hitler?*, eds. Knowlton and Cates, p. 14.

agenda, albeit associated for the time being with a German nationalist agenda.[10]

In the post-Cold War context, the question of comparability returned in an altered fashion. In unified Germany, the challenge of a nationalist historiography was seen off by a renewed interest in Nazism and the Holocaust, bolstered by the new wave of empirical studies facilitated by the opening of previously inaccessible archives. Particularly in French historiography, 'totalitarianism' came back into fashion as an analytical tool, and the Third Reich was again compared with the Soviet Union. François Furet's celebrated analysis of communism, *The Passing of an Illusion* (1995), though it did not undertake a systematic comparison and barely mentioned the murder of the Jews, inspired further comparative work.[11] Many historians, especially in France, noted the discrepancy between the

10. Jürgen Habermas, 'A Kind of Settlement of Damages: The Apologetic Tendencies in German History Writing' in *Forever in the Shadow of Hitler?*, eds. Knowlton and Cates, pp. 34–44; see also Habermas, *The New Conservatism: Cultural Criticism and the Historians' Debate* (Cambridge: Polity Press, 1989); A. Dirk Moses, *German Intellectuals and the Nazi Past* (New York: Cambridge University Press, 2007), ch. 5; Martin Broszat/Saul Friedländer, 'A Controversy about the Historicization of National Socialism', *New German Critique*, 44 (1988), pp. 85–126, and, for a discussion, Dan Stone, '*Nazi Germany and the Jews* and the Future of Holocaust Historiography' in *Years of Persecution, Years of Extermination: Saul Friedländer and the Future of Holocaust Studies*, eds. Paul Betts and Christian Wiese (London: Continuum, 2010), pp. 343–57. For analyses of the *Historikerstreit*, see Dan Diner, ed., *Ist der Nationalsozialismus Geschichte? Zu Historisierung und Historikerstreit* (Frankfurt/M: Fischer Taschenbuch Verlag, 1987); Geoff Eley, 'Nazism, Politics and the Image of the Past', *Past and Present*, 121 (1988), pp. 171–208; Charles S. Maier, *The Unmasterable Past: History, Holocaust, and German National Identity* (Cambridge, MA: Harvard University Press, 1988); Richard J. Evans, *In Hitler's Shadow: West German Historians and the Attempt to Escape the Nazi Past* (London: I. B. Tauris, 1989); Peter Baldwin, ed., *Reworking the Past: Hitler, the Holocaust, and the Historians' Debate* (Boston: Beacon Press, 1990); Alfred D. Low, *The Third Reich and the Holocaust in German Historiography: Toward the Historikerstreit of the Mid-1980s* (Boulder: East European Monographs, 1994); Dominick LaCapra, *Representing the Holocaust: History, Theory, Trauma* (Ithaca: Cornell University Press, 1994), ch. 2.
11. François Furet, *The Passing of an Illusion: The Idea of Communism in the Twentieth Century* (Chicago: University of Chicago Press, 1999); Ian Kershaw and Moshe Lewin, eds., *Stalinism and Nazism: Dictatorships in Comparison* (Cambridge: Cambridge University Press, 1997); Achim Siegel, ed., *The Totalitarian Paradigm After the End of Communism: Towards a Theoretical Reassessment* (Amsterdam: Rodopi, 1998); Henry Rousso, ed., *Stalinism and Nazism: History and Memory Compared* (Lincoln: University of Nebraska Press, 2004); Jörg Baberowski and Anselm Doering-Manteuffel, *Ordnung durch Terror: Gewaltexzesse und Vernichtung im nationalsozialistischen und im stalinistischen Imperium* (Bonn: Dietz, 2006); Michael Geyer and Sheila Fitzpatrick, eds., *Beyond Totalitarianism: Stalinism and Nazism Compared* (Cambridge: Cambridge University Press, 2009). See the excellent discussions in Richard Shorten, 'François Furet and Totalitarianism: A Recent Intervention in the Misuse of a Notion', *Totalitarian Movements and Political Religions*, 3, 1 (2002), pp. 1–34 and Carolyn J. Dean, 'Recent French Discourses on Stalinism, Nazism and "Exorbitant" Jewish Memory', *History & Memory*, 18, 1 (2006), pp. 43–85.

putative hyper-memory of the Holocaust and amnesia where communist crimes were concerned.[12] This kind of argument had already been exploited by the lawyer Jacques Vergès, who, in his defence of Klaus Barbie, argued that what the Nazis had done was no different from French crimes in Algeria. The debate over *The Black Book of Communism* gave rise to sophisticated discussions—but also some unfortunate polemics—about the place of the Holocaust in twentieth-century history and memory.[13] Stéphane Courtois, *The Black Book*'s editor, argued in his contributions and in other commentaries not just that the crimes of communism were no less worthy of attention that those of the Nazis but that 'Alas, there are people in the Jewish community who pretend to have a monopoly on crimes against humanity. It's a terrible shame. And, in the name of history, it's unacceptable.'[14] His comments caused a political storm in France, where communism has played a far more significant political role than in the UK or US. The result was that two of the book's main contributors, Nicolas Werth and Jean-Louis Margolin, publicly dissociated themselves from Courtois's position.[15]

But in many ways, Courtois's arguments were unremarkable; the problem in the French context was the accompanying subtext that uncomfortably implied that postwar memory of suffering had been monopolized by the Jews. Thus, a new debate emerged that sought to take seriously

12. See especially Alain Besançon, *Le malheur du siècle: sur le communisme, le nazisme et l'unicité de la Shoah* (Paris: Fayard, 1998), ch. 5, and Alain Brossat, *L'épreuve du désastre: Le XXe siècle et les camps* (Paris: Albin Michel, 1996).

13. Helmut Dubiel and Gabriel Motzkin, eds., *The Lesser Evil: Moral Approaches to Genocide Practices* (London: Routledge, 2004); Richard Shorten, 'Hannah Arendt on Totalitarianism: Moral Equivalence and Degrees of Evil in Modern Political Violence' in *Hannah Arendt and the Uses of History: Imperialism, Nation, Race and Genocide*, eds. Richard H. King and Dan Stone (New York: Berghahn, 2007), pp. 173–90. For an excellent review of *The Black Book*, see Vladimir Tismaneanu, 'Communism and the Human Condition: Reflections on *The Black Book of Communism*', *Human Rights Review*, 2, 2 (2001), pp. 125–34. Tismaneanu notes (p. 131) that the relative lack of attention paid to Stalinist crimes is not a result of one group monopolizing the memory of suffering in the twentieth century but of 'the fact that Communism was often regarded as progressive, anti-imperialist, and, more important still, anti-Fascist'. This is the flipside of Besançon's comment, in *Le malheur du siècle* (p. 63), that 'Universalism, which, before the seizure of power, is communism's great superiority over Nazi exclusivism, becomes, once in power, a universal menace.'

14. Stéphane Courtois, 'Crimes communistes: le malaise français', *Politique internationale* (1998), p. 372, cited in Shmuel Trigano, *The Democratic Ideal and the Shoah: The Unthought in Political Modernity* (Albany: State University of New York Press, 2009), p. 60.

15. See Martin Malia, 'Foreword: The Uses of Atrocity' and Stéphane Courtois, 'Introduction: The Crimes of Communism' and 'Conclusion: Why?' in Courtois et al., *The Black Book of Communism: Crimes, Terror, Repression* (Cambridge, MA: Harvard University Press, 1999), pp. ix–xx, 1–31, and 727–57.

the comparative project; after all, one can hardly assert that something is unique without comparing it to something else. Unfortunately, the polemics began anew and it took some time before they were replaced by a more appropriate scholarly sobriety. At the forefront of the new defenders of uniqueness were Yehuda Bauer and Steven T. Katz.

Bauer had already been an advocate of uniqueness for some time. In his 2001 book *Rethinking the Holocaust*, he set out his latest thoughts on the issue, arguing that 'one ought to differentiate between the intent to destroy a group in a context of selective mass murder and the intent to annihilate every person of that group . . . I would suggest retaining the term *genocide* for "partial" murder and the term *Holocaust* for total destruction.' This has the unfortunate consequence of making the Holocaust a 'genocide' but not a 'Holocaust', since the destruction was not total.[16] Besides, the Rwandan genocide also seems to offer an example of intended total destruction; that there were Tutsis in Burundi is no different from the fact that there were Jews in the USA during the Holocaust: the Hutu extremists and the Nazis would have targeted these groups had they been able to do so. The first volume of Katz's projected three-volume study, *The Holocaust in Historical Context*, appeared in 1994. In that book, Katz argued that the Holocaust is 'phenomenologically unique', a claim that has nothing to do with the philosophical school of phenomenology and apparently means nothing more than that the Holocaust was a unique phenomenon. Katz's basic position is that it is the 'unmediated, intended, complete *physical* eradication of every Jewish man, woman, and child that defines the particular, singular nature of this event that we call the Holocaust. It is this unconstrained, ideologically driven imperative that *every* Jew be murdered that distinguishes the Sho'ah from prior and to date subsequent, however inhumane, acts of collective violence, ethnocide, and mass murder.'[17] Unfortunately, this claim was the starting point of Katz's research and not its finding; his erudition was thus placed at the outset in the service of defending a preconceived conclusion.

16. Yehuda Bauer, *Rethinking the Holocaust* (New Haven: Yale University Press, 2001), p. 10. For his earlier, often more sophisticated considerations on the subject, see Bauer, *The Holocaust in Historical Perspective* (Seattle: University of Washington Press, 1978); Bauer, 'Genocide: Was it the Nazis' Original Plan?', *Annals of the American Academy of Political and Social Science*, 450 (1980), pp. 35–45.
17. Steven T. Katz, *The Holocaust in Historical Context, Vol. 1: The Holocaust and Mass Death Before the Modern Age* (New York: Oxford University Press, 1994), p. 10. One wonders whether the genocide in Rwanda, which occurred in the same year that Katz's book was published, has had an impact on the non-appearance of volumes 2 and 3.

Katz's position was taken up and critiqued in an edited volume of 1996, most notably and polemically by David Stannard, author of a book on the colonial settlement of the Americas called, tellingly, *American Holocaust*. In his contribution to *Is the Holocaust Unique?*, Stannard not only accused Katz, by calling the Holocaust unique, of engaging in a kind of genocide denial that exactly paralleled the strategies of Holocaust negationists, but claimed that the uniqueness position was 'fundamentally racist and violence-provoking'.[18] Stannard somewhat undermined his point, however, by arguing in his own book that 'The destruction of the Indians of the Americas was, far and away, the most massive act of genocide in the history of the world.'[19] The best known historian–activist of genocide in the Americas, Ward Churchill, also trumps Katz's unique Holocaust with a unique American genocide: 'The American holocaust was and remains unparalleled, both in terms of its magnitude and the degree to which its goals were met, and in terms of the extent to which its ferocity was sustained over time by not one but several participating groups.'[20] This kind of struggle for ultimate victimhood status is not only unseemly and unscholarly, it is divisive and dangerous.[21] Memory is not a zero-sum game in which all groups must engage in a kind of social Darwinist competition for which there is only one winner.

Fortunately, these polemics seem to be behind us now, at least in academia, where it is more widely acknowledged that 'far from blocking other historical memories from view in a competitive struggle for recognition, the emergence of Holocaust memory on a global scale has contributed to the articulation of other histories'.[22] Although claims of Holocaust 'unprecedentedness' or 'singularity' have been used in place of

18. David E. Stannard, 'Uniqueness as Denial: The Politics of Genocide Scholarship' in *Is the Holocaust Unique? Perspectives on Comparative Genocide*, ed. Alan S. Rosenbaum (Boulder: Westview Press, 1996), pp. 197, 167.
19. David E. Stannard, *American Holocaust: The Conquest of the New World* (New York: Oxford University Press), p. x.
20. Ward Churchill, *A Little Matter of Genocide: Holocaust and Denial in the Americas 1492 to the Present* (San Francisco: City Lights Books, 1997), p. 4.
21. Gavriel D. Rosenfeld, 'The Politics of Uniqueness: Reflections on the Recent Polemical Turn in Holocaust and Genocide Scholarship', *HGS*, 13, 1 (1999), pp. 28–61; Dan Stone, *Constructing the Holocaust: A Study in Historiography* (London: Vallentine Mitchell, 2003), ch. 5; Stone, 'The Historiography of Genocide: Beyond "Uniqueness" and Ethnic Competition' in *History, Memory and Mass Atrocity: Essays on the Holocaust and Genocide* (London: Vallentine Mitchell, 2006), pp. 236–51; Thomas W. Simon, 'The Holocaust's Moral "Uniqueness" ' in *Contemporary Portrayals of Auschwitz: Philosophical Challenges*, eds. Alan Rosenberg, James R. Watson, and Detlef Linke (Amherst, NY: Humanity Books, 2000), pp. 83–94.
22. Michael Rothberg, *Multidirectional Memory: Remembering the Holocaust in the Age of Decolonization* (Stanford: Stanford University Press, 2009), p. 6.

'uniqueness' by scholars sensitized to the problems associated with the latter word,[23] for the most part the debate has died down, as empirical research into the broader context of Nazi demographic policies—seeing the murder of the Jews as but one aspect of population plans for the Nazi empire—and into other cases of genocide—bringing to light details that were more or less unknown—has made the terms of the uniqueness debate irrelevant. Empirically, the most notable contribution to overcoming the unpleasantness of the uniqueness debate has been what we might call the 'new population studies'. Here, the Holocaust is historicized into the context not just of Stalinism but of ethnic cleansing and war in the first half of the twentieth century throughout Europe, and Nazi schemes for postwar demographic reordering. The latter are revealed most notably in the General Plan East (GPO, *Generalplan Ost*), which—in the plans drawn up in 1941–42 by racial experts Konrad Meyer-Hetling of the RKFDV and Erhard Wetzel of the Reich Ministry for the Occupied Eastern Territories—envisaged the murder of '*zig Million Menschen*' (x million people), usually estimated at some 30–45 million Slavs who would have been ruthlessly annihilated in order to make way for 10 million German settlers.[24] Benjamin Lieberman, Cathie Carmichael, Donald Bloxham, and Tim Snyder have all provided detailed studies of the prevalence of genocidal violence in post-World War I Europe, not with the aim of 'relativizing' the Holocaust (the fear of the anti-comparativists), but with the proper historian's intention of establishing lines of discontinuity as well as similarity.[25] The more polemical side of this debate centres on claims that Ukrainians suffered genocide as a result of

23. For example, Bob Brecher, 'Understanding the Holocaust: The Uniqueness Debate', *Radical Philosophy*, 96 (1999), pp. 17–28; Jean-Michel Chaumont, *La concurrence des victimes: Génocide, identité, reconnaissance* (Paris: La Découverte, 2002); Trigano, *The Democratic Ideal and the Shoah*.
24. Götz Aly, *'Final Solution': Nazi Population Policy and the Murder of the European Jews* (London: Arnold, 1999); Wolfgang Benz, 'Der Generalplan Ost: Zur Germanisierungspolitik des NS-Regimes in den besetzten Ostgebieten 1939–1945' in *Die Vertreibung der Deutschen aus dem Osten: Ursachen, Ereignisse, Folgen*, ed. Benz (Frankfurt/M: Suhrkamp Taschenbuch Verlag, 1995), pp. 45–57; Czeslaw Madajczyk, ed., *Vom Generalplan Ost zum Generalsiedlungsplan* (Munich: Saur, 1994); Bruno Wasser, *Himmlers Raumplanung im Osten: Der Generalplan Ost in Polen 1940–1944* (Basel: Birkhäuser, 1993); Mechtild Rössler and Sabine Schleiermacher, eds., *Der 'Generalplan Ost': Hauptlinien der nationalsozialistischen Planungs- und Vernichtungspolitik* (Berlin: Akademie, 1993); Mechtild Rössler, 'Applied Geography and Area Research in Nazi Society: Central Place Theory and Planning, 1933 to 1945', *Environment and Planning D: Society and Space*, 7, 4 (1989), pp. 419–31.
25. Benjamin Lieberman, *Terrible Fate: Ethnic Cleansing in the Making of Modern Europe* (Chicago: Ivan R. Dee, 2006); Cathie Carmichael, *Genocide Before the Holocaust* (New Haven: Yale University Press, 2009); Donald Bloxham, *The Final Solution: A Genocide* (Oxford: Oxford

the deliberately targeted famine of the 'Holodomor', and post-communist eastern European claims about martyrdom under communism, which frequently tend towards a rejection of liberalism and a rise in antisemitism.[26] Thus, comparative questions—and debates about the ethics of comparison—have by no means disappeared, and nor should they, for all history is comparative history, whether explicitly or not. But the notion that the Holocaust is unique has been replaced by detailed, scholarly examinations of the history of genocide, in which the Holocaust is neither set apart from nor reduced to broader trends in world history.

Genocide Studies and Holocaust Historiography

Although the term 'genocide' was coined in 1944 by the Polish-Jewish lawyer Raphael Lemkin, and then adopted in the 1948 United Nations Convention on the Prevention and Punishment of the Crime of Genocide (UNGC), scholarly study of the phenomenon, with a few exceptions, took several decades to get under way.[27] My aim in what follows is neither to present a comprehensive history of the genocide concept nor to analyse 'genocide studies' as a discipline in detail; rather, I seek to show how the emergence of genocide studies has been influenced by the extraordinary expansion of Holocaust historiography and to assess the extent to which genocide studies presents ways of providing historical explanations for the Holocaust that cannot be obtained from the other explanatory frameworks examined in this book. All too often, Holocaust historiography and the study of genocide have been separate enterprises; in the last decade, that state of affairs has—to a small extent, at least—begun to change.[28]

University Press, 2009); Tim Snyder, *Bloodlands* (New York: Basic Books, 2010). See also Norman M. Naimark, *Fires of Hatred: Ethnic Cleansing in Twentieth-Century Europe* (Cambridge, MA: Harvard University Press, 2002).

26. Nicolas Werth, 'The Crimes of the Stalin Regime: Outline for an Inventory and Classification' in *HG*, pp. 400–19, esp. 414–5; Florin Lobonţ, 'Antisemitism and Holocaust Denial in Post-Communist Eastern Europe' in *HH*, pp. 440–68; Vladimir Tismaneanu, *Fantasies of Salvation: Democracy, Nationalism and Myth in Post-Communist Europe* (Princeton: Princeton University Press, 1998).

27. Raphael Lemkin, *Axis Rule in Occupied Europe: Laws of Occupation, Analysis of Government, Proposals for Redress* (Washington, DC: Carnegie Endowment for International Peace, 1944), esp. the Preface and ch. 9.

28. See A. Dirk Moses, 'The Holocaust and Genocide' in *HH*, pp. 533–55.

By the early 1980s, an increasingly large number of scholars, mostly political scientists, were taking an interest in genocide. In this political science
paradigm, most scholarly attention was devoted to drawing up typologies
of genocides (for example, 'developmental', 'retributive', or 'ideological')
and working towards developing means of genocide prevention. The self-
styled 'pioneers of genocide studies' were a somewhat marginal group,
given that implicit in the whole project of genocide studies is the notion
that the Holocaust is but one case of genocide and is therefore amenable to
comparison and available for scholarly use as a building block for a general
theory of genocide.[29] Nevertheless, their work kept alive a comparative
component to scholarly discussions, which was otherwise rare in Holocaust
historiography.

The early political science paradigm was important for bringing Lemkin's
term to broader attention, especially within academia and activist circles.
But it actually departed substantially from both Lemkin's original concept
and the definition of genocide enshrined in the UNGC. The UNGC
differed from Lemkin mainly by removing (at least explicitly) the notion of
'cultural genocide', for it was felt by the UN delegates that the destruction
of a people's cultural artefacts and characteristics was of a different order
of persecution from the targeting of a people's biology. Nevertheless, the
definition that became the basis of international law is still criticized for

29. Important studies broadly in this paradigm (naturally, they are all different and I am
    aware of the problems involved in 'lumping' them together this way) include: Leo Kuper,
    Genocide: Its Political Use in the Twentieth Century (London: Penguin, 1981); Helen Fein,
    Genocide: A Sociological Perspective (London: Sage, 1993); Frank Chalk and Kurt Jonassohn,
    eds., *The History and Sociology of Genocide: Analyses and Case Studies* (New Haven: Yale
    University Press, 1990); Israel W. Charny, *How Can We Commit the Unthinkable? Genocide:
    The Human Cancer* (New York: Hearst Books, 1982); Robert Melson, *Revolution and
    Genocide: On the Origins of the Armenian Genocide and the Holocaust* (Chicago: University
    of Chicago Press, 1992); George J. Andreopoulos, ed., *Genocide: Conceptual and Historical
    Dimensions* (Philadelphia: University of Pennsylvania Press, 1994); Isidor Wallimann and
    Michael N. Dobkowski, eds., *Genocide and the Modern Age: Etiology and Case Studies of
    Mass Death* (Westport: Greenwood Press, 1987). See Samuel Totten and Steven L. Jacobs,
    eds., *Pioneers of Genocide Studies: Confronting Mass Death in the Century of Genocide* (New
    Brunswick: Transaction, 2002) and, more recently, Samuel Totten and Paul R. Bartrop,
    eds., *The Genocide Studies Reader* (New York: Routledge, 2009). They were all preceded
    by the still-inspiring Gil Elliot, *Twentieth Century Book of the Dead* (London: Allen Lane
    The Penguin Press, 1972). For discussions, see Ann Curthoys and John Docker, 'Defining
    Genocide', Anton Weiss-Wendt, 'Problems in Comparative Genocide Scholarship' and
    David Moshman, 'Conceptions of Genocide and Perceptions of History' in *HG*, pp. 9–41,
    42–70, and 71–92.

being at once too narrow and too broad. Article II of the UNGC defines genocide as:

> any of the following acts committed with intent to destroy, in whole or in part, a national, ethnical, racial or religious group, as such:
>
> (a) Killing members of the group;
> (b) Causing serious bodily or mental harm to members of the group;
> (c) Deliberately inflicting on the group conditions of life calculated to bring about its physical destruction in whole or in part;
> (d) Imposing measures intended to prevent births within the group;
> (e) Forcibly transferring children of the group to another group.

The omission of political groups can partly be explained by the Cold War context in which the convention was drawn up, but actually owes more to the fact that the four groups mentioned were obviously felt, in an assumption that makes the UNGC seem very dated, to be immutable. One could, the convention's framers assumed, choose one's political allegiance but not one's ethnicity or religion. Apparently, these are fixed markers of identity. So much for narrowness, but the UNGC is also excessively broad. Certainly from a legal point of view, 'intent' is the key term here, but who is to determine what constitutes the targeting of a group 'as such'? How significant a 'part' of a group must be targeted for persecution of a group 'in part' to count as genocide as opposed to any other human rights abuse? These are all questions that remain contested, although since the first cases were heard at the International Criminal Tribunals for the Former Yugoslavia and Rwanda and at the International Criminal Court, international law on genocide has developed rapidly and now provides a set of case law that offers precedents and judgments on which clarity can to some extent be founded.[30]

The 'pioneers of genocide studies' tended on the whole to come from a North American liberal social science tradition that viewed genocide as state policy (usually, a totalitarian state[31]) and that looked for intent as the key. Much of their work was devoted to genocide prevention, often with an over-inflated sense of what could be achieved. They took Article IIa (killing people) to be synonymous with genocide and overlooked the other

---

30. William A. Schabas, *Genocide in International Law: The Crime of Crimes* (Cambridge: Cambridge University Press, 2000).
31. Irving Louis Horowitz, *Taking Lives: Genocide and State Power*, 4th edn (New Brunswick: Transaction Books, 1997).

means by which genocide may be committed according to the UNGC (thus according with the popular dictionary definition of genocide too).[32] Empirically speaking, in the twentieth century, genocide has been a crime of the state—this is certainly true of the Holocaust, for although we have noted the extensive collaboration of groups and individuals across Europe in the murder of the Jews, this was collaboration that was invited under a state-organized genocidal campaign. However, there is nothing in the UNGC that says that genocide must be a state crime. And the question of intent—while it may be necessary in a court of law—can be understood flexibly by historians. Over twenty years ago, Tony Barta argued that historians should not, like political scientists, be satisfied with static typologies of genocide, but needed to explain how genocidal dynamics unfolded as they occurred; it would presumably be unhistorical to assume that a leader or a regime suddenly decides one day to commit genocide and, happily for the future scholar, leaves a paper trail to that effect behind them. Barta suggested that historians could look for evidence that would not necessarily stand up in a trial, for historians and lawyers were not doing quite the same thing. Intent, as Dirk Moses puts it, could be 'construed through action'. Historians need to understand 'relations of destruction', not search for incriminating documents. Genocide is a dynamic, unfolding process, not a single act.[33]

One can see the validity of Barta's claim by looking at the historiography of the Holocaust. The whole point about the scholarship on the decision-making process is to show that the Holocaust unfolded as a process and to understand the nature of that process. This is a key area where Holocaust historiography has informed genocide studies for the better. A greater awareness of historicity now lies at the heart of the study of genocide.

32. Chalk and Jonassohn, for example (*History and Sociology*, p. 23), defined genocide as 'a form of one-sided mass killing in which a state or other authority intends to destroy a group, as that group and membership in it are defined by the perpetrator'.
33. Tony Barta, 'Relations of Genocide: Land and Lives in the Colonization of Australia' in *Genocide and the Modern Age*, eds. Wallimann and Dobkowski, pp. 237–51. Barta's reflections on how those committed to a notion of genocide as 'explicit policy' either rejected or (more commonly) ignored his work, can be found in Barta, 'Decent Disposal: Australian Historians and the Recovery of Genocide' in *HG*, pp. 296–322. On 'construing intent through action', see A. Dirk Moses, 'An Antipodean Genocide? The Origins of the Genocidal Moment in the Colonization of Australia', *JGR*, 2, 1 (2000), pp. 89–106; Moses, 'Conceptual Blockages and Definitional Dilemmas in the "Racial Century": Genocides of Indigenous Peoples and the Holocaust', *Patterns of Prejudice*, 36, 2 (2002), pp. 7–36; Moses, 'Genocide and Settler Society in Australian History' in *Genocide and Settler Society: Frontier Violence and Stolen Indigenous Children in Australian History*, ed. Moses (New York: Berghahn, 2004), esp. pp. 28–35.

To give just one example, in his study of the Armenian genocide, Donald Bloxham is keen to stress that there was no single decision taken by the Ottoman authorities to kill the Armenians, a finding which renders the genocide more complex to understand, but provides a historically more accurate representation of the decision-making process. Bloxham borrows Hans Mommsen's term, 'cumulative radicalization', to show that the Armenian genocide 'emerged from a series of more limited regional measures' and only developed into 'a crystallized policy of empire-wide killing and death-by-attrition' by the early summer of 1915.[34] Bloxham sees the existence of pressure from certain quarters within the Committee for Union and Progress (CUP) regime—better known as the 'Young Turks'—towards extreme measures, but regards these less as proof of a 'plan', than 'of the ongoing search for a "solution" of the correct nature and magnitude'.[35] And explicitly connecting his inquiry into the Armenian genocide with the historiographical debates surrounding the Holocaust, Bloxham writes that 'it is unlikely that the CUP leaders instantly developed a precise template of how their inherently murderous scheme would unfold across the empire', a claim that he sees proven by 'the ongoing, rather improvised nature of the whole destruction process'.[36] Unsurprisingly then, he ends with the claim that the study of genocide can benefit from the more sophisticated insights of Holocaust historiography: 'Part of the interpretative problem is that "genocide" is more a legal term than a historical one, designed for the *ex post facto* judgements of the courtroom rather than the historian's attempt to understand events as they develop—that is, out of non-genocidal or latently murderous situations.'[37] Similar accounts can now be found for the Cambodian genocide, for the genocide of the Hereros in German Southwest Africa and, most impressively given its recent occurrence, for the Rwandan genocide.[38]

---

34. Donald Bloxham, 'The Armenian Genocide of 1915–1916: Cumulative Radicalization and the Development of a Destruction Policy', *Past and Present*, 181 (2003), p. 143.
35. Bloxham, 'The Armenian Genocide', p. 176.
36. Bloxham, 'The Armenian Genocide', pp. 181–2.
37. Bloxham, 'The Armenian Genocide', p. 189. For more detail, see Bloxham, *The Great Game of Genocide: Imperialism, Nationalism and the Destruction of the Ottoman Armenians* (Oxford: Oxford University Press, 2005). See also Mark Levene, 'Creating a Modern "Zone of Genocide": The Impact of Nation- and State-Formation on Eastern Anatolia, 1878–1923', *HGS*, 12, 3 (1998), pp. 393–433.
38. For key examples among the large literature, see Ben Kiernan, *The Pol Pot Regime: Race, Power, and Genocide in Cambodia under the Khmer Rouge, 1975–79* (New Haven: Yale University Press, 1996); David P. Chandler, *The Tragedy of Cambodian History: Politics, War,*

This heightened awareness of history—of genocide as a process, not as an event or a single decision—has gone hand in hand with the ongoing development of comparative genocide studies and, most important, of the attempt to go beyond comparisons to produce a general theory of genocide. Comparison of genocides was always, as noted, part of the genocide studies project; but recent synthetic works have started taking on board the criticisms of the 'liberal' school and, in the light of the end of the Cold War, the violence in Yugoslavia, Rwanda, and Sudan (Darfur) and the creation of the International Criminal Court, scholarship on genocide in general has expanded considerably. In the last few years, books by Ben Kiernan, Michael Mann, Benjamin Valentino, Eric Weitz, and Manus Midlarsky, among others, have given a new lease of life to comparative genocide studies.[39] Scholars have increasingly turned towards little known cases and expanded the repertoire of cases of 'subaltern' genocide, or pioneered the application of other disciplinary tools to the field, most notably anthropology and social psychology.[40] Even more noteworthy is

and Revolution since 1945 (New Haven: Yale University Press, 1991); Edward Kissi, *Revolution and Genocide in Ethiopia and Cambodia: A Comparative Study of Socialist Ethiopia and Democratic Kampuchea* (Lanham: Lexington Books, 2006); Alexander Laban Hinton, *Why Did They Kill? Cambodia in the Shadow of Genocide* (Berkeley: University of California Press, 2005); Mahmood Mamdani, *When Victims Become Killers: Colonialism, Nativism, and the Genocide in Rwanda* (Princeton: Princeton University Press, 2001); Scott Straus, *The Order of Genocide: Race, Power, and War in Rwanda* (Ithaca: Cornell University Press, 2006); Lee Ann Fujii, *Killing Neighbors: Webs of Violence in Rwanda* (Ithaca: Cornell University Press, 2009). For guides to the historiography, see Jürgen Zimmerer, 'Colonial Genocide: The Herero and Nama War (1904–8) in German South West Africa and Its Significance', Ben Kiernan, 'Documentation Delayed, Justice Denied: The Historiography of the Cambodian Genocide', and Scott Straus, 'The Historiography of the Rwandan Genocide' in *HG*, pp. 323–43, 468–86, and 517–42.

39. Ben Kiernan, *Blood and Soil: A World History of Genocide and Extermination from Sparta to Darfur* (New Haven: Yale University Press, 2007); Manus I. Midlarsky, *The Killing Trap: Genocide in the Twentieth Century* (Cambridge: Cambridge University Press, 2005); Michael Mann, *The Dark Side of Democracy: Explaining Ethnic Cleansing* (Cambridge: Cambridge University Press, 2005); Benjamin A. Valentino, *Final Solutions: Mass Killing and Genocide in the 20th Century* (Ithaca: Cornell University Press, 2004); Eric D. Weitz, *A Century of Genocide: Utopias of Race and Nation* (Princeton: Princeton University Press, 2003); Robert Gellately and Ben Kiernan, eds., *The Specter of Genocide: Mass Murder in Historical Perspective* (Cambridge: Cambridge University Press, 2003); Steven L. B. Jensen, ed., *Genocides: Cases, Comparisons and Contemporary Debates* (Copenhagen: Danish Center for Holocaust and Genocide Studies, 2003). For a helpful discussion, see Scott Straus, 'Second-Generation Comparative Research on Genocide', *World Politics*, 59, 3 (2007), pp. 476–501. Straus points to the absence of consensus about what constitutes genocide and the continued tendency to isolate genocide as a phenomenon from the study of violence in general. One of the main shortcomings of genocide studies is therefore an inability to explain how a violent situation becomes genocidal. Here, the example of Holocaust historiography is again instructive.

40. Nicholas A. Robins and Adam Jones, eds., *Genocides by the Oppressed: Subaltern Genocide in Theory and Practice* (Bloomington: Indiana University Press, 2009); Alexander Laban Hinton,

the attempt to move beyond comparative study and to work towards producing a theory of genocide *per se*, as is to be found in the works of Martin Shaw, Jacques Semelin, and, especially, Mark Levene. The latter sees genocide as a product of a world system in which nation–states are pitted against one another in a social Darwinist struggle for resources and power, and in which the weaker states resort to desperate measures to 'catch up' with the stronger.[41]

The status of the Holocaust in these general histories and theories of genocide is somewhat problematic. On the one hand, an interest in the Holocaust provided many scholars a way in to the study of genocide more generally; on the other hand, the Holocaust is not a very helpful 'ideal type' or yardstick for thinking about genocide, given the vastness of its geographical scope and the nature of the killing process, that is, the use of gas chambers. Nevertheless, these differences do not constitute grounds for a new 'uniqueness' thesis; first, the role of the state, of bureaucracy and technology and, most important, of an annihilationist intent is clear in other cases, most notably the Armenian, Cambodian, and Rwandan genocides; and second, we have already seen that the notion of the Holocaust as an 'industrial' or 'factory-line' genocide is only partly true.[42] The historiography of the Holocaust, then, has contributed to a 'historical turn' in genocide studies; as a result, an increasingly sophisticated genocide studies makes us understand that the Holocaust was no aberration but was part of a continuum in modern history, albeit a punctuated and crooked

ed., *Annihilating Difference: The Anthropology of Genocide* (Berkeley: University of California Press, 2002); Hinton, ed., *Genocide: An Anthropological Reader* (Oxford: Blackwell, 2002); Hinton and Kevin Lewis O'Neill, eds., *Genocide: Truth, Memory, and Representation* (Durham: Duke University Press, 2009); Christopher C. Taylor, *Sacrifice as Terror: The Rwandan Genocide of 1994* (Oxford: Berg, 1999); Victoria Sanford, *Buried Secrets: Truth and Human Rights in Guatemala* (New York: Palgrave Macmillan, 2003); John Docker, *The Origins of Violence: Religion, History and Genocide* (London: Pluto Press, 2008); James Waller, *Becoming Evil: How Ordinary People Commit Genocide and Mass Killing* (New York: Oxford University Press, 2002); Harald Welzer, *Täter: wie aus ganz normalen Menschen Massenmörder werden* (Frankfurt/M: S. Fischer, 2005); Philip Zimbardo, *The Lucifer Effect: Understanding How Good People Turn Evil* (New York: Random House, 2007); Steven K. Baum, *The Psychology of Genocide: Perpetrators, Bystanders, and Rescuers* (Cambridge: Cambridge University Press, 2008).

41. Martin Shaw, *What is Genocide?* (Cambridge: Polity Press, 2007); Jacques Semelin, *Purify and Destroy: The Political Uses of Massacre and Genocide* (London: Hurst and Company, 2007); Mark Levene, *Genocide in the Age of the Nation State. Vol. 1: The Meaning of Genocide* and *Vol. 2: The Rise of the West and the Coming of Genocide* (London: I. B. Tauris, 2005).

42. Besides, as David B. MacDonald notes (*Identity Politics in the Age of Genocide: The Holocaust and Historical Representation* (London: Routledge, 2008), p. 46), it is 'relatively easy to claim that Jews were subject to a unique universal and global focus, because Jews were a Diasporic people. They were globally dispersed.'

one, that includes slavery, imperial massacre, 'total war', and ethnic violence in the first half of the twentieth century.

These sorts of insights into the historicity of the genocidal decision-making process, the complexity of 'intent', the desirability of a comparative approach to genocide that avoids victim-centred competitions for suffering, and the value of a general theory of genocide, have largely come to fruition thanks to the 'rediscovery' of Lemkin's work, including his substantial unpublished papers, which include his plans for a major study of genocides throughout history. In his now canonical *Axis Rule in Occupied Europe* (1944)—the context of the Nazi occupation of Europe should not be forgotten—Lemkin defined genocide in the following way: 'Genocide has two phases: one, destruction of the national pattern of the oppressed group; the other, the imposition of the national pattern of the oppressor.' He also noted that genocide 'does not necessarily mean the immediate destruction of a nation, except when accomplished by mass killings of all members of a nation'; rather, genocide signifies 'a coordinated plan of different actions aiming at the destruction of essential foundations of the life of national groups, with the aim of annihilating those groups themselves'. Hence, genocide 'is directed against the national group as an entity, and the actions involved are directed against individuals, not in their individual capacity, but as members of the national group'.[43] Genocide is thus similar to homicide but targeted at groups; the aim of the persecutor, in Henry Huttenbach's insightful phrase, is 'to nullify' the oppressed group, making the world look as though that group had never existed. The aim of nullification or 'anti-creation', driven by 'ferocious narratives of redemption', is what distinguishes genocide from war crimes or other human rights abuses.[44]

Vitally, Lemkin's definition of genocide sounds much like a definition of colonialism, with its stress on the interaction of two distinct groups and the imposition of the pattern of life of the oppressor on to that of the oppressed.[45] At issue here is the question of intent. Barta's and Moses'

---

43. Lemkin, *Axis Rule*, p. 79. See Anson Rabinbach, 'The Challenge of the Unprecedented: Raphael Lemkin and the Concept of Genocide', *Simon Dubnow Institute Yearbook*, 4 (2005), 397–420; Dan Stone, 'Raphael Lemkin on the Holocaust', *JGR*, 7, 4 (2005), pp. 539–50; Moses, 'The Holocaust and Genocide'; Moses, 'Colonialism' in *Oxford Handbook of Holocaust Studies*, eds. Peter Hayes and John K. Roth (Oxford: Oxford University Press, 2010).
44. Henry R. Huttenbach, 'From the Editor: Towards a Conceptual Definition of Genocide', *JGR*, 4, 2 (2002), pp. 167–76 ('nullification', 'anti-creation'); Peter Fritzsche, 'Genocide and Global Discourse', *GH*, 23, 1 (2005), p. 109 ('ferocious narratives').
45. See, for example, Robert J. C. Young, *Postcolonialism: An Historical Introduction* (London: Wiley Blackwell, 2001); Jürgen Osterhammel, *Colonialism: A Theoretical Overview* (Princeton:

argument, that for historians there is more to proving intent than finding documents that will stand up in court, was directed first and foremost at colonial settler societies in North America and Australia. The 'liberal', political science approach that sees genocide as the commission of mass death by the state means that the question of whether genocide occurred in the white settler colonies is rejected from the start, for in those cases one cannot find orders given by state authorities to kill indigenous peoples, other than in certain confined cases.[46] In the case of Australia, one even finds the colonial authority, London, issuing orders to befriend and protect Aborigines. Hence, scholars, especially in the US, have been reluctant to utilize what many perceive as the 'blunt stick' of genocide for understanding the complexities of relationships between colonizer and colonized, frontier violence and nation-state building. Only very recently has this situation started to change, so that the question of genocide in North America is not left solely to marginal scholar–activists.[47]

So far we have seen that Holocaust historiography has had an impact on the study of genocide, providing it with a stronger historical sense. In terms of this book's context, the clearest case for studying the emergence of genocide studies as a discipline is the recent rise to prominence of the notion of the Holocaust as a 'colonial genocide'. Only by bearing in mind developments in genocide studies overall does this approach begin to make sense. In particular, questioning the notion that genocide is synonymous with state-sanctioned mass death and bringing in Lemkin's claim that genocide is a form of colonialism have opened up ways of approaching the Holocaust that are almost entirely new in the historiography of the

Princeton University Press, 1997); Wolfgang Reinhard, *Kleine Geschichte des Kolonialismus*, 2nd edn (Stuttgart: Kröner, 2008).

46. On 'liberal' and 'post-liberal' approaches to genocide, see Moses, 'Conceptual Blockages'.
47. Kiernan, *Blood and Soil*, chs 6 and 8; Benjamin Madley, 'Patterns of Frontier Genocide 1803–1910: The Aboriginal Tasmanians, the Yuki of California, and the Herero of Namibia', *JGR*, 6, 2 (2004), pp. 167–92; Ashley Riley Sousa, ' "They Will be Hunted Down Like Wild Beasts and Destroyed!" A Comparative Study of Genocide in California and Tasmania', *JGR*, 6, 2 (2004), pp. 193–209; Michael A. McDonnell and A. Dirk Moses, 'Raphael Lemkin as Historian of Genocide in the Americas' in *The Origins of Genocide: Raphael Lemkin as a Historian of Mass Violence*, eds. Dominik J. Schaller and Jürgen Zimmerer (London: Routledge, 2009), pp. 57–85, esp. 76–9. For a good discussion, see Alfred Cave, 'Genocide in the Americas', in *HG*, pp. 273–95. The literature on genocide in Australia is very large; for starting points see: Moses, ed., *Genocide and Settler Society*; Moses, ed., *Empire, Colony, Genocide*; Henry Reynolds, *An Indelible Stain? The Question of Genocide in Australia's History* (Ringwood, Vic: Viking, 2001); Colin Tatz, *With Intent to Destroy: Reflecting on Genocide* (London: Verso, 2003), ch. 4; *Aboriginal History*, 25 (2001), special issue: *'Genocide'? Australian Aboriginal History in International Perspective*, eds. Ann Curthoys and John Docker.

murder of the Jews. In the following section, I will examine the debate about colonialism and the Holocaust, and ask to what extent the concept of 'colonial genocide' helps us to understand the Holocaust.

Colonialism and the Holocaust

In contrast to the stress on the 'occupation' of Europe, historians have begun to talk of 'colonization', particularly in eastern Europe. They place the Nazi 'colonization' project in direct comparison with earlier European overseas practices, noting only that this time they applied to the creation of a continental empire in Europe. For postcolonial historians, this analysis is routine, as Vinay Lal, following Frantz Fanon and Aimé Césaire, provocatively argues: 'the Holocaust . . . visited upon the peoples of Europe the violence that colonial powers had routinely inflicted on the "natives" all over the world for nearly five hundred years'.[48] But for Holocaust historians, this remains a challenging proposition. Some historians, however, have responded, even noting that it was precisely the proximity of the 'colonies' and attendant anxieties about the lack of obvious differences between colonized and colonizer (such as skin colour), that made the German project more violent: 'The Nazis applied the binary distinctions typical of overseas colonialism to the East in order to turn marked similarity into absolute difference', as David Furber puts it.[49]

The debate about the Holocaust and colonialism makes especial use of Lemkin's juxtaposition of colonialism and genocide; the notion of 'colonial genocide' becomes more than just a term for 'genocide' that occurs in European overseas colonies—itself a contentious claim—in favour of the suggestion that genocide always involves some form of colonization (although the reverse proposition, that colonialism is inherently genocidal, remains disputed).[50] For example, Bloxham, echoing Lemkin, writes: 'The

---

48. Vinay Lal, 'Genocide, Barbaric Others, and the Violence of Categories: A Response to Omer Bartov', *American Historical Review*, 103, 4 (1998), pp. 1188–9.
49. David Furber, 'Near as Far in the Colonies: The Nazi Occupation of Poland', *International History Review*, 26, 3 (2004), p. 558.
50. See for example: Jürgen Zimmerer, 'Kolonialer Genozid? Vom Nutzen und Nachteil einer historischen Kategorie für eine Globalgeschichte' in *Von Windhuk nach Auschwitz? Beiträge zum Verhältnis zwischen Kolonialismus und Holocaust* (Münster: LIT, 2009), pp. 131–50; Alison Palmer, *Colonial Genocide* (Adelaide: Crawford House, 2000); John Docker, 'Are Settler-

justification for appropriating land in Africa, Australasia, or the Nazi eastern empire was that the native population had no civilization worthy of consideration, and that to put the land and its resources to proper use would entail the obliteration of native culture and its replacement by the cultural and economic patterns of the settlers.'[51] Robert Gellately notes: 'The mentality of the [Nazi] conquerors and the intellectuals who supported them reminds one of late nineteenth-century imperialists in Africa.'[52] In his major study of the decision-making process for the 'final solution', Christopher Browning writes that

> Hitler's belief in the need for German Lebensraum implied that the Nazis would construct an empire in eastern Europe analogous to what other European imperial powers had constructed overseas. Not surprisingly, this also meant that the Nazi regime stood ready to impose on conquered populations in Europe, especially Slavs in the east, the methods of rule and policies of population decimation that Europeans had hitherto inflicted only on conquered populations overseas.[53]

And Robert Cribb also asserts that there is 'a clear parallel, of course, between the actions of Western settlers in the lands of indigenous peoples and the policies of Nazi Germany in Eastern Europe, where displacement and extensive killing along with disease and starvation were intended to change demographic realities'.[54]

Historians have started to go beyond these casual, unsubstantiated mentions. Wendy Lower, for example, in her important study of the Holocaust in eastern Ukraine, goes to some length to fit the Holocaust into the 'colonial genocide' paradigm. The Nazi occupiers of Ukraine, she

Colonies Inherently Genocidal? Re-reading Lemkin' in *Empire, Colony, Genocide*, ed. Moses, pp. 81–101; Tony Barta, 'Mr Darwin's Shooters: On Natural Selection and the Naturalizing of Genocide' in *Colonialism and Genocide*, eds. Moses and Stone, pp. 20–41; Mike Davis, *Late Victorian Holocausts: El Niño Famines and the Making of the Third World* (London: Verso, 2001); Adam Hochschild, *King Leopold's Ghost: A Story of Greed, Terror and Heroism in Colonial Africa* (London: Pan, 2002); Patrick Wolfe, 'Settler Colonialism and the Elimination of the Native', *JGR*, 8, 4 (2006), pp. 387–409. Wolfe notes (pp. 398–9): 'In practice, it should go without saying, that the imposition on a people of the procedures and techniques that are generally glossed as "cultural genocide" is certainly going to have an impact on that people's capacity to stay alive'.

51. Bloxham, *The Final Solution*, p. 283.
52. Robert Gellately, 'The Third Reich, the Holocaust, and Visions of Serial Genocide' in *The Specter of Genocide*, eds. Gellately and Kiernan, p. 259.
53. Browning, *Origins*, p. 14.
54. Robert Cribb, 'Genocide in the Non-Western World: Implications for Holocaust Studies', in *Genocide*, ed. Jensen, p. 137.

argues, 'perceived their actions as legitimately linked to Europe's history of conquest and rule', a history that routinely included 'exploration, conquest, migration, and mass destruction of peoples'. Thus, the 'Nazi occupation of Eastern Europe demonstrated that such practices were not strictly overseas forms of conquest and rule, and that the worst aspects of colonialism—forced population movements, slave labor, and mass murder—could be combined and carried out on an enormous scale, in a matter of a few years, and in the heart of "civilized" Europe.'[55] In an important piece co-authored with David Furber, Lower writes that although the Jews were not typical of the 'colonial other'—because they were feared more than despised—the Nazis 'viewed them as natives in the classical colonial sense *and* as pernicious colonizers of supposed ancestral German land. The Jew thereby incarnated both the native other and the colonizing other, combining contempt and fear in a lethal cocktail.'[56] Elizabeth Harvey examines the settlement planners in occupied Poland, using the term 'colonization' as a matter of course.[57] And Elissa Mailänder Koslov shows how the behaviour of camp guards in Majdanek was influenced by their perception of taking part in a colonial enterprise.[58] Mark Mazower's latest synthesis brings these insights to a larger audience.[59] They are arguments that build on the unsystematic mentions by earlier historians of Nazi colonialism and, more importantly, on the claims of anti-colonial thinkers such as Césaire, Fanon, W. E. B. Du Bois, and Albert Memmi to the effect that fascism produced in Europe nothing that had not been visited upon 'natives' the world over. Fanon claimed: 'Not long ago Nazism transformed the whole of Europe into a veritable colony'; the outrage over Nazism's crimes merely resulted from this '*choc en retour*', as Du Bois put it.[60] Postcolonial theorists such as Vinay Lal, Achille Mbembe, and Paul Gilroy have developed these claims

55. Wendy Lower, *Nazi Empire-Building and the Holocaust in Ukraine* (Chapel Hill: University of North Carolina Press, 2005), pp. 6, 19–20.
56. David Furber and Wendy Lower, 'Colonialism and Genocide in Nazi-Occupied Poland and Ukraine' in *Empire, Colony, Genocide*, ed. Moses, pp. 375–6.
57. Elizabeth Harvey, 'Management and Manipulation: Nazi Settlement Planners and Ethnic German Settlers in Occupied Poland' in *Settler Colonialism in the Twentieth Century: Projects, Practices, Legacies*, eds. Caroline Elkins and Susan Pedersen (New York: Routledge, 2005), pp. 95–112.
58. Elissa Mailänder Koslov, ' "Going East": Colonial Experiences and Practices of Violence Among Female and Male Majdanek Camp Guards (1941–44)', *JGR*, 10, 4 (2008), pp. 563–82.
59. Mark Mazower, *Hitler's Empire: Nazi Rule in Occupied Europe* (London: Allen Lane, 2008).
60. Frantz Fanon, *The Wretched of the Earth* (London: Penguin, 1990 [1961]), p. 80; Rothberg, *Multidirectional Memory*, ch. 3.

more recently.[61] Gilroy, in particular, carefully shows how examining the interconnections between the Holocaust and colonial histories can contribute to understanding both without diminishing the significance of either.[62] Only now have historians, building on the insights of 'postcolonial studies', begun to provide empirical backing for them.

Historians have long known of Hitler's admiration for the British Empire, the regard with which he spoke of the annihilation of American Indians and his casual comparisons, in his so-called *Table Talk*, of Ukrainians and Russians with 'Negros' and other colonial subjects. Most famously, Hitler is supposed to have said:

> The struggle for hegemony in the world is decided for Europe by the possession of Russian territory; it makes Europe the place in the world most secure from blockade. . . . The Slavic peoples on the other hand are not destined for their own life. . . . The Russian territory is our India and, just as the English rule India with a handful of people, so will we govern this, our colonial territory. We will supply the Ukrainians with headscarves, glass chains as jewellery, and whatever else colonial peoples like.[63]

Similar remarks by other Nazi officials are not hard to find, many of them justifying German occupation and colonialism on the grounds that the eastern regions of Europe were authentically 'German' territory. For example, in 1939, Albert Brackmann of the University of Berlin wrote: 'The German people were the only bearers of culture in the East and in their role as the main power of Europe protected Western culture and carried it into uncultivated regions. For centuries, they constituted a barrier in the East against lack of culture [*Unkultur*] and protected the West against barbarity.'[64]

61. Achille Mbembe, *On the Postcolony* (Berkeley: University of California Press, 2001); Vinay Lal, 'The Concentration Camp and Development: The Pasts and Future of Genocide' in *Colonialism and Genocide*, eds. Moses and Stone, pp. 124–47. Earlier historians who talked about Nazism in colonial terms include Robert Koehl, Alexander Dallin, Hans Kohn, Klaus Hildebrand, Wolfe Schmokel, and Woodruff D. Smith. The latter's *The Ideological Origins of Nazi Imperialism* (New York: Oxford University Press, 1986) remains important.
62. Paul Gilroy, *The Black Atlantic: Modernity and Double Consciousness* (London: Verso, 1993); Gilroy, *Between Camps: Nations, Cultures, and the Allure of Race* (London: Penguin, 2000).
63. Hitler, *Monologe in Führerhauptquartier*, ed. Werner Jochmann (Hamburg, 1980), pp. 60–4 (17 September 1941), cited in Jürgen Zimmerer, 'Colonialism and the Holocaust: Towards an Archeology of Genocide' in *Genocide and Settler Society*, ed. Moses, p. 49. On Hitler's attitudes to the British Empire, see Gerwin Strobl, *The Germanic Isle: Nazi Perceptions of Britain* (Cambridge: Cambridge University Press, 2000), and Dan Stone, 'Britannia Waives the Rules: British Imperialism and Holocaust Memory' in *History, Memory and Mass Atrocity*, pp. 174–95.
64. Albert Brackmann, *Krisis und Aufbau in Osteuropa: Ein weltgeschichtliches Bild* (Berlin: Ahnenerbe-Stiftung, 1939), p. 11, cited in John Connelly, 'Nazis and Slavs: From Racial Theory to Racist Practice', *CEH*, 32, 1 (1999), p. 13.

Recent studies by Marcia Klotz, Diemut Majer, David Blackbourn, Robert L. Nelson, and many others confirm the idea that the Nazi occupation of 'the East' can meaningfully be conceptualized as a colonial project, taking colonialism as the imposition of one group's pattern of life on another's.[65] The differences between Nazi colonialism and, say, British or French, is that the latter held, however tenuously, to the notion of the 'civilizing mission' and hoped to assimilate the 'natives' to the 'benefits' of western 'civilization', all the while ensuring that the greatest benefits accrued to the metropole. As we have seen in Chapter 1, the brutal treatment of the 'natives' in eastern Europe meant that the Nazi variety of colonialism in Europe was of a different order of violence—a statement that is an indictment of Nazi rule and not meant as an exculpation of British of French, which employed massive violence when the Empires' rulers required it.[66] (Another difference is that in most definitions, colonialism requires this process to be carried on 'overseas', not in neighbouring lands, but this seems to be common usage rather than a hard and fast rule.)

Most of these studies focus on the Nazi *Lebensraum* project. We have already seen that the murder of the Jews is inseparable from the notion of *Lebensraum*, for in the Nazi imagination the Jews were responsible for denying Germany its natural expansion. John Connelly's important article, 'Nazis and Slavs', shows the racial hierarchy that governed Nazi conceptualizations of its occupied Slavic peoples—with Russians, Poles, and Ukrainians at the bottom, and Croats, Bulgarians, and Slovaks at the top—and explains how this racial schema was flexible enough to account for changing circumstances. Thus, attitudes towards assimilation, labour and food supply could vary depending on local conditions and military exigency. Importantly, though, Connelly notes that such concerns never extended to the Jews, for they were excluded from the start: 'Only in

65. Marcia Klotz, 'Global Visions: From the Colonial to the National Socialist World', *The European Studies Journal*, 16, 2 (1999), pp. 37–68; Diemut Majer, 'Das besetzte Osteuropa als deutsche Kolonie (1939–1944): Die Pläne der NS-Führung zur Beherrschung Osteuropas' in *Gesetzliches Unrecht: Rassistisches Recht im 20. Jahrhundert*, ed. Fritz Bauer Institut (Frankfurt/M: Campus, 2005), pp. 111–34; David Blackbourn, *The Conquest of Nature: Water, Landscape, and the Making of Modern Germany* (New York: W. W. Norton, 2006), ch. 5; Robert L. Nelson, ed., *Germans, Poland and Colonial Expansion to the East* (Basingstoke: Palgrave Macmillan, 2009).
66. For an interesting discussion, see Frank Biess, ' "Are We a Cruel Nation?" Colonial Practices, Perceptions and Scandals' in *Wilhelmine Germany and Edwardian Britain: Essays on Cultural Affinity*, eds. Dominik Geppert and Robert Gerwarth (Oxford: Oxford University Press, 2008), pp. 115–40.

the case of the Jews did Nazi racial ideology overpower every other consideration, whether of the economy, of military strategy, or of racial science. In the case of the Slavs Nazi ideology gradually adapted to the contours of conventional racial theory, though it was never officially codified.'[67] Thus, whilst the idea of the Nazi occupation of eastern Europe as a colonial project is relatively easy to accept, the question of what this has to do with the Holocaust is less obvious. If the Jews were written out of the picture from the outset, then the argument that there are links between colonial genocides of the late nineteenth and early twentieth centuries and the Holocaust is far harder to defend.

In order to understand the background to the debate, we first need to consider the 'colonial turn' in German history. A widespread lack of interest in colonial history, apart from indirectly in the contexts of 'social imperialism' and diplomatic—military relations, was until the last decade or so the norm amongst German historians. Because of the short life of the formal empire, historians, if they thought about it at all, believed that the 'impact' of colonialism on German life had been negligible.[68] Starting with the paradigm-shifting work of Susanne Zantop, who showed that the German colonial imagination long preceded and outlasted any formal imperial structures, historians have looked beyond a narrowly-focused imperial history to show that ideas and fantasies of empire—an 'intellectual colonialism'—penetrated deeply into German culture and society in every sphere, from advertising to sexuality to science.[69] There is not the space to go into detail here, but German imperial history now constitutes a sizeable historiography. There is still some way to go before this history comes of age—there are as yet few considerations of German colonialism from the point of view of the colonized and the lives of Afro-Germans are only now being written about, for example—but there

67. Connelly, 'Nazis and Slavs', p. 26. Also Doris L. Bergen, 'The Nazi Concept of "Volks-deutsche" and the Exacerbation of Anti-Semitism in Eastern Europe, 1939–45', *JCH*, 29, 4 (1994), pp. 569–82.
68. Pascal Grosse, 'What Does German Colonialism Have to Do with National Socialism? A Conceptual Framework' in *Germany's Colonial Pasts*, eds. Eric Ames, Marcia Klotz, and Lora Wildenthal (Lincoln: University of Nebraska Press, 2005), pp. 115–34; Uta G. Poiger, 'Imperialism and Empire in Twentieth-Century Germany', *History & Memory*, 17, 1/2 (2005), pp. 117–43; Birthe Kundrus, 'Blind Spots: Empire, Colonies, and Ethnic Identities in Modern German History' in *Gendering Modern German History: Rewriting Historiography*, eds. Karen Hagemann and Jean Quataert (New York: Berghahn, 2007), pp. 86–106.
69. Susanne Zantop, *Colonial Fantasies: Conquest, Family, and Nation in Precolonial Germany, 1770–1870* (Durham: Duke University Press, 1997). Zantop talks of 'intellectual colonialism' on p. 41.

has nevertheless been a remarkable 'globalization' of German history in the last two decades. And although there is, quite correctly, resistance to reading German imperial history solely in terms of its relationship to Nazism, much of the literature remains concerned to answer Zantop's question: 'can one posit a historical determinism that necessarily led from one stage of fantasizing to the next and that *had* to end in Nazi expansionism or racist extermination policies? Was there a teleological progression from nation without state to *Volk ohne Raum*, people without space?'[70]

Hannah Arendt claimed, in *The Origins of Totalitarianism*, that colonialism provided the building blocks for fascism in Europe, and scholars have recently begun testing this so-called 'boomerang thesis' empirically. Historians like Götz Aly and Robert Gellately, who stress that the murder of the Jews should be seen as but one—if the most urgent—stage in a broader genocidal vision, have provided a helpful way of understanding the link.[71] If one places the Holocaust into the context of Nazi genocides and mass killings (of Romanies and Soviet Prisoners of War, for example, or the largely unrealized plans of the GPO), then one can see a link between the 'colonial genocides' of Slavs and the destruction of the Jews. But this still suggests making the Holocaust fit the paradigm by association; are there more plausible connections to be found?

70. Zantop, *Colonial Fantasies*, p. 203. For some of the most significant works of recent German colonial history, see Geoff Eley and Bradley Naranch, eds., *German Cultures of Colonialism: Race, Nation, and Globalization 1884–1945* (Durham: Duke University Press, forthcoming); Sven Oliver Müller and Cornelius Torp, eds., *Das deutsche Kaiserreich in der Kontroverse* (Göttingen: Vandenhoeck & Ruprecht, 2008), esp. sections 3 and 4; Karsten Linne, *Deutschland jenseits des Äquators? Die NS-Kolonialplanungen für Afrika* (Berlin: Ch. Links, 2008); George Steinmetz, *The Devil's Handwriting: Precoloniality and the German Colonial State in Qingdao, Samoa, and Southwest Africa* (Chicago: University of Chicago Press, 2007); Matthew Jefferies, *Contesting the German Empire 1871–1918* (Oxford: Blackwell, 2007); Ames, Klotz and Wildenthal, *Germany's Colonial Pasts*; Sebastian Conrad and Jürgen Osterhammel, *Das Kaiserreich transnational: Deutschland in der Welt 1871–1914* (Göttingen: Vandenhoeck & Ruprecht, 2004); Birthe Kundrus, ed., *Phantasiereiche: Zur Kulturgeschichte des deutschen Kolonialismus* (Frankfurt/M: Campus, 2003); Lora Wildenthal, *German Women for Empire, 1884–1945* (Durham: Duke University Press, 2001); Sara Friedrichsmeyer, Sara Lennox, and Susanne Zantop, eds., *The Imperialist Imagination: German Colonialism and Its Legacy* (Ann Arbor: University of Michigan Press, 1998).
71. Gellately, 'The Third Reich, the Holocaust', pp. 241–63. On the 'boomerang thesis', see King and Stone, 'Introduction' in *Hannah Arendt and the Uses of History*, eds. King and Stone, pp. 1–17; Richard H. King, *Race, Culture, and the Intellectuals 1940–1970* (Washington, DC: Woodrow Wilson Center Press, 2004), ch. 4; Pascal Grosse, 'From Colonialism to National Socialism to Postcolonialism: Hannah Arendt's *Origins of Totalitarianism*', *Postcolonial Studies*, 9, 1 (2006), pp. 35–52; Dan Stone, 'Defending the Plural: Hannah Arendt and Genocide Studies', *New Formations*, 71 (2011), pp. 46–57.

Henning Melber suggested nearly twenty years ago not only that German rule in Southwest Africa provided the model for Apartheid but that Nazi rule represented the culmination of a process that began in the colonies: 'If at the turn of the century the African "subhuman" was being civilized in the German colonies (even if, in the most extreme case, this meant his extermination), then two decades after the pitiful end of the German colonial era, this definition of civilization as the protection of the purity of German blood was being practiced at home.'[72] Indeed, Southwest Africa, and most specifically the Herero and Nama War (1904–08) is the case that historians have found most persuasive when refining Arendt's intriguing and problematic thesis.[73] In turning to Southwest Africa, many historians have rejected the question implicit in Arendt's work—how could British colonialism lead to Nazism in Germany?—suggesting instead that the problem is better addressed by examining a specifically German trajectory.

The most commonly offered illustration of this link is that between race laws and racialized everyday practice in German Southwest Africa and Nazism. Jürgen Zimmerer, for example, writes that, although the genocide of the Herero and Nama is increasingly being remembered, 'by contrast, the everyday racism, which made German Southwest Africa an important precursor not only to the Apartheid regime in South Africa, but also to the racial policies of the Third Reich, has fallen entirely into oblivion.'[74] In the light of the apparent similarity between concern over miscegenation in the colonies and in Nazi Germany, many historians have drawn comparisons between laws concerning '*Mischehen*' and the Nuremberg Laws of 1935.[75] Appearing to prefigure the ban on sexual

---

72. Henning Melber, 'Kontinuitäten totaler Herrschaft: Völkermord und Apartheid in "Deutsch-Südwestafrika"': Zur kolonialen Herrschaftspraxis im deutschen Kaiserreich', *Jahrbuch für Antisemitismusforschung*, 1 (1992), p. 109.
73. On the Herero and Nama War, see Jan-Bart Gewald, *Herero Heroes: A Socio-Political History of the Herero of Namibia, 1890–1923* (Oxford: James Currey, 1999); Gewald, 'Imperial Germany and the Herero of Southern Africa: Genocide and the Quest for Recompense' in *Genocide, War Crimes and the West: History and Complicity*, ed. Adam Jones (London: Zed Books, 2004), pp. 59–77; Jürgen Zimmerer, *Deutsche Herrschaft über Afrikaner: Staatlicher Machtanspruch und Wirklichkeit im kolonialen Namibia* (Münster: LIT, 2004); Dominik Schaller, ' "Ich glaube, dass die Nation als solche vernichtet werden muss": Kolonialkrieg und Völkermord in Deutsch-Südwestafrika 1904–1907', *JGR*, 6, 3 (2004), pp. 395–430.
74. Jürgen Zimmerer, 'Ordnung, Entwicklung und Segregation in "Deutsch-Südwest" (1884–1915)' in *Gesetzliches Unrecht*, ed. Fritz Bauer Institute, p. 135.
75. Jürgen Zimmerer, 'Von Windhuk nach Warschau: Die rassische Privilegiengesellschaft in Deutsch-Südwestafrika, ein Modell mit Zukunft?' in *Von Windhuk nach Auschwitz?*,

relations between 'Germans' and 'Jews' in 1935, in Southwest Africa
'mixed marriages' were banned in 1905, in German East Africa in 1906,
and in Samoa in 1912.[76] What Elisa von Joeden-Forgey calls 'race power'
thus apparently constitutes a key link between Southwest Africa and
Nazism.[77]

One of the best known of these 'race-power' connections is the transfer
of eugenic knowledge from the colonies to Germany. As Michael Kater
puts it, a 'path can be mapped out that led directly from the experimental
laboratories of the late nineteenth century to the gas chambers of Auschwitz.
Four men were treading that path, all of them physicians, each one starting
as a genuine disciple of science and veering increasingly toward the irrational
as time progressed, eventually to cast shadows even beyond World War
II.'[78] These four were Theodor Mollison, who undertook a study trip to
German East Africa in 1904 and co-wrote an article on Maoris, 'Negroes',
and Aborigines as 'lower races'; Eugen Fischer, the co-author of Mollison's
piece, who also cut his teeth in Africa, with his famous anthropological

pp. 151–77; Pascal Grosse, *Kolonialismus, Eugenik und bürgerliche Gesellschaft in Deutschland 1850–1918* (Frankfurt/M: Campus, 2000), pp. 145–92; Fatima El-Tayeb, *Schwarze Deutsche: Der Diskurs um 'Rasse' und nationale Identität 1890–1933* (Frankfurt/M: Campus, 2001), pp. 118–31; Birthe Kundrus, *Moderne Imperialisten: Das Kaiserreich im Spiegel seiner Kolonien* (Cologne: Böhlau, 2003), pp. 219–79; Frank Becker, ed., *Rassenmischehen-Mischlinge-Rassentrennung: Zur Politik der Rasse im deutschen Kolonialreich* (Stuttgart: Franz Steiner, 2004).

76. Helmut Walser Smith, 'The Talk of Genocide, the Rhetoric of Miscegenation: Notes on Debates in the German Reichstag Concerning Southwest Africa, 1904–14' in *The Imperialist Imagination*, eds. Friedrichsmeyer, Lennox, and Zantop, pp. 107–23; Zimmerer, *Deutsche Herrschaft über Afrikaner*, pp. 94–109; Cornelia Essner, 'Zwischen Vernunft und Gefühl: Die Reichstagsdebatten von 1912 um koloniale "Rassenmischehe" und "Sexualität"', *Zeitschrift für Geschichtswissenschaft*, 45, 6 (1997), pp. 503–19; Franz-Josef Schulte-Althoff, 'Rassenmischung im kolonialen System: Zur deutschen Kolonialpolitik im letzten Jahrzehnt vor dem Ersten Weltkrieg', *Historisches Jahrbuch*, 105 (1995), pp. 52–94; Anegret Ehmann, 'From Colonial Racism to Nazi Population Policy: The Role of the So-Called Mischlinge' in *The Holocaust and History: The Known, the Unknown, the Disputed, and the Reexamined*, eds. Michael Berenbaum and Abraham J. Peck (Bloomington: Indiana University Press, 1998), pp. 115–33. Most critical on this assumed link is Birthe Kundrus, 'Von Windhoek nach Nürnberg? Koloniale "Mischehenverbote" und die nationalsozialistische Rassengesetzgebung' in *Phantasiereiche*, ed. Kundrus, pp. 110–31.

77. Elisa von Joeden Forgey, 'Race Power in Postcolonial Germany: The German Africa Show and the National Socialist State, 1935–40' in *Germany's Colonial Pasts*, eds. Ames, Klotz and Wildenthal, pp. 167–88; Joeden-Forgey, 'Race Power, Freedom, and the Democracy of Terror in German Racialist Thought' in *Hannah Arendt and the Uses of History*, eds. King and Stone, pp. 21–37; Grosse, 'What Does Colonialism', p. 118. See also Anne Dreesbach, *Gezähmte Wilde: Die Zurschaustellung 'exotischer' Menschen in Deutschland 1870–1940* (Frankfurt/M: Campus, 2005).

78. Michael H. Kater, *Doctors under Hitler* (Chapel Hill: University of North Carolina Press, 1989), p. 230.

study of the so-called Rehoboth Bastards, the 'mixed-race' children of black African women and Boer settlers;[79] Otmar von Verschuer, who succeeded Fischer at the KWIA in Berlin in 1942; and Josef Mengele as Verschuer's favourite assistant.[80] This direct line joining Fischer and Mengele has been cited many times as proof of the continuity of ideas and personnel between German colonialism and Nazism. To cite Kater again, to a large degree racial science:

> drew its illustrative material from imperial Germany's policies in its African colonies: Hereros (who were almost exterminated in 1904), Hottentots and so-called Rehoboth Bastards from German Southwest Africa. Fischer and Philalethes Kuhn, one of Ploetz's students, had acquired relevant knowledge in the colonial African theatre of war which they then bundled together to produce a scientific image of race. In the Third Reich, this allowed for a smooth transposition from Blacks to Jews as supposedly inferior objects of research.[81]

Although I have criticized the notion that physicians were responsible for the Holocaust, their involvement in the crimes of the Third Reich is indisputable and in the context of this chapter these career trajectories open up some productive lines of inquiry about the connections between the Holocaust and earlier experiences of colonialism. However, a few noteworthy examples such as this hardly accounts for the argument that colonialism and Nazism are profoundly joined, and historians thus put forward claims of more general underlying 'structural connections'.[82]

Some historians in fact see Germany's lack of colonial experience as more relevant for explaining the brutal occupation of eastern Europe than its brief history as an overseas imperial power. Bloxham, for example, writes: 'To the manifest ill-will of these new overlords should be added the deficit of any of the experience of imperial administration that benefited the other European

79. Eugen Fischer, *Die Rehobother Bastards und das Bastardierungsproblem beim Menschen: Anthropologische und ethnographische Studien an Rehobother Bastardvolk in Deutsch-Südwest-Afrika* (Jena: Verlag von Gustav Fischer, 1913).

80. Kater, *Doctors under Hitler*, pp. 230–5. Mollison can be compared with Philalethes Kuhn, also exposed to similar racist ideas in Southwest Africa, where he took part in the Herero war, and from which he gained his view of German superiority (Kater, *Doctors*, p. 113).

81. Michael H. Kater, 'Das Böse in der Medizin: Nazi-Ärzte als Handlanger des Holocaust' in *'Beseitigung des jüdischen Einflusses . . .' Antisemitische Forschung, Eliten und Karrieren im Nationalsozialismus*, ed. Fritz Bauer Institut (Frankfurt/M: Campus, 1999), pp. 219–39, here p. 223.

82. A notable exception is Zimmerer's work on geographers in the colonies and Nazi Germany: 'Im Dienste des Imperiums: Die Geographen der Berliner Universität zwischen Kolonialwissenschaften und Ostforschung', *Jahrbuch für Universitätsgeschichte*, 7 (2004), pp. 73–99.

colonial powers.'[83] Certainly this brutality undermined any belated attempts to induce deeper collaboration in the later stages of the war against the Soviet Union. Weimar Germany, in other words, was a postcolonial society, but one whose colonies had been lost not as a result of indigenous anti-colonial movements but at the hands of imperial rivals—another way of accounting for the perpetuation of a colonial mentality in the absence of colonies.[84]

From this broader rediscovery of German colonial history, the most heated debate to have emerged concerns the relationship between colonialism and the Holocaust. Foremost among the historians who propose such a connection is Jürgen Zimmerer. Primarily an expert on German Southwest Africa, Zimmerer has set out his argument in numerous studies; significantly, he has been instrumental in bringing the first genocide of the twentieth century to wider public attention in Germany (and beyond) and helped to spark a debate within Germany and between Germany and the Herero people (today a minority group in Namibia) about whether an apology should be offered to the Hereros (one was, in 2004) and whether financial reparations are in order.

Zimmerer does not advocate a simple line running from Africa to Auschwitz, as though colonialism were the only factor in the Holocaust, or as though the genocide of the Herero only has value insofar as Europeans today can view it as a 'trial run' for the Holocaust. As he states in his most recent work: 'There are no monocausal explanations for Nazi crimes, nor is there a linear progression from German colonialism to the murder of the Jews. Auschwitz was neither the logical consequence of the events in South-West Africa nor was it, as seen from Windhoek, inevitable.'[85] What he claims is that the 'colonial example illustrates the genocidal potential already present in parts of the bureaucratic and military institutions of Germany', that 'colonialism produced a reservoir of cultural practices that Nazi thugs could appropriate for themselves' and that 'Nazi perpetrators could, to a certain degree, legitimize their actions by pointing to similarities with colonial times'.[86]

83. Bloxham, *The Final Solution*, p. 208.
84. See Jared Poley, *Decolonization in Germany: Weimar Narratives of Colonial Loss and Foreign Occupation* (Bern: Peter Lang, 2005).
85. Jürgen Zimmerer, 'The First Genocide of the Twentieth Century: The German War of Destruction in South-West Africa (1904–1908) and the Global History of Genocide' in *Lessons and Legacies, Vol. 8: From Generation to Generation*, ed. Doris L. Bergen (Evanston: Northwestern University Press, 2008), p. 35.
86. Zimmerer, 'The First Genocide', p. 36.

Of his extensive writings, some already cited, perhaps the two most relevant here are his articles 'Colonialism and the Holocaust' and 'The Birth of the *Ostland* Out of the Spirit of Colonialism', for in those pieces Zimmerer sets out most thoroughly his arguments about the Holocaust's link with German colonial history.[87] In the first article, Zimmerer argues that, in broad terms, the underlying structural similarities between German colonialism and Nazism are 'race and space', racism and the conception of 'living space'. And more narrowly on the Herero genocide and the Holocaust, he sees both in terms of a German military tradition of 'racial extermination warfare' (*Rassen- und Vernichtungskrieg*), the latter essentially being a radicalized variant of the former. State-perpetrated colonial genocide thus constitutes an important precedent for Nazi genocide.[88] In the second piece, Zimmerer argues that, from the viewpoint of postcolonial studies, many of the aspects of Nazi rule that seem unique to Europeans were in fact radical versions of colonial practices, and he suggests that the history of German colonialism allowed Nazi perpetrators and 'ordinary Germans' to feel as though they were not engaging in taboo-breaking behaviour. He traces lines of continuity from Southwest Africa to Nazism, including a handful of 'Africa hands' who subsequently joined the *Freikorps*, and some fairly influential former colonial administrators. More important, Zimmerer notes that colonialism made a deep impression on German cultural life in general, especially through the press, films, monuments, lecture tours, exhibitions, and literature. The novels of Karl May are only the most obvious examples.[89]

Zimmerer's claims have engendered some strong criticisms. Dan Diner argues that the Holocaust is different from colonial genocides in that it was nothing more than 'pure annihilation, over and above war, conflict,

---

87. Zimmerer is but the most conspicuous of a growing number of historians advocating this argument; see, inter alia, Sven Lindqvist, *'Exterminate All the Brutes'* (London: Granta, 1996); Enzo Traverso, *The Origins of Nazi Violence* (New York: The New Press, 2003); Benjamin Madley, 'From Africa to Auschwitz: How German South West Africa Incubated Ideas and Methods Adapted and Developed by the Nazis in Eastern Europe', *European History Quarterly*, 35, 3 (2005), pp. 429–64.

88. Zimmerer, 'Colonialism and the Holocaust'.

89. Jürgen Zimmerer, 'The Birth of the *Ostland* Out of the Spirit of Colonialism: A Postcolonial Perspective on the Nazi Policy of Conquest and Extermination', *Patterns of Prejudice*, 39, 2 (2005), pp. 197–219. See also Zimmerer, 'Das Deutsche Reich und der Genozid: Überlegungen zum historischen Ort des Völkermordes an den Herero und Nama' in *Namibia-Deutschland: Eine geteilte Geschichte. Widerstand-Gewalt-Erinnerung*, eds. Larissa Förster, Dag Henrichsen, and Michael Bollig (Munich: Edition Minerva, 2004), pp. 106–21.

and enmity'.[90] Edward Ross Dickinson does not disagree that one of the roots of Nazi colonialism in Poland lay in Southwest Africa, but he finds it 'odd' that Zimmerer 'does not even mention two centuries of Prussian conquest and occupation, with attendant discriminatory regimes and justifications, in that very region'.[91] And Matthew Fitzpatrick suggests that the individuals whom Zimmerer highlights in order to demonstrate continuities between colonial and Nazi Germany, such as Franz Ritter von Epp (colonial governor and, under the Nazis, director of the colonial office) in fact highlight the discontinuities; Epp, it transpires, had some difficulty persuading former colonists to transfer their ambitions to Russia. And Fitzpatrick thinks that the difference between colonial and Nazi racism is too great to indicate a meaningful continuity; the former was founded on 'hierarchical', the latter on 'biological' racism: he distinguishes the Holocaust from colonial genocide by arguing that the Holocaust, 'unlike the genocidal Herero–Nama wars, might be considered a genocidal eugenicist program writ large'.[92]

In the light of Chapter 4, one can see how the focus on 'modernity' and its technologies—primarily eugenics—can, in the context of the history of colonialism, serve to isolate the Holocaust from the rest of modern history, and certainly leads to the opposite conclusion from the one hoped for by the advocates of the 'modernity' paradigm. For, ironically, in criticizing scholars who link colonial genocides and the Holocaust of reworking the old *Sonderweg* argument (this time in the context of German imperialism), they inadvertently let the *Sonderweg* argument slip in through the back door, by decoupling the Holocaust from the history of genocide in the modern world. Indeed, where they see a perverse *Sündenstolz* marking the argument of those who stress Germany's past, actually their own 'pride in sinfulness' is more Eurocentric still, since it suggests that European genocides are somehow more important and therefore more urgently in need of analysis, largely because of the 'achievements' of European technology. Whether because of a 'critical-liberal' approach that sees comparisons with the Holocaust as obscene, or because of a 'conservative-revisionist' desire to

90. Dan Diner, *Gegenläufige Geschichte: Über Geltung und Wirkung des Holocaust* (Göttingen: Vandenhoeck & Ruprecht, 2007), p. 81.

91. Edward Ross Dickinson, 'The German Empire: An Empire?', *History Workshop Journal*, 66 (2008), p. 139.

92. Matthew P. Fitzpatrick, 'The Pre-History of the Holocaust? The *Sonderweg* and *Historikerstreit* Debates and the Abject Colonial Past', *CEH*, 41, 3 (2008), pp. 489 (Epp), 498 (race), 501 ('eugenicist program').

quarantine the Holocaust, keeping it separate from an otherwise 'normal' if not positive German history, the effect is the same: a refusal to ask questions of colonialism's relationship with Nazism and the Holocaust, a '*Sonderweg* of the West'.[93]

One of the most pugnacious attacks on what has come to be known in Germany as the 'Zimmerer thesis' has been penned by Robert Gerwarth and Stefan Malinowski, in an article published in German in 2007 and in a slightly revised version in English in 2009. They call into question both the thesis of continuities between the Herero and Nama War and the Holocaust, on the one hand, and the designation of the Holocaust as a 'colonial genocide', on the other.

First, Gerwarth and Malinowski note that Germany was hardly the only colonial power to carry out massacres, even genocide, in its colonies. Citing the examples of the Americans in the Philippines, the Spanish in Cuba, and the French conquest of Algeria, they note that, by treating colonial massacre as a transnational phenomenon, the thesis of specifically German continuities becomes harder to uphold: 'the hypothesis of unbroken continuities between "Africa and Auschwitz" fails to account for the fact that Britain and France practiced policies of violent colonial suppression long before (and after) 1945, but simultaneously remained the bastions of democracy and never pursued policies of genocide *within* Europe.'[94] Rather than make diachronic connections based on flimsy evidence, it would be more sensible to make synchronic comparisons with other cases of colonial mass violence.[95] For Gerwarth and Malinowski, avoiding awkward comparisons across time and space means that historians pay attention instead to the truly key factors in the rise of Nazism, but also that they are better able to recognize that 'National Socialism and the German war of annihilation constituted a *break* with European traditions of colonialism rather than a continuation'.[96] Rather than the German experience of colonial genocide in Southwest Africa as the model for the Holocaust,

93. Zimmerer, 'Colonial Genocide: The Herero and Nama War', p. 337 ('critical-liberal' and 'conservative-revisionist'); Moses, 'Genocide and Modernity', p. 181 ('*Sonderweg* of the West').
94. Robert Gerwarth and Stephan Malinowski, 'Hannah Arendt's Ghosts: Reflections on the Disputable Path from Windhoek to Auschwitz', *CEH*, 42, 2 (2009), p. 290.
95. See, for example, Helmut Walser Smith, 'The Logic of Colonial Violence: Germany in Southwest Africa (1904–1907), the United States in the Philippines (1899–1902)' in *German and American Nationalism: A Comparative Perspective*, eds. Hartmut Lehmann and Hermann Wellenreuther (Oxford: Berg, 1999), pp. 205–31.
96. Gerwarth and Malinowski, 'Hannah Arendt's Ghosts', p. 285.

Gerwarth and Malinowski point to the catastrophe of World War I. This claim, they note, is not new, but has 'the advantage of being empirically confirmable'.[97]

Their arguments are compelling even if, as Zimmerer charges in his response to Gerwarth and Malinowski, the authors rely on an idealized notion of what European colonialism was like and even if they start from a sense of outrage that the Holocaust could be discussed in relation to colonialism at all.[98] However, although they mention it in passing as desirable, Gerwarth and Malinowski do not undertake a study of the continuities in biological racism from the colonial period onwards. This factor, whilst not the direct cause of the Holocaust, is nevertheless fundamental to understanding the Third Reich. Besides, separating World War I—a clash of imperial powers for whom colonies were strategically significant assets and which saw in Europe the sort of brutal warfare that had previously been reserved for the colonies—from colonial history is itself a questionable procedure; as Birthe Kundrus notes, the impact of colonial violence on the Great War and its aftermath has not yet been analysed.[99]

Indeed, the most sustained critique of the colonial approach to the Holocaust has come from Birthe Kundrus, in a number of important articles. Kundrus's main point is that to look at Nazism through the lenses of colonialism is to misunderstand both; Wilhelmine Germany was far more heterogeneous than Nazi Germany, and ultimately Nazism represented more of a break with what had gone before than a continuation: 'no continuity without change', as she puts it. 'The twenty years between the First and Second World Wars were not simply jumped'; the transfer of colonial conceptions across time and space fundamentally altered their meaning.[100] For example, in her detailed analysis of racial attitudes and

---

97. Robert Gerwarth and Stephan Malinowski, 'Der Holocaust als "kolonialer Genozid"? Europäische Kolonialgewalt und nationalsozialistische Vernichtungskrieg', *Geschichte und Gesellschaft*, 33, 3 (2007), p. 454. See also Benjamin Ziemann, 'Germany After the First World War—A Violent Society? Results and Implications of Recent Research on Weimar Germany', *Journal of Modern European History*, 1, 1 (2003), pp. 80–95.

98. Jürgen Zimmerer, 'Nationalsozialismus postkolonial: Plädoyer zur Globalisierung der deutschen Geschichte', *Zeitschrift für Geschichtswissenschaft*, 57, 6 (2009), pp. 529–48.

99. Birthe Kundrus, 'From the Herero to the Holocaust? Some Remarks on the Current Debate', *Afrika Spectrum*, 40, 2 (2005), p. 301. But cf. John Horne and Alan Kramer, *German Atrocities, 1914: A History of Denial* (New Haven: Yale University Press, 2001); Kramer, *Dynamic of Destruction: Culture and Mass Killing in the First World War* (Oxford: Oxford University Press, 2007).

100. Birthe Kundrus, 'Kontinuitäten, Parallelen, Rezeptionen: Überlegungen zur "Kolonialisierung" des Nationalsozialismus', *Werkstattgeschichte*, 15 (2006), p. 61.

laws in the German colonies, Kundrus comes to the conclusion that one should be wary of assuming continuities between colonial and Nazi practices: 'The contested debate over colonial "mixed marriages" is an especially impressive example of the heterogeneity and, ultimately, the polarized nature of Wilhelmine society, a society that cannot be reduced to anti-liberal or even "proto-fascist" attitudes and positions.'[101]

This argument is quite correct, although Kundrus perhaps overstates the degree of openness and heterogeneity that characterized Wilhelminian race discourse. But Kundrus seems to be tilting at windmills, for no one argues that Wilhelminian society can be reduced to a proto-fascist prelude to Nazism. As we have seen, the main target of Kundrus's objections, Zimmerer, is careful to emphasize precisely that point; rather, he is trying to open up previously unexpected lines of inquiry, not to shut down all others or to insist on a monocausal explanation for the rise of Nazism. He insists that a 'mental disposition'—one that believes in the right to a racially privileged social status (*rassische Privilegiengesellschaft*)—provides the link between colonialism and Nazism, and that this link 'does not posit causality or an irreversible *Sonderweg* leading from "Southwest" to occupied Europe'.[102] Further, on the particular point of race mixing, Kundrus writes that 'it would be incorrect to assume simple continuities between colonial bans on intermarriage and the Nuremberg Laws'; but it is not clear who does 'assume simple continuities' of that sort.[103]

Much of the debate turns on whether historians are advocating a new *Sonderweg*, as Kundrus alleges.[104] Some historians, such as Benjamin Madley and Isabel Hull, do indeed seem to be taking this tack, with Hull in particular suggesting that there were specifically German military traditions which predisposed Germans to genocidal 'absolute destruction'.[105] But most of the participants in the debate are careful to insist that reopening the *Sonderweg* debate is not their intention. Rather, as Andreas Eckert argues, the question of the links between the Herero genocide and the Holocaust helpfully reveal that developing comparative genocide scholarship needs to

---

101. Kundrus, *Moderne Imperialisten*, p. 279.
102. Zimmerer, *Von Windhuk nach Auschwitz?*, p. 84.   103. Kundrus, 'Blind Spots', p. 96.
104. Kundrus, 'Kontinuitäten, Parallelen, Rezeptionen', p. 49.
105. Isabel Hull, 'Military Culture and the Production of "Final Solutions" in the Colonies: The Example of Wilhelminian Germany' in *The Specter of Genocide*, eds. Gellately and Kiernan, pp. 141–62; Hull, *Absolute Destruction: Military Culture and the Practices of War in Imperial Germany* (Ithaca: Cornell University Press, 2005); see also the debate between Hull and Zimmerer in the *Bulletin of the German Historical Institute, Washington, DC*, 37 (2005).

engage in greater detail with the history of colonialism in general.[106] And
on the other side of the debate, Gerwarth and Malinowski claim: 'Mass
killings of indigenous civilian populations previously classified as racially or
culturally "inferior" were common currency in Europe's colonial empires
and are not indicative of a German colonial Sonderweg.'[107] This claim
seems to work against their main argument that there was no direct line
from the Hereros to the Holocaust; for apart from the fact that no one
asserts such a simplistic argument, the continual violence that Europeans
experienced (as perpetrators and victims) first in overseas colonies and
then in Europe from the late nineteenth century through to the early
1950s renders it wholly plausible that the genocide of the Jews has some
connections to practices, ideas, technologies, institutions, wars and visions
and blueprints that characterized the 'age of imperialism'. As with the
'uniqueness' question, the Sonderweg debate seems to be something of a red
herring, obscuring more productive lines of research.

It would be desirable to think that the two schools of thought are
approaching a consensus. Both recognize the validity of the other's claims,
and as a result place constraints on their own interpretations. Kundrus,
whilst she tends to reject the view that colonialism was a significant factor
in the development of the Holocaust, nevertheless admits: 'We might say
that the German overseas colonies were irrelevant to Hitler's plans, but that
the goals and interpretative framework in which Nazi expansion occurred
were inspired by European imperialism—as part of a renewed engagement
with the German imperial past and present by the Nazis.' And Zimmerer,
whilst maintaining the opposite view about links between colonialism and
the Holocaust, is still careful not to overstate his case: 'This is not to
claim that causal connections existed between colonial developments and
the Holocaust, but rather that a closer look at colonialism helps us to
understand how genocidal fantasies were developed and radicalized.'[108]

106. Andreas Eckert, 'Namibia—ein deutscher Sonderweg in Afrika? Anmerkungen zur inter-
    nationalen Diskussion' in Völkermord in Deutsch-Südwestafrika: Der Kolonialkrieg (1904–1908)
    in Namibia und seine Folgen, eds. Jürgen Zimmerer and Joachim Zeller (Berlin: Links, 2003),
    pp. 226–36. See also Zimmerer, 'Kein Sonderweg im "Rassenkrieg": Der Genozid an den
    Herero und Nama 1904–08 zwischen deutschen Kontinuitäten und der Globalgeschichte
    der Massengewalt' in Das deutsche Kaiserreich in der Kontroverse, eds. Müller and Torp,
    pp. 323–40; Zimmerer, 'The First German Genocide in Context: Towards a Postcolonial
    Reading of Germany's Racial Century' (forthcoming).
107. Gerwarth and Malinowski, 'Hannah Arendt's Ghosts', p. 298.
108. Kundrus and Zimmerer in 'Forum: The German Colonial Imagination', GH, 26, 2 (2008),
    pp. 270–1.

Such a consensus would be the most fortunate outcome. The insights of Zimmerer, Melber, and others concerning continuities need to be taken seriously, but so too do the objections of Dickinson, Kundrus, and Gerwarth and Malinowski. For there is something that makes the Holocaust different from earlier cases of colonial genocide, and this difference is neatly explained by Michael Rothberg. He argues that the 'colonial paradigm possesses less explanatory force when considering the deportation of Jews from Western or Southern Europe than when Nazi policy in Poland and the Soviet Union are at issue.'[109] Although the Nazi treatment of Slavs fits with established models of colonial genocide, 'When it comes to the Holocaust, race and space do not align themselves perfectly, since the first "race" scheduled for extermination was not found uniquely in the spaces slated for the most extreme form of colonization.'[110]

However, is that difference enough to justify making 'Holocaust' a separate category from 'genocide'? Why does it matter? What work does thinking about the Holocaust as 'genocide' or as 'colonialism' do? The most compelling argument for understanding the Holocaust in terms of colonial genocide is presented by Dirk Moses. Where Zimmerer presents World War II as a 'colonial war', but says it would be incorrect to see Nazi crimes, especially the Holocaust, 'as mere copies of colonial events', Moses takes the argument a step further, as do others who say that 'events such as the Jewish Holocaust are not aberrations, but rather a logical outcome and continuation of colonialism'.[111] As the main differences between the Holocaust and colonial genocide, Zimmerer cites the fact that the Jews were already part of the perpetrators' society and culture, and the bureaucratic, 'almost industrialized murder' that characterized the Holocaust in a way that was impossible in a colonial setting.[112]

Moses advances the debate, seeing the Holocaust not only as sharing many similarities with colonial genocide. Additionally, he regards the murder of the Jews as typical of genocide in general in that it was

109. The discovery of a kind of 'General Plan West' notwithstanding; see Peter Schöttler, 'Eine Art "Generalplan West": Die Stuckart-Denkschrift vom 14. Juni 1940 und die Planungen für eien neue deutsch-französische Grenze im Zweiten Weltkrieg', Sozial.Geschichte, 18, 3 (2003), pp. 83–131.
110. Rothberg, Multidirectional Memory, p. 105. Cf. Kundrus, 'From the Herero to the Holocaust?', p. 305.
111. Theofanis Verinakis, 'The (Un)civilizing Holocaust: From the Colony to the Lager', Social Identities, 14, 1 (2008), p. 53; see also Max Silverman, 'Interconnected Histories: Holocaust and Empire in the Cultural Imaginary', French Studies, 62, 4 (2008), pp. 417–28.
112. Zimmerer, 'The First Genocide', pp. 57–8.

carried out as a 'security' measure. Even more important, Moses sees the Holocaust in part as a 'subaltern' genocide, that is, a genocide undertaken by the (self-perceived) 'weak' out of fear of the supposed threat posed by their victims.[113] In this sense, the Holocaust can be seen as an 'anti-colonial' genocide—from the point of view of the perpetrators, of course. This view is not entirely novel; Herbert Strauss proposed the notion of the Germans as 'hostages of world Jewry' as the root of the Holocaust over twenty years ago; L. J. Hartog also emphasizes the role played in Hitler's decision-making process of the European Jews as 'hostages' should the US enter the war; and Peter Fritzsche writes: 'National Socialism was as murderous as it was, not because it was modern or efficient or bureaucratic, but because it saw itself to be the specific resolution of German history in which an imperiled people tried to make themselves unassailable.'[114] But it is the first time that the claim has been set into a comparative context.

The starting point of Moses' interpretation is the one with which I began this chapter: the intentionalist argument that the Holocaust resulted from antisemitism is fine, as far as it goes, but something must have happened to make the German variety of antisemitism result in genocide when the same cannot be said (other than under German supervision) for most of the rest of Europe. Moses asks what happens 'if we take a transnational or global approach that situates the Holocaust in processes that are universal in imperial and colonial situations'. His answer combines four different explanations. First, the 'genocidal policies against Slavic peoples in occupied Poland and Ukraine stood in the tradition of imperial conquests since antiquity'. The Nazis never intended totally to exterminate Poles and Ukrainians, but rather to eliminate the 'superfluous' population and retain the rest for labour. Second, when it comes to the Jews, a somewhat different approach is called for. The Holocaust, writes Moses, 'needs to be understood, to begin with, in terms of subaltern genocide'. The Nazis, he asserts, 'regarded Germans as an indigenous people who had been colonized

113. Robins and Jones, eds., *Genocides by the Oppressed*; Moses, ed., *Empire, Colony, Genocide*; Philippe R. Girard, 'Caribbean Genocide: Racial War on Haiti, 1802–4', *Patterns of Prejudice*, 39, 2 (2005), pp. 138–61.
114. Herbert A. Strauss, 'Hostages of "World Jewry": On the Origin of the Idea of Genocide in German History', *HGS*, 3, 2 (1988), pp. 125–36; L. J. Hartog, *Der Befehl zum Judenmord: Hitler, Amerika und die Juden* (Bodenheim: Syndikat Buchgesellschaft, 1997); Peter Fritzsche, *Life and Death in the Third Reich* (Cambridge, MA: The Belknap Press of Harvard University Press, 2008), pp. 5–6.

by Jews' who were undermining German national identity.[115] The Nazis, then, thought of themselves 'as a national liberation movement'. The claim is significant because it distinguishes the radicalism of Nazi antisemitism from what had gone before: 'If the Nazis' anti-Semitism was "redemptive", its particular intensity at this historical conjuncture cannot be read from centuries of anti-Semitism, which had not resulted in genocide like this before.'[116] The Holocaust can thus be seen as part of the history of antisemitism, to be sure, but can at the same time be trans-nationally contextualized in terms of 'both the political emotions common in central European nationalisms since the nineteenth century, and later anticolonial movements'.[117]

Moses does not remain content with the 'subaltern genocide' explanation, however. Third, he notes that the Holocaust 'shared elements of the security syndrome of other empires'. Especially after the collapse of the German empire in 1918, the sense that Jews were not merely colonizing 'others' but were enemies within threatening German stability was very real in the Nazis' feverish imaginations. 'The nationalist traumas of 1918 to 1920', Moses writes, 'drove many Germans to extreme measures to ensure that, like in so many other genocides, never again would inner enemies undermine the nation and war effort'. Genocide, in Moses' formulation, 'is as much an act of security as it is racial hatred'.[118] Finally, he also combines these aspects of the Nazi imagination with a more traditional image: of the *Ostjude* as a typical colonial 'other': 'dirty, lazy, stateless, uncivilized'.[119] He thus concurs with Furber and Lower that, for the Nazis, the Jews combined elements of the traditional colonial 'other' and a fearsome threat to German nationhood. The Holocaust, Moses concludes, 'was no colonial genocide in the common understanding of the term. It was an event, or multitude of events, that united four different, even contradictory imperial and colonial logics into one terrible paranoid mentality and praxis borne of a frustrated imperial nation struggling against a perceived colonizer.'[120]

115. Moses, 'Empire, Colony, Genocide: Keywords and the Philosophy of History' in *Empire, Colony, Genocide*, ed. Moses, p. 37.
116. Moses, 'Empire, Colony, Genocide', pp. 38–9. See also Moses, 'Redemptive Antisemitism and the Imperialist Imaginary' in *Years of Persecution, Years of Extermination*, eds. Betts and Wiese, pp. 233–54.
117. Moses, 'Empire, Colony, Genocide', p. 39.
118. A. Dirk Moses, 'Moving the Genocide Debate Beyond the History Wars', *Australian Journal of Politics and History*, 54, 2 (2008), p. 264.
119. Moses, 'Empire, Colony, Genocide', p. 39.
120. Moses, 'Empire, Colony, Genocide', p. 40.

Moses' arguments are thus aimed at allaying the anxieties of those who
do not see the Holocaust as a colonial genocide. To them, Moses concedes
that 'colonial genocide' offers only a partial explanation, which must be
supplemented by 'subaltern', 'security', and 'exterminatory' logics, all of
which form part of the 'imperial imaginary'. For the time being, Moses'
interpretation is the best attempt to demonstrate why thinking about the
Holocaust in terms of colonial practices is productive, though new work is
appearing all the time. Whether historians of the Holocaust in the narrower
sense will be persuaded remains to be seen. Some will no doubt see Moses'
work as diminishing the significance of Nazi ideology, replacing it with
'world structures'; some too will press Moses to explain the Holocaust in
western and southern Europe—does the 'security' aspect (the fear of Jewish
reprisals and of 'world Jewry') work hard enough here? Can it explain the
death camps as well as the *Einsatzgruppen* shootings? These are debates that
are still in their infancy, and we can expect to see many more attempts
to contextualize the Holocaust in world-historical terms—in the history
of colonialism, imperialism, nationalism, and war and ethnic violence—in
the future. How these will retain a sense of the importance of specifically
Nazi culture and ideology is an open question.

Conclusion

An analysis of the developing interrelationship between Holocaust historiography and genocide studies reveals that the comparative study of
genocide no longer requires participants to be pitted against one another in
a vulgar 'suffering Olympics'. Instead, the insights gained in both fields are
helping to illuminate each other. In the broader context of transnational,
even globalized Holocaust memory, this is no bad thing.[121]

This mutual reinforcement is most obvious in terms of the increasing
sophistication in genocide studies, in particular the turn to history among
genocide scholars. And in the case of the Holocaust, it means first of all
awareness that the uniqueness claim is an ethical rather than a historical

---

121. See, for example, Jan Eckel and Claudia Moisel, eds., *Universalisierung des Holocaust?*
     Erinnerungskultur und Geschichtspolitik in internationaler Perspektive (Göttingen: Wallstein,
     2008); Norbert Frei, ed., *Transnationale Vergangenheitspolitik: Der Umgang mit deutschen
     Kriegsverbrechen in Europa nach dem Zweiten Weltkrieg* (Göttingen: Wallstein, 2002); Daniel
     Levy and Natan Szneider, *Erinnerung im globalen Zeitalter: Der Holocaust* (Frankfurt/M:
     Suhrkamp, 2001).

one. If one wants to argue that the Holocaust is unique, at least do so on the basis of comparative study! More important, the recovery of Lemkin's writings and the debate about genocide in the context of settler colonies means that a globalization of the Holocaust has to some extent taken place. Even if this concerns only the initial stages of the murder process, the insight that the murder of the Jews in 1941–42—before the death camps were fully in operation—was part of a colonial-style sweep through eastern Europe has changed the way in which historians understand the place of Nazism in western history. It also allows us to see more clearly, on the one hand, that the murder of the Jews was but one part of a genocidal assault on eastern Europe's population and, on the other hand, that the Nazi attitude to Jews was different from its attitude to Slavs. Only the Jews were destined to be killed *in toto*, and this throughout Europe, not just in the area of German colonial settlement.

The Holocaust can indeed be understood as a colonial genocide, even as a subaltern genocide, but that finding heightens rather than diminishes our appreciation of the particular role played by Jews in the Nazis' imaginary universe. Rather than seeing the murder of the Jews as 'just' another colonial-style massacre, the Holocaust emerges from this line of inquiry as a product of a western tradition of violence, but also as a crime that differed from colonial genocides: the latter—for all the racist elements of fantasy that accompanied them—required the elimination of peoples in the interests of acquiring land, whereas the former was a war played out in the Nazi imagination. This makes no difference philosophically: the attempt to reorder the world so that the Hereros, the Jews, or the Tutsis no longer inhabit it constitutes the same crime against the human species; but historically speaking, it allows us clearly to delineate where the comparison works and where it breaks down. Clearly, Germany's colonial culture did to some extent influence the Nazis and can no longer be ignored as part of the background to the Holocaust. The colonies provided sources for shaping German culture that unquestionably remained salient—alongside other factors, of course—in determining the way in which the idea of genocide was formulated and then carried out by the Nazi regime.

The whole debate concerning genocide, colonialism, and the Holocaust is conducted on a meta-level of historical interpretation; it is less concerned with the mechanics of the Holocaust or the responses of the victims than with the ways in which historians set about interpreting empirical evidence. In the final chapter, I will try and bring together this meta-historical discussion about change and continuity in the past with more detailed empirical work by discussing perhaps the single most important carrier of continuities and changes through time: German culture. I will show how cultural history is helping historians not just to illustrate continuities from the colonial period—as well as others—but to illuminate the world created by the perpetrators. Whether discussing the colonial background or any other history of the Holocaust, attention to the narratives the perpetrators told themselves in their attempt to reshape the world provides insights into the perpetration of the Holocaust that cannot be gleaned from institutional, political, or social history. Ultimately, in attempting to think historically about the Holocaust, we must do more than recreate its unfolding; we must try, however distasteful it may seem, to enter into the minds of those who carried it out.

6

The Holocaust
as an Expression of Nazi
Culture

At stake is nothing less than to create anew in the light of consciousness a form of existence that hitherto resided in the unconscious . . . to nurture the irrational with rational means . . . proceeding from the purest impulses of the race.

Alfred Baeumler[1]

The Holocaust and Cultural History

The historiography of the Holocaust, as we have examined it so far, is as rich and sophisticated a body of literature as exists for any other significant historical event. However, its methodological tendency towards institutional, biographical, and structural approaches means that the most traumatic aspects of the Holocaust are often ignored. This outcome is especially marked in *Täterforschung*, as I showed in Chapter 2. If, instead of structures and institutions (whether the RSHA or the *Judenräte*), we examine instead the mental lives of those living through the Holocaust (whether perpetrators or victims), how does that change our

---

1. Alfred Baeumler, Gutachten (expert opinion) of 13 December 1940, cited in Uriel Tal, *Religion, Politics and Ideology in the Third Reich: Selected Essays* (London: Routledge, 2004), p. 90.

understanding? This is a question that takes us into the realm of cultural history.

Cultural history is a way of approaching the past through examining the discourses and practices of past actors, with the hope of explaining the ways in which they gave meaning to their lives. It is less interested in the factual reconstruction of events (though, as a historical method, it of course requires empirical accuracy) than in meaning-production in the past. This emphasis on meaning leads cultural historians to embrace methods deriving from anthropology, literary theory, and intellectual history. For meaning is found primarily in narratives. Whether written or not, these may be individual or collective narratives. And by 'narratives', cultural historians do not mean fictional stories but the many ways that exist to order the world, from religion to law, and the symbolic action of rituals such as commemorations, sporting events, or festivals.

In the historical profession in general, cultural history was one of the most successful disciplinary developments of the late twentieth century. Based on the work of anthropologist Clifford Geertz and sociologist Pierre Bourdieu, among others, a focus on narratives, microhistories, rituals, and symbols in the past became a familiar approach, and was made famous by works such as Natalie Zemon Davis's *The Return of Martin Guerre* (1985) and Carlo Ginzburg's *The Cheese and the Worms* (1982). Indeed, medievalists and early modernists were especially productive in their approach to cultural history. But, as Lynn Hunt noted:

> the theoretical impetus of interpretive anthropology was lost in the crush to study cultural *topics*. Geertz had been concerned to reconstitute anthropology as a discipline based on interpretation, with a grounding in hermeneutical philosophy and literary theory. Historians who followed his lead focused instead on the cultural forms that he and other anthropologists had studied as their point of departure. Festivals, rituals, and charivaris were discovered everywhere, but for historians who studied them they seemed to constitute an end in themselves rather than an occasion for the construction of new social theoretical understandings.[2]

Indeed, cultural history has become so pervasive amongst historians that its ubiquity is its most noticeable characteristic. An exception, however, has been, until recently, the historiography of the Holocaust. Although there are a significant number of studies, especially by Israeli historians, of Jewish

---

2. Lynn Hunt, 'History Beyond Social Theory' in *The States of 'Theory': History, Art, and Critical Discourse*, ed. David Carroll (Stanford: Stanford University Press, 1990), p. 99.

culture as a historical topic (theatre in the ghetto or art in Theresienstadt, for example), as we saw in Chapter 2, they have not been devoted to rethinking social meaning in Hunt's terms.[3]

Since the 1960s and the pioneering work of George L. Mosse, Nazi culture has been a subject of interest for historians.[4] However, this early work on culture was always considered something of a self-defined topic, one that was an adornment to the more insightful political history that explained the rise and nature of Nazism. 'Culture', in this understanding, was just one facet of Nazism. And even though Mosse did a great deal to try and disabuse his colleagues of this view, his approach remained somewhat marginalized. The more recent flourishing of cultural history—which Mosse, of course, lived to see and did much to encourage—has brought change to the historiographical scene. Now Nazi culture is seen as fundamental to understanding the Third Reich, and the danger is the opposite one: not that culture is 'tacked on' to economic, social, and political studies, but that it is seen as an all-encompassing category that, by explaining everything, explains nothing. Yet, if we want to understand the Holocaust, we need to treat it as a problem of cultural history, that is, to understand the symbolic webs of meaning that the Nazis created for themselves that permitted their values to interact with longer-established German narratives in a way that made radical exclusion and, finally, genocide, a meaningful possibility.[5] Thus, what might at first glance appear to be more relevant to studying the internal structure of the Third Reich turns out on closer inspection to be inseparable from histories of the Holocaust, of both the perpetrators and their victims.

With respect to the victims too perhaps we can acquire a clearer sense of what the Holocaust did to Jewish individuals and communities if we approach it with the question of meaning production and destruction in

3. See Dan Stone, 'Holocaust Historiography and Cultural History', *Dapim*, 23 (2009), pp. 52–68 for further discussion.
4. George L. Mosse, *The Crisis of German Ideology: Intellectual Origins of the Third Reich* (London: Weidenfeld & Nicholson, 1970); Hermann Glaser, *The Cultural Roots of National Socialism* (London: Croom Helm, 1978). On Mosse, see Saul Friedländer, 'Mosse's Influence on the Historiography of the Holocaust' in *What History Tells: George L. Mosse and the Culture of Modern Europe*, eds. Stanley Payne, David Sorkin, and John Tortorice (Madison: University of Wisconsin Press, 2004), pp. 134–47, and Mosse's *Confronting History: A Memoir* (Madison: University of Wisconsin Press, 2000).
5. Alon Confino, 'A World Without Jews: Interpreting the Holocaust', *GH*, 27, 4 (2009), pp.531–59; Helmut Walser Smith, 'Anti-Semitic Violence as Reenactment: An Essay in Cultural History', *Rethinking History*, 11, 3 (2007), pp. 335–51.

mind. What many of the writings of Jews during the Holocaust reveal is precisely this desperate struggle to hold on to meaning and, for the most part, their failure. Indeed, what we see by approaching the Holocaust's victims as a problem in cultural history is a very clear sense of 'the destabilization and at times collapse of the victim's symbolic world'.[6] This approach is not just a complement to existing ways of writing the history of the Holocaust; it allows historians to deal, in a non-sensationalist way, with the trauma and horror that is overlooked in *Täterforschung* and institutional histories.

Nazi Culture

According to Claudia Koonz:

> Nazism offered all ethnic Germans, whether or not they joined the party, a comprehensive system of meaning that was transmitted through powerful symbols and renewed in communal celebrations. It told them how to differentiate between friend and enemy, true believer and heretic, non-Jew and Jew. In offering the faithful a vision of sanctified life in the Volk, it resembled a religion.[7]

There is much to consider here, but let us for the moment concentrate on Koonz's statement that Nazism 'resembled a religion'. With the end of the Cold War and the return to fashion of totalitarianism theory, one of the most influential ways of interpreting Nazism was as a 'political religion'.[8] This term, which traces its origins back to Eric Voegelin, Carl Schmitt, Raymond Aron, and Jules Monnerot, was popularized by scholars such as Emilio Gentile and Michael Burleigh in the 1990s.[9]

---

6. Amos Goldberg, 'The History of the Jews in the Ghettos: A Cultural Perspective' in *The Holocaust and Historical Methodology*, ed. Dan Stone (New York: Berghahn, forthcoming).
7. Claudia Koonz, *The Nazi Conscience* (Cambridge, MA: The Belknap Press of Harvard University Press, 2003), p. 273.
8. Hans Maier, ' "Totalitarismus" und "Politische Religionen": Konzepte des Diktaturvergleichs', *VfZ*, 43 (1995), pp. 387–405.
9. Eric Voegelin, *Die politischen Religionen* (Munich: Wilhelm Fink, 1996 [1938]); Carl Schmitt, *Political Theology: Four Chapters on the Concept of Sovereignty* (Cambridge, MA: MIT Press, 1988 [1922]); Jules Monnerot, *Sociology of Communism* (London: George Allen & Unwin, 1953); Emilio Gentile, *The Sacralization of Politics in Fascist Italy* (Cambridge, MA: Harvard University Press, 1996); Gentile, 'Political Religion: A Concept and its Critics—A Critical Survey', *Totalitarian Movements and Political Religions*, 6, 1 (2005), pp. 19–32; Gentile, *Politics as Religion* (Princeton: Princeton University Press, 2006); Michael Burleigh, *The Third Reich: A New History* (London: Macmillan, 2000).

Seeing Nazism as a 'religion' means focusing first on the same sort of texts that I described in Chapter 4 as mystical antisemitism. The writings of Jörg Lanz von Liebenfels, Guido von List, Theodor Fritsch, Artur Dinter, and Dietrich Eckart, the activities of the Thule Society, the theosophists and ariosophists all provide an 'occult' background to Nazism.[10] Claus-Ekkehard Bärsch analyses the writings of Hitler, Himmler, Goebbels, and Rosenberg in terms of 'political religion', and Klaus Vondung proposes the concept of 'apocalypse' as a broad framework for interpreting Nazism.[11] Uriel Tal's essays, in particular, have been influential here. Tal drew widely on the writings of the antisemitic research institutes, theologians, lawyers, and philosophers, and argued that 'Nazism appropriated the messianic structure of monotheism, especially of Christian monotheism, deprived it of its authentic content, reversed the meaning of the redemptive rhythm of Christianity, and went on to exploit that new pseudo-religion for its own political ends, in a most effective way.'[12] But one also needs to examine the rituals and structures of Nazi institutions. Apart from 'the transposition of the Christian idea of resurrection to a certain nation', as Philippe Burrin usefully defines political religion, the Nazis 'recycled symbols and disparate themes', including clothing, oath-taking, liturgy, architecture, and the general 'feel' of the sacred to such an extent that 'It is difficult to refrain from giving the name "religion" to the belief of Hitler and his lieutenants.'[13]

The theory of 'ersatz', 'secular', or 'political' religion has thus attracted influential followers and given rise to some thoughtful and fascinating literature. It undeniably—through its focus on ritual and the symbolic—provides many useful insights into the nature of the Third Reich and, usually by implication, the Holocaust. However, with a few exceptions, scholars have been reluctant to apply 'political religion' theory to

10. Nicholas Goodrick-Clarke, *The Occult Roots of Nazism: Secret Aryan Cults and Their Influence on Nazi Ideology* (London: I. B. Tauris, 1992); Peter Staudenmaier, 'Occultism, Race and Politics in German-Speaking Europe, 1880–1940: A Survey of the Historical Literature', *European History Quarterly*, 39, 1 (2009), pp. 47–70.
11. Claus-Ekkehard Bärsch, *Die politische Religion des Nationalsozialismus: Die religiöse Dimension der NS-Ideologie in den Schriften von Dietrich Eckart, Joseph Goebbels, Alfred Rosenberg und Adolf Hitler* (Munich: Wilhelm Fink, 1998); Klaus Vondung, *Die Apokalypse in Deutschland* (Munich: Deutscher Taschenbuch Verlag, 1988).
12. Tal, *Religion, Politics and Ideology*, p. 178. See also Philippe Lacoue-Labarthe and Jean-Luc Nancy, 'The Nazi Myth', *Critical Inquiry*, 16 (1990), pp. 291–312.
13. Philippe Burrin, 'Political Religion: The Relevance of a Concept', *History & Memory*, 9, 1/2 (1997), pp. 334, 337. In general, see the essays in Michael Ley and Julius H. Schoeps, eds., *Der Nationalsozialismus als politische Religion* (Bodenheim: Philo, 1997).

the Holocaust itself. Michael Ley, rising to his task with enthusiasm, writes:

> The extermination camps were National Socialism's holy places of worship, where the holy ritual of human sacrifice was carried out. . . . In the eyes of Hitler and his true-believing supporters, the murder of the European Jews was, in terms of salvation-theology, the necessary prerequisite for the 'thousand-year Reich'. This apocalyptic theology is the kernel of National Socialism's apocalyptic politics.[14]

Bärsch, similarly, sees the Holocaust as the logical outcome of Hitler's transformation of 'Christology' into National Socialist ideology:

> Why Auschwitz? Auschwitz is no mystery. On the basis of his political religion, Hitler had no other choice than to decide to murder the Jews. The one thing that bound and obligated all National Socialists was their political religion. National Socialists had no choice other than to accept Hitler's decision and to carry it out, or to stop being National Socialists.[15]

In this reading, the murder of the Jews does not simply follow from Nazi eschatology but is the central component of it; a Nazi who rejects the decision to kill the Jews neither understands nor can truly belong to the movement.

Hitler, then, in this interpretation, was a kind of 'magician' or 'rainmaker' whose millions of followers sought redemption in melding themselves to the collective, making the *Volk* community the site of the transcendent. In this sense, as Eric Wolf argues, 'National Socialism is better understood as a movement akin to the cargo cults and ghost dances studied by anthropologists than as a rational deployment of means to pragmatic ends.'[16]

However, there are also criticisms of the political religion concept. First of all, some historians feel that the history of ideas approach, exemplified by Ley and Bärsch, takes place 'in a timeless space, free of political

14. Michael Ley, 'Auschwitz—ein historischer Essay' in *Auschwitz: Versuche einer Annäherung*, eds. Charlotte Kohn-Ley and Michael Ley (Vienna: Verlag für Gesellschaftskritik, 1996), pp. 125–6; see also Ley, *Genozid als Heilserwartung: Zum nationalsozialistischen Mord am europäischen Judentum*, 2nd edn (Vienna: Picus, 1995); Ley, *Holokaust als Menschenopfer: Vom Christentum zur politischen Religion des Nationalsozialismus* (Münster: LIT, 2002).
15. Bärsch, *Die politische Religion*, p. 382.
16. Eric R. Wolf, *Envisioning Power: Ideologies of Dominance and Crisis* (Berkeley: University of California Press, 1999), pp. 197–8. See also Eric Voegelin, *Hitler and the Germans* (Columbia: University of Missouri Press, 1999); Dan Stone, 'Nazism as Modern Magic: Bronislaw Malinowski's Political Anthropology' in *History, Memory and Mass Atrocity: Essays on the Holocaust and Genocide* (London: Vallentine Mitchell, 2006), ch. 3.

or social structures'.[17] In other words, the analysis of 'apocalyptic' or 'redemptive' texts or rituals tends to remain at an aesthetic level and does not go far enough in terms of the production of social reality. It might overlook, for example, the fact that, early on in the movement's history, Hitler forbade criticism of established religion for fear of alienating voters. Other historians criticize the concept itself. Kevin Passmore questions the intellectual heritage of the 'political religion' notion, seeing it as bound up with sexist and elitist early theories of collective psychology.[18] Others query the use of the term 'religion'. Stanley Stowers, for example, suggests that describing Nazism as a 'political religion' not only inadvertently presupposes a notion of an 'authentic' religion—usually Christianity—from which Nazism sought to break but many of whose characteristics it borrowed. It also, more worryingly, goes some way to accepting Nazism's self-description as connecting with 'the sacred', and thus remains wedded to a romantic understanding of religion that is itself more religious than analytical.[19] Yet others follow Hannah Arendt in claiming that 'There is no substitute for God in the totalitarian ideologies', for in them 'the metaphysical place for God has remained empty'.[20]

Uriel Tal argued that 'Nazism intended to develop, groom, educate, and mould a new type of man, a man who did not need the power of the police or any other kind of *Anwendung von Zwang* ("application of coercion") to make him conform to the norms of the state or society.'[21] Thus, irrespective of whether or not this constituted a 'religious' ambition, one needs to supplement the insights of 'political religions theory' with an emphasis on how the Nazis created their world. In particular, we need to consider the role played by 'the Jew' in creating the Nazi universe and destroying the Jewish one. As Saul Friedländer puts it, 'we are hard put to identify the importance of charisma in a modern society functioning

17. Ulrike Ehret, 'Understanding the Popular Appeal of Fascism, National Socialism and Soviet Communism: The Revival of Totalitarianism Theory and Political Religion', *History Compass*, 5, 4 (2007), p. 1245.
18. Kevin Passmore, 'The Gendered Genealogy of Political Religions Theory', *Gender & History*, 20, 3 (2008), pp. 644–68.
19. Stanley Stowers, 'The Concepts of "Religion", "Political Religion" and the Study of Nazism', *JCH*, 42, 1 (2007), pp. 9–24.
20. Arendt, 'A Reply to Eric Voegelin' in *Essays in Understanding 1930–1954* (New York: Harcourt Brace, 1994), p. 406. See, for example, Neil Gregor, 'Nazism—A Political Religion? Rethinking the Voluntarist Turn' in *Nazism, War and Genocide: Essays in Honour of Jeremy Noakes*, ed. Gregor (Exeter: Exeter University Press, 2005), pp. 1–21
21. Tal, *Religion, Politics, and Ideology*, p. 2.

along the rules of instrumental rationality and bureaucratic procedures. There remains but one plausible interpretation: Modern society does remain open to—possibly in need of—the ongoing presence of religious or pseudoreligious incentives within a system otherwise dominated by thoroughly different dynamics. . . . Unavoidably the question leads us back once again to the phantasmal role played by "the Jew" in Hitler's Germany and the surrounding world.'[22]

To begin with Hitler, O. K. Werckmeister describes Hitler's self-important sense of being the 'sculptor' of Germany; for Hitler, art could become reality and the reshaping of Germany was conceived as an aesthetic project.[23] Hans Rudolf Vaget has recently argued that the Third Reich was largely driven by Hitler's aesthetic sensibility. Hitler's 'Wagnerian self-fashioning'—based on psychologically adolescent grandiose fantasies—was transposed onto the level of the nation as *Gesamtkunstwerk* (total work of art). Not only that, but Vaget argues that 'antisemitism was indeed the decisive link in the fateful metapolitical concatenation of Wagner, Bayreuth, and the ruler of the Third Reich.'[24] As Hilberg once put it, 'For Hitler everything was architecture. The war itself was an aesthetic phenomenon, the destruction of the Jews an edifice, the whole *Götterdämmerung* a controlled Wagnerian process.'[25] Combining this aesthetic fantasy with the notion of 'Hitler as philosophe' and of charismatic leadership, one has an image of 'the Führer' dramatically embodying the deepest desires of the *Volk* for rebirth and regeneration.[26] The elimination of the Jews was central to this aesthetic vision.

This 'self-fashioning' extended even to the bodies of Germans. SS men, in particular, can be understood as a 'project' for embodying the new values of the Third Reich. As Paula Diehl shows, the SS men themselves were conceived as symbolic representations of Aryan values, encompassing

22. Saul Friedländer, *The Years of Extermination: Nazi Germany and the Jews, 1939–1945* (London: HarperCollins, 2007), pp. 657, 658.
23. O. K. Werckmeister, 'Hitler the Artist', *Critical Inquiry*, 23, 2 (1997), pp. 270–97. See also Eric Michaud, *The Cult of Art in Nazi Germany* (Stanford: Stanford University Press, 2004); Frederic Spotts, *Hitler and the Power of Aesthetics* (New York: Overlook, 2003).
24. Hans Rudolf Vaget, 'Wagnerian Self-Fashioning: The Case of Adolf Hitler', *New German Critique*, 101 (2007), p. 113.
25. Cited in Robert Jan van Pelt and Carroll William Westfall, *Architectural Principles in the Age of Historicism* (New Haven: Yale University Press, 1991), p. 348.
26. Lawrence Birken, *Hitler as Philosophe: Remnants of the Enlightenment in National Socialism* (Westport: Greenwood, 1995); Philippe Lacoue-Labarthe, *Heidegger, Art and Politics: The Fiction of the Political* (Oxford: Basil Blackwell, 1990).

not only violence and power but also the racial utopia of the 'new man'.[27] The synchronized anonymity of the black–clad marching troops of the elite 'Leibstandarte-SS Adolf Hitler' unit, originally set up as Hitler's personal bodyguard, symbolized the protection of the Aryan community. The display of black leather with the death's head cross, especially, 'clothed the SS men in symbolic connotations which signaled closeness to and contempt for death, asceticism, the presence of power, and belonging to an unreachable elite'.[28] As Mosse put it, the SS was a 'bizarre, exclusive brotherhood, an odd mixture of sectarian fantasy, feudal habits, romantic German cult and modern political-economic management as well as the cold-blooded reason of the state'.[29]

Most importantly, the German *Volk* as a whole was to be fashioned anew. First, this was to be achieved on a physical basis. Boaz Neumann writes: 'National Socialism did not offer its followers ideas, but a life experience.' There was, he explains, 'no gap between the idea/ideology and practice'.[30] Nazism was not an ideology but a *Weltanschauung*, an ontological category, from which those who were a priori excluded from the *Volksgemeinschaft* had to be radically removed. The Jew or the 'other' who was conceived by the Nazis as not 'belonging to life' was excluded not because of anything he had done but because of his very existence: 'His belonging to this category was ontological: it had nothing to do with his actual and concrete being, but with his ontological state of Being, and as such no explanation or justification was necessary.'[31] In other words, the Nazis 'attempted to construct a German society based on a new subjective consciousness',[32] one in which there was no distinction between 'conventional' and 'moral'

27. Paula Diehl, *Macht-Mythos-Utopie: Die Körperbilder der SS-Männer* (Berlin: Akademie Verlag, 2005), p. 232.
28. Diehl, *Macht-Mythos-Utopie*, p. 233. Cf. Daniel Wildmann, *Begehrte Körper. Konstruktion und Inszenierung des 'arischen' Männerkörpers im 'Dritten Reich'* (Würzburg: Königshausen & Neumann, 1998).
29. Cited in Peter Reichel, 'Festival and Cult: Masculine and Militaristic Mechanisms of National Socialism' in *Shaping the Superman: Fascist Body as Political Icon—Aryan Fascism*, ed. J. A. Mangan (London: Frank Cass, 1999), p. 166.
30. Boaz Neumann, 'The National Socialist Politics of Life', *New German Critique*, 85 (2002), p. 109.
31. Neumann, 'The National Socialist Politics of Life', p. 124; see also Andreas Musolff, 'What Role do Metaphors Play in Racial Prejudice? The Function of Antisemitic Imagery in Hitler's *Mein Kampf*', *Patterns of Prejudice*, 41, 1 (2007), pp. 21–43.
32. Alon Confino, 'Death, Spiritual Solace, and Afterlife: Between Nazism and Religion' in *Between Mass Death and Individual Loss: The Place of the Dead in Twentieth-Century Germany*, eds. Confino, Paul Betts, and Dirk Schumann (New York: Berghahn, 2008), p. 220.

norms, so that every sphere of life was 'moralized'.[33] The Third Reich was not an 'amoral' society or regime, as postwar accounts such as Friedrich Meinecke's *The German Catastrophe* (1946) charged; rather, the success of the Nazi *Weltanschauung* in attracting supporters, according to Raphael Gross, was that it intimately joined morality to religion.[34]

How was this reshaping to be achieved? In every sphere of life, from architecture to schooling, from the symbols surrounding factory workers to the maps produced by German geographers, the Nazi world view permeated everyday consciousness. Young people were trained not just in Nazi ideology but to bear themselves as—*to be*—Nazis. The creation of a pantheon of Nazi 'heroes' helped to inculcate these values and literally to re-constitute people as Nazis. Peter Lambert notes that 'Nazi cults of heroism appear to have worked best when they were constructed exclusively by and for the Nazis' own elites', such as Holocaust perpetrators, where they confirmed the claim that their acts were 'objectively heroic'; yet the Nazis worked hard to persuade the population at large to share its propaganda.[35] Even in the realm of popular culture, Nazism penetrated daily life. Popular renditions of the story of the SA 'martyr' Horst Wessel, for example, resemble nothing so much as saints' lives, thus indicating how Nazi 'political religion' was constructed 'from below'.[36]

Nazi schooling brought race theory into every sphere of education. Famous children's books such as *Der Giftpilz* (The Poisonous Mushroom) and *Der Pudelmopsdackelpinscher* (The Poodlepugdachshundpinscher) are only the tip of an enormous iceberg. From mathematics to geography, the school curriculum was Nazified.[37] Girls in the *Bund Deutscher Mädel*

33. Raphael Gross, ' "Treue" im Nationalsozialismus: Ein Beitrag zur Moralgeschichte der NS-Zeit' in *Treue: Politische Loyalität und militärische Gefolgschaft in der Moderne*, eds. Nikolaus Buschmann and Karl Borromäus Murr (Göttingen: Vandenhoeck & Ruprecht, 2008), p. 262.
34. Raphael Gross, 'Gott und Religion in der Ethik des Nationalsozialismus' in *Nachleben der Religionen: Kulturwissenschaftliche Untersuchungen zur Dialektik der Säkularisierung*, eds. Martin Treml and Daniel Weidner (Munich: Wilhelm Fink, 2007), pp. 177–87; Werner Konitzer, 'Antisemitismus und Moral: Einige Überlegungen', *Mittelweg 36*, 14, 2 (2005), pp. 24–35.
35. Peter Lambert, 'Heroisation and Demonisation in the Third Reich: The Consensus-Building Value of a Nazi Pantheon of Heroes', *Totalitarian Movements and Political Religions*, 8, 3 (2007), p. 542. On propaganda, see David Welch, *The Third Reich: Politics and Propaganda* (London: Routledge, 1993).
36. Heiko Luckey, 'Believers Writing for Believers: Traces of Political Religion in National Socialist Pulp Fiction', *Totalitarian Movements and Political Religions*, 8, 1 (2007), pp. 77–92.
37. Gregory Paul Wegner, *Anti-Semitism and Schooling under the Third Reich* (New York: RoutledgeFalmer, 2002); Gilmer W. Blackburn, *Education in the Third Reich: Race and History in Nazi Textbooks* (Albany: SUNY Press, 1985); Änne Bäumer-Schleinkofer, *Nazi Biology*

(League of German Maidens) were imbued with the Nazi *Weltanschauung*, as were boys in the Hitler Youth.[38] Nazi poets such as Josef Magnus Wehner and Hans Zöberlein glorified the 'German revolution' through their own 'revolution' in culture.[39] Factory workers internalized Nazi symbols, at the same time as they superimposed them onto existing everyday practices.[40] German mapping incorporated Nazi views of national self-determination and racial distribution in Europe to justify territorial expansion and the elimination of the 'superfluous'.[41] Nazi landscape and architecture, for example, at the Nazi party rally grounds in Nuremberg, sought to give the *Weltanschauung* material embodiment. The massive size of the marching grounds were 'supposed to generate emotions of *Begeisterung* and *Faszination*—a heady mix of enthusiasm, awe, fascination and excitement', in other words, a sense of taking part in a sacred, yet at the same time earthly movement.[42] Nazi film and theatre was a key site for spreading the message.[43] And whilst it is true that 'the class structure in Germany was not essentially changed' and that the Nazi regime 'was not entirely successful in achieving its aims to homogenize society and to create consensus for its rule',[44] nevertheless the scale of their success in the mere six years before the outbreak of war is remarkable.

As Lothar Kroll shows, the Nazi regime even gave the concept of history a new meaning. Hitler believed that the year 1933 was 'nothing other

and Schools (Frankfurt/M: Peter Lang, 1995); Marjorie Lamberti, 'German Schoolteachers, National Socialism and the Politics of Culture at the End of the Weimar Republic', *CEH*, 34, 1 (2001), pp. 53–82.

38. Lisa Pine, 'Creating Conformity: The Training of Girls in the *Bund Deutscher Mädel*', *European History Quarterly*, 33, 3 (2003), pp. 367–85; Michael H. Kater, *The Hitler Youth* (Cambridge, MA: Harvard University Press, 2004).
39. Jay W. Baird, *Hitler's War Poets: Literature and Politics in the Third Reich* (Cambridge: Cambridge University Press, 2008).
40. Alf Lüdtke, 'German Work and German Workers: The Impact of Symbols on the Exclusion of Jews in Nazi-Germany' in *Probing the Depths of German Antisemitism: German Society and the Persecution of the Jews, 1933–1941*, ed. David Bankier (Jerusalem: Yad Vashem, 2000), pp. 298–311.
41. Guntram Henrik Herb, *Under the Map of Germany: Nationalism and Propaganda 1918–1945* (London: Routledge, 1997).
42. Sharon Macdonald, 'Words in Stone? Agency and Identity in a Nazi Landscape', *Journal of Material Culture*, 11, 1/2 (2006), pp. 105–26, here p. 111. See also Paul B. Jaskot, *The Architecture of Oppression: The SS, Forced Labor and the Nazi Monumental Building Economy* (London: Routledge, 2000).
43. Peter Reichel, *Erfundene Erinnerung: Weltkrieg und Judenmord in Film und Theater* (Frankfurt/M: Suhrkamp Taschenbuch Verlag, 2007).
44. Lisa Pine, *Hitler's 'National Community': Society and Culture in Nazi Germany* (London: Hodder Arnold, 2007), p. 27.

than the restoration of a millennial age'.[45] The Nazis saw the coming of their 'revolution' as a *Zeitenwende* of world-historical proportions, thus lending their actions the sense of being fated and inevitable. In overcoming the 15 years of the *Systemzeit*, the 150 years of the dominance of the bourgeoisie, and the 1,500 years of Christian hegemony, Hitler's diagnosis of the present simultaneously carried a historical narrative that presented the rise of Nazism as historically unique, and his coming to power as the dawn of a new epoch.[46] Kroll goes as far as to say that 'Hitler's antisemitism only took on its fatal political effect as a theory of history, that is to say, when wrapped in a far-reaching and all-encompassing fiction of the whole course of historical becoming and historical development.'[47] Certainly historians in Nazi Germany lent their support to the regime, and the 'majority also lent support to exterminationist antisemitism'.[48]

What all the historical research into these various areas of life in Nazi Germany shows is that the Nazis intended not just to change the nature of society but fundamentally to remould the 'people's body'. The term *Volkskörper* has often been understood metaphorically as a Nazi synonym for the nation or the race. But, as Boaz Neumann shows, the Nazis meant it literally; since it is clear that the *Fremdkörper* (foreign body) was treated anything but metaphorically, it makes little sense to see its antithesis, the organic people's body, only in symbolic terms. For them, 'it was the *Volkskörper*, and not individual bodies, which formed the corporeal ontology in the Nazi Weltanschauung, that by which both "worthy" and "unworthy" individual bodies were defined and by which policies of cultivation and enhancement, on the one hand, or neglect, removal, and extermination, on the other, were determined.'[49] Neumann insightfully indicates why the work on Nazi culture is so essential to understanding the Holocaust: not just because the Nazis thought that Jews threatened German society and culture but because they literally poisoned and diseased the people's body, like a cancer. The two things—people's body and Jewish

45. Lothar Kroll, *Utopie als Ideologie: Geschichtsdenken und politisches Handeln im Dritten Reich*, 2nd ed. (Paderborn: Schöningh, 1999), p. 33.
46. Kroll, *Utopie als Ideologie*, p. 40.   47. Kroll, *Utopie als Ideologie*, p. 50.
48. Willi Oberkrome, 'German Historical Scholarship under National Socialism' in *Nazi Germany and the Humanities*, eds. Wolfgang Bialas and Anson Rabinbach (Oxford: Oneworld, 2007), pp. 210–1. See also Joachim Lerchenmueller, 'Die "SD-mäßige" Bearbeitung der Geschichtswissenschaft' in *Nachrichtendienst, politische Elite und Mordeinheit: Der Sicherheitsdienst des Reichsführers SS*, ed. Michael Wildt (Hamburg: Hamburger Edition, 2003), pp. 160–89.
49. Boaz Neumann, 'The Phenomenology of the German People's Body (*Volkskörper*) and the Extermination of the Jewish Body', *New German Critique*, 106 (2009), p. 150.

body—cannot be understood separately from each other. In other words, 'the Jewish body was an essential element in Nazi body politics, as well as being essential for a politics of the body in relation to the other. The *Volkskörper* could not (co)exist with the Jewish body.'[50] Neumann thus provides an analysis of the *Volkskörper* that helps to explain the violence of the Nazi attack on the Jews, and shows why the Holocaust is not simply the end of a continuum that begins with the harassment or street violence that is commonly associated with racial hatred:

> That mission was born of the fervent conviction that the Jews were actually losing their otherness, that they were capable of penetrating the *Volkskörper*, which, in fact, they were doing. As long as the Jews were seen as other, they remained the object of traditional attacks. Once they began to lose their alienness, they emerged as an existential threat to the *Volkskörper*.[51]

Auschwitz, then, the *anus mundi*, was the place 'where the Jewish body, the ultimate *Fremdkörper*, was flushed out of the *Volkskörper*'.[52]

The Nazis' *Weltanschauung* penetrated all areas of life in Germany. After years of historical scholarship that stressed terror, coercion, and propaganda, the historiography now indicates that the majority of the population enthusiastically embraced Nazism. This claim must not be exaggerated, for many areas of life—such as class and local relationships—remained relatively stable. Yet the Nazis' success lay precisely in overlaying their radical philosophy of history onto existing narratives. Nazism gave a new meaning to German society and culture, but this meaning did not come from nowhere; rather, it corresponded to the desires and fears of large swathes of the population concerning national glory, racial degeneration, international conspiracies against Germany, and community revival. These narratives are inseparable from antisemitism and the murder of the Jews. Nowhere is this mix of old and new more apparent—and more shocking—than in the example of the Churches in the Third Reich.

The historiography of the Churches in the Third Reich—and the responses of churches outside Germany to Nazism and the Holocaust—constitutes an enormous body of literature. It dates back to the very origins of Nazism and, during the 1930s and 1940s, the position of the Churches in Nazi Germany was one of the most discussed questions in the

---

50. Neumann, 'Phenomenology', p. 170.   51. Neumann, 'Phenomenology', p. 174.
52. Neumann, 'Phenomenology', p. 178. In light of Neumann's brilliant article, it is worth revisiting Terence Des Pres' classic essay, 'Excremental Assault' in his *The Survivor: An Anatomy of Life in the Death Camps* (New York: Oxford University Press, 1976), pp. 51–71.

scholarly and popular literature. Here I cannot give an overview of that
historiography,[53] but want to indicate how recent work on the Churches
and the Holocaust intersects with the historiography of Nazi culture and
the dominance or otherwise of Nazi narratives in the Third Reich. Of
course, the roles played by the Churches in the Holocaust—whether in
terms of omission or commission—are hotly disputed, and I will also
not ignore such questions. But there is room here neither for detailed
institutional histories nor for considering the (unseemly) debate about
which confession, Protestant or Catholic, was 'worse'.

That Christians were heavily influenced by Nazism is now indisputable,
however much postwar historians and Christians sought to deny any
such links. Whilst the Nazis undeniably made some attempts to limit the
influence of the Churches—holding Hitler Youth meetings on Sunday
mornings, for example—they also accommodated them to a great extent,
whether out of cynicism or genuine faith. And whilst most histories of the
Churches under Nazism stop before World War II, Doris Bergen points
out that 'it was precisely in the war years that the partnership between
Christianity and National Socialism achieved its firmest form. . . . The
Churches were useful—indeed, indispensable, in wartime, and examination
of the archival record suggests that this was as true for the Catholic as the
Protestant Church, both of which remained loyal pillars of support.'[54]

Numerous standard works now show the extent to which the Protestant denominations coordinated themselves with the requirements of the
regime.[55] Bergen's work on the German Christians shows how deeply
the affinities between Nazism and Protestantism went, as does Susannah
Heschel's recent study of the Institute for the Study and Eradication of

---

53. See Robert P. Ericksen and Susannah Heschel, 'The German Churches and the Holocaust'
    in *HH*, pp. 296–318 for an excellent guide.
54. Doris L. Bergen, 'Nazism and Christianity: Partners and Rivals? A Response to Richard
    Steigmann-Gall, *The Holy Reich: Nazi Conceptions of Christianity, 1919–1945*', *JCH*, 42,
    1 (2007), pp. 31–2. See Robert P. Ericksen and Susannah Heschel, eds., *Betrayal: German
    Churches and the Holocaust* (Minneapolis: Augsburg Fortress, 1999) and Kevin P. Spicer, ed.,
    Antisemitism, Christian Ambivalence and the Holocaust (Bloomington: Indiana University Press,
    2007) for general surveys.
55. For example: Clemens Vollnhals, *Evangelische Kirche und Entnazifizierung, 1945–1949: Die Last
    der nationalsozialistischen Vergangenheit* (Munich: R. Oldenbourg, 1989); Wolfgang Gerlach,
    And the Witnesses Were Silent: The Confessing Church and the Persecution of the Jews (Lincoln:
    University of Nebraska Press, 2000); Manfred Gailus, *Protestantismus und Nationalsozialis-
    mus: Studien zur nationalsozialistischen Durchdringung des protestantischen Sozialmilieus in Berlin*
    (Cologne: Böhlau, 2001); Gailus, *Kirchliche Amtshilfe: Die Kirche und die Judenverfolgung im
    'Dritten Reich'* (Göttingen: Vandenhoeck & Ruprecht, 2008).

Jewish Influence on German Religious Life, established in 1939 with the aim of proving and popularizing the notion of the 'Aryan Jesus'.[56] More local studies have begun appearing, as well as studies of the Nazification of clergy and pastors.[57] Catholicism too has come in for something of a battering in recent years, with the publication of books with titles like *Hitler's Pope* or *The Popes Against the Jews*.[58] Debates about the role played by Pius XII, the Vatican or the Catholic Church more broadly have been mired in controversy, and sensitive Vatican archives are still not yet open to all historians.[59] Saul Friedländer is scandalized that Pius XII remained silent about the deportations, even when they were taking place in Rome, but points out that many Jews were aided by Catholics and found hiding places throughout Italy (and beyond), even in the Vatican itself.[60] These goings-on must have been known about and tolerated by the Pope.[61] Yet it seems that Pius XII was more frightened of communism than he was of Nazism, and thus whatever he thought or said in private, 'would abstain from any step that would harm Germany'.[62] Little has yet been written about the Orthodox Churches' role during the Holocaust, however, and

56. Doris L. Bergen, *Twisted Cross: The German Christian Movement in the Third Reich* (Chapel Hill: University of North Carolina Press, 1996); Susannah Heschel, *The Aryan Jesus: Christian Theologians and the Bible in Nazi Germany* (Princeton: Princeton University Press, 2008).

57. Birgit Gregor, 'Zum protestantischen Antisemitismus: Evangelische Kirchen und Theologen in der Zeit des Nationalsozialismus' in '*Beseitigung des jüdischen Einflusses . . .' Antisemitische Forschung, Eliten und Karrieren im Nationalsozialismus*, ed. Fritz Bauer Institut (Frankfurt/M: Campus, 1999), pp. 171–200; Manfred Gailus, 'Overwhelmed By Their Own Fascination with the "Ideas of 1933": Berlin's Protestant Social Milieu in the Third Reich', *GH*, 20, 4 (2002), pp. 462–93; Christopher Probst, ' "An Incessant Army of Demons": Wolf Meyer-Erlach, Luther, and "the Jews" in Nazi Germany', *HGS*, 23, 3 (2009), pp. 441–60.

58. John Cornwell, *Hitler's Pope: The Secret History of Pius XII* (London: Viking, 1999); David Kertzer, *The Popes Against the Jews: The Vatican's Role in the Rise of Modern Antisemitism* (New York: Knopf, 2001).

59. Compare Pierre Blet, *Pius XII and the Second World War: According to the Archives of the Vatican* (New York: Paulist Press, 1999) with Robert S. Wistrich, 'The Vatican Documents and the Holocaust: A Personal Report', *Polin: Studies in Polish Jewry*, 15 (2002), pp. 413–43. See also Menachem Shelah, 'The Catholic Church in Croatia, the Vatican and the Murder of the Croatian Jews', *HGS*, 4, 3 (1989), pp. 323–39.

60. Friedländer, *The Years of Extermination*, pp. 561–74.

61. Susan Zuccotti, *Under His Very Windows: The Vatican and the Holocaust in Italy* (New Haven: Yale University Press, 2000), pp. 307–8.

62. Friedländer, *The Years of Extermination*, p. 568; see also Michael Phayer, *The Catholic Church and the Holocaust, 1930–1965* (Bloomington: Indiana University Press, 2000); Carol Rittner and John K. Roth, *Pius XII and the Holocaust* (Leicester: Leicester University Press, 2002); Beth A. Griech-Polelle, *Bishop von Galen: German Catholicism and National Socialism* (New Haven: Yale University Press, 2002); Kevin P. Spicer, *Resisting the Third Reich: The Catholic Clergy in Hitler's Berlin* (DeKalb: Northern Illinois University Press, 2004); Suzanne Brown-Fleming, *The Holocaust and Catholic Conscience: Cardinal Aloisius Muench and the Guilt Question in Germany* (Notre Dame: University of Notre Dame Press, 2005).

this is a key desideratum if real comparative conclusions are to be drawn.[63] Given the general silence of the Churches, in particular of their leaderships, with respect to the persecution and murder of the Jews, it should be no surprise that ordinary Germans were able to find ways in their daily lives to mix their Christianity and their support for the Nazi regime.

Julius Schoeps writes: 'Not only was the majority of the population taken in by Nazism's merging of politics and religion, but so, significantly, were numerous Christian theologians.'[64] Indeed, the troubling question of the Churches' relationship with Nazism is exacerbated when one considers the claim—taking political religion theory to its logical conclusion—that Nazism was itself a religion. Instead of starting with the question of how Nazified Christians became, this way of proceeding begins by asking how Christian the Nazis were. Those who have asked this question argue that the Third Reich was not just structured like a religion, it was fundamentally religious. David Redles describes 'Hitler's millennial Reich', and argues that the Holocaust was the necessary result of Nazi eschatology.[65] And Richard Steigmann-Gall has courted controversy with his claim that Nazism was not antithetical to Christianity, but that many Nazis wanted to create a Nazified form of Protestantism.[66] Furthermore, we still know very little about how religion affected the behaviour of Holocaust perpetrators. Military chaplains in the Wehrmacht perpetuated the connection between faith and fatherland, there were theologians among the *Einsatzgruppen*, and many leading Nazis, such as camp commandants Rudolf Hoess and Franz Stangl, had important links to the Catholic Church.[67] The problematic

---

63. George Margaritis, 'The Greek Orthodox Church and the Holocaust', online at http://hcc.haifa.ac.il/Departments/greece/events/holocaust_greece/margaritis.pdf (accessed 25 August 2009).

64. Julius H. Schoeps, 'Erlösungswahn und Vernichtungswille: Die sogennante "Endlösung der Judenfrage" als Vision und Programm des Nationalsozialismus' in *Der Nationalsozialismus als politische Religion*, eds. Ley and Schoeps, p. 266.

65. David Redles, *Hitler's Millennial Reich: Apocalyptic Belief and the Search for Salvation* (New York: New York University Press, 2005).

66. Richard Steigmann-Gall, *The Holy Reich: Nazi Conceptions of Christianity 1919–1945* (Cambridge: Cambridge University Press, 2003); see *JCH*, 42, 1 (2007), which is partly devoted to this book, which, despite not being quite as novel as Steigmann-Gall claims, nevertheless demands serious engagement.

67. Bergen, 'Nazism and Christianity', p. 32. See also Bergen, ed., *The Sword of the Lord: Military Chaplains from the First to the Twenty-First Century* (Notre Dame: University of Notre Dame Press, 2004); Bergen, 'Religion and Genocide: A Historiographical Survey' in *HG*, pp. 194–227 for an important comparative essay; and the essays by Ericksen, Heschel, Griech-Polelle, and Bergen in Omer Bartov and Phyllis Mack, eds., *In God's Name: Genocide and Religion in the Twentieth Century* (New York: Berghahn, 2001).

case of Kurt Gerstein exemplifies the dilemma of a perpetrator with a Christian conscience.[68] All in all, one is forced to conclude, with Bergen, that 'it would be hard to deny that many Nazis, élite and rank-and-file, regarded themselves as good Christians and continued to do so throughout the Third Reich.'[69] But did their Christianity motivate them to kill Jews? This is an assumption that is regularly made about the 'primitive' or 'superstitious' Ukrainians or Belorussians; could it not also be true for Germans, over 95% of whom were still paid-up church members in 1939? In order to help answer that question, one needs to consider the creation of the *Volksgemeinschaft*, and examine the ways in which Nazism constituted both a break and a continuity with the past. The radical reconstruction of morality, consciousness, and race was superimposed on established mores and norms so that popular support could be based simultaneously on the feeling of taking part in revolution and on protecting cherished Germanic values.

Antisemitism and the Creation of the *Volksgemeinschaft*

Historians have written many studies on the development of Nazi anti-semitism after 1933.[70] The Nazis enacted a slew of laws and decrees that progressively immiserated and excluded the Jews, culminating in the onset of violence against them in the Kristallnacht pogrom of 9–10 November 1938. At the same time that what we might call 'classical intentionalism' has disappeared, historians are increasingly confident in placing the anti-Jewish action and legislation of the pre-1938 period in a causal relationship with the Holocaust. This does not mean, as in an older historiography, seeing the years 1933–38 as a process of 'necessary dehumanization' that prepared the way for murder—few historians now believe in the existence

68. Saul Friedländer, *Counterfeit Nazi: The Ambiguity of Good* (London: Weidenfeld & Nicolson, 1969).
69. Bergen, 'Nazism and Christianity', p. 28.
70. Notably: Eberhard Jäckel, *Hitler's World View: A Blueprint for Power* (Cambridge, MA: Harvard University Press, 1981); Hermann Graml, *Antisemitism in the Third Reich* (Oxford: Blackwell, 1992); Bankier, ed., *Probing the Depths of German Antisemitism*; Robert Gellately, *Backing Hitler: Consent and Coercion in Nazi Germany* (Oxford: Oxford University Press, 2001); Philippe Burrin, *Nazi Anti-Semitism: From Prejudice to the Holocaust* (New York: The New Press, 2005); Saul Friedländer, *Nazi Germany and the Jews: The Years of Persecution, 1933–39* (London: Weidenfeld & Nicolson, 1997).

of a preconceived plan to kill the Jews of Europe, as we have already seen. Besides, in typical Nazi style, petty legislation such as prohibiting German Jews from owning pets was still being announced even after the death camps had begun operating. Rather, historians now see these years as telling us something about the inner logic of Nazism, so that, whilst there was no concrete plan for genocide, a genocidal fantasy was present from the start. Thus, Kershaw, not noted for departing from the empirical evidence, writes: 'In the anti-Jewish climate in Germany around the time of the Reichskristallnacht pogrom of November 9–10, 1938—a climate more menacing than ever before—"marks of a genocidal mentality" were in clear evidence in the Nazi leadership.'[71] Indeed, examining pre-1933 Nazi texts, one can easily argue that this genocidal mentality was there from the very beginning of the movement. From the first programme of the newly founded NSDAP, Jews were explicitly to be deprived of their citizenship. The apocalyptic frame of mind is neatly summed up in Alfred Rosenberg's obsessional anti-Jewish writings of the 1920s, and in this passage in which the all-or-nothing nature of Nazism is clearly expressed: 'the leaders of National Socialism have unequivocally let it be understood that they would either help the new idea of state to victory, in spite of all opposition and necessary disappointments, or, if necessary, perish with the entire German people'.[72]

Furthermore, various recent studies show the significance of persecution to everyday life in Nazi Germany. In the early 1990s, following German unification, fears abounded that the increasing interest in *Alltagsgeschichte* (the history of everyday life) would lead German historians to focus on aspects of life that were 'normal' and hence to overlook antisemitism and other forms of Nazi persecution.[73] In fact, what has happened is that studies have revealed in ever greater depth the extent to which a racialized world view permeated all aspects of society. Going hand in hand, we now have detailed accounts of the deliberate pauperization and persecution of Jews in the German provinces as well as extensive evidence for the rapidity and enthusiasm with which most Germans made Nazi race theories part of

71. Ian Kershaw, 'Hitler's Role in the Final Solution', *YVS*, 34 (2006), p. 29.
72. Alfred Rosenberg, 'The Folkish Idea of State' in *Nazi Ideology Before 1933: A Documentation*, eds. Barbara Miller Lane and Leila J. Rupp (Manchester: Manchester University Press, 1978), p. 69.
73. For example, Karl Heinz Roth, 'Revisionist Tendencies in Historical Scholarship into German Fascism', *International Review of Social History*, 39, 3 (1994), pp. 429–55.

their everyday lives.[74] In other words, the historiography shows the rapid creation of communities of radical inclusion and exclusion. In Michael Wildt's terms, the *Volksgemeinschaft* was a form of 'self-empowerment'; the flip side of the creation of the 'people's community' was the necessity of excluding those who were not *Volksgenossen*, or 'racial comrades'. 'What is often overlooked', writes Harald Welzer, confirming Raphael Gross's argument, 'is that, while the wrongs of the "Third Reich" primarily targeted the "them" groups such as the Jews, Sinti and Roma, the opposition, the disabled and others, traditional concepts of morality and law continued to be in force for the members of the national community.'[75]

As the sociologist Franz Janka shows, the *Volksgemeinschaft* was a kind of 'permanent staging' (*permanente Inszenierung*), something that had to be continually realized rather than something that could be found ready made. He cites Melita Maschmann's words as typical: 'No slogan fascinated me so much as that of the *Volksgemeinschaft*. . . . What bound me to this fantastical ideal was the hope that it could bring about a state of affairs in which people of all strata could live together like brothers and sisters.'[76] In other words, the facts were less important (and we should note that Maschmann's dream of social equality was certainly never realized under Nazism[77]) than the fantasy of a life in common. Realizing the dream required total commitment, as demonstrated through the work camps, where Germans of all social backgrounds would become simply members of the *Volk*. And hence the significance of the Nazi celebrations such as the *Tag des Machtantritts* (Day of Accession to Power) celebrated on 30 January each year, or the *Heldentag* (Heroes' Day), celebrated in March, which commemorated the fallen of the Great War and the 'martyrs' of the National Socialist movement. May Day was reformulated as the *Fest der*

74. Wolf Gruner, 'Poverty and Persecution: The Reichsvereinigung, the Jewish Population, and Anti-Jewish Policy in the Nazi State, 1939–1945', *YVS*, 27 (1999), pp. 23–60; Klaus Hesse and Philippe Springer, *Vor aller Augen: Fotodokumente des nationalsozialistischen Terrors in der Provinz* (Essen: Klartext, 2002); Birthe Kundrus and Beate Meyer, eds., *Deportation der Juden aus Deutschland: Pläne, Praxis, Reaktionen 1938–1945* (Göttingen: Wallstein, 2004).
75. Harald Welzer, 'On Killing and Morality: How Normal People Become Mass Murderers' in *Ordinary People as Mass Murderers: Perpetrators in Comparative Perspective*, eds. Olaf Jensen and Claus-Christian Szejnmann (Basingstoke: Palgrave Macmillan, 2008), p. 169.
76. Melita Maschmann, *Fazit: Mein Weg in die Hitler-Jugend* (Munich: Deutscher Taschenbuch Verlag, 1981), cited in Franz Janka, *Die braune Gesellschaft: Ein Volk wird formatiert* (Stuttgart: Quell, 1997), p. 364.
77. Frank Bajohr and Michael Wildt, 'Einleitung' in *Volksgemeinschaft: Neue Forschungen zur Gesellschaft des Nationalsozialismus*, eds. Bajohr and Wildt (Frankfurt/M: Fischer Taschenbuch Verlag, 2009), pp. 7–23.

Volksgemeinschaft, no longer a celebration of the workers' movement but of the community as a whole, and Mothers' Day in May was used to inculcate the value of motherhood in the new Reich. Above all, the *Reichsparteitag*, held at Nuremberg every year, reveals the Nazis' goals.[78] Janka notes that the *Volksgemeinschaft* needed these large-scale stagings and use of symbols because it was 'a society which owed its existence not to the guidance of reason but to an emotional coming together'.[79]

In other words, Nazism cannot be understood solely as a problem in political or social history but needs to be analysed as a problem in culture too, if its popular success is to be understood. Through symbols such as the uniforms, songs, the swastika, 'fire', 'blood', and the flags (especially the *Blutfahne*, or 'blood flag'), the merging of the individual with the whole becomes more comprehensible. The *Volksgemeinschaft* was the Nazi version of the permanent revolution, an endless process of 'becoming the Volk'. The more the process was realized, the more alternative conceptions of ways of living became marginalized.[80] Especially the martial aspects of the *Volksgemeinschaft*—the *Schicksalsgemeinschaft* (community of fate)—required the elimination of those who stood in the way of the vision. Hence 'The concentration camps and the Second World War were in no way "slip-ups", accidents, or the monstrous products of a few madmen. The bestiality and the horror were a product of this social organization named the *Volksgemeinschaft*, and these measures were required as a result of its pretension to totality.' The creation of the 'permanent staging' required the permanent struggle against the enemy.[81] Indeed, the war marks not a departure from the symbols of the *Volksgemeinschaft*—blood, convictions, struggle, work—but their high point.[82] So too, the Holocaust is part of this history: 'The annihilation of the Jews and ruthless war against others were inseparably bound to this social formation; this holds true not only from today's retrospective viewpoint but was already inherent in an organization based on *völkisch* thinking, which drew a decisive dividing line between the self and the other.'[83] Or, as Helmut Walser Smith has recently put it: 'German anti-Semitism became a still deeper structuring force when paired with the construction of community.'[84] Nazi ideology

78. Janka, *Die braune Gesellschaft*, pp. 370–3.   79. Janka, *Die braune Gesellschaft*, pp. 394–5.
80. Janka, *Die braune Gesellschaft*, pp. 395–401.   81. Janka, *Die braune Gesellschaft*, p. 407.
82. Janka, *Die braune Gesellschaft*, p. 417.   83. Janka, *Die braune Gesellschaft*, p. 420.
84. Helmut Walser Smith, *The Continuities of German History: Nation, Religion, and Race across the Long Nineteenth Century* (Cambridge: Cambridge University Press, 2008), p. 220. See also

was successful not only because it marked a break with what had gone before but also because it tapped into long-held common assumptions of German culture.

Nowhere is this argument about the creation of the *Volksgemeinschaft* more clearly illustrated than in the historiography of Kristallnacht (a term, incidentally, invented not by the Nazis themselves but by Berliners ironically commenting on Nazi actions). Historians have in recent years debated the roles played by Goebbels, Goering, Himmler, Heydrich, and Hitler, often concluding that Goering was less opposed to the pogrom than was earlier believed and that the SS were more deeply involved than had been realized. One historian argues, on the basis of hints in Goebbels' diaries, that Hitler was the real instigator of the nationwide attack on the Jews on 9–10 November 1938.[85] But more revealing than debates about the chain of command—which tell us something about power politics in the heart of the Third Reich, but not much else—are studies of the events of Kristallnacht throughout the German provinces.[86] These demonstrate that the pogrom was a complex event (or better, set of events), especially where its onset is concerned. Wolfgang Benz gives details of local citizens engaging in acts of violence and destruction, noting that Kristallnacht was characterized by a 'release of energy' that permitted participants 'to indulge in sadistic, infantile, sexist, aggressive behaviour'. Benz gives as examples Treuchtlingen (Middle Franconia), where a striking number of women were involved in inciting and carrying out violent attacks on Jews and their property; and Rimbach (Odenwald), where a group of local NSDAP members physically abused a Jewish family and then burned down their

Avraham Barkai, 'The German *Volksgemeinschaft* from the Persecution of the Jews to the "Final Solution" ' in *Confronting the Nazi Past: New Debates on Modern German History*, ed. Michael Burleigh (London: Collins & Brown, 1986), pp. 84–97.

85. Angela Hermann, 'Hitler und sein Stoßtrupp in der "Reichskristallnacht" ', *VfZ*, 56, 4 (2008), pp. 603–19. Cf. Stefan Kley, 'Hitler and the Pogrom of November 9–10, 1938', *YVS*, 28 (2000), pp. 87–112.

86. For example, Bastian Fleermann and Angela Genger, eds., *Novemberpogrom 1938 in Düsseldorf* (Essen: Klartext, 2008); Ben Barkow, Raphael Gross, and Michael Lenarz, eds., *Novemberpogrom 1938: Augenzeugenberichte der Wiener Library, London* (Frankfurt/M: Jüdischer Verlag im Suhrkamp Verlag, 2008). A particularly fascinating example is Herbert Ruland, ' "Die Tatsache scheint zu erschrecken, daß so etwas in Aachen möglich ist": Unbekannte Fotografien vom Morgen nach der Pogromnacht' in *Bürokratien: Initiative und Effizienz*, eds. Wolf Gruner and Armin Nolzen (Berlin: Assoziation A, 2001), pp. 211–22, which discusses photographs of the aftermath of Kristallnacht in Aachen. There are many other similar publications covering the German regions. In general, see Martin Gilbert, *Kristallnacht: Prelude to Destruction* (London: HarperCollins, 2006) and, now, Alan E. Steinweis, *Kristallnacht 1938* (Cambridge, MA: The Belknap Press of Harvard University Press, 2009).

house.[87] In the light of the evidence, Benz concludes that there was 'an alarming degree of consensus and cooperation among local inhabitants'.[88]

According to Wolf-Arno Kropat, anti-Jewish demonstrations were already taking place in Kassel and other places in northern Hesse on the night of 7–8 November, before spreading to other parts of Hesse and then to the country at large. The question is whether these initial attacks were the work of radical local antisemites or whether they were ordered from on high. In other words, the question of whether Goebbels acted spontaneously and alone is key, not only in terms of his interaction with the other Nazi leaders but, as with later decision-making processes, in the sense of centre–periphery relations.[89] What seems most likely is that Kristallnacht was not Goebbels' spontaneous reaction to the murder in Paris of the Nazi diplomat Ernst vom Rath by the Polish Jew Herschel Grynszpan; rather, the murder—turned into an attack on the Germans by the 'international Jew'—was used as the opportunity to unleash 'acts of revenge' (*Racheakte*) on the Jews, thus bringing to a culmination the process of economic dispossession and social exclusion of the Jews in Germany. Furthermore, if it was not exactly ordered by Hitler, the evidence suggests that Goebbels acted with the full knowledge and support of the Führer: 'The Reich Propaganda Minister's remark in his speech on the evening of 9 November in Munich, that anti-Jewish demonstrations had already taken place in the *Gaus* of Kurhesse and Magdeburg-Anhalt, and that the "Führer" had decided not to take steps against them, suggests that at this point Goebbels was already operating in full agreement with Hitler.'[90] In other words, as with the historiography of the decision-making process for the 'Final Solution', one sees important two-way traffic between the centre and the periphery, but always within a framework of an antisemitic consensus—'I would not like to be a Jew in Germany', Goebbels chillingly

---

87. Wolfgang Benz, 'The November Pogrom of 1938: Participation, Applause, Disapproval' in *Exclusionary Violence: Antisemitic Riots in Modern German History*, eds. Christhard Hoffmann, Werner Bergmann, and Helmut Walser Smith (Ann Arbor: University of Michigan Press, 2002), p. 151.
88. Benz, 'The November Pogrom', p. 152.
89. Wolf-Arno Kropat, '*Reichskristallnacht': Der Judenpogrom vom 7. bis 10. November 1938—Urhebern, Täter, Hintergründe* (Wiesbaden: Kommission für die Geschichte der Juden in Hessen, 1997), pp. 5–6.
90. Kropat, '*Reichskristallnacht*', p. 173. See also Philippe Burrin, *Hitler and the Jews: The Genesis of the Holocaust* (London: Edward Arnold, 1994), p. 57: 'While Hitler could only have endorsed the concept of exacting reprisals, he seems to have been surprised by the extent of the destruction'; Burrin goes on to note that Goebbels' relationship with Hitler became increasingly strained over the next few years.

remarked at the 12 November conference of Nazi leaders held at Goering's Air Ministry—and with the Third Reich's small leadership group being firmly in the driving seat. The record of that meeting reveals that there was no crisis in the Third Reich's leadership as a result of Kristallnacht, as has sometimes been argued.[91] This model was as true in 1938 as it was in 1941–42, the difference being that by the later date Himmler and the SS were decisively in the ascendant.

Retrospectively, this sort of analysis is quite convincing. Dan Diner has developed it by showing that events that followed November 1938 provide a link between Kristallnacht and the Final Solution. In particular, the Nazi policy of forced emigration, especially as it was implemented in post-Anschluss Austria, illustrates the 'connecting threads', since the 'process commencing with forced emigration, or expulsion, eventually led to and culminated in the death camps'.[92] Among the consequences of Kristallnacht were the massive incarcerations of Jewish men in concentration camps, the development of plans to expel the Jews from Germany, the acceleration of the expulsion process and, most significant, the handing of control over the 'Jewish question' from Goering to the SS, represented by Heydrich, all of which 'marked a qualitatively new step in the move toward a "final solution" that was gradually taking shape'.[93] The resulting hardening of attitudes to Jewish refugees among Germany's neighbours, especially France, Switzerland, and Poland, but also the international response articulated at the Evian Conference of July 1938, radicalized attitudes within the Reich about what to do with the Jews. And as the Reich expanded eastwards and 'acquired' more Jews, in the light of the failure of expulsion policies, the Nazis arrived at more radical solutions. 'The connection', Diner notes, 'between the German Nazis' outward expansion and the radicalizing of their approach to the "Jewish problem" is clearly evident.'[94]

We do well to bear in mind Kropat's statement that Kristallancht was not 'a preliminary stage of the "Final Solution" ', irrespective of how inhumane the treatment of the Jews was during the pogrom and in the concentration camps later, where at least 30,000 were taken. 'To the extent

91. Dieter Obst, 'Reichskristallnacht': Ursachen und Verlauf des antisemitischen Pogroms vom November 1938 (Frankfurt/M: Peter Lang, 1991).
92. Dan Diner, 'The Catastrophe Before the Catastrophe: 1938 in Historical Context' in Beyond the Conceivable: Studies on Germany, Nazism, and the Holocaust (Berkeley: University of California Press, 2000), p. 79.
93. Diner, 'Catastrophe', p. 81.   94. Diner, 'Catastrophe', p. 84.

that the Nazi-leadership's "act of revenge" had a concrete political goal,'
writes Kropat, 'it was the attempt to get the Jews to leave Germany, as
party and state had intended since at least 1936.'[95] Nevertheless, several
leading historians want to make the evidence work harder. Fritzsche writes:
'As far as the Nazis were concerned, Germany's Jews had become utterly
disposable, and their physical elimination could be contemplated: this was
the revolutionary consequence of the pogroms of November 1938.'[96] And
Wildt claims: 'We can therefore understand why it is that the mob violence
unleashed in November 1938, rather than the deportations to death of late
autumn 1941, is more often remembered as the decisive event.'[97]

In much of this historiography, the response of the victims themselves is
overlooked. In the understandable desire to explain the background to the
Holocaust, the focus has been squarely on the perpetrators, especially on the
spreading of culpability throughout the German population and the attempt
to include as wide a section of the German population as plausible in anti-
Jewish activities. To the extent that this approach is problematic, it is so if
it suggests that Jews were simply people to whom things happen, passive
victims of history; people, as Hannah Arendt put it, who 'are regarded
a priori, so to speak, as potential inhabitants of concentration camps'.[98]
Whilst this was so from a Nazi point of view, it behoves historians today
not unwittingly to replicate that perspective.

For this reason, it is important to consider the German Jews' responses to
persecution, for several clichés need to be questioned. The most important
of these is that, following the 1935 Nuremberg laws, stripping Jews of
their German citizenship and de facto reversing the nineteenth-century
emancipation process, many German Jews felt that the persecution had
peaked and that, with a return to the pre-emancipation condition, there
would be a slowdown in the legislative and physical onslaught against
them. But this canard—which is a standard trope of the literature—does
not bear scrutiny. Merely the fact that fully half of Germany's 500,000 Jews
had left the country by the outbreak of the war is a clear indication that
they were not confident that matters had reached a conclusion. Internal
discussions from the Jewish press confirm this view. In her analysis of *Der*

95. Kropat, 'Reichskristallnacht', p. 179.   96. Fritzsche, *Life and Death*, p. 141.
97. Michael Wildt, *Volksgemeinschaft als Selbstermächtigung: Gewalt gegen Juden in der deutschen
    Provinz 1919 bis 1939* (Hamburg: Hamburger Edition, 2007), p. 347.
98. Arendt to Karl Jaspers, 17 August 1946, in *Arendt/Jaspers Correspondence 1926–1969*, eds. Lotte
    Kohler and Hans Saner (San Diego: Harcourt Brace & Company, 1992), p. 54.

Morgen, a scholarly German-Jewish journal, Sarah Fraiman shows how the question of Diaspora versus Zionism came to dominate the debates, with articles on Jewish life in Palestine and other countries featuring regularly, until the Nazis shut the periodical down in November 1938.[99] The liberal *CV-Zeitung* (the organ of the *Centralverein*) and the Zionist *Jüdische Rundschau* struggled throughout the 1930s to find a way of allowing Jewish identity to negotiate the trials of the Nazi onslaught. These 'embattled (re-)constructions' of the categories of Jewishness and Germanness reveal that such categories were shifting in response to rapidly-changing circumstances, and that German Jews were fully engaged with Nazism, even though they could not resolve the dilemma of reiterating Nazi discourse in defining Jews 'racially', as a *Volk* of their own.[100]

Another area where we may glimpse some understanding of the desperate circumstances in which the victims found themselves is in the massive bureaucracy of 'Aryanization' and expropriation. As Dean notes, tackling head on the notion of Jewish passivity: 'The detailed analysis of questions relating to emigration and the preservation of property reveals great energy and activism in the way Jewish families tackled the problems they faced.' What is striking in this context is that, following the measures the Nazis introduced to strip Jews of their wealth before emigration (such as the *Reichsfluchtsteuer*, the Reich Flight Tax, or currency transfer restrictions), so few Jews 'resorted to the "illegal" methods the Nazis repeatedly denounced as "typically Jewish" '. Dean's conclusion is that 'The ingrained habit of obedience to legal authority made it difficult for many Jews to adjust to the reality of a state-organized threat to their very existence.'[101] Finally, Marion Kaplan shows how German Jews responded in a variety of ways to their persecution, and proves that it is a 'profound and cruel distortion' to criticize them for not having left in time.[102]

Likewise, we must consider the German Jews' responses to Kristallnacht. Benz notes that the pogrom 'was staged as a ritual of public degradation'

99. Sarah Fraiman, 'The Transformation of Jewish Consciousness in Nazi Germany as Reflected in the German Jewish Journal *Der Morgen*, 1925–1938', *Modern Judaism*, 20, 1 (2000), pp. 41–59.

100. Thomas Pegelow, ' "German Jews", "National Jews", "Jewish *Volk*" or "Racial Jews"? The Construction and Contestation of "Jewishness" in Newspapers of Nazi Germany, 1933–1938', *CEH*, 35, 2 (2002), pp. 195–221.

101. Martin Dean, *Robbing the Jews: The Confiscation of Jewish Property in the Holocaust, 1933–1945* (Cambridge: Cambridge University Press, 2008), pp. 12, 65, 68.

102. Marion Kaplan, *Between Dignity and Despair: Jewish Life in Nazi Germany* (New York: Oxford University Press, 1998), p. 231.

and writes that, for its victims, it was a 'traumatic experience of humiliation, maltreatment, and loss of identity' that expedited the process of their total exclusion from German life.[103] Stefanie Schüler-Springorum shows this process in excruciating detail for the Berlin Jewish community, which had to bear the cost of maintaining all community welfare institutions, such as foster homes, after 19 November 1938. Unsurprisingly, the overwhelming response of most Jews to Kristallnacht was to try and get out of the country; as Schüler-Springorum notes, the poor—and those who had been made destitute by Nazi policies—were least likely to find an escape route.[104] In her excellent narrative of the Kristallnacht pogrom, Kaplan employs a gender perspective to show that, although more women than men wanted to leave Germany, in fact fewer women than men did actually leave, largely because it was easier for women to find work and because parents were more willing to send sons than daughters away to unknown countries. By 1941, those standing in the queue outside the Gestapo for exit visas were 'All old people, old women'.[105] Under the almost impossible circumstances, one of the only places left in the world where one could enter without a visa was Shanghai, and, by the end of 1939, some 18,000 Jews had reached the city. The Japanese, under German pressure, created a ghetto there in 1943, but this was nothing like Warsaw or Łódź, and most of the Jews survived the war. Whilst Kristallnacht should then not be seen from a post hoc perspective as the start of the 'Final Solution', most Jews in the Third Reich clearly understood that it was the beginning of the end for German Jewry, and they responded by emigrating wherever they could.[106]

Nazi culture, then, meant the entwinement of the cosy and *gemütlich* with extraordinary violence. As Michael Wildt reminds us:

> from the start, the *Volksgemeinschaft*'s inclusivity was bound up with the violent exclusion of so-called 'asocials', the allegedly hereditarily inferior and, above all, Jews. Those things which former '*Volksgenossen*' loved to keep apart later on, namely the persecution of the Jews and the experience of community under National Socialism, belong inseparably together. They

103. Benz, 'The November Pogrom', p. 157.
104. Stefanie Schüler-Springorum, 'Fear and Misery in the Third Reich: From the Files of the Collective Guardianship Office of the Berlin Jewish Community', *YVS*, 27 (1999), pp. 61–103.
105. Kaplan, *Between Dignity and Despair*, pp. 138–44, quoting (p. 144) Elisabeth Freund. See also Kaplan, 'Jewish Women in Nazi Germany: Daily Life, Daily Struggles, 1933–1939', *Feminist Studies*, 16, 3 (1990), pp. 579–606.
106. Yehuda Bauer, *Jewish Reactions to the Holocaust* (Tel-Aviv: MOD Books, 1989), pp. 54–6.

form the two sides of a political project: the destruction of bourgeois society and the building of a new, racist order. . . . Antisemitic violence therefore does not represent a means of achieving National Socialist policies; violence against Jews was the core of these policies.[107]

Or, as he writes elsewhere, 'The Nazi regime communalized violence and permitted the "*Volksgenossen*" to take part in it.'[108]

Similarly, Roger Griffin talks of the *Volksgemeinschaft* in Durkheimian terms, seeing the national community 'as the basis for a recreated socio-logical experience, ordered according to a perceived racial health'.[109] This meant eradicating the perceived forces of degeneration and urgently expe-diting the forces of rebirth. This in turn meant fundamentally re-conceiving the story that Germans told about themselves: 'The Nazi revolution thus took the form of an elaborate process of transforming reality by spreading and normalizing the National Socialist *Weltanschauung*, the "grand narra-tive" of how history was unfolding, to a point where rival value-systems were silenced or drowned out by the sheer volume of official Newspeak and the invasion of civic space by their symbology of the New Order.' What Griffin refers to unproblematically as the 'Nazi revolution' was thus not only a political process but a process that was conceived psychologically and cosmologically; its 'ultimate aim' was not just to build a new state, but 'to give birth to a new type of man (and woman) and so carry out totali-tarianism's "anthropological revolution" '.[110] Tellingly, with respect to the Holocaust, Griffin notes that the existence of a *Führerbefehl* is 'a legalistic rather than a historical issue'. His point is that the murder of the Jews must be seen as a product of the shared utopian goal of national rebirth: 'Had the Third Reich not been collectively "imagined" as the rebirth of the national community, the Final Solution could never have been conceived or executed as one of its potential strategies of implementation.'[111] This

107. Wildt, *Volksgemeinschaft als Selbstermächtigung*, p. 68.
108. Michael Wildt, 'Gewalt als Partizipation: Der Nationalsozialismus als Ermächtigungsregime', in *Staats-Gewalt: Ausnahmezustand und Sicherheitsregimes. Historische Perspektiven*, eds. Alf Lüdtke and Wildt (Göttingen: Wallstein, 2008), p. 239.
109. Roger Griffin, 'Hooked Crosses and Forking Paths: The Fascist Dynamics of the Third Reich' in *A Fascist Century: Essays by Roger Griffin*, ed. Matthew Feldman (Basingstoke: Palgrave Macmillan, 2008), p. 96.
110. Griffin, 'Hooked Crosses', p. 97. See also Dan Stone, 'The Holocaust and the Human' in *Hannah Arendt and the Uses of History: Imperialism, Nation, Race and Genocide*, eds. Richard H. King and Stone (New York: Berghahn, 2007), pp. 232–49.
111. Griffin, 'Hooked Crosses', p. 99. See also Griffin, 'Withstanding the Rush of Time: The Prescience of Mosse's Anthropological View of Fascism' in *What History Tells*, eds. Payne, Sorkin, and Tortorice, pp. 110–33.

is a statement that clearly shows the imprint of a Mosse-inspired cultural approach, focusing on symbolic meanings rather than events. It reveals that one way of trying to understand the origins of the Holocaust is through the Nazis' self-identity claims, an approach that usefully complements the more strictly empirical task of recreating the sequence of events.

As we have seen with respect to the 'voluntaristic turn', the wave of studies into racism in everyday life is remarkable. From the involvement of Germans in genealogical research to the prosecution of *Rassenschande* cases (in which ordinary Germans acted as denouncers, court witnesses or assistants to the police and justice apparatuses),[112] huge numbers made race part of their everyday experience of living in Nazi Germany, even if they were not (as Richard Evans rightly notes) fanatical Nazis. The same is true of German soldiers, who fought so bitterly not only because they were hardened antisemites or because they unquestioningly followed orders, but, as Thomas Kühne shows, because of their desire to create a community, which they did through mass violence. Kühne cites Michael Geyer's concept of the '*Vergesellschaftung der Gewalt*' (the 'socialization of violence'), and argues that '*Kameradschaft*' ('comradeship') is a guiding concept through which to provide a history of experience (*Erfahrungsgeschichte*) not only of National Socialism but of Germany's transition from Nazism to democracy.[113] In other words, *Kameradschaft* is a symbolic form that 'represented the self-image of the "war generation", even if not all its members identified with it'.[114] That is to say, not all soldiers identified with the myth of *Kameradschaft* to the same extent. Kühne argues that, even if his study brings out the plurality of experiences, he sees as a conclusion not 'cultural variety' but 'social unity: the cohesion of the National Socialist "*Volksgemeinschaft*" and its soldiers in the war'. *Kameradschaft* is the model and myth that held the *Volksgemeinschaft* and the Third Reich's soldiers

112. Alexandra Przyrembel, '*Rassenschande': Reinheitsmythos und Vernichtungslegitimation im National-sozialismus* (Göttingen: Vandenhoeck & Ruprecht, 2003); Patricia Szobar, 'Telling Sexual Stories in the Nazi Courts of Law: Race Defilement in Germany, 1933 to 1945', *Journal of the History of Sexuality*, 11, 1/2 (2002), pp. 131–63; Szobar, 'The Prosecution of Jewish-Gentile Sex in the Race Defilement Trials' in *Lessons and Legacies, Vol. 7: The Holocaust in International Perspective*, ed. Dagmar Herzog (Evanston: Northwestern University Press, 2006), pp. 159–68; Michael Ley, 'Rassenschande Prozesse im Dritten Reich' in *Wie ein Monster entsteht: Zur Konstruktion des anderen in Rassismus und Antisemitismus*, eds. Kirstin Breitenfellner and Charlotte Kohn-Ley (Bodenheim: Philo, 1998), pp. 216–28.
113. Thomas Kühne, *Kameradschaft: Die Soldaten des nationalsozialistischen Krieges und das 20. Jahrhundert* (Göttingen: Vandenhoeck & Ruprecht, 2006), pp. 14–15.
114. Kühne, *Kameradschaft*, p. 16.

together, and provided this conjunction with continuity. Thus, he expands his argument out from the military to say that the *Volksgemeinschaft* 'presented itself as a total community of comrades'.[115] *Kameradschaft* became official state doctrine under Nazism. Whilst the home front was of course not equivalent to a barracks on the eastern front, this is an insightful concept.

Finally, one can see that, with the decline in significance of the 'structuralist' perspective, the Holocaust's affective dimensions come more clearly into view. One should not claim that the Holocaust was some sort of 'outburst of affect', for this would be to deny altogether the bureaucratic–technical aspects of the genocide. But, the historiography has tended to overlook altogether—other than in heuristically problematic cases, such as Goldhagen's—this vital dimension of the murder.

It is important to note, for example, that the use of the term 'barbarism' continues to be used by historians to describe the brutality of the Nazi regime. To take one example among many, consider this passage, a description of Kristallnacht: 'The breakdown of all law that night, the domination of absolute violence, could have appeared to the victims as nothing but a descent into barbarism.'[116] Of course, the term in this context is quite appropriate as a description of the violence. But it also carries with it implications of a wider relapse, a societal aberration.

In actual fact, the enjoyment of violence is hardly an aberrant emotion; rather, it appears to be a common human characteristic. Yet the Holocaust cannot only be seen in these terms. With respect to the Holocaust, what Dominick LaCapra calls 'sacrificialism' went hand in hand with the eugenic, medicalizing discourses of blood and race. 'Perhaps', he writes, 'only this disconcerting conjunction helps to explain the incredible excesses of brutality, cruelty, and at times carnivalesque or "sublime" elation in Nazi behaviour towards Jews.'[117] Precisely this conjunction is what cultural history should aim to explain. But historians have, until recently, been reluctant to entertain notions of 'enjoyment', perhaps because of

115. Kühne, *Kameradschaft*, pp. 18, 19, 97. See also Kühne, 'Male Bonding and Shame Culture: Hitler's Soldiers and the Moral Basis of Genocidal Warfare' in *Ordinary People*, eds. Jensen and Szejnmann, pp. 55–77.
116. Wildt, *Volksgemeinschaft als Selbstermächtigung*, p. 347.
117. Dominick LaCapra, 'Lanzmann's Shoah: Here There Is No Why', *Critical Inquiry*, 23, 2 (1997), pp. 268–9, n4; LaCapra, *History in Transit: Experience, Identity, Critical Theory* (Ithaca: Cornell University Press, 2004), p. 146. Cf. Bernd Weisbrod, 'Violence and Sacrifice', in *The Third Reich Between Vision and Reality: New Perspectives on German History, 1918–1945*, ed. Hans Mommsen (New York: Berg, 2001), pp. 5–21.

the 'Auschwitz syndrome' mentioned above, perhaps because it is just too shocking. Yet Omer Bartov talks of 'festive enrichment and socioeconomic improvement' going hand in hand in eastern Europe, producing genocide as 'a mechanism for social mobility'.[118] Gordon Horwitz claims that, in the early days of the occupation of Łódź, 'The richest of degradations involved the staging of rituals that were scatological or misogynistic in overtone: "Cleaning toilets with bare hands, scrubbing floors with fingernails were daily occurrences. Women were told to take off their underwear and use it to clean the floors, the windows, and toilets." '[119]

These references tend to be to individual acts of cruelty, although LaCapra also refers in this context to the *Einsatzgruppen* and the death marches following the closure of the camps. Historians have tended to dismiss such cases as incidental to the larger story of 'industrial murder', brushing them off as the acts of 'sadists'. Few have wanted to follow Primo Levi in trying to understand what he called 'useless violence'.[120] But it is possible to see the Holocaust as such in these terms, as Berel Lang importantly does. He talks of the transgressive aspects of the Holocaust, whereby one sees 'a moral awareness of the particular practice in its wrongfulness, its transgression of a norm—with the will to do it anyway and thus, quite consistently, also to elaborate or embellish the wrong, as artists do in their medium: a consciousness of the violation being committed, together with its affirmation. An intention of such actions thus becomes the process of transgression itself and the assertion of power accompanying it.'[121]

One can demonstrate the validity of this assertion in numerous ways. For example, when SS General Erich von dem Bach-Zelewski was asked at Nuremberg about the mental prerequisites for the execution of the 'war of annihilation', he replied: 'If one preaches for years and decades that the Slavic race is an inferior race, that the Jews are not human at all, then such an explosion must be the outcome.'[122] Frank Bajohr writes: 'The

118. Omer Bartov, 'Eastern Europe as the Site of Genocide', *JMH*, 80, 3 (2008), p. 576.
119. Gordon J. Horwitz, *Ghettostadt: Łódź and the Making of a Nazi City* (Cambridge, MA: The Belknap Press of Harvard University Press, 2008), pp. 11–12, citing 'The History of the Litzmannstadt Ghetto' in Alan Adelson and Robert Lapides, *Łódź Ghetto: Inside a Community under Siege* (London: Viking, 1989), p. 23.
120. Primo Levi, *The Drowned and the Saved* (London: Abacus, 1989), ch. 5.
121. Berel Lang, *Post-Holocaust: Interpretation, Misinterpretation, and the Claims of History* (Bloomington: Indiana University Press, 2005), p. 14.
122. Bach-Zelewski cited in Wolfram Wette, ' "Rassenfeind": Antisemitismus und Antislawismus in der Wehrmachtpropaganda' in *Die Wehrmacht im Rassenkrieg: Der Vernichtungskrieg hinter der Front*, ed. Walter Manoschek (Vienna: Picus, 1996), p. 62.

deportations and public denunciations were imbued with an aura of the sensational, exercising an almost magical fascination for the young.'[123] And Konrad Kwiet asserts: 'A festive atmosphere prevailed at the killings.'[124] Thus, when Dana Villa argues, in response to Horkheimer and Adorno's use of Nietzsche's concept of 'festive cruelty', that 'Such spontaneous cruelty can, perhaps, account for pogroms, but it can hardly explain a massively planned and meticulously executed project of extermination', it is by no means clear that the distinction is quite so watertight.[125]

The Victims' Understanding as a Problem in Cultural History

According to Eelco Runia: 'People start to make history not despite the fact that it is at odds with—yes, destroys—the stories they live by, but because it destroys the stories they live by.'[126] As David Theo Goldberg explains in the case of race construction, race:

> emerges out of the creations, the fabrications, of real social actors in their constructed reproductions and transformations of given discursive formations and expressions. . . . Racial constitution is what gives one racial identity, what makes one a racial member, what identifies one racially in society, in law, and gives substance to one's social being.[127]

Hence the persistence of racial thinking throughout the twentieth century.[128] We have seen this process most clearly with respect to the perpetrators of the Holocaust. But is it applicable to the victims too?

Although the main focus of this chapter—and the book as a whole—has been on the perpetrators, I would like to end by discussing the ways in

---

123. Frank Bajohr, 'The "Folk Community" and the Persecution of the Jews: German Society under National Socialist Dictatorship, 1933–1945', *HGS*, 20, 2 (2006), p. 195.
124. Konrad Kwiet, 'Perpetrators and the Final Solution' in *The Memory of the Holocaust in the 21st Century: The Challenge for Education*, ed. Stephanie McMahon-Kaye (Jerusalem: Yad Vashem, 2001), p. 79.
125. Dana Villa, 'Genealogies of Total Domination: Arendt, Adorno, and Auschwitz', *New German Critique*, 100 (2007), pp. 23–4.
126. Eelco Runia, 'Burying the Dead, Creating the Past', *History and Theory*, 46, 3 (2007), p. 319.
127. David Theo Goldberg, 'The Semantics of Race', *Ethnic and Racial Studies*, 15, 4 (1992), p. 561.
128. S. O. Y. Keita and Rick A. Kettles, 'The Persistence of Racial Thinking and the Myth of Racial Divergence', *American Anthropologist*, 99, 3 (1997), pp. 534–44; Faye V. Harrison, 'The Persistent Power of "Race" in the Cultural and Political Economy of Racism', *Annual Review of Anthropology*, 24 (1995), pp. 47–74.

which the victims responded to their persecution. Jews were not simply passive victims of Nazi genocide even if their fate was, for the vast majority, out of their hands. The turn towards a cultural history of the perpetrators leads one to think in similar terms about the victims. German history tends to be written in dispassionate, '*wissenschaftliche*' terms, with a strong emphasis on archival, documentary evidence; but cultural history, as we have seen in Chapter 2, has already to some extent made an impact on the history of the Jews during the Holocaust, especially in the analysis of diaries, music, and testimonies, precisely the sorts of narratives that permit an analysis of meaning-production and meaning-destruction within a group. Is Runia's claim about the destruction of meaning at all relevant to the response of the Jews to their persecution by the Nazis?

In his memoir, Imo Moszkowicz writes: 'Only persecution turned the Jews in Germany into an undifferentiated group; this is exactly how it had been earlier in the Polish and Russian ghettos, under Torquemada's torture in Spain, and under Haman, who recommended exterminating the Jews to King Ahasuerus.'[129] His reference to previous cases of persecution, bridging the millennia, brings to mind David Roskies' argument that Jewish tradition has means at its disposal for understanding the Holocaust. The *Churban*, to use the Yiddish term that connects the Holocaust to the destruction of the temples in 586 BCE and 70 CE, can be incorporated into existing narratives of suffering.[130] With reference to the poetry of Abraham Sutzkever, a survivor of the Vilna ghetto, Roskies writes that 'the greater the loss, the greater one's need to transcend it with selective memory, emphatic rhyme, and natural beauty'.[131] The writing of history, by contrast, tends towards the opposite direction. Suspiciously seeing claims to transcendence and wholeness as refusals to engage with the reality of the horror of the Holocaust, historians increasingly assert the meaninglessness of the Holocaust from a Jewish point of view—other than in ultra-orthodox claims that the Holocaust was a punishment for turning away from God—and have worked hard to eradicate 'selective memory'. Indeed, as this book shows, there are few areas of the Holocaust experience

---

129. Imo Moszkowicz, *Der grauende Morgen: Erinnerungen* (Münster: LIT, 2004), p. 136. Thanks to Robert O'Neill for this reference.

130. David Roskies, *Against the Apocalypse: Responses to Catastrophe in Modern Jewish Culture* (Cambridge, MA: Harvard University Press, 1984); Roskies, *The Jewish Search for a Usable Past* (Bloomington: Indiana University Press, 1999). See also Alan Mintz, *Hurban: Responses to Catastrophe in Jewish Literature* (Syracuse: Syracuse University Press, 1996).

131. Roskies, *Against the Apocalypse*, p. 257.

left that remain under a taboo. Whether it is appropriate to control such horror using established traditions that reassert 'natural beauty' is a question of aesthetic sensibility. But most historians would probably feel that doing so imposes an order on the events that does not reflect reality. And one result of that position is to note that many Jews—again, with the partial exception of the ultra-orthodox and possibly some communists—did not have narratives and traditions to hand that were entrenched enough to allow them to comprehend what was happening to them.

One powerful example of this destruction of symbolic meaning is provided by Amos Goldberg. In his analysis of Chaim Kaplan's well-known diary from the Warsaw ghetto, Goldberg shows how the triumph of Nazism undermined the victims' ability to make sense of what was happening. In fact, in certain instances, Kaplan noticed a tendency to identify with Nazism, out of a sense of desperation. Kaplan wrote this in his diary on 18 May 1941:

> Nazism came to annihilate us. It is the enemy of Judaism in its spirit and in its practice. We fight it and await its defeat. However—the human spirit is inexplicable. Unconsciously, we accept its ideology and follow in its ways. Nazism has conquered our entire world. It severely damages our public life. And yet we do not cease to declare day and night that it is ugliness and that one ought to distance oneself from it.

This split in Jewish consciousness that Kaplan identifies is very telling. Nazism is, quite obviously, reviled; but at the same time, it has 'conquered our entire world', including the inner life. It has disrupted the normal ways of making sense of the world, giving rise to what Goldberg calls an 'epistemological grey zone'.[132]

It does not suffice, however, to note that the Holocaust destroyed the Jews' symbolic universe. Recent historiography concerning women and the Holocaust, children's experiences, hiding and rescue all indicate that Jews experienced the Holocaust very differently. This should come as no surprise, given that we are talking about populations that varied enormously in terms of language, culture, class, national belonging, and political and religious affiliation. But it remains an important point in the face of the overwhelmingly large historiography that remains firmly focused on the perpetrators and the mechanics of destruction.

132. Amos Goldberg, ' "Nazism Has Conquered Our Entire World": The Epistemological Grey Zone in Chaim Kaplan's Wartime Diaries' (unpublished ms, 2009). I am very grateful to the author for permission to cite this article.

The debate about women and the Holocaust, for example, that exploded
in the early 1990s, and has now become more or less mainstream within
the literature, revealed that women and men—and within the first group,
women in different places and of varying means—experienced the Holocaust very differently. Early proponents of the study of women, such as
Sybil Milton and Joan Ringelheim, provocatively argued that 'it has been
too difficult to contemplate the extent to which gender counted in the
exploitation and murder of Jewish women, and the extent to which the
sexism of Nazi ideology and the sexism of the Jewish community met in
a tragic and involuntary alliance.'[133] Some scholars objected to what they
regarded as an intrusion of a 'feminist agenda' into Holocaust Studies, and
argued that the Nazi targeting of all Jews, regardless of gender, meant
that gendered behaviour played a 'severely diminished role' during the
Holocaust.[134]

What we might call a 'first generation' of scholars working on women
and the Holocaust emphasized gender distinctions, and argued—curiously
contradicting the 'feminist' ideology that was supposedly driving their
work—that women survived better because they were better 'carers and
sharers'; where men behaved individualistically, women formed sororities
and substitute families. They drew attention to gendered issues in the
ghettos and camps, and to the roles played by women in cultural activities
in the camps, in partisan activity, in resistance movements, and in hiding.
These studies showed, for example, that women could more easily 'pass'
as Aryan in occupied Warsaw, not only because men could be identified
as Jewish with a simple 'trouser inspection', but because women tended
to speak better Polish, thanks to their secular schooling and more regular
interactions with Gentiles on shopping trips.[135] More recent scholarship
on this issue offers a more sophisticated methodology. Zoë Waxman notes

133. Joan Ringelheim, 'The Split between Gender and the Holocaust' in *Women in the Holocaust*,
eds. Dalia Ofer and Lenore J. Wietzman (New Haven: Yale University Press, 1998), p. 345.
For the first studies, see Ringelheim, 'The Unethical and the Unspeakable: Women and the
Holocaust', *Simon Wiesenthal Center Annual*, 1 (1984), pp. 69–87; Ringelheim, 'Women
and the Holocaust: A Reconsideration of Research', *Signs*, 10, 4 (1985), pp. 741–61; Myrna
Goldenberg, ' "From a World Beyond": Women in the Holocaust', *Feminist Studies*, 22, 3
(1996), pp. 667–87.
134. Lawrence L. Langer, 'Gendered Suffering? Women in Holocaust Testimonies' in *Women in
the Holocaust*, eds. Ofer and Weitzman, p. 351.
135. Apart from *Women in the Holocaust*, see also Judith Tydor Baumel, *Double Jeopardy: Gender
and the Holocaust* (London: Vallentine Mitchell, 1998); Elizabeth R. Baer and Myrna
Goldenberg, eds., *Experience and Expression: Women, the Nazis, and the Holocaust* (Detroit:
Wayne State University Press, 2003).

that ascribing only domestic, mothering, and care-giving roles to women leads one to 'obscure the diversity of women's Holocaust experiences'.[136] Scholars are thus no longer surprised to find that women could be brutal or aggressive, and no longer automatically describe such women as 'deviant females'.[137] There has been little work on masculinity, however, and so far the concept of 'gender' as applied to Holocaust research has meant in practice women and, increasingly, family studies.

Conceptual and methodological advances in applying gender to the study of the Holocaust means that research into gender is gradually being decoupled from the study of children, as scholars realize that mothering does not encompass the full range of female experiences during the Holocaust years, and as the study of children becomes more sophisticated in its own right. Perhaps no other area of Holocaust historiography has developed so quickly over the last five years. Where a decade ago there were two noteworthy studies, now the literature has mushroomed.[138] This situation no doubt owes something to the fact that few survivors other than child survivors remain alive, as well as to the Wilkomirski scandal, in which the man who claimed to speak for child survivors, getting them heard where previously they had been overlooked, turned out to be a fraud, thus fuelling a desire for accurate information about children.[139] It means that scholarship on children and the Holocaust is as important to recent developments in literary studies as it is in historical ones, and there have also been a number of significant publications of children's diaries and testimonies.[140]

136. Zoë Waxman, 'Unheard Testimony, Untold Stories: The Representation of Women's Holocaust Experiences', *Women's History Review*, 12, 4 (2003), pp. 661–77; Anna Hardman, *Women and the Holocaust* (London: Holocaust Educational Trust, 2000).

137. Heschel, 'Does Atrocity Have a Gender?', p. 311.

138. George Eisen, *Children and Play in the Holocaust: Games Among the Shadows* (Amherst, MA: University of Massachusetts Press, 1988); Debórah Dwork, *Children with a Star: Jewish Youth in Nazi Europe* (New Haven: Yale University Press, 1991).

139. Binjamin Wilkomirski, *Fragments: Memories of a Childhood, 1939–1948* (London: Picador, 1996). See Stefan Maechler, *The Wilkomirski Affair: A Study in Biographical Truth* (London: Picador, 2001).

140. Nicholas Stargardt, *Witnesses of War: Children's Lives under the Nazis* (London: Jonathan Cape, 2005); Sue Vice, *Children Writing the Holocaust* (Basingstoke: Palgrave Macmillan, 2004); Andrea Reiter, ed., *Children and the Holocaust* (London: Vallentine Mitchell, 2006); Anita Brostoff, ed., *Flares of Memory: Stories of Childhood During the Holocaust* (Oxford: Oxford University Press, 2001); Laurel Holliday, ed., *Children's Wartime Diaries: Secret Writings from the Holocaust and World War II* (London: Piatkus, 1995); *Children and the Holocaust: Symposium Presentations* (Washington, DC: United States Holocaust Memorial Museum, 2004); Hélène Beer, *Journal* (London: MacLehose Press, 2008).

Outside of Nazi-occupied Europe, the best histories of Jewish responses, as Marrus noted, have 'focused on particular groups, rooting their reactions in an identifiable culture and political outlook'.[141] This observation is most clearly confirmed in the historiography of the Yishuv, the Jewish community in Palestine before 1948. As recently as a 1983 conference, Dina Porat observed that the historiography of the Yishuv's response to the Holocaust was in its infancy, with scholarship still beset by raw emotions.[142] But what was already emerging, and what has been confirmed since, is that Jews in the Yishuv, despite many having relatives in, or having themselves come from occupied Europe, responded to the persecution and murder of the Jews as Jewish communities elsewhere did.[143] The polemical assertion that Jews in Palestine condemned their European brethren for 'going like sheep to the slaughter' or that Ben-Gurion lacked pity and was interested in the European Jews only insofar as they helped advance the Zionist cause,[144] have been subjected to strong criticism. A large Hebrew-language historiography has grown up around these issues.

Careful studies by Dina Porat, Tuvia Friling, and others have argued that Ben-Gurion and the Yishuv leadership actually did far more to try and save the Jews of Europe than has been recognized.[145] Scholars still note various negative aspects of the Yishuv's response, including attitudes towards the Diaspora and towards survivors, as well showing how post-1948 Israeli trials of supposed collaborators were fraught with emotional baggage and often displayed limited or very partisan understanding of the actualities of Nazi Europe. At the same time, a specifically Israeli, strongly intentionalist

141. Michael R. Marrus, *The Holocaust in History* (London: Penguin, 1989), p. 169.
142. Dina Porat, 'The Historiography of the Yishuv and the Holocaust' in *The Historiography of the Holocaust Period*, ed. Yisrael Gutman and Gideon Greif (Jerusalem: Yad Vashem, 1988), pp. 549–69.
143. For Britain and the USA, see Tony Kushner, 'Britain, the United States and the Holocaust: In Search of a Historiography' in *HH*, pp. 253–75.
144. Yoav Gelber, 'Zionist Policy and European Jewry (1939–1942)', *YVS*, 13 (1979), pp. 169–210; Bela Vago, 'Some Aspects of the Yishuv Leadership's Activities during the Holocaust' in *Jewish Leadership in the Nazi Era: Patterns of Behavior in the Free World*, ed. Randolph L. Braham (New York: City University of New York, 1985), pp. 45–65. See also Tom Segev, *The Seventh Million: The Israelis and the Holocaust* (New York: Hill and Wang, 1993).
145. Dina Porat, *The Blue and the Yellow Stars of David: The Zionist Leadership in Palestine and the Holocaust* (Cambridge, MA: Harvard University Press, 1990); Abraham J. Edelheit, *The Yishuv in the Shadow of the Holocaust: Zionist Politics and Rescue Aliya, 1933–1939* (Boulder: Westview Press, 1996); Tuvia Friling, *Arrows in the Dark: David Ben-Gurion, the Yishuv Leadership, and Rescue Attempts during the Holocaust*, 2 vols. (Madison: University of Wisconsin Press, 2003).

approach to the Holocaust was developing.[146] The role played by the Holocaust in Israeli life, in particular with respect to the Israel/Palestine conflict, is also much discussed, with many commentators arguing that Holocaust memory has contributed to the apocalyptic tone of Middle East politics.[147] But the sort of withering criticisms of several decades ago have—as with debates about the *Judenräte* or Jewish resistance—given way to a more mature, dispassionate scholarship. There is greater understanding that, for young people in the Yishuv, for example, their reaction could be 'a mixture of rage and thirst for revenge on the gentiles and revulsion and shame for the Jews'.[148] With respect to Zionist policy towards the war and the fate of the Jews, as Ofer notes, many felt that 'the British should be pressured to do more to ease restrictions on entry to Palestine and to show greater generosity about helping Jews escape from the Balkans. Nevertheless, cooperation with the British in the war against Hitler must not be rejected.'[149] But it is also noted that 'The facts are grim but have to be recognized as they were. None of the classic disputes between the Zionists and the non-Zionists, or between the different Zionist factions, or between the diverse movements in non-Zionist Jewish society, or the patterns of relations between Jews and Gentiles, were significantly influenced as a result of the Jewish tragedy unfolding in Europe',[150] perhaps because 'The Holocaust highlighted the fact that, despite fifty years of a Zionist enterprise

146. Dalia Ofer, 'Linguistic Conceptualization of the Holocaust in Palestine and Israel, 1942–53', *JCH*, 31, 3 (1996), pp. 567–95; Hanna Yablonka, 'The Development of Holocaust Consciousness in Israel: The Nuremberg, Kapos, Kastner, and Eichmann Trials', *Israel Studies*, 8, 3 (2003), pp. 1–24; Ruth Linn, 'Genocide and the Politics of Remembering: The Nameless, the Celebrated, and the Would-Be Holocaust Heroes', *JGR*, 5, 4 (2003), pp. 565–86; Roni Stauber, *The Holocaust in Israeli Public Debate in the 1950s: Ideology and Memory* (London: Valletine Mitchell, 2007).

147. Idith Zertal, *Israel's Holocaust and the Politics of Nationhood* (Cambridge: Cambridge University Press, 2005); Avraham Burg, *The Holocaust is Over; We Must Rise from its Ashes* (Basingstoke: Palgrave Macmillan, 2008).

148. Anita Shapira, 'The Holocaust and World War II as Elements of the Yishuv Psyche until 1948' in *Thinking about the Holocaust After Half a Century*, ed. Alvin H. Rosenfeld (Bloomington: Indiana University Press, 1997), p. 71.

149. Dalia Ofer, 'Fifty Years After: The Yishuv, Zionism, and the Holocaust, 1933–1948' in *Major Changes within the Jewish People in the Wake of the Holocaust*, eds. Yisrael Gutman and Avital Saf (Jerusalem: Yad Vashem, 1996), p. 482. See also Ofer, 'Enmity, Indifference or Cooperation: The Allies and Yishuv's Rescue Activists' in *The Final Solution: Origins and Implementation*, ed. David Cesarani (London: Routledge, 1994), pp. 268–87; Dina Porat, *Israeli Society, the Holocaust and its Survivors* (London: Vallentine Mitchell, 2007).

150. Jehuda Reinharz and Evyatar Friesel, 'The Zionist Leadership Between the Holocaust and the Creation of the State of Israel' in *Thinking*, ed. Rosenfeld, pp. 99–100. See also Israel Bartal, 'Yishuv and Diaspora in Changing Perspectives' in *Major Changes*, eds. Gutman and Saf, pp. 387–97.

in Eretz Israel and the possibilities of a national home opened by the British mandate, the Zionist movement was incapable of presenting a serious answer to the existential problems of European Jewry.'[151] Such conclusions may be debatable, but they show a greater sense of historical consciousness than dominated the debates a few decades ago.

Despite all these discussions—and others, including rescue activities, hiding, and partisans—a curious split continues to exist between the writing of Jewish history and Holocaust history. Historians of the Jews have tended to leave the writing of the Holocaust to 'specialists', who, it is assumed, are often not conversant with the religious and cultural history of the Jews over a longer timeframe.[152] This is an ironic situation, given that, in the popular imagination, it is assumed that most historians working on the Holocaust must be Jews, and given the extent to which the Holocaust is perceived as a 'problem for the Jews' rather than for wider, Gentile society.[153] With the increasing emphasis on the broad problem of Jewish responses, including issues of religion, education, resistance, and rescue, this situation looks set to change, at least to some extent. The general sphere of cultural history, especially its emphasis on meaning-production and destruction, means that Holocaust history is becoming more firmly integrated into Jewish history. Yet perhaps only when a larger repertoire of methods is utilized will this conjunction be realized.

In particular, there is a need to incorporate oral history in order 'to expand the reach of the social history of the Holocaust', since, as Steve Hochstadt notes, most Jews experienced the Holocaust as a 'family crisis':

> As they were swept up in events beyond their control and comprehension, they were preoccupied with family; if they survived, they conceived of their traumatic past within familial terms. Forced by the Nazis out of their participation in communal, commercial, and public life, Jews constructed their narrowed lives around family. When it is composed, based on both written and oral sources, the Jewish history of the Holocaust will be dominated by family.[154]

---

151. Ofer, 'Fifty Years After', p. 494. See also *Israel Studies*, 14, 1 (2009), special issue on *Israelis and the Holocaust*.
152. David Engel, *Historians of the Jews and the Holocaust* (Stanford: Stanford University Press, 2009).
153. See Dan Diner, 'Varieties of Narration: The Holocaust in Historical Memory' in *Beyond the Conceivable*, pp. 173–200.
154. Steve Hochstadt, 'Review Article: Recent Contributions to Holocaust Historiography', *German Studies Review*, 31, 2 (2008), pp. 371–2.

Thus, we can expect more studies on fatherhood and masculinity, inspired by the important work on women and femininity during the Holocaust, on childhood, and, especially, on life in the immediate aftermath of the Holocaust. Work on DP camps has brought a whole range of experiences into the sphere of Holocaust historiography that was previously marginal, and contributes to the breaking of our usual chronologies. Testimonies have long shown that the Holocaust did not simply 'end' in 1945; now a body of historical literature confirms that point, with many fine, sensitive studies appearing that deal with religion, gender, death and mourning, emigration, Zionism, communal politics, and post-war international politics.[155] The focus on family and the aftermath of the Holocaust as continued problems marks a fitting place to end this study, for these are topics—and life experiences—that have no end, and that continually pose new questions. Like life itself, histories of the Holocaust should always remain to be written and the past should stay ceaselessly unfinished.

155. Yisrael Gutman and Avital Saf, eds., *She'erit Hapletah, 1944–1948: Rehabilitation and Political Struggle* (Jerusalem: Yad Vashem, 1990); David Wyman, *DPs: Europe's Displaced Persons 1945–1951* (Ithaca, NY: Cornell University Press, 1998); Michael Brenner, *After the Holocaust: Rebuilding Jewish Lives in Postwar Germany* (Princeton: Princeton University Press, 1999); Angelika Königseder and Juliane Wetzel, *Waiting for Hope: Jewish Displaced Persons in Post-World War II Germany* (Evanston: Northwestern University Press, 2001); Arieh J. Kochavi, *Post-Holocaust Politics: Britain, the United States, and Jewish Refugees, 1945–1948* (Chapel Hill: University of North Carolina Press, 2001); Zeev W. Mankowitz, *Life Between Memory and Hope: The Survivors of the Holocaust in Occupied Germany* (Cambridge: Cambridge University Press, 2002); Eva Kolinsky, *After the Holocaust: Jewish Survivors in Germany after 1945* (London: Pimlico, 2004); Jay Howard Geller, *Jews in Post-Holocaust Germany, 1945–1953* (Cambridge: Cambridge University Press, 2004); Atina Grossmann, *Jews, Germans, and Allies: Close Encounters in Occupied Germany* (Princeton: Princeton University Press, 2007); Avinoam J. Patt and Michael Berkowitz, eds., *We Are Here: New Approaches to Jewish Displaced Persons in Postwar Germany* (Detroit: Wayne State University Press, 2009).

Conclusion
Into the Abyss

He who fights with monsters should look to it that he does not become a monster. And when you gaze long into an abyss the abyss also gazes into you.

Friedrich Nietzsche[1]

T he historiography of the Holocaust is vast; what I have covered in this book gives an indication of the main lines of inquiry, but is still necessarily only a starting point. Anyone desiring to conduct research on any aspect of the Holocaust, no matter how apparently minor, will immediately discover innumerable studies that offer far greater detail than I can discuss in these pages. For all this extensive literature, my examination of the historiography of the last two decades has reinforced my sense of the achievement of the early historians of Nazism and the Holocaust. We know far more about the mechanics of persecution and murder in all regions of Europe, about the roles played by the Allied and neutral countries, the churches and NGOs, about the extent of Nazi persecution of forced labourers, occupied nations and those excluded from the *Volksgemeinschaft* in the Third Reich's prisons and labour camps, and about the responses of Nazism's victims to their persecution, whether in hiding or in the resistance, and the actions of the small minority who tried to save them. Yet in outline, the narratives offered by Poliakov, Reitlinger, Hilberg, Krausnick,

---

1. Friedrich Nietzsche, *Beyond Good and Evil: Prelude to a Philosophy of the Future* (London: Penguin, 1973), p. 84.

Wulf, and others in the 1950s and 1960s were remarkably insightful and durable.

Many of the frameworks that have shaped the historiography of the Holocaust from the period of the war onwards are only now being shaken.[2] Nolzen shows that Weber's distinction between bureaucratic and charismatic leadership is too limited; Lindenfeld that the Holocaust can be understood simply as neither a legacy of the Enlightenment nor of mysticism; and LaCapra that technology and science in the Third Reich went hand in hand with transgressive, boundary-breaking behaviour. The binaries that frame historical scholarship—centre/periphery, efficiency/polycracy, intentionalism/functionalism, modernity/irrationality, race science/racial mysticism—are too neatly drawn to be able to encompass the real motors and dynamic forces behind the Third Reich and the Holocaust.

Naturally, the early historians' texts can be criticized.[3] Yet in essence, the bulk of today's historiography confirms many of their findings. Even the undreamt-of details into regional occupation policies, the looting of artworks, or local collaboration—all of which were topics inaccessible or as yet not anticipated by historians—confirm in key respects the findings of the first generation of scholars. Debates about the nature of Nazism have returned full circle to terms such as 'gangsterism' and 'corruption' as the notion of a tightly controlled dictatorship has been called into question by the 'voluntaristic turn' and the idea of a 'consensus dictatorship'. The key role of the Nazi leadership has been reaffirmed by historians who have researched Nazi agencies, propaganda, and indoctrination; antisemitism, albeit in a far more sophisticated context of 'cumulative radicalization' and structural or inter-agency competition and organization, retains its centrality; and discussions of 'modernity' and 'race' build on earlier insights into the bureaucratic nature of the killing process. Of course, Holocaust historiography has drawn strength from many new methodologies that have energized historical scholarship in general over the last half century: social, intellectual, and economic history, but also, belatedly, approaches informed by gender analysis, discourse analysis, the history of the emotions,

2. The wartime origins of the historiography of the Holocaust, partly in well-known texts such as those of Hermann Rauschning, Konrad Heiden, Ernst Fraenkel, Franz Neumann, and Raphael Lemkin, and partly in long-forgotten texts, is the subject of my future research.
3. See my *Constructing the Holocaust: A Study in Historiography* (London: Vallentine Mitchell, 2003); more specifically, Nicolas Berg, *Der Holocaust und die westdeutschen Historiker: Erforschung und Erinnerung* (Göttingen: Wallstein, 2003).

the family, the body, and other terms that fall under the broad rubric of 'cultural history'. As the last chapter shows, there are many ways in which the Holocaust can yet be explored, ways that a new generation of historians will develop, from microhistories of Shtetls and ghettos to histories of Jewish responses, drawing on oral history. It is unlikely that new documents that fundamentally change our understanding of what the Holocaust was or how it happened will be discovered. But every important historical event is rewritten according to the needs of the present ('all history is contemporary history'), and the Holocaust is certainly no exception. What remains to be seen is how, as we reach the culmination of 'traditional' historiography in works such as Friedländer's *Years of Extermination*, new insights into what the Holocaust means will be generated through the employment of different methodological approaches. Perhaps the time has come not to slow the pace of empirical study—this will always be worthwhile for without it there is nothing to discuss—but to complement the mass of archival work with greater reflection on the reasons that brought this scholarship into being in the first place.[4] Buried under the footnotes, it is sometimes easy to forget that the Holocaust, as the now hackneyed phrase goes, has 'shattered the elementary bases of civilization and culture'.[5] We historians often go about our business as if this were not the case, for historiography is also a key component of this very culture that has supposedly been shattered. When we recap what Nazism was as a movement and an ideology, and think plainly about what Nazism 'achieved' in the Holocaust, we can recapture that sense of shock, the sense that drives the search for new and unfamiliar ways of representing it.

Nazism was not just an attack on the Jews, or on the Romanies, or Slavs, or other despised peoples. It was not 'merely' an attempt to create a Nazi Empire in Europe in the manner of the European overseas empires, nor was it 'only' an attempt to reshape the demography of Europe along racial lines. It was all these things, but also something more. Nazism was, as Yehuda Bauer says, a 'total rebellion' against 'what we inaccurately call western civilization'.[6] Or, we might say, it was a radicalization of

4. For a starting point, see Dan Stone, ed., *The Holocaust and Historical Methodology* (New York: Berghahn, forthcoming).
5. Dan Diner, *Gegenläufige Gedächtnisse: Über Geltung und Wirkung des Holocaust* (Göttingen: Vandenhoeck & Ruprecht, 2007), p. 7.
6. Yehuda Bauer, 'Overall Explanations: German Society and the Jews or: Some Thoughts about Context' in *Probing the Depths of German Antisemitism: German Society and the Persecution of the Jews, 1933–1941*, ed. David Bankier (New York: Berghahn, 2000), p. 16.

characteristics of 'western civilization' that had already been seen, in more incipient form, in slavery and colonialism and intra-European warfare in the early twentieth century. What accounts for the horror of Nazism, and our enduring fascination with it, is Nazism's attempt to redefine what is meant by the term 'human being'. Nazism was an anthropological project that wanted to reshape the world by declaring a limited understanding of who was to count as human. In this it of course drew on the resources of the west, which as a result have been terribly impugned: Enlightenment dreams of 'forcing people to be free', Utopian visions of the 'New Man' common from the Renaissance onwards; Romantic notions of racial chosenness. But Nazism, whilst it drew strength from these movements, also 'o'erleaped' them with its 'vaulting ambition' to make such fantasies real.

In a remarkable letter to her mentor and friend Karl Jaspers of 17 December 1946, the exiled German-Jewish philosopher Hannah Arendt wrote the following:

> I haven't understood what actually happened. Perhaps what is behind it all is only that individual human beings did not kill other individual human beings for human reasons, but that an organized attempt was made to eradicate the concept of the human being.

More than sixty years later, this insight has yet to be bettered. In it we see how the modern themes of race science, technology, and bureaucracy coalesced with the transgressive ideological violence of conspiracy theory, mysticism, and 'thinking with the blood'. The Holocaust chills us to the bone because its resources are ones that remain familiar to us in late modernity—censuses and the categorization of people, technology, medicalization, 'biopower'—and because we see daily how our 'rational' lives are in fact suffused with 'magical' thinking that under the right circumstances can be put to terrible use: fear of immigrants and disease, hygiene fetishism, body-culture obsession. Romanies, whether in Italy, Hungary, or Romania, continue to know full well the truth of this claim; the continuities in their experience from the *Porrajmos* to the present are astounding when one considers the assault on antisemitism that became an integral part of the postwar consensus in Europe.[7]

The narrative of the Holocaust itself is an endless concatenation of horror, whether one encounters this in the personal stories of survivor testimonies or

---

7. Ian Hancock, 'Romanies and the Holocaust: A Re-evaluation and an Overview' in *HH*, 383–96.

in the relatively dispassionate language of the historian. The attempt to find a redemptive meaning to the Holocaust, whether in narrative denouements of liberation, the creation of the state of Israel, or the reconstitution of family life, makes a mockery of the vastness of the destruction, of individuals and ancient cultures. To teach it to schoolchildren necessarily involves sanitizing its worst aspects and thus to some extent falsifying the record. Not to sanitize it impugns their childhoods. Why then is teaching and commemorating the Holocaust being promoted so forcefully by western governments and educational agencies as necessary to promote good citizenship? What makes these people sure they are not breeding a generation of cynics? It is indeed the case that as one gazes into the abyss the abyss gazes back into you. The Holocaust teaches nothing about human rights. In this book, inspired by *The Holocaust in History*, I am happy to give the last word to Michael Marrus: 'It seems to me that the study and the popular presentation of the Holocaust run into difficulties when they have been deliberately undertaken to make us "feel better"—to confirm our political judgments, to enhance understanding of the Jewish predicament, or even to improve "human understanding" . . . That such things could have happened is to me reason enough to ponder them in awe and study them with scientific curiosity. I doubt that we should "feel better" after coming to grips with such horrors, and I am sometimes very uneasy when people seem to undertake the exercise with this in mind.'[8]

---

8. Michael R. Marrus, 'The Use and Misuse of the Holocaust' in *Lessons and Legacies: The Meaning of the Holocaust in a Changing World*, ed. Peter Hayes (Evanston: Northwestern University Press, 1991), p. 119.

Further reading

The size of the historiography of the Holocaust means that English-language readers are well served. Accordingly, I have chosen to stick to English works here and have tried to be as concise as possible.

GENERAL

There are now a number of comprehensive scholarly collections that provide useful ways in to particular topics: Peter Hayes and John Roth, eds., *The Oxford Handbook of Holocaust Studies* (Oxford: Oxford University Press, 2010); Dan Stone, ed., *The Historiography of the Holocaust* (Basingstoke: Palgrave Macmillan, 2004); and David Cesarani, *The Holocaust: Critical Concepts in Historical Studies*, 6 vols. (London: Routledge, 2004), the last a helpful collection of previously published articles. The *Lessons and Legacies* series (Evanston: Northwestern University Press, 1991–), though eclectic, consistently presents cutting-edge research.

On Holocaust historiography itself, Michael Marrus, *The Holocaust in History* (London: Penguin, 1989) remains very useful, but can now be supplemented by Tom Lawson, *Debates on the Holocaust* (Manchester: Manchester University Press, 2010). On the early historiography (the 1950s and 1960s), David Bankier and Dan Michman, eds., *Holocaust Historiography in Context: Emergence, Challenges, Polemics and Achievements* (Jerusalem: Yad Vashem, 2008) is an important, original volume, well worth consulting. Dan Michman's *Holocaust Historiography: A Jewish Perspective* (London: Vallentine Mitchell, 2003) offers a way into many topics primarily from the point of view of Jewish history. Dan Diner, *Beyond the Conceivable: Studies on Germany, Nazism, and the Holocaust* (Berkeley: University of California Press, 2000) is a fine collection of essays on theoretical problems associated with writing the history of the Holocaust.

As for document collections, there are several standard works, but we await a comprehensive selection that covers the whole of Europe.

On the Third Reich, the historiography is equally voluminous, and the best standard work is Ian Kershaw, *The Nazi Dictatorship: Problems and Perspectives of Interpretation*, 4th edn (London: Hodder Arnold, 2000). The more recent *Nazi Germany* (Oxford: Oxford University Press, 2008), edited by Jane Caplan, is a

helpful collection of essays on major themes. The four-volume collection of
documents with commentary edited by Jeremy Noakes and Geoffrey Pridham,
Nazism, 1919–1945: A Documentary History (Exeter: Exeter University Press,
1983–98) is indispensable. Older studies, such as Martin Broszat, *The Hitler
State: The Foundation and Development of the Internal Structure of the Third Reich*
(London: Longman, 1981) and Karl-Dietrich Bracher's *The Nazi Dictatorship:
The Origins, Structure and Consequences of National Socialism* (London: Penguin,
1978), are still well worth consulting. Neil Gregor's reader, *Nazism* (Oxford:
Oxford University Press, 2000) includes a wide selection of texts.

There are many single-volume histories of the Holocaust, ranging from those
aimed at children to those that assume some knowledge. A superb introduction,
which packs an enormous amount into very few pages, is David Engel, *The
Holocaust: The Third Reich and the Jews* (London: Longman, 1999). Other useful
works include John Weiss, *Ideology of Death: Why the Holocaust Happened in
Germany* (Chicago: Ivan R. Dee, 1997) and Leni Yahil, *The Holocaust: The
Fate of European Jewry* (New York: Oxford University Press, 1990). The best
single-volume works, however, are those that are analytically strong as well as
empirically wide-ranging, and these include: Peter Fritzsche, *Life and Death in the
Third Reich* (Cambridge, MA: The Belknap Press of Harvard University Press,
2008); Doris L. Bergen, *War and Genocide* (Lanham: Rowman and Littlefield,
2003); Debórah Dwork and Robert Jan van Pelt, *Holocaust: A History* (London:
John Murray, 2002), which is idiosyncratic but highly readable.

On the theoretical problems of writing history, the touchstone remains
Saul Friedländer, ed., *Probing the Limits of Representation: Nazism and the 'Final
Solution'* (Cambridge, MA: Harvard University Press, 1992). This should now
be read alongside Paul Betts and Christian Wiese, eds., *Years of Persecution, Years
of Extermination* (London: Continuum, 2010), which offers theoretical responses
to Friedländer's two-volume *Nazi Germany and the Jews*; Dan Stone, ed., *The
Holocaust and Historical Methodology* (New York: Berghahn, forthcoming), and
Alon Confino, *Foundational Pasts* (New York: Cambridge University Press,
forthcoming).

On the subject of post-Holocaust memory and interpretation, which I
have been unable to cover in this book, there is much to choose from.
Among the most significant works are Dominick LaCapra's books, especially
Representing the Holocaust: History, Theory, Trauma (Ithaca: Cornell University
Press, 1994), *History and Memory after Auschwitz* (Ithaca: Cornell University Press,
1998), and the 'Interview for Yad Vashem' in *Writing History, Writing Trauma*
(Baltimore: Johns Hopkins University Press, 2001). Other thought-provoking
studies include: Moishe Postone and Eric Santner, eds., *Catastrophe and Meaning:
The Holocaust and the Twentieth Century* (Chicago: University of Chicago Press,

2003); Omer Bartov, *Murder in Our Midst: The Holocaust, Industrial Killing, and Representation* (New York: Oxford University Press, 1996) and *Mirrors of Destruction: War, Genocide, and Modern Identity* (New York: Oxford University Press, 2000); Berel Lang, *The Future of the Holocaust: Between History and Memory* (Ithaca: Cornell University Press, 1999); Barbie Zelizer, *Remembering to Forget: Holocaust Memory Through the Camera's Eye* (Chicago: University of Chicago Press, 1998); James E. Young, *The Texture of Memory: Holocaust Memorials and Meaning* (New Haven: Yale University Press, 1993) and *At Memory's Edge: After-Images of the Holocaust in Contemporary Art and Architecture* (New Haven: Yale University Press, 2000); Lawrence Douglas, *The Memory of Judgment: Making Law and History in the Trials of the Holocaust* (New Haven: Yale University Press, 2001); Michael Rothberg, *Traumatic Realism: The Demands of Holocaust Representation* (Minneapolis: University of Minnesota Press, 2000); Brett Ashley Kaplan, *Unwanted Beauty: Aesthetic Pleasure in Holocaust Representation* (Urbana: University of Illinois Press, 2007); Gary Weissman, *Fantasies of Witnessing: Postwar Efforts to Experience the Holocaust* (Ithaca: Cornell University Press, 2004); Robert Eaglestone, *The Holocaust and the Postmodern* (Oxford: Oxford University Press, 2004); Sara Guyer, *Romanticism after Auschwitz* (Stanford: Stanford University Press, 2007). A useful collection of theoretical responses to the Holocaust can be found in Neil Levi and Michael Rothberg, eds., *The Holocaust: Theoretical Readings* (Edinburgh: Edinburgh University Press, 2003).

In my opinion, historians gain a great deal from reading Holocaust fiction. Not necessarily for empirical accuracy, but for their insights into the nature of Nazism and the Holocaust, I especially recommend: Jonathan Littell, *The Kindly Ones* (London: Chatto & Windus, 2009); Jorge Semprun, *What a Beautiful Sunday!* (London: Abacus, 1984) and *The Cattle Truck* (London: Serif, 1993); Ida Fink, *A Scrap of Time and Other Stories* (Evanston: Northwestern University Press, 1995); Tadeusz Borowski, *This Way for the Gas, Ladies and Gentlemen* (London: Penguin, 1976); Sara Nomberg-Przytyk, *Auschwitz: True Tales from a Grotesque Land* (Chapel Hill: University of North Carolina Press, 1985); Bogdan Wojdowski, *Bread for the Departed* (Evanston: Northwestern University Press, 1997); Piotr Rawicz, *Blood from the Sky* (New Haven: Yale University Press, 2003); Yoram Kaniuk, *Adam Resurrected* (New York: Grove Press, 2000); David Grossman, *See Under: Love* (London: Pan, 1991); André Schwarz-Bart, *The Last of the Just* (London: Penguin, 1977), and the novels of Raymond Federman, especially *Aunt Rachel's Fur: A Novel Improvised in Sad Laughter* (Normal: FC2, 2001) and *Return to Manure* (Tuscaloosa: FC2, 2006). Isaac Bashevis Singer, *Shadows on the Hudson* (London: Penguin, 1999) is a superb novel, examining the after-effects of the Holocaust on survivors in the US. On the relationship between fiction, history, and memory, see Susan Rubin Suleiman, *Crises of*

Memory and the Second World War (Cambridge, MA: Harvard University Press, 2006).

CHAPTER I

David Bankier and Israel Gutman, eds., *Nazi Europe and the Final Solution* (Jerusalem: Yad Vashem, 2003) is an excellent collection that covers most of Europe. David Wyman, ed., *The World Reacts to the Holocaust* (Baltimore: Johns Hopkins University Press, 1996) is a substantial book, but with some notable omissions in its coverage. There are now numerous regional and country studies; among the most important are: Yitzhak Arad, *The Holocaust in the Soviet Union* (Lincoln: University of Nebraska Press, 2009); Ray Brandon and Wendy Lower, eds., *The Shoah in Ukraine: History, Testimony, Memorialization* (Bloomington: Indiana University Press, 2008); Wendy Lower, *Nazi Empire-Building and the Holocaust in Ukraine* (Chapel Hill: University of North Carolina Press, 2005); Andrew Ezergailis, *The Holocaust in Latvia 1941–1944* (Riga: Historical Institute of Latvia, 1996); Randolph L. Braham, *The Politics of Genocide: The Holocaust in Hungary*, condensed edn (Detroit: Wayne State University Press, 2000); Dan Michman, ed., *Belgium and the Holocaust: Jews, Belgians, Germans*, 2nd edn (Jerusalem: Yad Vashem, 2000); Radu Ioanid, *The Holocaust in Romania: The Destruction of Jews and Gypsies under the Antonescu Regime, 1940–1944* (Chicago: Ivan R. Dee, 2000); Susan Zuccotti, *The Holocaust, the French and the Jews* (Lincoln: University of Nebraska Press, 1999). Martin Dean, *Collaboration in the Holocaust: Crimes of the Local Police in Belorussia and Ukraine, 1941–44* (Basingstoke: Macmillan, 2000) is essential reading. It can be complemented by the more wide-ranging *Collaboration and Resistance During the Holocaust: Belarus, Estonia, Latvia, Lithuania*, eds. David Gaunt, Paul A. Levine, and Laura Palosuo (Bern: Peter Lang, 2004). Raul Hilberg, *Perpetrators, Victims, Bystanders: The Jewish Catastrophe 1933–1945* (London: Secker and Warburg, 1995) is an impressive survey.

On theft and plunder, the standard work, setting the bar very high for future scholarly endeavour, is Martin Dean, *Robbing the Jews: The Confiscation of Jewish Property in the Holocaust, 1933–1945* (Cambridge: Cambridge University Press, 2008). Other useful studies include Martin Dean, Constantin Goschler, and Philipp Ther, eds., *Robbery and Restitution: The Conflict over Jewish Property in Europe* (New York: Berghahn, 2007) and Avi Beker, ed., *The Plunder of Jewish Property During the Holocaust: Confronting European History* (New York: New York University Press, 2001), which are both collections of illuminating essays. More focused studies include Frank Bajohr, *'Aryanization' in Hamburg: The Economic Exclusion of Jews and the Confiscation of Their Property in Nazi Germany* (New York: Berghahn, 2002) and Gerard Aalders, *Nazi Looting: The Plunder of Dutch Jewry During the Second World War* (Oxford: Berg, 2004). The role played by plunder in supporting the quality of life of the Third Reich's population is provocatively discussed in Götz Aly, *Hitler's Beneficiaries: Plunder, Racial War, and the Nazi Racial State* (New York: Metropolitan Books, 2006). But compare Aly's interpretation with Adam Tooze, *The Wages of Destruction: The Making and Breaking of the Nazi Economy* (London: Allen Lane, 2006). For the 'voluntaristic turn', see Robert Gellately, *The Gestapo and German Society: Enforcing Racial Policy, 1933–1945* (Oxford: Clarendon Press, 1990); Eric A. Johnson, *Nazi Terror: The Gestapo, Jews, and Ordinary Germans* (New York: Basic Books, 1999).

In understanding the Holocaust in Europe, the surviving diaries of key witnesses are invaluable. Several remarkable diaries have been published in the last few years, including: Mihail Sebastian, *Journal 1935–1944: The Fascist Years* (Chicago: Ivan R. Dee, 2000); Raymond-Raoul Lambert, *Diary of a Witness 1940–1943: The Ordeal of the Jews of France During the Holocaust* (Chicago: Ivan R. Dee, 2007); *The Diary of Dawid Sierakowiak: Five Notebooks from the Łódź Ghetto* (London: Bloomsbury, 1996); Hélène Beer, *Journal* (London: MacLehose Press, 2008); Victor Klemperer's diaries, *I Shall Bear Witness* (London: Weidenfeld & Nicolson, 1998) and *To the Bitter End* (London: Weidenfeld & Nicolson, 1999). Michał Grynberg, ed., *Words to Outlive Us: Eyewitness Accounts from the Warsaw Ghetto* (London: Granta, 2003) offers powerful accounts.

Among the huge number of testimonies, I recommend the following as especially noteworthy: Adina Blady Szwajger, *I Remember Nothing More: The Warsaw Children's Hospital and the Jewish Resistance* (New York: Pantheon Books, 1990); Roman Frister, *The Cap, or The Price of a Life* (London: Weidenfeld & Nicolson, 1999); Paul Steinberg, *Speak You Also: A Survivor's Reckoning* (London: Allen Lane, 2001); Ruth Klüger, *Landscapes of Memory: A Holocaust Childhood Remembered* (London: Bloomsbury, 2003). Primo Levi's accounts, *If This Is a Man* and *The Truce* (London: Abacus, 1987), and his essays, *The Drowned and the Saved* (London: Abacus, 1989), are essentials, as is Jean Améry, *At the Mind's Limits: Contemplations By a Survivor on Auschwitz and Its Realities* (New York: Schocken Books, 1986). A few *Yizker-Bikher* (memorial books) have been translated into English, including Feigl Bisberg-Youkelson and Rubin Youkelson, eds., *The Life and Death of a Polish Shtetl* (Lincoln: University of Nebraska Press, 2000), which is the Strzegowo memorial book. The best study of the *Yizker-Bikher* is Jack Kugelmass and Jonathan Boyarin, *From a Ruined Garden: The Memorial Books of Polish Jewry*, 2nd edn (Bloomington: Indiana University Press, 1998).

CHAPTER 2

Among the vast literature on the decision-making process for the Final Solution, a handful of works stand out. Ian Kershaw, *Hitler, the Germans and the Final Solution* (New Haven: Yale University Press, 2008) is a collection of Kershaw's enormously influential essays; Peter Longerich, *The Unwritten Order: Hitler's Role in the Final Solution* (Stroud: Tempus, 2001) and *Holocaust: The Nazi Persecution and Murder of the Jews* (Oxford: Oxford University Press, 2010); Christopher R. Browning with Jürgen Matthäus, *The Origins of the Final Solution: The Evolution of Nazi Jewish Policy, September 1939–March 1942* (London: William Heinemann, 2004); and Saul Friedländer, *Years of Extermination: Nazi Germany and the Jews 1939–1945* (London: HarperCollins, 2007) are the standard works by the leading historians of the subject. Browning's essay collections, *Fateful Months: Essays on the Emergence of the Final Solution*, rev. edn (New York: Holmes & Meier, 1991), *The Path to Genocide: Essays on Launching the Final Solution* (Cambridge: Cambridge University Press, 1992), and *Nazi Policy, Jewish Workers, German Killers* (Cambridge: Cambridge University Press, 2000) are all indispensable. Donald Bloxham, *The Final Solution: A Genocide* (Oxford: Oxford University Press, 2009) combines sophisticated analysis of the decision-making process with a wider, pan-European perspective. Ulrich Herbert, *National Socialist Extermination Policies: Contemporary German Perspectives and Controversies* (New York: Berghahn, 2000) is a key text for understanding the 'neo-functionalist' school that has produced so many remarkable 'regional studies', very few of which have been translated into English. Mark Roseman, *The Villa, the Lake, the Meeting: Wannsee and the Final Solution* (London: Penguin, 2003) is the surest guide to understanding the place of the Wannsee Conference in the Nazi decision-making process.

With respect to the victims, the historiography of the ghettos is especially rich. Yisrael Gutman, *The Jews of Warsaw 1939–1943: Ghetto, Underground, Revolt* (Brighton: Harvester Press, 1982) is a classic work, as is Isaiah Trunk, *Judenrat: The Jewish Councils in Eastern Europe under Nazi Occupation* (Lincoln: University of Nebraska Press, 1996). Gustavo Corni, *Hitler's Ghettos: Voices from a Beleaguered Society 1939–1944* (London: Arnold, 2003) is the most accessible synthetic work on the ghettos. Among the recent publications, Sara Bender, *The Jews of Białystok During World War II and the Holocaust* (Waltham: Brandeis University Press, 2008), Barbara Epstein, *The Minsk Ghetto 1941–1943: Jewish Resistance and Soviet Internationalism* (Berkeley: University of California Press, 2008), Gordon J. Horwitz, *Ghettostadt: Łódź and the Making of a Nazi City* (Cambridge, MA: The Belknap Press of Harvard University Press, 2008), Samuel Kassow, *Who Will Write Our History? Rediscovering a Hidden Archive from the Warsaw Ghetto*

(London: Penguin, 2009), and Barbara Engelking and Jacek Leociak, *The Warsaw Ghetto: A Guide to the Perished City* (New Haven: Yale University Press, 2009) deserve to be singled out. Lucjan Dobroszycki, ed., *The Chronicle of the Łódź Ghetto* (New Haven: Yale University Press, 1984) and Isaiah Trunk, *Łódź Ghetto: A History* (Bloomington: Indiana University Press, 2006) are important earlier works, the latter recently translated from Yiddish. Yehuda Bauer, *The Death of the Shtetl* (New Haven: Yale University Press, 2010) is a reminder of the importance of pre-war Jewish life and culture to Holocaust historiography. With particular reference to resistance, see Ruby Rohrlich, ed., *Resisting the Holocaust* (Oxford: Berg, 1998) and James M. Glass, *Jewish Resistance During the Holocaust: Moral Uses of Violence and Will* (Basingstoke: Palgrave Macmillan, 2004). A rare and fascinating account by a Jewish policeman is Calel Perechodnik, *Am I a Murderer? Testament of a Jewish Policeman* (Boulder: Westview Press, 1996).

There are now many important studies of perpetrators. Christopher R. Browning, *Ordinary Men: Reserve Police Battalion 101 and the Final Solution in Occupied Poland* (London: HarperCollins, 1992) is the starting point for the debates. Michael Wildt, *An Uncompromising Generation: The Nazi Leadership of the Reich Security Main Office* (Madison: University of Wisconsin Press, 2010) is a key text in perpetrator research. Gerald Feldman and Wolfgang Seibel, eds., *Networks of Nazi Persecution: Bureaucracy, Business and the Organization of the Holocaust* (New York: Berghahn, 2005) is one of the most original and intellectually-stimulating works in the field of recent years. Of the political biographies, Peter Longerich, *Heinrich Himmler: Biographie* (Munich: Siedler, 2008) will soon be available in English. A very useful collection is Olaf Jensen and Claus-Christian Szejnmann, eds., *Ordinary People as Mass Murderers: Perpetrators in Comparative Perspective* (Basingstoke: Palgrave Macmillan, 2008), which, despite the title, focuses mostly on the Holocaust.

CHAPTER 3

Zygmunt Bauman, *Modernity and the Holocaust* (Cambridge: Polity Press, 1989) is the key text in the debate about 'modernity'. More empirically informed studies include: Götz Aly and Susanne Heim, *Architects of Annihilation: Auschwitz and the Logic of Destruction* (London: Weidenfeld & Nicolson, 2003); Detlev J. K. Peukert, 'The Genesis of the "Final Solution" from the Spirit of Science' in *Nazism and German Society, 1933–1945*, ed. David F. Crew (London: Routledge, 1994), pp. 274–99; Michael Thad Allen, *The Business of Genocide: The SS, Slave Labor, and the Concentration Camps* (Chapel Hill: University of North Carolina Press, 2002) and Wolf Gruner, *Forced Labor under the Nazis: Economic Needs and Racial Aims, 1938–1944* (New York: Cambridge University Press, 2006). Jane Caplan and Nikolaus Wachsmann, eds., *Concentration Camps in Nazi*

Germany: The New Histories (London: Routledge, 2009) presents some of the most research work on the camp system. Yitzhak Arad, *Belzec, Sobibor, Treblinka: The Operation Reinhard Death Camps* (Bloomington: Indiana University Press, 1987) is still the only monograph on Operation Reinhard. On Chełmno, see Shmuel Krakowski, *Chelmno: A Small Village in Europe. The First Nazi Mass Extermination Camp* (Jerusalem: Yad Vashem, 2009). And on Auschwitz, see Sybille Steinbacher, *Auschwitz: A History* (London: Penguin, 2005) and Debórah Dwork and Robert Jan van Pelt, *Auschwitz 1270 to the Present* (New Haven: Yale University Press, 1996). Gideon Greif, *We Wept Without Tears: Testimonies of the Jewish Sonderkommando from Auschwitz* (New Haven: Yale University Press, 2005) is a remarkable book of interviews with surviving members of the Auschwitz *Sonderkommando*. The *Sonderkommando* men's extraordinary writings can be found in Ber Mark, *The Scrolls of Auschwitz* (Tel Aviv: Am Oved, 1985).

CHAPTER 4

The literature on eugenics and racial hygiene in Germany and their links with the T4 programme and the Holocaust is enormous. The standard works are: Paul Weindling, *Health, Race and German Politics Between National Unification and Nazism, 1870–1945* (Cambridge: Cambridge University Press, 1989); Henry Friedlander, *The Origins of Nazi Genocide: From Euthanasia to the Final Solution* (Chapel Hill: University of North Carolina Press, 1995); Benno Müller-Hill, *Murderous Science: Elimination by Scientific Selection of Jews, Gypsies, and Others, Germany 1933–1945* (Oxford: Oxford University Press, 1988); Robert N. Proctor, *Racial Hygiene: Medicine under the Nazis* (Cambridge, MA: Harvard University Press, 1988). The more recent exhibition catalogue, *Deadly Medicine: Creating the Master Race*, ed. Dieter Kuntz (Washington, DC: United States Holocaust Memorial Museum, 2004), contains superb essays and is richly illustrated. On eugenics in a broader context, see Alison Bashford and Philippa Levine, eds., *The Oxford Handbook of the History of Eugenics* (Oxford: Oxford University Press, 2010).

Claudia Koonz, *The Nazi Conscience* (Cambridge, MA: The Belknap Press of Harvard University Press, 2003); Alan E. Steinweis, *Studying the Jew: Scholarly Antisemitism in Nazi Germany* (Cambridge, MA: Harvard University Press, 2006); Jeffrey Herf, *The Jewish Enemy: Nazi Propaganda During World War II and the Holocaust* (Cambridge, MA: The Belknap Press of Harvard University Press, 2006); and Eric Ehrenreich, *The Nazi Ancestral Proof: Genealogy, Racial Science, and the Final Solution* (Bloomington: Indiana University Press, 2007) all explain the limitations of approaching the Holocaust from the perspective of racial science.

On German scholarship's contribution to the Holocaust, see Ingo Haar and Michael Fahlbusch, eds., *German Scholars and Ethnic Cleansing, 1919–1945* (New

York: Berghahn, 2005). Christopher M. Hutton, *Race and the Third Reich: Linguistics, Racial Anthropology and Genetics in the Dialectic of Volk* (Cambridge: Polity Press, 2005) is the only sustained examination of academic debates concerning 'race' in the Third Reich, and deserves to be much more widely known.

CHAPTER 5

For general works on genocide, Donald Bloxham and A. Dirk Moses, eds., *The Oxford Handbook of Genocide Studies* (Oxford: Oxford University Press, 2010) and Dan Stone, ed., *The Historiography of Genocide* (Basingstoke: Palgrave Macmillan, 2008) are the most comprehensive. Robert Gellately and Ben Kiernan, eds., *The Specter of Genocide: Mass Murder in Historical Perspective* (New York: Cambridge University Press, 2003) is among the best essay collections. Of the synthetic works, Eric D. Weitz, *A Century of Genocide: Utopias of Race and Nation* (Princeton: Princeton University Press, 2003) is a useful starting point, and should be read alongside Mark Levene, *Genocide in the Age of the Nation State*, 2 vols. (London: I. B. Tauris, 2005) and Jacques Semelin, *Purify and Destroy: The Political Uses of Massacre and Genocide* (London: Hurst & Company, 2007).

On the relationship of colonialism and genocide, A. Dirk Moses, ed., *Empire, Colony, Genocide: Conquest, Occupation, and Subaltern Resistance in World History* (New York: Berghahn, 2008) is the most up-to-date collection; A. Dirk Moses and Dan Stone, eds., *Colonialism and Genocide* (London: Routledge, 2007), and Dominik J. Schaller and Jürgen Zimmerer, eds., *The Origins of Genocide* (London: Routledge, 2009) are also useful.

On the imperial dimension of Nazi rule in Europe, see: Tim Snyder, *Bloodlands* (New York: Basic Books, 2010); Norman Rich, *Hitler's War Aims, Vol. 2: The Establishment of the New Order* (New York: W. W. Norton, 1974); and the recent synthesis by Mark Mazower, *Hitler's Empire: Nazi Rule in Occupied Europe* (London: Allen Lane, 2008).

Hannah Arendt, *The Origins of Totalitarianism*, rev. edn (San Diego: Harcourt Brace, 1979) is the classic starting point for the thesis that fascism was 'colonialism come back home' and has given rise to an enormous literature. For a way into it, see Richard H. King and Dan Stone, eds., *Hannah Arendt and the Uses of History: Imperialism, Nation, Race, and Genocide* (New York: Berghahn, 2007); and, for a thoughtful analysis of the Holocaust in relationship to decolonization, see Michael Rothberg, *Multidirectional Memory: Remembering the Holocaust in the Age of Decolonization* (Stanford: Stanford University Press, 2009).

CHAPTER 6

George L. Mosse, *The Crisis of German Ideology: Intellectual Origins of the Third Reich* (London: Weidenfeld & Nicolson, 1970), as well as Mosse's many other later books, are wonderful introductions to thinking about Nazism in terms of cultural history. On 'political religion', the most stimulating approach is offered by Uriel Tal, *Religion, Politics and Ideology in the Third Reich: Selected Essays* (London: Routledge, 2004). It can profitably be read alongside *Probing the Depths of German Antisemitism: German Society and the Persecution of the Jews, 1933–1941*, ed. David Bankier (Jerusalem: Yad Vashem, 2000), which is more focused on social and political history. On the German Churches, Robert Ericksen and Susannah Heschel, eds., *Betrayal: German Churches and the Holocaust* (Minneapolis: Augsburg Fortress, 1999) and Kevin P. Spicer, ed., *Antisemitism, Christian Ambivalence, and the Holocaust* (Bloomington: Indiana University Press, 2007) are wide-ranging collections of essays. More specific are Robert P. Ericksen, *Theologians under Hitler: Gerhard Kittel, Paul Althaus, and Emanuel Hirsch* (New Haven: Yale University Press, 1985); Doris L. Bergen, *Twisted Cross: The German Christian Movement in the Third Reich* (Chapel Hill: University of North Carolina Press, 1996); and Susannah Heschel, *The Aryan Jesus: Christian Theologians and the Bible in Nazi Germany* (Princeton: Princeton University Press, 2008). The topic of Pius XII and the Vatican encourages partisanship; for balanced accounts, see Susan Zuccotti, *Under His Very Windows: The Vatican and the Holocaust in Italy* (New Haven: Yale University Press, 2001) and Michael Phayer, *The Catholic Church and the Holocaust, 1930–1965* (Bloomington: Indiana University Press, 2000).

On Jewish responses to persecution, good starting points are David Roskies, *Against the Apocalypse: Responses to Catastrophe in Modern Jewish Culture* (Cambridge, MA: Harvard University Press, 1984) and Marion Kaplan, *Between Dignity and Despair: Jewish Life in Nazi Germany* (New York: Oxford University Press, 1998). On gender, Dalia Ofer and Lenore J. Wietzman, eds., *Women in the Holocaust* (New Haven: Yale University Press, 1998) is still the best starting point. Shirli Gilbert, *Music in the Holocaust: Confronting Life in the Nazi Ghettos and Camps* (Oxford: Clarendon Press, 2005) is a thoughtful analysis of the problems of culture and resistance. Jonathan Rose, ed., *The Holocaust and the Book: Destruction and Preservation* (Amherst, MA: University of Massachusetts Press, 2001) is an unusual and moving collection of expertly written essays.

On the Nazi *Volksgemeinschaft*, the most recent and important work has not yet appeared in English, but it is to be hoped that Michael Wildt,

Volksgemeinschaft als Selbstermächtigung: Gewalt gegen Juden in der deutschen Provinz 1919 bis 1939 (Hamburg: Hamburger Edition, 2007) and Frank Bajohr and Michael Wildt, eds., *Volksgemeinschaft: Neue Forschungen zur Gesellschaft des Nationalsozialismus* (Frankfurt/M: Suhrkamp Taschenbuch Verlag, 2009) will soon be translated.

Index

CPSIA information can be obtained at www.ICGtesting.com
Printed in the USA
LVOW071852180112

264510LV00002B/64/P

9 780199 566808